D0422168

# HOMOSEXUALITY BIBLIOGRAPHY:

## Supplement, 1970-1975

by

## WILLIAM PARKER

The Scarecrow Press, Inc.
Metuchen, N.J.   1977

Library of Congress Cataloging in Publication Data

Parker, William, fl. 1966-
    Homosexuality bibliography.

    Includes indexes.
    1.  Homosexuality--Bibliography.  I.   Parker,
William, fl. 1966-        Homosexuality.  II.   Title.
Z7164.S42P35      suppl.     [HQ76]      016.30141'57
ISBN 0-8108-1050-6                              77-1114

*3-1303-00044-2070*

*215322*

*10-17-1978*

## CONTENTS

iii

# PREFACE

A vast amount of additional material has appeared since my original bibliography on homosexuality, covering materials written in English through 1969, was published in 1971. This new Supplement, which includes all the significant material published in English during the six years from 1970 through 1975, uses the same organization, as the Table of Contents shows, as was used in the earlier volume. The sections on books, pamphlets, and dissertations and the articles in religious, legal, medical, scientific, and other specialized journals are as complete as I have been able to make them. But the materials for the other sections, especially for articles from newspapers and from homophile publications (and also for gay literature) are highly selective. (An entire volume could easily be assembled for these last mentioned categories alone.) Except in a few instances, letters to editors, reviews of books and movies, and articles in pulp magazines have been omitted.

As a glance at the Index of Subjects will reveal, the content of this Supplement differs from the original volume in the following ways: there is less emphasis on homosexuality as sin, sickness or crime, and more on homosexuality as an increasingly acceptable life style; there is less emphasis on homosexuals as offenders against society and more on homosexuals as a minority group struggling to acquire the status and liberties enjoyed by other groups; and there is less emphasis on the views of "experts" and more on the views of homosexuals themselves.

Although the quality of research and writing on homosexuality has improved in the last few years, the reader must still be critical and cautious in the evaluation and use of the materials referred to in this volume. It is hoped that this Supplement, like the original bibliography, will prove useful and timely for both the general reader and the research specialist.

W. P.

## BOOKS (NON-FICTION)

1) Aaron, William. Straight: A Heterosexual Talks
About His Homosexual Past. Garden City, N. Y. :
Doubleday and Co. , 1972. 216 pp. (Paperback ed. :
Bantam)

2) Abbott, Sidney and Love, Barbara. Sappho Was a
Right-On Woman: A Liberated View of Lesbianism.
New York: Stein and Day, 1972. 251 pp. (Hardback
and paperback editions)

3) Acosta, Mercedes de. Here Lies the Heart. New
York: Arno Press, 1975. 372 pp. (Autobiography)
(Reprint of work published in 1960)

4) Aldrich, Ann. Take a Lesbian to Lunch. New York:
Macfadden-Bartell Co. , 1972. 192 pp. (Paperback)

5) Altman, Dennis. Homosexual: Oppression and Liberation. New York: Outerbridge and Dienstfrey, 1971.
242 pp. (Paperback ed. : Avon)

6) Alvarez, Walter G. and March, Sue. Homosexuality
vs. Gay Liberation--Gay Liberation vs. Homosexuality.
New York: Pyramid Books, 1974. 259 and 105 pp.
(Paperback)

7) Anonymous. Lesbian Love: the Intimate Story of a
Strange Friendship. Windsor, Victoria, Australia:
Peer Books, 1972.

8) Bailey, Derrick S. Homosexuality and the Western
Christian Tradition. Hamden, Conn. : Archon Books,
1975. 181 pp. (Reprint of work published by Long-
mans, Green, London, 1955)

9) Baisden, Major J. , Jr. The Dynamics of Homosexuality. Edited by Joanne R. Tubbs. Sacramento,

1

Calif.: Allied Research Society, 1975. 197 pp.

10) Bancroft, John. Deviant Sexual Behavior. London:
Oxford University Press, 1974. 233 pp.

11) Barnes, Djuna. Ladies Almanack. New York: Harper and Row, 1972. 84 pp. (Reprint of work published
in 1928)

12) Barnett, Leonard. Homosexuality: Time to Tell the
Truth. London: Gollancz, 1975. 159 pp. (Paperback)

13) Barnett, Walter. Sexual Freedom and the Constitution:
An Inquiry into the Constitutionality of Repressive Sex
Laws. Albuquerque: University of New Mexico Press,
1973. 333 pp.

14) Bell, Alan P. and Hall, Calvin S. The Personality of
a Child Molester. Chicago: Aldine, Atherton Press,
1971. 162 pp.

15) Bell, Arthur. Dancing the Gay Lib Blues: A Year in
the Homosexual Liberation Movement. New York: Simon and Schuster, 1971. 191 pp.

16) Birkby, Phyllis and others (eds.). Amazon Expedition:
A Lesbian Feminist Anthology. New York: Times
Change Press, 1973. 93 pp. (Paperback) (See nos.
311, 447, 491, and 614)

17) Blake, James. The Joint. Garden City, N.Y.:
Doubleday and Co., 1971. 382 pp. (Autobiography)
(Paperback ed.: Dell)

18) Boggan, E. Carrington; Haft, Marilyn; Lister, Charles;
and Rupp, John P. An American Civil Liberties Union
Handbook: The Rights of Gay People. New York:
Avon Books, 1975. 268 pp. (Paperback) (See nos.
195, 223, 303, 304, 415, and 659)

19) Braybrooke, Neville (ed.). The Letters of J. R. Ack-
erley. London: Duckworth, 1975. 354 pp.

19a) Bridgman, Richard. Gertrude Stein in Pieces. New
York: Oxford University Press, 1970. 411 pp.

20)     Brinkley, Roland A. and others. The Laws against
        Homosexuality. ("Criminal Justice Monograph," v. 2,
        no. 4.) Huntsville, Tex.: Institute of Contemporary
        Corrections and Behavioral Sciences, Sam Houston
        University, 1973. 93 pp.

21)     Brown, Rita M. Rubyfruit Jungle. Plainfield, Vt.:
        Daughters, Inc., 1973. 217 pp. (Paperback) (Auto-
        biography)

22)     Carpenter, Edward. Intermediate Types among Primi-
        tive Folk: A Study in Social Evolution. New York:
        Arno Press, 1975. 185 pp. (Reprint of work pub-
        lished in 1919)

23)     Casal, Mary. The Stone Wall: An Autobiography.
        New York: Arno Press, 1975. 227 pp. (Reprint of
        work published in 1930)

24)     Caserta, Peggy and Knapp, Dan. Going down with
        Janis. Secaucus, N.J.: Lyle Stuart, 1973. 298 pp.
        (Paperback ed.: Dell) (Biography)

25)     Chardans, Jean-Louis. History and Anthology of Homo-
        sexuality. Paris: British Group of Sexological Re-
        search, 1970.

26)     Clanton, Gordon and Downing, Chris (eds.). Face to
        Face: An Experiment in Intimacy. New York: Dut-
        ton, 1975. 241 pp.

27)     Clarke, Lige and Nichols, Jack. I Have More Fun
        with You than Anybody. New York: St. Martin's
        Press, 1972. 152 pp.

28)     _____ and _____. Roommates Can't Always be
        Lovers: An Intimate Guide to Male-Male Relationships.
        New York: St. Martin's Press, 1974. 194 pp. Intro-
        duction by George Weinberg.

29)     Cory, Donald W. The Homosexual in America: A
        Subjective Approach. New York: Arno Press, 1975.
        334 pp. (Reprint of work published in 1951, with
        preface and appendix of 1960 edition)

30)     Croft-Cooke, Rupert. The Unrecorded Life of Oscar
        Wilde. New York: David McKay Co., 1972. 289 pp.

31)    Cunningham, Barry. Gay Power: the Homosexual
       Revolution. New York: Tower Books, 1971. (Paper-
       back)

32)    Damon, Gene; Watson, Jan; and Jordan, Robin. The
       Lesbian in Literature: A Bibliography. 2nd ed.
       Reno: The Ladder, 1975. 96 pp. (Paperback) (1577
       items)

33)    Daughters of Bilitis. The Ladder. New York: Arno
       Press, 1975. 9 v. (Reprint of vols. 1-16, Oct.
       1956-Sep. 1972)

34)    Davidson, Alex. The Returns of Love: Letters of a
       Christian Homosexual. London: Inter-Varsity Press,
       1970. 93 pp.

35)    Davidson, Michael. Some Boys: A Homosexual Odys-
       sey. London: Bruce and Watson, 1970. 199 pp.

36)    Douglas, Alexander (pseud.). Friends: A True Story
       of Male Love. New York: Coward, McCann, and
       Geoghegan, 1973. 224 pp.

37)    Douglas, Jason. Bisexuality. London: Canova, 1970.
       191 pp.

38)    Drakeford, John W. Forbidden Love: A Homosexual
       Looks for Understanding and Help. Waco, Tex.:
       World Books, 1971. 149 pp.

39)    Ellis, Havelock and Symonds, John A. Sexual Inver-
       sion. New York: Arno Press, 1975. 164 pp. (Re-
       print of work published in 1897) (See nos. 140 and
       141)

40)    Enroth, Ronald M. and Jamison, Gerald E. The Gay
       Church. Grand Rapids, Mich.: William B. Eerdmans
       Publishing Co., 1974. 144 pp. (Paperback)

41)    Evans, Barbara and Boone, Pat. Joy! A Homosexual's
       Search for Fulfillment. Carol Stream, Ill.: Creation
       House, 1973. 144 pp. (Autobiography)

42)    Falk, Ruth B. Women Loving: A Journey Toward
       Being an Independent Woman. New York: Random
       House, 1975. 550 pp. (Paperback)

43) Falkon, Felix L. A Historic Collection of Gay Art. San Diego: Greenleaf Publishing Co., 1972. 225 pp. (Paperback)

44) Fast, Julius and Wells, Hal. Bisexual Living. New York: M. Evans and Co., 1975. 240 pp. (Paperback ed.: Pocket Books)

45) Feldman, M. P. and MacCulloch, M. J. Homosexual Behaviour: Therapy and Assessment. Oxford: Pergamon Press, 1971. 288 pp. (Vol. 14 of "International Series of Monographs on Experimental Psychology")

46) Fisher, Peter. The Gay Mystique: the Myths and Reality of Male Homosexuality. New York: Stein and Day, 1972. 258 pp. (Hardback and paperback editions)

47) Foster, Marion and Murray, Kent. A Not So Gay World: Homosexuality in Canada. Toronto: McClelland and Stewart, 1972. 240 pp.

48) Fox, Chris; Hill, Charles; Pinkett, Cil; and Young, Ian. A Selected Bibliography Concerning Male and Female Homosexuality, Consisting of Gay Liberation, Sociological, Psychological, and Literary Works. Toronto: CHAT, 1972.

49) Frederics, Diana (pseud.). Diana: A Strange Autobiography. New York: Arno Press, 1975. 284 pp. (Reprint of work published in 1939)

50) Freedman, Mark. Homosexuality and Psychological Functioning: Exploring a Valid Sexual Choice. Belmont, Calif.: Brooks-Cole Publishing Co., 1971. 124 pp. (Paperback)

51) Gay Academic Union. The Universities and the Gay Experience: Proceedings of Conference. New York: Gay Academic Union, 1974. 105 pp. (Paperback) (See nos. 346, 393, 401, 407, 446, 493, and 562)

52) A Gay Bibliography: Eight Bibliographies on Lesbianism and Male Homosexuality. New York: Arno Press, 1975. 479 pp. (See nos. 184, 340, 341, 374, 411, and 590)

53)    A Gay News Chronology: January 1969-May 1975: In-
       dex and Abstracts of Articles from the New York
       Times. New York: Arno Press, 1975. 158 pp. (562
       items)

54)    Gearhart, Sally and Johnson, William R. Loving Wo-
       men/Loving Men: Gay Liberation and the Church.
       San Francisco: Glide Publications, 1974. 165 pp.

55)    Goode, Erich and Troiden, Richard R. (eds.). Sexual
       Deviance and Sexual Deviants. New York: Morrow
       and Co., 1974. 277 pp. (See nos. 336, 372, 376,
       431, 513, 544, 643, 673, 1348, and 1999)

56)    Government versus Homosexuals. New York: Arno
       Press, 1975. 126 pp. (Reprint of (1) U.S. Senate,
       67th Congress, 1st Session, Report of Committee on
       Naval Affairs, Alleged Immoral Conditions at Newport
       (R.I.) Naval Training Station, 1921; (2) U.S. Senate,
       81st Congress, 2nd Session, Report of Committee on
       Expenditures in the Executive Departments, Employ-
       ment of Homosexuals and Other Sex Perverts in Gov-
       ernment, 1950; and (3) Florida Legislature, Report of
       Florida Investigation Committee, Homosexuality and
       Citizenship in Florida, 1964)

57)    Grosskurth, Phyllis. John Addington Symonds. New
       York: Arno Press, 1975. 370 pp. (Biography) (Re-
       print of work published in 1964)

58)    Gunn, Peter. Vernon Lee: Violet Paget, 1856-1936.
       New York: Arno Press, 1975. 244 pp. (Biography)
       (Reprint of work published in 1964)

59)    Gurwell, John K. Mass Murder in Houston. Houston:
       Cordovan Press, 1974. 160 pp. (Paperback)

60)    Hamilton, Wallace. Christopher and Gay: A Partisan's
       View of the Greenwich Village Homosexual Scene. New
       York: Saturday Review Press, 1973. 216 pp.

61)    Harris, Mervyn. The Dilly Boys: Male Prostitution
       in Piccadilly. London: Croom Helm, 1973. 126 pp.

62)    Harvey, Ian. To Fall Like Lucifer. London: Sidg-
       wick and Jackson, 1971. 171 pp. (Autobiography)

63)    Hatterer, Lawrence J.   Changing Homosexuality in the
       Male:   Treatment for Men Troubled by Homosexuality.
       New York:   McGraw-Hill, 1970.   492 pp.

64)    Heilbrun, Carolyn G.   Toward a Recognition of Andro-
       gyny.   New York:   Knopf, 1973.   189 pp.   (Paperback
       ed. :   Harper and Row)

65)    A Homosexual Emancipation Miscellany, c. 1835-1952.
       New York: Arno Press, 1975.   172 pp.   (See nos. 307,
       344, 456, 538, and 588

66)    Hoving, Axel.   Lesbos:   A Photobook of Lesbian Love.
       London:   Riverhaven Ltd. -Luxor Press, 1971.   199 pp.

67)    Hudson, Billy.   Christian Homosexuality.   North Holly-
       wood, Calif. :   Now Library Press, 1970.   240 pp.
       (Paperback)

68)    Humphreys, Laud.   Out of the Closets:   the Sociology
       of Homosexual Liberation.   Englewood Cliffs, N. J. :
       Prentice-Hall, 1972.   176 pp.   (Paperback ed. :   Spec-
       trum)

69)    _____.   Tearoom Trade:   Impersonal Sex in Public
       Places.   Chicago:   Aldine Publishing Co. , 1970.
       180 pp.   Revised ed. :   Chicago:   Aldine Publishing
       Co. , 1975.   (Paperback)

70)    Hunter, John F.   The Gay Insider:   A Hunter's Guide
       to New York and a Thesaurus of Phallic Lore.   New
       York:   Traveller's Companion, 1971.   300 pp.   (Paper-
       back)

71)    _____.   The Gay Insider:   USA.   New York:   Stone-
       hill Publishing Co. , 1972.   629 pp.   (Paperback)

72)    Hurwood, Bernhardt J.   The Bisexuals.   Greenwich
       Conn. :   Fawcett Publications, 1974.   208 pp.   (Paper-
       back ed. :   Gold Medal)

73)    Hyde, H. Montgomery.   The Love That Dared Not
       Speak Its Name:   A Candid History of Homosexuality
       in Britain.   Boston:   Little, Brown and Co. , 1970.
       323 pp.

74)    _____.   Oscar Wilde:   A Biography.   New York:

Farrar, Straus and Giroux, 1975.   410 pp.

75)    Inglis, Brian.   Roger Casement.   London:  Hodder and
       Stoughton, 1973.   448 pp.

76)    Jay, Karla and Young, Allen (eds. ).   After You're
       Out:  Personal Experiences of Gay Men and Lesbian
       Women.   New York:  Links Books, 1975.   296 pp.
       (Paperback)  (See nos.  298, 306, 327, 349, 369, 370,
       386, 391, 392, 437, 472, 473, 484, 485, 486, 521,
       523, 534, 540, 560, 576, 583, 592, 618, 620, 627,
       628, 640, 690, and 704)

77)    _____ and _____ (eds. ).   Out of the Closets:
       Voices of Gay Liberation.   New York:  Douglas, 1972.
       403 pp.   (See nos.  299, 326, 333, 343, 348, 355, 361,
       362, 384, 390, 412, 414, 416, 445, 457, 458, 474,
       483, 496, 511, 527, 541, 574, 600, 602, 603, 604,
       608, 609, 610, 630, 634, 637, 641, 647, 648, 669,
       670, 671, 689, 693, 697, and 705)

78)    Johnston, Jill.   Lesbian Nation:  the Feminist Solution.
       New York:  Simon and Schuster, 1973.   283 pp.   (Pa-
       perback ed. :  Touchstone-Clarion)

79)    Jones, Clinton R.   Homosexuality and Counseling.
       Philadelphia:  Fortress Press, 1974.   132 pp.   (Paper-
       back)

80)    _____.   What about Homosexuality?   ("Youth Forum
       Series, " no.  4F21 )  Nashville:  Thomas Nelson, Inc. ,  ·
       1972.   86 pp.   (Paperback)

81)    Jones, Rhoda.   Left-handed in Love, as told by Rhoda
       Jones.   London:  Panther Books, 1970.   127 pp.

82)    Karlen, Arno.   Sexuality and Homosexuality:  A New
       View.   New York:  W. W. Norton Co. , 1971.   666 pp.

83)    Kelly, George A.   The Political Struggle of Active
       Homosexuals to Gain Social Acceptance.   Chicago:
       Franciscan Herald Press, 1975.

84)    Kirkwood, James.   American Grotesque:  An Account
       of the Clay Shaw-Jim Garrison Affair in the City of
       New Orleans.   New York:  Simon and Schuster, 1970.
       669 pp.

85)  Klaich, Dolores.  Woman Plus Woman:  Attitudes To-
     ward Lesbianism.  New York:  Simon and Schuster,
     1974.  287 pp.  (Paperback ed. :  Morrow)

86)  Kranz, Sheldon (ed. ).  The H Persuasion:  How Per-
     sons Have Permanently Changed from Homosexuality
     through the Study of Aesthetic Realism.  New York:
     Definition Press, 1971.  136 pp.  (Paperback)

87)  Lauritsen, John and Thorstad, David.  The Early Ho-
     mosexual Rights Movement (1864-1935).  New York:
     Times Change Press, 1974.  93 pp.  (Paperback)

88)  Lehman, J. Lee (ed. ).  Gays on Campus.  Washington,
     D. C. :  U. S. National Student Association, 1975.  86
     pp.  (Paperback) (See nos. 196, 304, 309, 358, 417,
     418, 419, 524, 539, 571, 580, 619, 631, 633, and 687)

89)  Liddell, Robert.  Cavafy:  A Critical Biography.  Lon-
     don:  Duckworth, 1974.  222 pp.

90)  Lind, Earl (pseud. ).  Autobiography of an Androgyne.
     New York:  Arno Press, 1975.  265 pp.  (Reprint of
     work published in 1918)

91)  _____.  The Female Impersonators.  Edited by Al-
     fred W. Herzog.  New York:  Arno Press, 1975.
     295 pp.  (Autobiography) (Reprint of work published
     in 1922)

92)  Livingood, John M. (ed. )  National Institute of Mental
     Health Task Force on Homosexuality:  Final Report
     and Background Papers.  (Publication No. HSM 72-
     9116)  Washington, D. C. :  U. S. Government Printing
     Office, 1972.  79 pp.  (Paperback) (See nos. 404,
     421, 465, 497, 542, 572, and 632.)

93)  Loeffler, Donald L.  An Analysis of the Treatment of
     the Homosexual Character in Dramas produced in the
     New York Theater from 1950 to 1968.  New York:
     Arno Press, 1975.  201 pp.  (Reprint of doctoral dis-
     sertation submitted to Bowling Green State University
     in Ohio, 1969)

94)  Loovis, David.  Gay Spirit:  A Guide to Becoming a
     Sensuous Homosexual.  New York:  Strawberry Hill-
     Grove Press, 1974.  171 pp.

95)     Loraine, John A. (ed. ).  Understanding Homosexual-
        ity: Its Biological and Psychological Bases.  New
        York:  American Elsevier Publishing Co. , 1974.
        214 pp.  (See nos.  339, 368, 398, 406, 436, 501,
        504, 536, and 607)

96)     Martin, Del and Lyon, Phyllis.  Lesbian/Women.
        San Francisco:  Glide Publications, 1972.  282 pp.
        (Paperback ed. :  Bantam)

97)     Mattachine Society.  The Mattachine Review.  New
        York:  Arno Press, 1975.  5 v.  (Reprint of vols.
        1-12, Jan. 1955-Jul. 1966)

98)     Maugham, Robin.  Escape from the Shadows.  New
        York:  McGraw-Hill, 1973.  273 pp.  (Autobiography)

99)     Mayne, Xavier (pseud. ).  Imre:  A Memorandum.
        New York:  Arno Press, 1975.  205 pp.  (Autobio-
        graphy)  (Reprint of work published in 1906)

100)    _____.  The Intersexes:  A History of Similsexu-
        alism as a Problem in Social Life.  New York:  Ar-
        no Press, 1975.  641 pp.  (Reprint of work published
        in 1908)

101)    McCaffrey, Joseph A. (ed. ).  The Homosexual Dia-
        lectic.  Englewood Cliffs, N. J. :  Prentice-Hall,
        1972.  218 pp.  (Paperback ed. :  Spectrum)  (See
        nos.  329, 373, 403, 432, 450, 461, 506, 555, 587,
        666, 691, 697, 1243, 1929, 2324, and 2797)

101a)   Mellow, James R.  Charmed Circle:  Gertrude Stein
        and Company.  New York:  Praeger, 1974.  528 pp.
        (Biography)

102)    Miller, Merle.  On Being Different:  What It Means
        to Be a Homosexual.  New York:  Random House,
        1971.  65 pp.  (Autobiography)  (Paperback ed. :
        Popular Library)  (See nos. 992, 993, 1266, and
        1267)

103)    Millett, Kate.  Flying.  New York:  Knopf, 1974.
        546 pp.  (Autobiography)

104)    Miss Marianne Woods and Miss Jane Pirie against
        Dame Helen Cumming Gordon.  New York:  Arno

Press, 1975. (Reprint of records of 19th century
trial for Lesbianism)

105) Murphy, John. Homosexual Liberation: A Personal
View. New York: Praeger, 1971. 182 pp.

106) Myron, Nancy and Bunch, Charlotte (eds.) Lesbianism and the Women's Movement. Baltimore: Diana
Press, 1975. 104 pp. (Paperback) (See nos. 328,
347, 351, 385, 601, 612, 650, 653, and 674)

107) _____ and _____ (eds.). Women Remembered:
A Collection of Biographies from "The Furies."
Baltimore: Diana Press, 1974. 89 pp. (Paperback)
(See nos. 313, 350, 448, and 694)

108) Nachman, Elana. Riverfinger Women. Plainfield,
Vt.: Daughters, Inc., 1974. 183 pp. (Paperback)

109) Negrin, Su. Begin at Start: Some Thoughts on Personal Liberation and World Change. Washington,
N.J.: Times Change Press, 1972. 174 pp. (Autobiography)

110) Newton, Esther. Mother Camp: Female Impersonators in America. Englewood Cliffs, N.J.: Prentice-
Hall, 1972. 136 pp. (Paperback)

111) Norton, Rictor. The Homosexual Literary Tradition:
An Interpretation. New York: Revisionist Press,
1974. 399 pp.

112) Oberholtzer, W. Dwight (ed.). Is Gay Good: Ethics,
Theology, and Homosexuality. Philadelphia: West-
minster Press, 1971. 287 pp. (Paperback) (See
nos. 366, 434, 449, 451, 492, 543, 552, 584, 585,
589, 593, 597, 679, and 691)

113) Olson, Jack. The Man with the Candy: the Story of
the Houston Mass Murders. New York: Simon and
Schuster, 1974. 255 pp.

114) Onge, Jack. The Gay Liberation Movement: A History. Chicago: Alliance Press, 1971. 90 pp. (Paperback)

115) Parker, William. Homosexuality: A Selective Bib-

liography of over 3,000 Items.  Metuchen, N. J.:
Scarecrow Press, 1971.  323 pp.  (3,225 items)

116)    Perry, Troy and Lucas, Charles.  The Lord Is My
        Shepherd and He Knows I'm Gay.  Los Angeles: Nash
        Publishing Co., 1972.  232 pp.  (Paperback ed.:
        Bantam)

117)    Philpott, Kent.  The Third Sex?  Six Homosexuals
        Tell Their Story.  Plainfield, N. J.:  Logos Interna-
        tional, 1975.  208 pp.

118)    Pittinger, W. Norman.  Time for Consent:  A Chris-
        tian's Approach to Homosexuality.  2nd ed.  London:
        Student Christian Movement Press, 1970.  124 pp.
        (Paperback)

119)    Plummer, Kenneth.  Sexual Stigma:  An Interaction-
        ist Account.  London:  Routledge and Kegan Paul,
        1975.  258 pp.

120)    Reid, Don and Gurwell, John K.  Eyewitness.  Hous-
        ton:  Cordovan Press, 1973.  232 pp.

121)    Reid, John (pseud.).  The Best Little Boy in the
        World.  New York:  Putnam's, 1973.  247 pp.  (Au-
        tobiography)

122)    Richmond, Len and Noguerra, Gary (eds.).  The Gay
        Liberation Book.  San Francisco:  Ramparts Press,
        1973.  208 pp.  (Paperback)  (See nos. 300, 301,
        302, 324, 325, 343, 353, 397, 400, 413, 432, 440,
        441, 442, 475, 477, 479, 488, 518, 535, 553, 581,
        616, 665, 675, 684, and 703)

123)    Rodgers, Bruce.  The Queens' Vernacular:  A Gay
        Lexicon.  San Francisco:  Straight Arrow Books,
        1972.  254 pp.  (Paperback)  (Over 12,000 items)

124)    Rorem, Ned.  The Final Diary, 1961-72.  New York:
        Holt, Rinehart, and Winston, 1974.  439 pp.

125)    Rosen, David H.  Lesbianism:  A Study of Female
        Homosexuality.  Springfield, Ill.:  Thomas, 1974.
        123 pp.  Foreword by Evelyn Hooker.  (Paperback)

126)    Rosenfels, Paul.  Homosexuality:  the Psychology of

the Creative Process. New York: Libra Publishers,
Inc., 1971. 169 pp.

127)  Ruitenbeek, Hendrik M. (ed. ). Homosexuality: A
Changing Picture. London: Souvenir Press, 1973.
218 pp. (See nos. 365, 389, 531, 566, 569, 575,
626, 644, 654, 729, 737, 1134, 1829, 1924, 1929,
2086, and 2123)

128)  Rule, Janet. Lesbian Images. Garden City, N. Y. :
Doubleday and Co. , 1975. 246 pp. (Includes chap-
ters on: Radclyffe Hall, Gertrude Stein, Willa Cather, Vita Sackville-West, Ivy Compton-Burnett, Elizabeth Bowen, Colette, Violette Leduc, Margaret
Anderson, Dorothy Baker, May Sarton, and Maureen
Duffy)

129)  Sagarin, Edward. Structure and Ideology in an Association of Deviants. New York: Arno Press, 1975.
446 pp. (Reprint of doctoral dissertation submitted
to New York University, 1966)

130)  Saghir, Marcel T. and Robins, Eli. Male and Female Homosexuality: A Comprehensive Investigation.
Baltimore: Williams and Wilkins, 1973. 341 pp.

131)  Saxon, Grant T. (pseud. ). The Happy Hustler. New
York: Warner Publishing Co. , 1975. 189 pp. (Paperback)

131a)  Secrest, Meryle. Between Me and Life: A Biography
of Romaine Brooks. Garden City, N. Y. : Doubleday,
1974. 432 pp.

132)  Sharma, Umesh D. and Rudy, Wilfrid C. Homosexuality: A Select Bibliography. Waterloo, Ontario:
Waterloo Lutheran University, 1970. 114 pp. (Paperback) (2,537 items)

133)  Simpson, Ruth. From the Closet to the Courts: The
Lesbian Transition. New York: Viking Press, 1975.
180 pp.

134)  Smith, Timothy d'A. Love in Earnest: Some Notes
on the Lives and Writings of English 'Uranian' Poets
from 1889 to 1930. London: Routledge and Kegan
Paul, 1970. 280 pp.

135)    Steakley, James D.  The Homosexual Emancipation
        Movement in Germany.  New York:  Arno Press,
        1975.  121 pp.  (Includes translations of many Ger-
        man texts)

136)    Strachey, Giles Lytton.  Lytton Strachey by Himself:
        A Self Portrait.  Edited by Michael Holroyd.  New
        York:  Holt, Rinehart, and Winston, 1971.  184 pp.
        (Autobiography)

137)    Sturgeon, Mary C.  Michael Field.  New York:  Ar-
        no Press, 1975.  245 pp.  (Biography) (Reprint of
        work published in 1921)

138)    Sweet, Roxanne T.  Political and Social Action in
        Homophile Organizations.  New York:  Arno Press,
        1975.  252 pp.  (Reprint of doctoral dissertation sub-
        mitted to University of California at Berkeley, 1968)

139)    Swicegood, Thomas L. P.  Our God Too.  New York:
        Pyramid Books, 1974.  379 pp.  (Paperback)

140)    Symonds, John A.  A Problem in Greek Ethics, Be-
        ing an Inquiry into the Phenomenon of Sexual Inver-
        sion.  New York:  Haskell House, 1971.  73 pp.
        (Reprint of work published in 1901)

141)    _____.  A Problem of Modern Ethics, Being an
        Inquiry into the Phenomenon of Sexual Inversion.
        New York:  B. Blom, 1971.  91 pp.  (Reprint of
        work published in 1896)

142)    Tanner, John.  Sex and the Homosexual.  New York:
        Macfadden, Bartell Co., 1971.  192 pp.  (Paperback)

143)    Teal, Donn.  The Gay Militants.  New York:  Stein
        and Day, 1971.  355 pp.

144)    Thayer, Paul.  To Carthage I Came.  New York:
        Vantage Press, 1974.  333 pp.

145)    Theodor, Evelyn.  Lesbian Secrets.  London:  Luxor
        Press, 1970.  190 pp.

146)    Tiefenbrun, Ruth.  Moment of Torment:  An Interpre-
        tation of Franz Kafka's Short Stories.  Carbondale,
        Ill. :  Southern Illinois University, 1973.  160 pp.

147)   Tobin, Kay and Wicker, Randy.  The Gay Crusaders.
       New York: Paperback Library, 1972.  238 pp.  (Pa-
       perback)  (Reprinted:  New York:  Arno Press, 1975)

148)   Trainer, Russell.  The Male Homosexual Today.
       New York:  Macfadden-Bartell Co., 1970.  160 pp.
       (Paperback)

149)   Tripp, Clarence A.  The Homosexual Matrix.  New
       York:  McGraw-Hill, 1975.  314 pp.

150)   Twenty-five to Six Baking and Trucking Co.  Great
       Gay in the Morning:  One Group's Approach to Com-
       munal Living and Sexual Politics.  Washington, N. J.:
       Times Change Press, 1972.  95 pp.  (Paperback)

151)   Tyler, Parker.  Screening the Sexes:  Homosexuality
       in the Movies.  New York:  Holt, Rinehart, and Win-
       ston, 1972.  367 pp.  (Paperback ed.:  Anchor)

152)   Vanggaard, Thorkil.  Phallos:  A Symbol and Its His-
       tory in the Male World.  Translated from the Danish
       by the author.  New York:  International Universities
       Press, 1972.  208 pp.  (Paperback ed.:  Simon and
       Schuster)

152a)  Vassall, John.  Vassall:  The Autobiography of a Spy.
       London:  Sidgwick and Jackson, 1975.  200 pp.

153)   Vincenza, Una [Lady Troubridge].  The Life of Rad-
       clyffe Hall.  New York:  Arno Press, 1975.  189 pp.
       (Biography)  (Reprint of work published in 1963)

154)   Warren, Carol A. B.  Identity and Community in the
       Gay World.  New York:  Wiley and Sons, 1974.  191
       pp.  (Paperback)  (See no. 290)

155)   Weinberg, George.  Society and the Healthy Homo-
       sexual.  New York:  St. Martin's Press, 1972.  150
       pp.  (Paperback ed.:  Anchor)

156)   Weinberg, Martin S. and Bell, Alan P.  Homosexu-
       ality:  An Annotated Bibliography.  New York:  Har-
       per and Row, 1972.  550 pp.  (1, 263 items)

157)   _____ and Williams, Colin J.  Male Homosexuals:
       Their Problems and Adaptations.  New York:  Oxford

University Press, 1974. 316 pp. (Paperback ed.:
Penguin)

158)   Weiss, Carl and Friar, David J. Terror in the
Prisons: Homosexual Rape and Why Society Condones
It. Indianapolis: Bobbs-Merrill Co., 1974. 247 pp.

159)   Werther, Ralph (pseud.). The Female Impersonators. New York: Arno Press, 1975. 295 pp. (Reprint of work published in 1922)

159a)  Wickliff, Jim (ed.). In Celebration: Integrity's
First National Convention. Chicago: Integrity, 1975.
91 pp. (See nos. 390a and 598a)

160)   Williams, Colin J. and Weinberg, Martin S. Homosexuals and the Military: A Study of Less than Honorable Discharge. New York: Harper and Row,
1971. 221 pp. Foreword by Evelyn Hooker.

161)   Williams, Tennessee. Memoirs. Garden City, N.Y.:
Doubleday and Co., 1975. 264 pp. (Autobiography)

162)   Wilton, Karena. Women in Love with Women. London: Olympia Press, 1971. 180 pp.

163)   Wittig, Monique. The Lesbian Body. New York:
Morrow and Co., 1975. 165 pp.

164)   Wolff, Charlotte. Love between Women. New York:
St. Martin's Press, 1971. 230 pp. (Paperback ed.:
Colophon)

165)   Wysor, Bettie. The Lesbian Myth. New York: Random House, 1974. 438 pp.

166)   Young, Ian. The Male Homosexual in Literature:
A Bibliography. Metuchen, N.J.: Scarecrow Press,
1975. 242 pp. (2,921 items) (Also four essays--
see nos. 478, 582 and 706)

## PAMPHLETS AND DOCUMENTS

167) Aherne, David. Hindsight of One Gay Student.
("Otherwise Monograph Series," No. 18) New York:
National Task Force on Student Personnel Services
and Homosexuality, 1972. 13 pp.

168) American Armed Forces Association. The Gay Service Man and Woman's Rebuttal. Pensacola, Flda.:
American Armed Forces Association, 1975. 20 pp.

169) American Library Association, Social Responsibilities
Round Table, Task Force on Gay Liberation. A Gay
Bibliography. 5th ed. Philadelphia: American Library Association Task Force on Gay Liberation,
1975. 8 pp. (Reprinted in Lehman, no. 88, pp. 77-
85)

170) Ann Arbor, Mich., Code of City of. Title IX, chap.
112, sec. 9-151 to 9-155. (Ordinance prohibiting
discrimination against homosexuals in city employment)

171) Anonymous. I am a Homosexual. Waterloo, Ontario,
Canada: Waterloo University's Gay Liberation Movement, 1973. 14 pp.

172) Bamford, Julian. Information on Veneral Disease for
Gay Women and Men. Los Angeles: Gay Community
Services Center, 1975. (Reprinted in Jay and Young,
no. 76, pp. 256-66).

173) Barnett, Walter and Warner, Arthur C. Why Reform
the Sodomy Laws? Princeton: National Committee
for Sexual Civil Liberties, 1971. 24 pp.

174) Bell, Alan P. Homosexuality. Revised ed. ("SIECUS
Study Guide," No. 2) New York: Sex Information
and Education Council of U.S., 1973. 16 pp.

17

175)     A Bibliography of Lesbian-related Materials.  Min-
         neapolis:  Lesbian Resources Center, 1974.  (60
         items)

176)     Birenbaum, William M.  On Opening an Admission
         of Being Different:  A College President Looks at
         Homosexuality and College Public Relations.  ("Other-
         wise Monograph Series," No. 1) New York:  Na-
         tional Task Force on Student Personnel Services and
         Homosexuality, 1972.  6 pp.

177)     Blair, Ralph.  Etiological and Treatment Literature
         on Homosexuality.  ("Otherwise Monograph Series,"
         No. 5) New York:  National Task Force on Student
         Personnel Services and Homosexuality, 1972.  49 pp.

178)     _____.  An Evangelical Look at Homosexuality.
         ("Otherwise Monograph Series") New York:  Nation-
         al Task Force on Student Personnel Services and
         Homosexuality, 1975.  12 pp.

179)     _____.  Homosexuality and Psychomatic Assess-
         ment.  ("Otherwise Monograph Series," No. 15)
         New York:  National Task Force on Student Person-
         nel Services and Homosexuality, 1972.  9 pp.

180)     _____.  Student Personnel Services and Homosex-
         uality:  A National Review of Provisions and Opinions
         of Deans of Students, Directors of Counseling, and
         Homosexual College Students.  ("Otherwise Monograph
         Series," No. 2) New York:  National Task Force on
         Student Personnel Services and Homosexuality, 1972.
         7 pp.

181)     _____.  Vocational Guidance and Gay Liberation.
         ("Otherwise Monograph Series," No. 19) New York:
         National Task Force on Student Personnel Services
         and Homosexuality, 1972.  18 pp.

182)     _____; Rash, John P.; Rogers, Herbert; and
         "Paul."  Homosexuality and Religion.  ("Otherwise
         Monograph Series," No. 13) New York:  National
         Task Force on Student Personnel Services and Homo-
         sexuality, 1972.  21 pp.

183)     Blamires, David.  Homosexuality from the Inside.
         London:  Social Responsibility Council of the Religious
         Society of Friends, 1973.  45 pp.

184)  Bradley, Marion Z. and Damon, Gene.  "Checklist:
      A Complete Cumulative Checklist of Lesbian, Variant,
      and Homosexual Fiction in English, " in A Gay Biblio-
      graphy, no. 52, pp. 75-235.  (1,021 items)  (Reprint
      of work published in 1960, with supplements for 1961
      and 1962)

185)  Brown, James R. and Butwill, N.  Religion, Society,
      and the Homosexual.  New York:  Manuscript Infor-
      mation Corporation, 1973.  44 pp.

186)  Buffum, Peter C.  Homosexuality in Prisons.  Wash-
      ington, D.C.:  National Institute of Law Enforcement
      and Criminal Justice, 1972.  48 pp.

187)  Butcher, Patricia S.  Readers' Advisory Service:
      Selected Topical Booklist Number 69:  Human Sexual-
      ity.  New York:  Science Associates International,
      Inc., 1974.  18 pp.  (46 items on homosexuality)

188)  A Catholic Bibliography on Homosexuality.  Boston:
      Dignity, 1974.  (46 items)

189)  Chicago Gay People's Legal Committee.  Pocket Le-
      gal Guide for Gay People.  Chicago:  Chicago Gay
      People's Legal Committee, 1973.  (Reprinted in Jay
      and Young, no. 76, pp. 161-68).

190)  Come Out Staff.  Come Out:  Selections from the
      Radical Gay Liberation Newspaper.  New York:
      Times Change Press, 1971.  62 pp.

191)  Copely, Ursula (ed.).  Directory of Homosexual Or-
      ganizations and Publications Annotated.  Hollywood,
      Ca.:  Homosexual Information Center, 1975.  32 pp.

192)  Crew, Louie (ed.).  "Gay Male Writing and Publish-
      ing."  Special issue of Margins:  A Review of Little
      Magazines and Small Press Books.  May 1975.  80
      pp.  (See nos. 2220, 2254, 2259, 2261, 2269, 2279,
      2281, 2288, 2305, 2314, 2315, 2382, 2395, 2407,
      2432, 2439, 2455, and 2473)

193)  _____ and Norton, Rictor (eds.).  "The Homosex-
      ual Imagination."  Special issue of College English,
      v. 36, no. 3, Nov. 1974.  132 pp.  (See nos. 2221,
      2224, 2249, 2251, 2262, 2301, 2303, 2332, 2341,
      2388, 2391, 2425, 2445, and 2449)

194)      District of Columbia. District Code. Title 34.
          (Human Rights ordinance prohibiting discrimination
          against homosexuals)

195)      East Lansing, Mich., City of. City Code. Ordin-
          ance no. 325 amending Title I, chapter 4, sections
          1.126 and 1.127. (Reprinted in ACLU Handbook, no.
          18, pp. 255-56.) (Ordinance prohibiting discrimina-
          tion against homosexuals)

196)      Fairchild, Betty. Parents of Gays. Washington,
          D.C.: Parents of Gays, 1975. 14 pp. (Reprinted
          in Lehman, no. 88, pp. 43-47)

197)      Farrell, Ronald A. and Morrione, Thomas J. Social
          Interaction and Stereotypic Responses to Homosexuals.
          Washington, D.C.: Department of Health, Education,
          and Welfare, 1972. 38 pp.

198)      Findlay, Dennis and others. Operation Socrates
          Handbook. Waterloo, Ontario, Canada: Federation
          of Students, University of Waterloo, 1973. 39 pp.

199)      Gair, Cindi; Toy, Jim; and Blair, Ralph. Gay Peer
          Counseling at Michigan. ("Otherwise Monograph
          Series," No. 9) New York: National Task Force on
          Student Personnel Services and Homosexuality, 1972.
          9 pp.

200)      Gay Activists Alliance. Twenty Questions about Ho-
          mosexuality: A Political Primer. New York: Gay
          Activists Alliance, 1973. 24 pp. (Reprinted in
          March and Alvarez, no. 6, pp. 69-105.)

201)      Gay Ministry Task Force of the Salvatorian Fathers.
          A Model for Ministry to the Homosexual Community.
          Milwaukee: Salvatorian Fathers, 1974. 38 pp.

202)      Gay Yellow Pages Number 6. New York: Renais-
          sance House, 1975. 80 pp. (Listing by state of gay
          organizations, churches, publications, bars,
          businesses, counseling services, legal resources,
          community service centers, guides, directories, etc.
          Over 100 national publications and over 400 organiza-
          tions are listed)

203)      Hansel, Robert R. The Homosexual Problem-Theirs

or Ours? New York: Executive Council of the Episcopal Church, Section for Experimental and Specialized Services, 1970. 17 pp.

204)     Hart, George. The Straight or Gay Book. Los
         Angeles: Price-Stern-Sloan, 1974. 30 pp. (Cartoons)

205)     Health and Veneral Disease: Guide for Gay Men.
         New York: Gay Men's Health Project, 1975. 28 pp.

206)     Hemric, Benjamin (ed. ). Male Homosexual Students
         Speak for Themselves. ("Otherwise Monograph Series,"
         No. 4) New York: National Task Force on Student Per-
         sonnel Services and Homosexuality, 1972. 5 pp.

207)     Hickey, Owen. Law and Laxity. London: Times
         Newspapers, 1970. 20 pp.

208)     Hodges, Andrew. Psychiatry and the Homosexual:
         A Brief Analysis of Oppression. ("Gay Liberation
         Pamphlet," No. 1) London: London Gay Liberation,
         1973. 32 pp.

209)     _____ and Hunter, David. With Downcast Gays:
         Aspects of Homosexual Self-Oppression. London:
         Pomegranate Press, 1974. 40 pp.

210)     Hodges, Beth (ed. ). "Lesbian Feminist Writing and
         Publishing. " Special issue of Margins: A Review of
         Little Magazines and Small Press Books. Aug. 1975.
         72 pp. (See nos. 2243, 2257, 2265, 2266, 2271,
         2333, 2343, 2351, 2371, 2386, 2398, 2444, 2465, 2468,
         2475, and 2477)

211)     Homosexual Information Center. A Selected Biblio-
         graphy of Homosexuality. 5th edition. Los Angeles:
         Homosexual Information Center, 1972. 4 pp. (89 items)

212)     Homosexuality in Literature. (Catalog No. 7) Elm-
         hurst, N. Y. : Elysian Fields, Booksellers, 1975.
         42 pp. (1328 items) (Bibliography)

213)     Homosexuality in South Australia: A Collection of
         Writings. Adelaide, Australia: Adelaide University
         Students' Association, 1972. 50 pp.

214)     Kenyon, Frank E. Homosexuality. London: British
         Medical Association, 1973. 31 pp.

215)    Kuda, Marie J. (ed. ).  Women Loving Women:  A
        Select and Annotated Bibliography of Women Loving
        Women in Literature.  Chicago:  Lavender Press,
        1974.  28 pp.  (Approximately 200 items)

216)    Lauritsen, John.  Religious Roots of the Taboo on
        Homosexuality:  A Materialist View.  New York:
        Gay Liberation Front, 1974.  26 pp.

217)    Lee, Ron; Melleno, Frank; and Mullis, Robert.  Gay
        Men Speak.  San Francisco:  Multi-Media Resource
        Center, 1973.  42 pp.

218)    MacInnes, Colin.  Loving Them Both:  A Study of Bi-
        sexuality and Bisexuals.  London:  Martin Brian and
        O'Keefe, 1973.  55 pp.

219)    Martin, Del and Lyon, Phyllis.  Lesbian Love and
        Liberation.  San Francisco:  Multi-Media Resource
        Center, 1973.  40 pp.

220)    Mathews, Walter M.  Homosexuality:  An Educational
        Confrontation.  Washington, D. C. :  Department of
        Health, Education, and Welfare, 1973.  8 pp.

221)    May, Eugene P.  Perceptions in Homosexuals and Non-
        Homosexuals:  A Study of Counselors', Psychologists',
        and Homosexuals' Perceptions.  ("Otherwise Monograph
        Series, " No.  2) New York:  National Task Force on Stu-
        dent Personnel Services and Homosexuality, 1972.  10 pp.

222)    Milligan, Don.  The Politics of Homosexuality.  Lon-
        don:  Pluto Press, 1973.  19 pp.

223)    Minneapolis, City of.  Code of Ordinances relating
        to Civil Rights.  Ordinance amending Chapter 945. 010,
        adopted March 29, 1974.  (Reprinted in ACLU Hand-
        book, no. 18, pp. 251-54, and in Congressional Re-
        cord, v. 120, no. 61, p. E2732, May 2, 1974. )

224)    Mostly for Men:  Homosexuality in Literature.  (Catalog
        No. 9. ) Elmhurst, N. Y. :  Elysian Fields, Booksellers,
        1975.  34 pp.  (875 items)  (Bibliography)

225)    National Conference of Catholic Bishops.  Principles
        to Guide Confessors in Questions of Homosexuality.
        Washington, D. C. :  National Conference of Catholic
        Bishops, 1973.  15 pp.

226)     National Gay Task Force. Gay Parent Support Pack-
         et. New York: National Gay Task Force, 1973.
         12 pp. (Statements from Ralph Blair, Evelyn Hooker,
         Judd Marmor, John Money, Wardell Pomeroy, Ben-
         jamin Spock, and George Weinberg)

227)     National Gay Task Force. Resolutions in Support of
         Rights of Homosexuals. New York: National Gay
         Task Force, 1975. 19 pp. (American Anthropologi-
         cal Association, 1970; American Association for the
         Advancement of Science, 1975; American Bar Asso-
         ciation, 1973; American Federation of Teachers,
         1970; American Library Association, 1971; American
         Personnel and Guidance Association, 1971 and 1973;
         American Psychiatric Association, 1973; American
         Psychological Association, 1975; Council of the Epis-
         copal Diocese of New York, 1971; Executive Council
         of the Episcopal Diocese of Michigan, 1974; Lutheran
         Church in America, Fifth Biennial Convention, 1970;
         National Board of the YWCA Association of the U.S.A.,
         26th National Convention, 1973; National Council of
         Churches in the U.S.A., n.d.; National Education
         Association, 1974; National Federation of Priests
         Councils, Roman Catholic Church, 1972; National Or-
         ganization of Women, National Conference, 1973;
         Unitarian Universalist Association of Churches and
         Fellowships in North America, 1970 and 1973; and
         United Church of Christ, Council for Christian Social
         Action, 1969)

228)     Nolte, M. Chester (ed.). Gender and Sexual Mores
         in Educational Employment: A Legal Memorandum.
         Washington, D.C.: National Association of Secondary
         School Principals, 1974. 7 pp.

229)     Ogg, Elizabeth. Homosexuality in Our Society.
         ("Public Affairs Pamphlet," No. 484) New York:
         Public Affairs Committee, 1972. 28 pp.

230)     One, Varda. The Image of Women in Homophile Nov-
         els. Venice, Ca.: Everywoman Press, 1971. 29 pp.

231)     Quinn, Brian D. A Different Drummer: Metaphysics
         and the Homosexual. San Francisco: Nevelow and
         Brower Printing Co., 1975. 41 pp.

232)     Righton, Peter (ed.). Counselling Homosexuals: A
         Study of Personal Needs and Public Attitudes. Lon-

don:  Bedford Square Press, 1973.  35 pp.

233)   Roskam, Philip; Bebe; and Jeff.  Gay Community at
       Queens College.  ("Otherwise Monograph Series, "
       No.  16)  New York:  National Task Force on Student
       Personnel Services and Homosexuality, 1972.  8 pp.

234)   Rubin, Isadore.  Homosexuality.  ("SIECUS Guide, "
       No.  2)  New York:  Sex Information and Education
       Council of the United States, 1970.  20 pp.

235)   San Francisco, City and County of.  Administrative
       Code.  Ordinance No.  96-72.  Sections 12 B. 1 and
       12 B. 2 (a) and (b).  (Employment rights for homo-
       sexuals)

236)   Society for Individual Rights, Religious Committee.
       Statements by Churches and Church Committees on
       Homosexuality.  San Francisco:  Society for Indivi-
       dual Rights, 1971.  12 pp.  (Recommendation to Par-
       liament by Archbishop Griffith of the Roman Catholic
       Church, 1957; New Dutch Catechism, 1969; Statement
       of Council for Christian Social Action of United
       Church of Christ, 1969; Report of Task Force on
       Sexuality, United Presbyterian Church, USA, 1970;
       Statement of Lutheran Church in America Convention,
       1970; Statement of Unitarian General Assembly, 1970;
       and Statement of Committee on Social Justice of Arch-
       diocese of San Francisco, 1971. )

237)   Spitzer, Robert L.  A Proposal about Homosexuality
       and the American Psychiatric Association Nomencla-
       ture.  Washington, D. C. :  American Psychiatric As-
       sociation, 1973.  6 pp.

238)   United Methodist Church, Division of Higher Educa-
       tion of the Board of Education.  "Gay Men's Libera-
       tion. "  Special issue of Motive, vol. 32, issue 2,
       winter, 1972.  64 pp.  (See nos.  1407, 1408, 1416,
       1420, 1435, 1444, 1448, 1455, 1496, 1537, 1541,
       1549, 1560, and 1562)

239)   _____.  "Lesbian/Feminist Issue. "  Special issue
       of Motive, v. 32, issue 1, winter, 1972.  64 pp.
       (See nos.  1406, 1413, 1421, 1422, 1425, 1471, 1473,
       1476, 1501, 1511, 1530, 1534, and 1553)

240)     United Presbyterian Church, U.S.A., Program Agen-
         cy. "Homosexuality: Neither Sin nor Sickness."
         Special issue of Trends, Jul.-Aug. 1973.  50 pp.
         (See nos. 1423, 1424, 1482, 1499, 1512, 1528, 1557,
         and 1561)

241)     United States Federal Register.  Proposed Changes
         of Civil Service Commission Regulations concerning
         Disqualification for and Dismissal from Federal Em-
         ployment.  Dec. 3, 1973, pp. 33315-16.  (Proposed
         changes to 5 CFR [Code of Federal Regulations], par.
         731)

242)     Walters, David M.  Homophiles of Penn State.
         ("Otherwise Monograph Series," No. 14)  New York:
         National Task Force on Student Personnel Services
         and Homosexuality, 1972.  10 pp.

243)     _____.  Student Teaching and Gay Liberation.
         ("Otherwise Monograph Series," No. 10)  New York:
         National Task Force on Student Personnel Services and
         Homosexuality, 1972. 11 pp.  (Joseph Acanfora case)

244)     West, Celeste (ed.).  "Gay Liberation."  Special is-
         sue of Synergy, no. 29, Sep.-Oct. 1970.  44 pp.
         (See nos. 2241, 2263, 2376, 2459, and 2469)

245)     Women and Literature: An Annotated Bibliography of
         Women Writers.  2nd ed.  Revised and enlarged.
         Cambridge, Mass.: The Sensibility Collective, 1973.
         58 pp.  (43 items on lesbianism)

246)     Young, Allen.  Gay Sunshine Interview with Allen
         Ginsberg.  Bolinas, Ca.: Grey Fox Press, 1973.
         42 pp.  (Reprinted from Gay Sunshine, no. 16, Jan.-
         Feb. 1973)

# THESES AND DISSERTATIONS

247) Annon, Jack S. The Extension of Learning Principles to the Analysis and Treatment of Sexual Problems. Ph.D., Psychology, University of Hawaii, 1971. 570 pp. University Microfilm no. 72-290. (Summary in Dissertation Abstracts International, 32/05-B, p. 3627, 1971)

248) Anthony, Robert M. Conflict in the Male Homosexual and Non-homosexual and Its Relationship to Intrapersonal, Interpersonal, and Vocational Adjustment. M.A., Psychology, University of California, 1964. 111 pp.

249) Bauer, Alan J. A Study of Self-Concept in Women Who Identify with Either a Gay Lib or Women's Lib Organization. Ed.D., Psychology, University of North Colorado, 1973. 97 pp. University Microfilm no. 74-1600. (Summary in Dissertation Abstracts International, 34/07-A, p. 3977, 1974)

250) Blair, Ralph E. Student Personnel Perspectives and Homosexually Interested College Students. Ed.D., Counseling and Guidance, Pennsylvania State University, 1971. 296 pp. University Microfilm no. 72-19277. (Summary in Dissertation Abstracts International, 33/01-A, p. 151, 1972)

251) Brown, Donald A. A Study of the Educational and Vocational Decision-making of Four Groups of Homosexuals. Ph.D., Educational Psychology, University of Michigan, 1973. 150 pp. University Microfilm no. 74-15678. (Summary in Dissertation Abstracts International, 35/01-A, p. 252, 1974)

252) Caffrey, Thomas A. Assaultive and Troublesome Behavior among Adolescent Homosexual Prison Inmates.

Ph. D. , Psychology, City University of New York, 1974.   118 pp.   University Microfilm no. 74-16977. (Summary in Disseration Abstracts International, 35/02-B, p. 1038, 1974)

253)    Carrier, Joseph M.   Urban Mexican Male Homosexual Encounters:  An Analysis of Participants and Coping Strategies.   Ph. D. , Psychology, University of California at Irvine, 1972.   335 pp.   University Microfilm no. 72-32339.   (Summary in Dissertation Abstracts International, 33/06-B, p. 2787, 1972)

254)    Dank, Barry M.   The Development of a Homosexual Identity:  Antecedents and Consequents.   Ph. D. , Sociology, University of Wisconsin, 1973.   270 pp. University Microfilm no. , 73-10706.   (Summary in Dissertation Abstracts International, 34/01-A, p. 423, 1973)

255)    Eisenberg, Mark A.   The Process of Homosexual Identification and the Effect of the Homosexual Subculture on the Lifestyle of the Homosexual.   Ph. D. , Psychology, University of Massachusetts, 1974. 182 pp.   University Microfilm no. 75-6016.   (Summary in Dissertation Abstracts International, 35/09-B, p. 4648, 1975)

256)    Elkin, Ann J.   Early Recollections of Male Homosexuals.   Ph. D. , Psychology, United States International University, 1974.   162 pp.   University Microfilm no. 74-14311.   (Summary in Dissertation Abstracts International, 35/01-B, p. 499, 1974)

257)    Farrell, Ronald A.   Societal Reaction of Homosexuals:  Toward a Generalized Theory of Deviance. Ph. D. , Sociology, University of Cincinnati, 1972. 228 pp.   University Microfilm no. 72-31729.   (Summary in Dissertation Abstracts International, 33/06-A, p. 3035, 1972)

258)    Finkelstein, Bonnie B.   The Role of Women in the Novels in E. M. Forster with Parallels to the Role of Homosexuals in "Maurice. "   Ph. D. , Modern Language and Literature, Columbia University, 1972. 207 pp.   University Microfilm no. 72-31207.   (Summary in Dissertation Abstracts International, 33/06-A, p. 2931, 1972)

259)     Freeman, William M.    The Alteration of Sexual Pre-
         ference in the Human Male:  A Conditioning Therapy
         for Male Homosexuals.    Ph. D. , Psychology, Univer-
         sity of Louisville, 1972.    177 pp.    University Micro-
         film no. 73-05812.    (Summary in Dissertation Ab-
         stracts International, 33/09-B, p. 4503, 1973)

260)     Gigl, John L.    The Overt Male Homosexual:  A Pri-
         mary Description of a Self-selected Population.  Ph. D. ,
         Counseling and Guidance, University of Oregon, 1970.
         113 pp.    University Microfilm no. 71-16811.    (Sum-
         mary in Dissertation Abstracts International, 32/01-
         A, p. 174, 1971)

261)     Grevatt, Margaret V.    Lesbian/Feminism:  A Re-
         sponse to Oppression.    Ph. D. , Sociology, Case West-
         ern Reserve University, 1975.    457 pp.    University
         Microfilm no. 75-27916.    (Summary in Dissertation
         Abstracts International, 36/01-A, p. 4772, 1976)

262)     Hendlin, Steven J.    Rorschach Indices of Homosex-
         uality in Overt Adjusted Male Homosexuals:  A Study
         of Validity and Reliability.    Ph. D. , Psychology,
         United States International University, 1975.    126 pp.
         University Microfilm no. 75-19114.    (Summary in
         Dissertation Abstracts International, 36/09-B, pp.
         1407-08, 1975)

263)     Herman, Steven H.    An Experimental Analysis of Two
         Methods of Increasing Heterosexual Arousal in Homo-
         sexuals.    Ph. D. , Psychology, University of Missisip-
         pi, 1972.    135 pp.    University Microfilm no. 72-
         20232.    (Summary in Dissertation Abstracts Interna-
         tional, 33/01-B, p. 439, 1972)

264)     Hoffman, Andrew J.    The Freudian Theory of the Re-
         lationship between Paranoia and Repressed Homosex-
         ual Wishes in Women.    Ph. D. , Psychology, Case
         Western Reserve University, 1975.    93 pp.    Univer-
         sity Microfilm no. 75-19212.    (Summary in Disserta-
         tion Abstracts International, 36/09-B, pp. 1436-37,
         1975)

265)     Horstman, William R.    Homosexuality and Psycho-
         pathology:  A Study of the MMPI Responses of Homo-
         sexual and Heterosexual Male College Students.
         Ph. D. , Psychology, University of Oregon, 1971.

116 pp. University Microfilm no. 72-28153. (Summary in Dissertation Abstracts International, 33/05-B, p. 2347, 1972)

266) Kalman, Barbara A. Differences in the Emotional Adjustment and Self-concepts among Institutionalized Delinquent Girls Relative to the Kinship System and Homosexuality. Ph. D., Psychology, Ball State University, 1970. 134 pp. University Microfilm no. 71-09522. (Summary in Dissertation Abstracts International, 31/10-B, p. 6259, 1971)

267) Kelly, James J. III. Brothers and Brothers: The Gay Man's Adaptation to Aging. Ph. D., Social Work, Brandeis University, 1974. 244 pp. University Microfilm no. 74-24234. (Summary in Dissertation Abstracts International, 36/11-A, p. 3130, 1975)

268) Kwawer, Jay S. An Experimental Study of Psychoanalytic Theories of Overt Male Homosexuality. Ph. D., Psychology, New York University, 1971. 108 pp. University Microfilm no. 72-13380. (Summary in Dissertation Abstracts International, 32/10-B, p. 6053, 1972)

269) Lell, Gordon. The Rape of Ganymede: Greek-love Themes in Elizabethan Friendship Literature. Ph. D., English, University of Nebraska, 1970. 303 pp. University Microfilm no. 71-09573. (Summary in Dissertation Abstracts International, 31/10-A, pp. 5367-68, 1971)

270) Lumby, Malcolm E. Sociolinguistic Code-switching and Sexual Orientation: A Content Analysis of Homoerotic Stories. Ph. D., Speech, Southern Illinois University, 1974. 206 pp. University Microfilm no. 75-16273. (Summary in Dissertation Abstracts International, 36/08-A, pp. 600-01, 1975)

271) May, Eugene P. A Study of Therapists' and Homosexuals' Philosophies of Human Nature and Attitudes toward Deviant Behavior. Ph. D., Psychology, University of Illinois at Champagne-Urbana, 1971. 131 pp. University Microfilm no. 72-12290. (Summary in Dissertation Abstracts International, 32/10-B, p. 6056, 1972)

272)     Mundorff, Jan E.   Personality Characteristics of Se-
         lected College Male Heterosexuals, Homosexual Ac-
         tivists, and Non-activists.   Ed. D. , Northern Illinois
         University, 1973.   153 pp.   University Microfilm no.
         73-20558.   (Summary in Dissertation Abstracts Inter-
         national, 34/03-A, p. 1137, 1973)

273)     Murphy, Norman C.   Anxiety, Homosexual Attitude,
         Duration of Time since Initial Explicitly Sexual Re-
         sponses:  Admitted Homosexual and Heterosexual
         Samples.   Ph. D. , Psychology, University of Wash-
         ington, 1971.   172 pp.   University Microfilm no.
         72-07397.   (Summary in Dissertation Abstracts Inter-
         national, 32/08-B, p. 4848, 1972)

274)     Nelson, Catherine I.   A Study of Homosexuality among
         Women Inmates at Two State Prisons. Ph. D. , Sociol-
         ogy-Criminology, Temple University, 1974.   225 pp.
         University Microfilm no. 74-28243.   (Summary in
         Dissertation Abstracts International, 35/06-A, p.
         3908, 1974)

275)     Norton, Rictor C.   Studies of the Union of Love and
         Death:  I.   Heracles and Hylas:  The Homosexual
         Archetype.   II.   The Pursuit of Ganymede in Renais-
         sance Pastoral Literature.   III.   Folkore and Myth
         in "Who's Afraid of Virginia Woolf?"   IV.   "The
         Turn of the Screw":  Coincidenta Oppositorum.
         Ph. D. , Modern Language and Literature, Florida
         State University, 1972.   275 pp.   University Micro-
         film no. 73-04697.   (Summary in Dissertation Ab-
         stracts International, 33/09-A, p. 5190, 1973)

276)     Nyberg, Kenneth L.   Homosexual and Homoerotic Be-
         havior Differences in Men and Women.   Ph. D. , So-
         ciology, University of Utah, 1973.   174 pp.   Univer-
         sity Microfilm no. 73-32032.   (Summary in Disserta-
         tion Abstracts International, 34/07-A, p. 4438, 1974)

277)     Oberstone, Andrea K.   Dimensions of Psychological
         Adjustment and Style of Life in Single Lesbians and
         Single Heterosexual Women.   Ph. D. , Psychology,
         California School of Professional Psychology, 1974.
         244 pp.   University Microfilm no. 75-8510.   (Sum-
         mary in Dissertation Abstracts International, 35/10-
         B, p. 5088, 1975)

278)     Okum, Marjorie E.   Personal Space as a Reaction
         to the Threat of an Interaction with a Homosexual.
         Ph. D. , Psychology, Catholic University of America,
         1975.   115 pp.   University Microfilm no. 75-21536.
         (Summary in Dissertation Abstracts International,
         36/10-B, p. 1973, 1975)

279)     Parker, William C.   Male Homosexuality in the Pris-
         on Setting.   Master's essay, School of Criminal Jus-
         tice, State University of New York at Albany, 1971.

280)     Pineda, Elia B.   Stated Attitudes and Behaviors of
         Registered Nurses Regarding Homosexuality.   M. S. ,
         Nursing, University of Arizona, 1975.   55 pp.

281)     Poole, Kenneth A.   A Sociological Approach to the
         Etiology of Female Homosexuality and the Lesbian
         Social Scene.   Ph. D. , Sociology, University of South-
         ern California, 1970.   203 pp.   University Microfilm
         no. 70-25057.   (Summary in Dissertation Abstracts
         International, 31/06-A, p. 3068, 1970)

282)     Pritt, Thomas E.   A Comparative Study between Male
         Homosexuals' and Heterosexuals' Perceived Parental
         Acceptance-Rejection Self-Concepts and Self-Evalua-
         tion Tendencies.   Ph. D. , Educational Psychology,
         University of Utah, 1971.   194 pp.   University Micro-
         film no. 72-00531.   (Summary in Dissertation Ab-
         stracts International 32/06-A, p. 3100, 1971)

283)     Raphael, Sharon M.   "Coming Out, " the Emergence of
         the Movement Lesbian.   Ph. D. , Sociology, Case West-
         ern Reserve University, 1974.   153 pp.   University Mi-
         crofilm no. 75-5084.   (Summary in Dissertation Ab-
         stracts International, 35/08-A, p. 5336, 1975)

284)     Rethford, William R.   A Descriptive Field Research
         of the Male Homosexual as a Requisite toward a Stra-
         tegy of Christian Ministry.   Ed. D. , Southern Baptist
         Seminary, 1972.   169 pp.   University Microfilm no.
         73-06752.   (Summary in Dissertation Abstracts Inter-
         national, 33/09-B, p. 4494, 1973)

285)     Robinson, David J.   The Rhetoric of Troy Perry:  A
         Case Study of the Los Angeles Gay Rights Rally, No-
         vember 16, 1969.   Ph. D. , Speech, University of

Southern California, 1972.   263 pp.   University Microfilm no. 73-09321.   (Summary in Dissertation Abstracts International, 33/10-A, p. 5870, 1973)

286)   Salsberg, Sheldon.   Membership and Participation in Formal Voluntary Associations by Urban Male Homosexuals.   Ph. D., Sociology, New York University, 1971.   207 pp.   University Microfilm no. 72-03125. (Summary in Dissertation Abstracts International, 32/07-A, p. 4132, 1972)

287)   Skippon, Ronald J.   A Multivariate Analysis of Popular Conceptions and Attitudes Regarding the Etiology of Male Homosexuality.   Ph. D., University of Ottawa, 1974.

288)   Tanner, Barry A.   The Modification of Male Homosexual Behavior by Avoidance Learning.   Ph. D., Psychology, University of North Carolina, 1972. 103 pp.   University Microfilm no. 73-04880.   (Summary in Dissertation Abstracts International, 33/08-B, p. 3923, 1973)

289)   Thompson, Norman L.   Family Background and Sexual Identity in Male and Female Homosexuals.   Ph. D., Psychology, Emory University, 1971.   97 pp.   University Microfilm no. 71-22879.   (Summary in Dissertation Abstracts International, 32/03-B, p. 1863, 1971)

290)   Warren, Carol A. B.   Identity and Community in the Gay World.   Ph. D., Sociology, University of California at San Diego, 1972.   248 pp.   University Microfilm no. 73-04430.   (Summary in Dissertation Abstracts International, 33/08-A, p. 4554, 1972)

291)   Watson, James L.   Understanding and Counseling the Homosexual.   Ph. D., Religion and Theology, Claremont School of Religion, 1972.

292)   Westmoreland, Catherine.   A Study of Long-term Relationships among Male Homosexuals.   Ph. D., Psychology, United States International University, 1975. 156 pp.   University Microfilm no. 75-29424.   (Summary in Dissertation Abstracts International, 36/12-B, p. 3132, 1976)

293) Williams, Colin J. Discharges from the Military: An Examination of Labelling Theory. Ph. D. , Sociology, Rutgers University, 1970. 381 pp. University Microfilm no. 70-16960. (Summary in Dissertation Abstracts International, 31/03-A, p. 1393, 1970)

294) Wilson, Marilyn L. A New Female Homosexuality Scale. Ed. D. , Psychology, University of Northern Colorado, 1973. 116 pp. University Microfilm no. 74-1657. (Summary in Dissertation Abstracts International, 34/08-B, p. 4065, 1974)

## ARTICLES IN BOOKS

295)  Abbott, Sidney and Love, Barbara. "Is Women's Liberation a Lesbian Plot?" in Vivian Gornick and Barbara K. Moran (eds. ), Woman in Sexist Society: Studies in Power and Powerlessness (New York: Basic Books, 1971), pp. 436-51 (chap. 26).

296)  "The Acanfora Case, " in Barbara Yates, Steve Werner, and David Rosen (eds. ), We'll Do It Ourselves: Combatting Sexism in Education (Lincoln, Nebr. : Study Commission on Undergraduate Education and the Education of Teachers, 1974), pp. 291-321. (Partial reprint of decisions in the U.S. District Court for Maryland and the 4th Circuit Court of Appeals. ) (See no. 1643)

297)  Adler, Kurt A. "Homosexuality from the Standpoint of Individual Psychology," in William S. Sahakian (ed. ), Psychopathology Today: Experimentation, Theory and Research (Itaska, Ill. : Peacock Publishers, 1970), pp. 511-18. (Reprinted from Adler, "Life Style, Gender Role, and the Symptom of Homosexuality," Journal of Individual Psychology, 23:67-78, 1967)

298)  Alinder, Gary. "Entries in a Journal," in Jay and Young, no. 76, pp. 73-82.

299)  _____. "Gay Liberation meets the Shrinks, " in Jay and Young, no. 77, pp. 141-45.

300)  _____. "My Gay Soul, " in Richmond and Noguerra, no. 122, pp. 139-41; and in Jay and Young, no. 77, pp. 282-83.

301)  _____. "Off Dr. Bieber," in Richmond and Noguerra, no. 122, pp. 105-09.

302)    Altman, Dennis.  "Introduction, " in Richmond and
        Noguerra, no. 122, pp. 14-18.

303)    "American Laws applicable to Consensual Adult Ho-
        mosexual Acts, " in ACLU Handbook, no. 18, pp. 163-
        209.

304)    American Library Association, Task Force on Gay
        Liberation, Social Responsibilities Roundtable.  "A
        Gay Bibliography--3rd Revison, " in ACLU Handbook,
        no. 18, pp. 241-49; and in Yates, Werner, and Ro-
        sen, no. 296, pp. 124-33.  (105 items)

305)    Anderson, J. N. D.  "Homosexuality, " in Morality,
        Law, and Grace (London:  Tyndale Press, 1972),
        pp. 67-74.  (Paperback)

306)    Anonymous.  "Butch or Fem:  The Third World Les-
        bian's Dilemma, " in Jay and Young, no. 76, pp. 68-69.

307)    Anonymous.  "Don Leon:  A Poem by Lord Byron and
        Forming a Part of a Political Journal by His Lord-
        ship, Supposed to Have Been Entirely Destroyed by
        Thomas Moore, London [1930], " in Homosexual Eman-
        cipation Miscellany, no. 65, pp. 1-107.

308)    Anonymous.  "Lesbians Belong in the Women's Move-
        ment, " in Women Unite!  An Anthology of the Cana-
        dian Women's Movement (Toronto:  Canadian Women's
        Educational Press, 1972), pp. 171-73.

309)    Anonymous.  "Some Notes of a Homosexual Teaching
        Assistant in His First Summer of Ph. D. Work, " in
        Lehman, no. 88, pp. 16-18.

310)    Ard, Ben N. Jr.  "Problematic Behavior (Homosex-
        uality), " in Treating Psychosexual Dysfunction (New
        York:  Jason Aronson, 1974), pp. 157-70 (chap. 13).

311)    Atkinson, Ti-Grace.  "Lesbianism and Feminism, "
        in Amazon Odyssey (New York:  Links Books-Quick
        Fox, 1974), pp. 83-88 and 131-89.

312)    _____.  "Lesbianism and Feminism, " in Birkby
        and Others, no. 16, pp. 11-14.

313)    Baker, Susan.  "Anne Bonny and Mary Read, " in

Myron and Bunch, no. 107, pp. 77-89.

314)    Bancroft, John.    "A Comparative Study of Aversion
        and Desensitization in the Treatment of Homosexual-
        ity, " in Laurence E. Burns and James L. Worsley
        (eds. ), Behaviour Therapy in the 1970s:  A Collection
        of Original Papers (Bristol, Eng. :  John Wright and
        Sons, 1970), pp. 12-33.

315)                    .   "The Relationship between Gender Identity
        and Sexual Behavior:  Some Clinical Aspects, " in
        Christopher Ounsted and David C. Taylor (eds. ),
        Gender Differences:  Their Ontogony and Significance
        (Edinburgh:  Churchill Livingstone, 1972), pp. 57-
        72 (chap. 4).

316)    Barlow, David H.    "The Treatment of Sexual Devia-
        tion:  Toward a Comprehensive Behavioral Approach,"
        in Karen S. Calhoun, Henry E. Adams, and Kevin
        M. Mitchell (eds. ), Innovative Treatment Methods in
        Psychopathology (New York:  Wiley and Sons, 1974),
        pp. 121-47 (chap. 4).

317)    Bartell, Gilbert D.    "More Action, " in Group Sex
        (New York:  Peter H. Wyden, Inc. , 1971), pp. 146-
        62 (chap. 8).

318)    Bell, Alan.    "The Homosexual as Patient" and "The
        Homosexual as Physician, " in Richard Green (ed. ),
        Human Sexuality:  A Health Practitioner's Text (Bal-
        timore:  Williams and Wilkins, 1974), pp. 35-74 and
        75-82 (chaps. 5-6).

319)    Bell, Robert R.    "Male Homosexuality" and "Female
        Homosexuality, " in Social Deviance:  A Substantive
        Analysis (Homewood, Ill:  Dorsey Press, 1971), pp.
        248-305 (chaps. 10 and 11).

320)    Bender, David and McCuen, Gary.    "Comparing Al-
        ternate Family Structures" and "Analyzing Gay Rights, "
        in Determing Family and Sexual Roles (Anoka, Minn. :
        Greenhaven Press, 1973).

321)    Bengis, Ingrid.    "Lesbianism, " in Combat in the
        Erogenous Zone (New York:  Knopf, 1972), pp. 115-
        94.    (Paperback ed. :  Bantam)

322)     Benson, Leonard.  "Sex and Restraint ... Homosex-
         uality," in The Family Bond:  Marriage, Love and
         Sex in America (New York:  Random House, 1971),
         pp. 71-102 at 86-90 (chap. 5).

323)     Bentley, Eric R.  "Men's Liberation," in Theatre of
         War (New York:  Viking Press, 1972), pp. 326-33.

324)     Benton, Nick.  "The Same Old Game," "David," and
         "Don't Call Me Brother," in Richmond and Noguerra,
         no. 122, pp. 36-37, 57-59, and 181-83.

325)     Berlandt, Konstantin.  "Bring the Beautiful Boys
         Home," in Richmond and Noguerra, no. 122, pp.
         147-49.

326)     _____.  "My Soul Vanished from Sight:  A Cali-
         fornia Saga of Gay Liberation," in Jay and Young,
         no. 77, pp. 38-55.

327)     _____.  "Search for Words," in Jay and Young,
         no. 76, pp. 70-72.

328)     Berson, Ginny.  "The Furies," in Myron and Bunch,
         no. 106, pp. 15-19.

329)     Bieber, Irving and Others.  "Conclusions," in McCaf-
         frey, no. 101, pp. 84-100.  (Reprinted from Bieber
         and others, Homosexuality:  A Psychoanalytic Study
         of Male Homosexuals [New York:  Basic Books,
         1962], pp. 303-19.)

330)     Bieber, Toby.  "Group Therapy with Homosexuals,"
         in Harold I. Kaplan and Benjamin J. Sadock (eds.),
         Group Treatment of Mental Illness (New York:  Dut-
    ·    ton, 1972), pp. 25-40 (chap. 2).

331)     Blaine, Graham B. Jr. and McArthur, Charles C.
         "Basic Character Disorders and Homosexuality," in
         Emotional Problems of Students (2nd ed.; New York:
         Appleton, Century, Crofts, 1971), pp. 94-108 (chap. 6).

332)     Bleuel, Hans P.  "Ernst Roehm, A Taste for Men"
         and "Drowned in a Bog," in Sex and Society in Nazi
         Germany, translated from the German by J. Maxwell
         Brownjohn (Philadelphia:  Lippincott, 1973), pp. 95-
         101 and 217-25.

333)     Blixton, Sandy. "Viewpoint of an Anti-sexist Marx-
         ist," in Jay and Young, no. 77, pp. 323-27.

334)     Block, William A.  "Homosexuality," in What Your
         Child Really Wants to Know about Sex--and Why (En-
         glewood Cliffs, N.J.:  Prentice-Hall, 1972), pp. 213-
         21 (chap. 14).

335)     Blumenfeld, Warren.  "The Oppression of Gay Peo-
         ple," in Yates, Werner, and Rosen, no. 296, pp.
         81-102.

336)     Blumstein, Philip W. and Schwarz, Pepper.  "Les-
         bianism and Bisexuality," in Goode and Troiden, no.
         55, pp. 278-95.

337)     Bogdan, Robert.  "A New Life," in Being Different:
         The Autobiography of Jane Fry (New York:  Wiley and
         Sons, 1974), pp. 161-67 (chap. 13).

338)     Boston Women's Health Book Collective.  "In Ameri-
         ka They Call Us Dykes," in Our Bodies, Ourselves:
         A Book Especially for Women (Boston:  Simon and
         Schuster, 1971), pp. 56-73 (chap. 5).

339)     Boyd, Kenneth M.  "Homosexuality and the Church,"
         in Loraine, no. 95, pp. 165-86 (chap. 7).

340)     Bradley, Marion Z.  "Astra's Tower: Special Leaf-
         lets Nos. 2 and 3," in A Gay Bibliography, no. 52,
         pp. 7-71.  (290 items)  (Reprint of annotated biblio-
         graphy published in 1958-59)

341)     _____ and Damon, Gene.  "Checklist 1960, 1961,
         and 1962" in A Gay Bibliography, no. 52, pp. 73-235.
         (1,399 items)  (Reprint of annotated bibliography pub-
         lished in 1960, 1961, and 1962)

342)     Brasch, Rudolf.  "Out of the Ordinary," in How Did
         Sex Begin? (New York:  David McKay Co., 1973),
         pp. 202-34 at 202-14 (chap. 14).

343)     Brass, Perry.  "Cruising: Games Men Play" and
         "Games Male Chauvinists Play," in Jay and Young,
         no. 77, pp. 264-65; and in Richmond and Noguerra,
         no. 122, pp. 39-41.

344)     British Society for the Study of Sex Psychology.
         "Policy and Principles--General Aims" and "The So-
         cial Problem of Sexual Inversion," in <u>Homosexual</u>
         <u>Emancipation Miscellany</u>, no. 65, pp. 1-10 and 1-12.
         (Reprinted from pamphlets published in London in
         1920 and 1923)

345)     Brown, Fred and Kempton, Rudolf T.  "Homosexual-
         ity and Variations in Sexual Expression," in <u>Sex</u>
         <u>Questions and Answers</u> (2nd ed.; New York:  Mc-
         Graw-Hill, 1970), pp. 224-45 (chap. 12).

346)     Brown, Harold; Cooper, Janet; Hansen, Bert; Par-
         man, Leah; Manford, Morty; and Stanley, Julia P.
         "Coming Out," in <u>Universities and the Gay Experi-</u>
         <u>ence</u>, no. 51, pp. 59-87.

347)     Brown, Rita M.  "Living with Other Women" and
         "The Shape of Things to Come," in Myron and Bunch,
         no. 106, pp. 63-67 and 69-77.

348)     _____.  "Take a Lesbian to Lunch" and "Hanoi to
         Hoboken:  A Round Trip Ticket," in Jay and Young,
         no. 77, pp. 189-95 and 195-201.

349)     _____.  "We'd Better All Hang Together or Surely
         We'll All Hang Separately," in Jay and Young, no.
         76, pp. 227-31.

350)     Bunch, Charlotte.  "Dona Catalina de Erauso," in
         Myron and Bunch, no. 107, pp. 43-50.

351)     _____.  "Lesbians in Revolt," in Myron and Bunch,
         no. 106, pp. 21-26.

352)     Burke, Tom.  "The New Homosexuality," in Philip
         Nobile (ed.), <u>The New Eroticism</u> (New York:  Ran-
         dom House, 1970), pp. 77-97.  (Reprinted from <u>Es-</u>
         <u>quire</u>, 73:178, 304-18, Dec. 1969)

353)     Burroughs, William.  "Sexual Conditioning," in Rich-
         mond and Noguerra, no. 122, pp. 194-95.

354)     Burt, John and Brower, Linda.  "Homosexuality,"
         in <u>Education for Sexuality:  Concepts and Programs</u>
         <u>for Teaching</u> (Philadelphia:  W. B. Saunders Co.,
         1970), pp. 148-61 (chap. 10).

355)     Byron, Stuart.   "The Closet Syndrome," in Jay and
         Young, no. 77, pp. 58-65.

356)     Campbell, Robert J.   "Alienation and Homosexuality,"
         in William C. Bier (ed. ), Alienation:  Plight of Mod-
         ern Man? (New York:   Fordham University Press,
         1972), pp. 219-29.

357)     Cantor, Donald J.   "The Homosexual Revolution--A
         Status Report," in Lester A. Kirkendall and Robert
         N. Whitehurst (eds. ), The New Sexual Revolution
         (New York:  Donald W. Brown, Inc. , 1971), pp. 85-
         96 (chap. 7).   (Reprinted from The Humanist, 27:
         160-63, Fall 1967)

358)     Carr, Tom.   "How to Get Publicity for Campus Gay
         Groups," in Lehman, no. 88, pp. 34-36.

359)     Chesser, Eustace.   "Homosexuality," in Young Adults'
         Guide to Sex (New York:   Drake Publishers, 1972),
         pp. 97-104 (chap. 10).

360)     _____ .   "Society and the Homosexual," "The Ho-
         mosexual Dilemma," and "Female Homosexuality,"
         in Strange Loves:  The Human Aspects of Sexual De-
         viations (London:   Jarrolds Publishers, 1971), pp.
         125-45, 146-61, and 162-78 (chaps. 8-10).

361)     Chicago Gay Liberation.   "Working Paper for the
         Revolutionary People's Constitutional Convention," in
         Jay and Young, no. 77, pp. 346-52.

362)     Chicago Gay Liberation Front.   "A Leaflet for the Amer-
         ican Medical Association," in Jay and Young, no. 77,
         pp. 145-47.

363)     Chou, Eric.   "The Manchus Indulge in Homosexuali-
         ty," in The Dragon and the Phoenix (New York:  Ar-
         bor House, 1971), pp. 112-15.

364)     Clark, Donald.   "Homosexual Encounters in All-Male
         Groups," in Lawrence Solomon and Betty Berzon (eds.),
         New Perspectives in Encounter Groups (San Francisco:
         Jossey-Bass, 1972), pp. 368-82; and in Joseph H. Pleck
         and Jack Sawyer (eds.), Men and Masculinity (Englewood
         Cliffs, N.J.:  Prentice-Hall, 1974), pp. 88-93.

365)     Coleman, James.   "My Homosexuality and My Psy-

chotherapy, " in Ruitenbeek, no. 127, pp. 191-98.

366)     Coleman, P. E. "Changing the Law and the English Ex-
         perience, " in Oberholtzer, no. 112, pp. 185-98 (chap. 8).

367)     Colton, Helen. "Homosexuality and Bisexuality, " in
         Sex after the Sexual Revolution (New York: Associa-
         tion Press, 1972), pp. 67-75.

368)     Cooper, Alan J. "Aetiology of Homosexuality, " in
         Loraine, no. 95, pp. 1-23 (chap. 1).

369)     Cordova, Jeanne. "What's a Dyke to Do? And What
         the Dyke Is Doing" and "How to Come Out without
         Being Thrown Out, " in Jay and Young, no. 76, pp.
         16-21 and 89-95.

370)     Crew, Louie. "Inherit the Earth, " in Wickliff, no.
         159a, pp. 68-77.

370a)    _____. "Thriving Decloseted in Rural Academe, "
         in Jay and Young, no. 76, pp. 96-102.

371)     Crompton, Louis. "Literature and Our Gay Minor-
         ity, " in Yates, Werner, and Rosen, no. 296, pp.
         105-23. (Reprinted from Iowa English Bulletin Year-
         book, Fall 1973, pp. 3-21)

372)     Cronin, Denise M. "Coming Out among Lesbians, "
         in Goode and Troiden, no. 55, pp. 268-77.

373)     Curzon, Daniel. "Something You Do in the Dark, "
         in McCaffrey, no. 101, pp. 198-204. (Reprinted from
         Curzon, no. 2957, pp. 18-25.)

374)     Damon, Gene and Stuart, Lee. "The Lesbian in Lit-
         erature: A Bibliography, " in A Gay Bibliography,
         no. 52, pp. 237-323. (2,047 items) (Reprint of an-
         notated bibliography published in 1967)

375)     Daniels, Arlene K. "The Social Construction of Mil-
         itary Psychiatric Diagnoses, " in Hans P. Dreitzel
         (ed.), Recent Sociology No. 2: Patterns in Commun-
         icative Behavior (New York: Macmillan, 1970), pp.
         182-205 at 200-02.

376)     Dank, Barry M. "The Homosexual, " in Goode and
         Troiden, no. 55, pp. 174-210.

377)        _____. "The Homosexual," in Don Spiegel and
            Patricia Keith-Spiegel (eds.), Outsiders USA: Orig-
            inal Essays on 24 Outgroups in American Society
            (San Francisco: Rinehart, 1973), pp. 269-97.

378)        d'Arcangelo, Angelo. "The Homosexual Handbook,"
            in Maurice Girodias (ed.), The New Olympia Reader
            (New York: Olympia Press, 1970).

379)        Daunton, Elizabeth. "Treatment of a Bisexual Con-
            flict in Prepuberty and Adolescence," in Marjorie
            Harley (ed.), The Analyst and the Adolescent at Work
            (New York: Quadrangle, 1974), pp. 40-67.

380)        Davis, Alan J. "Sexual Assaults in the Philadelphia
            Prison System," in John H. Gagnon and William Si-
            mon (eds.), The Sexual Scene (Chicago: Aldine
            Press, 1970), pp. 107-24. (Reprinted from Trans-
            Action, 6:8-16, Dec. 1968)

381)        Davis, Katherine B. and Kopp, Mario E. "Homo-
            sexuality: The Unmarried College Woman" and "Ho-
            mosexuality: The Married Woman," in Katherine B.
            Davis, Factors in the Sex Life of 2200 Women (New
            York: Arno Press, 1972), pp. 238-96 and 297-328
            (chaps. 10-11). (Reprint of original work published
            in 1929)

382)        Davison, Gerald C. and Neale, John M. "Homosex-
            uality," in Abnormal Psychology: An Experimental
            Clinical Approach (New York: Wiley and Sons, 1974),
            pp. 293-322 (chap. 12).

383)        Day, Beth. "The White Man's Way: Homosexuality
            across the Color Line," in Sexual Life between Blacks
            and Whites (New York: World Publishing Co., 1972),
            pp. 323-37 (chap. 19).

384)        "Declaration by the First National Congress on Edu-
            cation and Culture," in Jay and Young, no. 77, pp.
            246-50. (Translated from the Spanish)

385)        Deevey, Sharon. "Such a Nice Girl," in Myron and
            Bunch, no. 106, pp. 21-26.

386)        Della Rosa, Laura. "The Bi-sexual Potential," in
            Jay and Young, no. 76, pp. 62-64.

387) D'Emilio, John. "Introduction," in Universities and the Gay Experience, no. 51, pp. 9-18.

388) Deming, Barbara. "An Exchange of Letters: Confronting One's Own Oppression," in We Cannot Live without Our Lives (New York: Grossman Publishers, 1974), pp. 117-48.

389) DeMott, Benjamin. "But He's a Homosexual ... ," in Irving Buchen (ed.), The Perverse Imagination: Sexuality and Literary Culture (New York: New York University Press, 1970), pp. 147-64; and in Ruitenbeek, no. 127, pp. 37-52. (Reprinted from New American Review, 1:166-82, 1967)

390) Diaman, N. A. "On Sex Roles and Equality," in Jay and Young, no. 77, pp. 262-64.

391) Dobinski, Karla. "Lesbians and the Law," in Jay and Young, no. 76, pp. 152-60.

392) Dotten, Thomas. "Niggers in the Woodpile," in Jay and Young, no. 76, pp. 218-26.

393) Duberman, Martin and Gittings, Barbara. "Keynote Addresses," in Universities and the Gay Experience, no. 51, pp. 23-28 and 29-32.

394) Duyckaerts, Francois. "Homosexual Attraction and Heterosexual Fears," in The Sexual Bond, translated from the French by John A. Kay (New York: Dell Publishing Co., 1970), pp. 131-63 (chap. 5).

395) Edwards, Samuel (pseud.). "Chapter Five," in George Sand: A Biography of the First Modern Liberated Woman (New York: McKay, 1972), 73-91.

396) Elliott, Neil. "Homosexuality" and "Lesbians, Pederasts, and Boy Prostitution," in Sensuality in Scandinavia (New York: Weybright and Talley, 1970), pp. 186-99 (chap. 17) and 200-07 (chap. 18).

397) Evans, Arthur. "How to Zap Straights," in Richmond and Noguerra, no. 122, pp. 111-15.

398) Fairburn, Nicholas H. "Homosexuality and the Law," in Loraine, no. 95, pp. 160-64 (chap. 6).

399)     Farrell, Ronald A. and Hardin, Clay W. "Legal
         Stigma and Homosexual Career Deviance," in Marc
         Riedel and Terence P. Thornberry (eds.), Crime and
         Delinquency: Dimensions of Deviance (New York:
         Praeger, 1974), pp. 128-40.

400)     "Father Knows Best," in Richmond and Noguerra,
         no. 122, pp. 165-68.

401)     Fee, Elizabeth. "Science and Homosexuality," in
         Universities and the Gay Experience, no. 51, pp.
         35-39.

402)     Feldman, M. P. "Abnormal Sexual Behavior in
         Males," in Hans J. Eysenck (ed.), Handbook of Ab-
         normal Psychology (2nd ed.; London: Pitman Medi-
         cal Books, 1973), pp. 131-43 and 152-60.

403)     "Final Report of Task Force on Homosexuality," in
         McCaffrey, no. 101, pp. 145-55. (Excerpts from
         Livingood, no. 92)

404)     Frank, Jerome. "Treatment of Homosexuals," in
         Livingood, no. 92, pp. 63-68.

405)     Freedman, Alfred M.; Kaplan, Harold F.; and Sad-
         dock, Benjamin J. "Homosexuality." in Modern Syn-
         opsis of Psychiatry: A Comprehensive Textbook (Bal-
         timore: Williams and Wilkins, 1972), pp. 413-19.

406)     Freund, Kurt W. "Male Homosexuality: An Analysis
         of the Pattern," in Loraine, no. 95, pp. 26-81
         (chap. 2).

407)     Friedenberg, Edgar Z. "Homophobic Society," in
         Universities and the Gay Experience, no. 51, pp. 40-43.

408)     Gagnon, John H. "On Being in the 'Community,'"
         in Jack D. Douglas (ed.), Observations of Deviance
         (New York: Random House, 1970), pp. 112-14 (chap.
         8). (Reprinted from William Simon and John H.
         Gagnon, Sexual Deviance [New York: Harper and Row,
         1967], pp. 261-63)

409)     _____ and Simon, William. "Male Homosexuality,"
         "The Lesbian," and "Homosexual Conduct in Prison,"
         in Sexual Conduct: The Social Sources of Human

Sexuality (Chicago: Aldine Publishing Co., 1973), pp. 129-75 (chap. 5), 176-216 (chap. 6), and 235-59 (chap. 8).

410)     _____ and _____. "The Social Meaning of Prison Homosexuality," in Richard D. Knudtsen (ed.), Crime, Criminology, and Contemporary Society (Homewood, Ill.: Dorsey Press, 1970), pp. 367-77. (Reprinted from Federal Probation, 32:23-29, Mar. 1968).

411)     Garde, Noel I. (pseud.). "The Homosexual in Literature: A Chronological Bibliography, circa 700 B.C.-- 1958," in A Gay Bibliography, no. 52, pp. 327-62. (587 items) (Reprint of work published in 1959)

412)     Gay Liberation Front Women (New York City). "Lesbians and the Ultimate Liberation of Women," in Jay and Young, no. 77, pp. 201-03.

413)     "Gay Liberation Theatre," in Richmond and Noguerra, no. 122, pp. 97-104.

414)     A Gay Male Group. "Notes on Gay Male Consciousness-raising," in Jay and Young, no. 77, pp. 293-301.

415)     "Gay Organizations," in ACLU Handbook, no. 18, pp. 263-68. (65 items)

416)     "Gay Revolutionary Party Manifesto," in Jay and Young, no. 77, pp. 342-45.

417)     "Gay Student Groups," in Lehman, no. 88, pp. 36-39. (List of 150 groups in United States and 11 in Canada)

418)     "Gay Studies Syllabi," in Lehman, no. 88, pp. 59-66. (University of Nebraska, Rutgers University, California State University at Sacramento, California State at Long Beach, Swarthmore College, Concordia College, University of Montreal, University of Toronto--St. Michael's College, California State University at Los Angeles, University of Massachusetts, and Queens College)

419)     Gearhart, Sally and Martin, Del. "Afterthought: Lesbians as Gays and as Women," in Lehman, no.

88, pp. 69-74. (Reprinted with additions in Yates, Werner, and Rosen, no. 296, pp. 268-87)

420)    Gebhard, Paul H.  "Homosexuality," in Paul H. Gebhard, Jan Raboch, and Hans Giese, The Sexuality of Women (New York:  Stein and Day, 1970), pp. 33-37 (chap. 8).

421)    _____.  "Incidences of Overt Homosexuality in the United States and Western Europe," in Livingood, no. 92, pp. 22-29.

422)    Geis, Gilbert.  "Consensual Homosexuality," in Not the Law's Business:  An Examination of Homosexuality, Abortion, Prostitution, and Gambling in the United States (Rockville, Md. :  National Institute of Mental Health, Center for Studies of Crime and Delinquency, 1972), pp. 15-52 (chap. 2).  (Reprinted as One Eyed Justice [New York:  Drake Publishers, 1974])

423)    Giese, Hans.  "Narcissism, Homosexuality," in Paul H. Gebhard, Jan Raboch and Hans Giese, The Sexuality of Women, translated from the German by Colin Bearne (New York:  Stein and Day, 1970), pp. 106-17 (chap. 12).

424)    Gilder, George.  "The Perils of Androgyny," in Sexual Suicide (New York:  Quadrangle, 1972), pp. 225-37 at 226-28.

425)    _____.  "Single Man Blues," in The Naked Nomads (New York:  Quadrangle, 1974), pp. 8-21 (chap. 1).

426     Ginder, Richard.  "The Other Love," in Binding with Briars:  Sex and Sin in the Catholic Church (Englewood Cliffs, N. J. :  Prentice-Hall, 1975), chap. 13.

427)    Ginsberg, Allen.  "At the Conspiracy Trial," in Richmond and Noguerra, no. 122, pp. 200-02.

428)    Goldfried, Marvin R.  "Homosexual Signs," in Marvin R. Goldfried, George Stricker, and I. B. Weiner (eds. ), Rorschach Handbook of Clinical and Research Applications (Englewood Cliffs, N. J. :  Prentice-Hall, 1971), pp. 188-216.

429)    Goldstein, Martin and Haeberle, Erwin J.   "Homo-
        sexuality," in The Sex Book (New York:  Herder and
        Herder, 1971), pp. 82-84.

430)    Goldstein, Michael J. and Kant, Harold S.   "Peak
        Adolescent Experience with Erotica:  Homosexuals,
        Transsexuals, Users" and "Peak Adult Experience
        with Erotica:  Homosexuals, Transsexuals, Users,"
        in Pornography and Sexual Deviance:  A Report of
        the Legal and Behavioral Institute (Berkeley:  Univer-
        sity of California Press, 1973), pp. 83-97 (chap. 7)
        and 110-21 (chap. 9).

431)    Goode, Erich and Troiden, Richard R.   "Male Ho-
        mosexuality" and "Lesbianism," in Goode and Troi-
        den, no. 55, pp. 149-60 and 229-37.

432)    Goodman, Paul.   "Memoirs of an Ancient Activist,"
        in McCaffrey, no. 101, pp. 175-81; and in Richmond
        and Noguerra, no. 122, pp. 23-29.

433)    Green, Richard.   "The Behaviorally Feminine Male
        Child:  Pretranssexual?  Pretransvestite?  Preho-
        mosexual?  Preheterosexual?" in Richard C. Fried-
        man, Ralph M. Richart, and Raymond L. Vande
        Wiele (eds.), Sex Differences in Behavior (New York:
        Wiley and Sons, 1974), pp. 301-14 (chap. 16).

434)    Grey, Antony.   "The Church's Role after Law Re-
        form," in Oberholtzer, no. 112, pp. 199-203.

435)    _____.   "Homosexual Law Reform," in Brian
        Frost (ed.), The Tactics of Pressure (London:  Gail-
        lard, 1975).

436)    _____.   "Homosexuality--Some Social and Legal
        Aspects," in Loraine, no. 95, pp. 143-49 (chap. 5).

437)    Guthmann, Edward.   "Bottoms Up:  An In-depth Look
        at V.D.," in Jay and Young, no. 76, pp. 267-76.

438)    Guttag, Bianca.   "Homophobia in Library School,"
        in Celeste West and Elizabeth Katz (eds.), Revolting
        Librarians (San Francisco:  Booklegger Press, 1972),
        pp. 37-38.

439)    Hadden, Samuel B.   "Group Psychotherapy with Ho-

mosexual Men," in H. L. P. Resnick and Marvin E. Wolfgang (eds.), Sexual Behavior: Social, Clinical, and Legal Aspects (Boston: Little, Brown and Co., 1972), pp. 267-80 (chap. 13).

440)    Haggerty, Patrick. "Out, Out Damn Faggot," in Richmond and Noguerra, no. 122, pp. 69-78.

441)    Hall, Joel. "Growing up Black and Gay," in Richmond and Noguerra, no. 122, pp. 51-56.

442)    Hall, Ralph. "Confessions of an All-American Boy," in Richmond and Noguerra, no. 122, pp. 31-35.

443)    Hampson, John L. "Changing Views on Homosexuality, Transvestism, and Transsexualism," in Robert H. Williams (ed.), To Live and to Die: When, Why, and How (New York: Springer Verlag, 1973), pp. 306-18 (chap. 25).

444)    Hansen, Waldemar. "Naked to His Enemies," in The Peacock Throne (New York: Holt, Rinehart, and Winston, 1972), pp. 396-412 (chap. 24).

445)    Hanson, Craig A. "The Fairy Princess Exposed," in Jay and Young, no. 77, pp. 266-69.

446)    Harris, Bertha. "The Lesbian in Literature: Or Is There Life on Mars?" in Universities and the Gay Experience, no. 51, pp. 44-52.

447)    _____. "More Profound Nationality of Their Lesbianism: Lesbian Society in Paris in the 1920's," in Birkby and Others, no. 16, pp. 77-88.

448)    Harris, Helaine. "Queen Christina [of Sweden]," in Myron and Bunch, no. 107, pp. 11-17.

449)    Harvey, John F. "Pastoral Responses to Gay World Questions," in Oberholtzer, no. 112, pp. 123-39 (chap. 5).

450)    Hedblom, Jack H. "The Female Homosexual: Social and Attitudinal Dimensions," in McCaffrey, no. 101, pp. 31-64.

451)    Henry, Carl F. H. "In and Out of the Gay World," in Oberholtzer, no. 112, pp. 104-15 (chap. 3).

452) Hess, Eckhard; Seltzer, Allan L.; and Schlien, John
      M. "Pupil Response of Hetero-and Homosexual Males
      to Pictures of Men and Women: A Pilot Study," in
      B. L. Kintz and James L. Bruning (eds.), Research
      in Psychology: Readings from the Introductory Course
      (Glenview, Ill.: Scott, Foresman and Co., 1970),
      pp. 427-31. (Reprinted from Journal of Abnormal
      and Social Psychology, 70:165-68, 1965)

453) Hettlinger, Richard. "Gay Can Be Good," in Sex
      Isn't That Simple: The New Sexuality on Campus
      (New York: Seabury Press, 1974), pp. 138-54
      (chap. 5).

454) _____. "Homosexuality," in Growing Up with Sex
      (New York: Seabury Press, 1970), pp. 46-54 (chap.
      4). (Paperback)

455) _____. "Sexual Immaturity ... Homosexuality,"
      in Sexual Maturity (Belmont, Ca.: Wadsworth Pub-
      lishing Co., 1970), pp. 25-28 (chap. 3). (Paperback)

456) Hirshfeld, Magnus. "Autobiographical Sketch," in
      Homosexual Emancipation Miscellany, no. 65, 5 pp.
      (Reprinted from Victor Robinson [ed.], Encyclopedia
      Sexualis [New York: Dingwall-Rock, 1936], pp.
      317-21)

457) Hobson, Christopher Z. "Surviving Psychotherapy,"
      in Jay and Young, no. 77, pp. 147-53.

458) Hoeffding, Virginia. "Dear Mom," in Jay and Young,
      no. 77, pp. 34-37.

459) Hoffman, Martin. "The Gay World," in Arlene S.
      and Jerome H. Skolnick (eds.), Family in Transition
      (Boston: Little, Brown and Co., 1971), pp. 443-50.
      (Reprinted from Hoffman, The Gay World [New York:
      Basic Books, 1968], chap. 2)

460) _____. "Homosexuality and Social Evil," in Read-
      ings in Psychology Today (2nd ed.; Del Mar, Ca.:
      Communications Research Machines, Inc., 1972),
      pp. 484-87.

461) _____. "Homosexuals and the Law," in McCaffrey,
      no. 101, pp. 121-36. (Reprinted from Hoffman, The
      Gay World [New York: Basic Books, 1968], chap. 5)

462)     Hoffman, Stanton. "The Cities of Night: John
         Rechy's 'City of Night' and the American Literature
         on Homosexuality," in Irving Buchen (ed.), The Per-
         verse Imagination: Sexuality and Literary Culture
         (New York: New York University Press, 1970), pp.
         165-78.

463)     Holbrook, David. "The Truth about Perversions,"
         in Sex and Dehumanization in Art, Thought, and Life
         in Our Times (London: Pitman Publishing Co.,
         1972), pp. 94-111 (chap. 6).

464)     Hooker, Evelyn. "The Homosexual Community," in
         Jack D. Douglas (ed.), Observations of Deviance
         (New York: Random House, 1970), pp. 115-28 (chap.
         9). (Reprinted from William Simon and John H.
         Gagnon [eds.], Sexual Deviance [New York: Harper
         and Row, 1967], pp. 167-84)

465)     _____. "Homosexuality," in Livingood, no. 92,
         pp. 11-21. (Reprinted from International Encyclo-
         pedia of the Social Sciences, IV [1968], 222-33)

466)     Horner, Tom. "Prostitution: Female and Male,"
         "Eunuchs and Transvestites," and "Homosexuality,"
         in Sex in the Bible (Rutland, Vt.: Charles E. Tuttle
         Co., 1974), pp. 65-73, 76-80, 81-92 (chaps. 8, 10-
         11). (Pertinent Passages from the Bible)

467)     Hosford, Ray E. and Rifkin, Harvey B. "Application
         of Behavior Therapy to Compulsive Exhibitionism and
         Homosexuality," in Ray E. Hosford and C. S. Moss
         (eds.), The Crumbling Walls: Treatment and Coun-
         seling of Prisoners (Urbana: University of Illinois,
         1975).

468)     Hudson, John P. "Sexual Latitude: For and Against,"
         in Harold H. Hart and Others, Sexual Latitude: For
         and Against (New York: Hart Publishing Co., 1972),
         pp. 162-89.

469)     Humphreys, Laud. "Impersonal Sex and Perceived
         Satisfaction," in James M. Henslin (ed.), Studies in
         the Sociology of Sex (New York: Appleton, Century,
         Crofts, 1971), pp. 351-74 (chap. 14).

470)     _____. "Impersonal Sex in Public Places," in

Jhan and June Robbins (eds.), An Analysis of Human Sexual Inadequacy (New York: New American Library, 1970), pp. 205-35.

471)     Hunt, Morton.  "Homosexuality," in Sexual Behavior in the 1970s (Chicago: Playboy Press, 1974), pp. 303-26.

472)     Hurley, Tom.  "Gay Couples and Straight Law," in Jay and Young, no. 76, pp. 145-51.

473)     "Hustler: A Boy for All Seasons--An Interview between a Hustler and His Customer," in Jay and Young, no. 76, pp. 117-24.

474)     "An International Directory of Gay Organizations," in Jay and Young, no. 77, pp. 475-503.  (329 organizations)

475)     "Italian Gay Literature," in Richmond and Noguerra, no. 122, pp. 154-55.

476)     Jackson, Bruce.  "Queens, Punks, and Studs," in In the Life: Versions of the Criminal (New York: Holt, Rinehart, and Winston, 1972), pp. 353-412. (Autobiographical)

477)     Jackson, Don.  "Dachau for Queers" and "Treatment of a Gay Militant," in Richmond and Noguerra, no. 122, pp. 42-49 and 79-86.

478)     Jackson, Graham.  "The Theater of Implication: Homosexuality in Drama," in Ian Young, The Male Homosexual in Literature: A Bibliography (Metuchen, N.J.: Scarecrow Press, 1975), pp. 162-74.

479)     Jacobs, Paul.  "What Do You Mean I'm Prejudiced?" in Richmond and Noguerra, no. 122, pp. 173-75.

480)     James, Basil.  "Homosexuality," in Charles G. Costello (ed.), Symptoms of Psychopathology: A Handbook (New York: Wiley and Sons, 1970), pp. 574-93 (chap. 23).

481)     Janov, Arthur.  "Homosexuality," in The Primal Revolution: Toward a Real World (New York: Simon and Schuster, 1972), pp. 83-97 (chap. 7).

482)          . "Sexuality, Homosexuality, and Bisexuality," in The Primal Scream:  Primal Therapy - The
Cure for Neurosis (New York:  Putnam's Sons, 1970),
pp. 281-321 (chap. 11).  (Paperback ed.:  Dell)

483)     Jay, Karla.  "A Gay Critique of Modern Literary
Criticism" and "Portrait of the Lesbian as a Young
Dyke," in Jay and Young, no. 77, pp. 66-68 and
275-77.

484)          . "Identity and Lifestyles," "Surviving Gay
Coupledom," "Creating Community and Helping Ourselves," "Oppression is Big Business:  Scrutinizing
Gay Therapy," and "The Spirit Is Liberationist but
the Flesh Is ..., or, You Can't Always Get in Bed
with Your Dogma," in Jay and Young, no. 76, pp.
3-4, 35-43, 171-72, 205-10, and 211-14.

485)          ; Jordan, Rose; Manford, Morty; and Young,
Allen.   "Can Gay Men and Women Work Together?--
A Forum," in Jay and Young, no. 76, pp. 173-94.

486)     Jem.  "A Bi-sexual Offers Some Thoughts on Fen-
ces," in Jay and Young, no. 76, pp. 65-67.

487)     Jensen, Gordon.  "Homosexuality," in Youth and Sex,
Pleasure and Responsibility (Chicago:  Nelson-Hall,
1974), pp.  127-40.

488)     Johnson, Dick (pseud.).  "Sexism in the Army," in
Richmond and Noguerra, no. 122, pp. 190-93.

489)     Johnson, Eric W.  "Another Problem of Sex:  Homosexuality," in Sex:  Telling It Straight (Philadelphia:
Lippincott, 1970), pp.  71-74 (chap. 13).

490)          . "Homosexuality--Being Gay," in Love and
Sex in Plain Language (New rev. ed.; Philadelphia:
Lippincott, 1973).  (Paperback ed.:  Bantam)

491)     Johnston, Jill.  "Return of the Amazon Mother" and
"The Comingest Womanifesto," in Birkby and Others,
no. 16, pp. 66-76 and 89-92.

492)     Jones, H. Kimball.  "Homosexuality--A Provisional
Christian Stance," in Oberholtzer, no. 112, pp. 140-
62 (chap. 6).

493)   Kantrowitz, Arnie.   "I Heard a Promise," in Univer-
       sities and the Gay Experience, no. 51, pp. 99-105.

494)   Katchadourian, Herant.   "Variations and Deviations
       of Sexual Behavior," in Human Sexuality:  Sense and
       Nonsense (San Francisco:  Witt-Freeman and Co.,
       1974), pp. 55-63.

495)   _____ and Lunde, Donald.   "Variations and Devia-
       tions in Sexual Behavior," in Fundamentals of Human
       Sexuality (New York:  Holt, Rinehart, and Winston,
       1972), pp. 263-80.

496)   Katz.   "Smash Phallic Imperialism," in Jay and
       Young, no. 77, pp. 259-62.

497)   Katz, Robert L.   "Notes on Religious History, Atti-
       tudes, and Laws Pertaining to Homosexuality," in
       Livingood, no. 92, pp. 58-62.

498)   Kay, F. George.   "Experimental Family Structures
       Today [Homosexual Marriages]," in The Family in
       Transition:  Its Past, Present, and Future Patterns
       (New York:  Wiley and Sons, 1972), pp. 142-48
       (chap. 8).

499)   Kelsey, Morton T.   "The Homosexual and the Church,"
       in Michael J. Taylor (ed.), Sex Thoughts for Contem-
       porary Christians (Garden City, N.Y.:  Doubleday and
       Co., 1972), pp. 223-43.   (Reprinted from Journal of
       Religion and Health, 7:61-78, Jan. 1968)

500)   Kennedy, Eugene C.   "The Gay Myth," in The New
       Sexuality:  Myths, Fables, and Hang-ups (Garden
       City, N.Y.:  Doubleday and Co., 1972), pp. 172-
       89 (chap. 11).

501)   Kenyon, F. Edwin.   "Female Homosexuality:  A Re-
       view," in Loraine, no. 95, pp. 83-119 (chap. 3).

502)   _____.   "Some Characteristics of Female Patients
       referred with Homosexual Problems," in Norman
       Morris (ed.), Psychosomatic Medicine in Obstetrics
       and Gynaecology (Basel:  Karger, 1972), pp. 379-81.

503)   Kilander, Holger F.   "Special Topics:  Homosexual-
       ity," in Sex Education in the Schools (London:  Mac-

millan Co., 1970), pp. 306-10 (chap. 19).

504)    King, Ambrose J. "Homosexuality and Veneral Di-
        sease," in Loraine, no. 95, pp. 187-214 (chap. 8).

505)    Kinsey, Alfred C.; Pomeroy, Wardell B.; and Mar-
        tin, Clyde. "The Heterosexual-Homosexual Balance,"
        in William S. Sahakian (ed.), Psychopathology Today:
        Experimentation, Theory and Research (Itasca, Ill.:
        Peacock Publishing Co., 1970), pp. 508-10. (Re-
        printed from Kinsey, Pomeroy, and Martin, Sexual
        Behavior in the Human Male [Philadelphia: Saunders
        Co., 1968], from chap. 21)

506)    _____; _____; and _____. "Homosexual Out-
        let," in McCaffrey, no. 101, pp. 3-30. (Reprinted
        from Kinsey, Pomeroy, and Martin, Sexual Behavior
        in the Human Male [Philadelphia: Saunders Co.,
        1968], from chap. 21)

507)    Kirkham, George L. "Homosexuality in Prison," in
        James M. Henslin (ed.), Studies in the Sociology of
        Sex (New York: Appleton, Century, Crofts, 1971),
        pp. 325-50 (chap. 13).

508)    Klein, Carole. "Homosexual Parents," in The Single
        Parent Experience (New York: Walker, 1973), pp.
        77-90. (Paperback ed.: Avon)

509)    Knapp, Whitman and Others. "Bars," in Commission
        to Investigate Allegations of Police Corruption and the
        City's Anti-Corruption Procedures: Commission Re-
        port (New York: George Braziller, 1974), pp. 133-
        48 (chap. 8).

510)    Knight, Robert S. "The Relationship of Latent Ho-
        mosexuality to the Mechanism of Paranoid Delusion,"
        in Stuart C. Miller (ed.), Clinician and Therapist:
        Selected Papers of Robert P. Knight (New York: Ba-
        sic Books, 1972), pp. 99-109. (Reprinted from Bul-
        letin of the Menninger Clinic, 4:149-59, 1940)

511)    Knoebel, John. "Somewhere in the Right Direction:
        Testimony of My Experience in a Gay Male Living
        Collective," in Jay and Young, no. 77, pp. 301-15.

512)    Koedt, Ann. "Lesbianism and Feminism," in Anne

Koedt, Ellen Levine, and Anita Rapone (eds.), Radical Feminism (New York: Quadrangle Books, 1973), pp. 246-58.

513)  _____. "Loving Another Woman," in Goode and Troiden, no. 55, pp. 247-55.

514)  Kogan, Benjamin A. "Divergent Sexual Behavior," in Human Sexual Expression (New York: Harcourt, Brace, Jovanovich, 1970), pp. 297-329 (chap. 10).

515)  Kolb, Lawrence C. "Homosexuality," in Modern Clinical Psychiatry (Philadelphia: Saunders, 1973), pp. 504-05.

516)  Krop, Harry D. "Behavior Therapy of Sexual Deviancy," in Jules H. Masserman (ed.), Current Psychiatric Therapies (New York: Grune and Stratton, 1972), v. 14, pp. 59-66.

517)  Lamb, Lawrence E. "Homosexuality, Male and Female," in Dear Doctor: It's about Sex (New York: Walker and Co., 1973), pp. 134-51 (chap. 7).

518)  Landerson, Louis. "France's Own Gay Liberation," in Richmond and Noguerra, no. 122, pp. 156-60.

519)  Landis, Carney and Others. "The Homoerotic Woman," in Sex in Development (College Park, Md.: McGrath Publishing Co., 1970), pp. 146-54 (chap. 12).

520)  LaPonte, Meredith R. "Life in a Parking Lot: An Ethnography of a Homosexual Drive-In," in Jerry Jacobs (ed.), Deviance: Field Studies and Self-Disclosure (Palo Alto, Ca.: National Press Books, 1974), pp. 7-29 (chap. 1).

521)  LaRiviere, Robert. "Bundles of Twigs in New Hamshire: A High School Teacher's Report," in Jay and Young, no. 76, pp. 105-12.

522)  Lawrence, Jodi. "One Is a Lonely Number," in The Search for the Perfect Orgasm (Los Angeles: Nash Publishing Co., 1973), pp. 197-212 (chap. 16).

523)  Lee, Julie. "Some Thoughts on Monogamy," in Jay and Young, no. 76, pp. 44-51.

524)     Lehman, J. Lee. "Introduction," "Coming Out Mid-
         west," and "Funding of Campus Groups," in Lehman,
         no. 88, pp. 5, 13-15, and 33-34.

525)     Leon, Gloria R. "Michael Boland: A Study of Sex-
         ual Deviation," in Case Histories of Deviant Behav-
         ior: A Social Learning Analysis (Boston: Holbrook
         Press, 1974), pp. 143-61 (chap. 9).

526)     LeShan, Eda J. "Homosexuality," in Natural Parent-
         hood: Raising Your Child Without a Script (New York:
         New American Library, 1970). (Paperback ed. :
         Signet)

527)     "Letter from Cuban Gay People to the North Ameri-
         can Gay Liberation Movement," in Jay and Young,
         no. 77, pp. 244-46.

528)     Levy, Howard and Miller, David. "Homosexuality,"
         in Going to Jail: The Political Prisoner (New York:
         Grove Press, 1972), pp. 137-63 (chap. 16).

529)     Leznoff, Maurice and Westley, William A. "The
         Homosexual Community," in John N. Edwards (ed. ),
         Sex and Society (Chicago: Markham Publishing Co. ,
         1972), pp. 79-88 (chap. 6). (Reprinted from Social
         Problems, 3:257-63, 1956)

530)     Lieberman, E. James and Peck, Ellen. "Homosex-
         uality," in Sex and Birth Control: A Guide for the
         Young (New York: Crowell Co. , 1973), pp. 229-33.

531)     Liebert, Robert. "The Gay Student: A Psychopoli-
         tical View," in Ruitenbeek, no. 127, pp. 53-69
         (chap. 4).

532)     Lilliston, Lynn. "The Feminine Homosexual," in
         Arlene and Jerome H. Skolnick (eds. ), The Family
         in Transition (Boston: Little, Brown and Co. , 1971),
         pp. 451-56.

533)     Lister, Charles. "The Right to Control the Use of
         One's Body," in Norman Dorsen (ed. ), The Rights
         of Americans (New York: Pantheon Books, 1971),
         pp. 348-64 at 350-55.

534)     Loftin, Edward E. and Others. "The Life and Death

of a Gay Prisoner," in Jay and Young, no. 76, pp. 135-44.

535)  "London Gay Liberation Front Manifesto," in Richmond and Noguerra, no. 122, pp. 117-27.

536)  Loraine, John A.; Chew, Iain; and Dyer, Tim. "The Population Explosion and the Status of the Homosexual in Society," in Loraine, no. 95, pp. 205-14 (chap. 9).

537)  Love, Nancy. "The Invisible Sorority," in The Improper Philadelphians (New York: Weybright and Talley, 1970), pp. 169-95.

538)  MacDonald, Eann (pseud.). "Preliminary Concepts," in Homosexual Emancipation Miscellany, no. 65, 6 pp. (Reprinted from pamphlet; Los Angeles: Bachelors Anonymous, 1950)

539)  Mager, Don. "On the Need for Gay Studies," in Lehman, no. 88, pp. 51-52.

540)  _____. "Out in the Workplace" and "Faggot Father," in Jay and Young, no. 76, pp. 103-04 and 128-34.

541)  Marlene. "Problems of an Inter-racial Relationship," in Jay and Young, no. 77, pp. 315-18.

542)  Marmor, Judd. "Notes on Some Psychodynamic Aspects of Homosexuality," in Livingood, no. 92, pp. 55-57 and 78-79.

543)  Martin, Del and Lyon, Phyllis. "A Lesbian Approach to Theology," in Oberholtzer, no. 112, pp. 213-20 (chap. 11).

544)  _____ and _____. "Lesbian Love and Sexuality," in Goode and Troiden, no. 55, pp. 238-46. (Extract from Martin and Lyon, no. 96)

545)  _____ and _____. "Lesbian Love and Sexuality," in Francine Klagsbrun (ed.), The First Ms. Reader (New York: Warner Communications Co., 1972), pp. 135-44. (Paperback) (Extract from Martin and Lyon, no. 96)

546)         _____ and _____. "The New Sexuality and the
            Homosexual," in Herbert A. Otto (ed.), The New
            Sexuality (Palo Alto, Ca.: Science and Behavior
            Books, 1971), pp. 198-214.

547)         _____ and _____. "The Realities of Lesbian-
            ism," in Joanne Cooke, Charlotte Bunch-Weeks, and
            Robin Morgan (eds.), The New Woman: A Motive
            Anthology on Women's Liberation (Indianpolis: Bobbs-
            Merrill Co., 1970), pp. 78-88 (Paperback ed.: Faw-
            cett); and in Carolyn C. Perrucci and Dena B. Tang
            (eds.), Marriage and the Family: A Critical Analysis
            and Proposals for Change (New York: D. McKay Co.,
            1974), pp. 233-41.

548)         _____ and _____. "Sexual Latitude: For," in
            Harold Hart and others (eds.), Sexual Latitude: For
            and Against (New York: Hart Publishing Co., 1971),
            pp. 143-61.

549)         _____ and Mariah, Paul. "Homosexual Love--
            Woman to Woman, Man to Man," in Herbert A. Otto
            (ed.), Love Today: A New Exploration (New York:
            Association Press, 1972), pp. 120-34 (chap. 10).
            (Paperback ed.: Delta)

550)         Masters, William H. and Johnson, Virginia E. "Sec-
            ondary Impotence with Homosexuality as Contributing
            Etiological Factor" and "Homosexual Influence," in
            Human Sexual Inadequacy (Boston: Little, Brown and
            Co., 1970), pp. 179-83 and 244-47.

551)         Mathis, James L. "Homosexuality," in Clear Think-
            ing about Sexual Deviations (Chicago: Nelson-Hall
            Co., 1972), pp. 13-28 (chap. 2).

552)         Maurer, Thomas. "Toward a Theology of Homosex-
            uality--Tried and Found Trite and Tragic," in Ober-
            holtzer, no. 112, pp. 98-103 (chap. 2).

553)         May, Step. "High School Days," in Richmond and
            Noguerra, no. 122, pp. 129-32.

554)         Mazur, Ronald. "The Double Standard and People's
            Liberation ... Heterosexuals versus Homosexuals,"
            in The New Intimacy: Open-ended Marriage and Al-
            ternative Lifestyles (Boston: Beacon Press, 1973),
            pp. 28-31 (chap. 2).

555)    McCaffrey, Joseph A. "Homosexuality: The Stereo-
        type and the Real," in McCaffrey, no. 101, pp. 137-44.

556)    McCary, James L. "Homosexuality," in Sexual
        Myths and Fallacies (New York: Van Nostrand Rein-
        hold Co., 1971), pp. 85-107 (chap. 4).

557)    _____. "Sexual Variance," in Human Sexuality
        (2nd ed.; New York: Van Nostrand Co., 1973), pp.
        369-76.

558)    McConaghy, N. "Aversion Therapy of Homosexual-
        ity," in Jules H. Masserman (ed.), Current Psychi-
        atric Therapies (New York: Grune and Stratton,
        1972), v. 12, pp. 38-47.

559)    McDougall, Joyce. "Homosexuality in Women," in
        Janine Chassequet-Smirgel (ed.), Female Sexuality:
        New Psychoanalytic Views (Ann Arbor: University
        of Michigan Press, 1970), pp. 171-212.

560)    McGirr, Kevin J. "Alcohol Use and Abuse in the
        Gay Community: A View toward Alternatives," in
        Jay and Young, no. 76, pp. 277-88.

561)    McIntosh, Mary. "The Homosexual Role," in Arlene
        S. and Jerome H. Skolnick (eds.), The Family in
        Transition (Boston: Little, Brown and Co., 1971),
        pp. 231-42 (Reprinted from Social Problems, 16:
        182-92, Fall 1968)

562)    McNeill, John J. "Demythologizing Sodom and Go-
        morrah," in Universities and the Gay Experience,
        no. 51, pp. 53-56.

563)    Mellen, Joan. "Lesbianism in the Movies," "Vis-
        conti's Death in Venice," and "Outfoxing Lawrence,"
        in Women and Their Sexuality in the New Film (New
        York: Horizon Press, 1973), pp. 74-105 (chap. 3),
        203-15 (chap. 9), and 216-28 (chap. 10).

564)    Meyers, Jeffrey. "D. H. Lawrence and Homosexu-
        ality," in Stephen Spender (ed.), D. H. Lawrence:
        Novelist, Poet, Prophet (New York: Harper and
        Row, 1973), pp. 135-46.

565)    Michael, Richard P.; Wilson, Margo I.; and Zumpe, D.
        "The Bisexual Behavior of Female Rhesus Monkeys,"

in Richard C. Friedman, Ralph M. Richart, Raymond
L. Vande Wiele, and L. O. Stern (eds.), Sex Differences in Behavior (New York: Wiley and Sons, 1974),
pp. 399-412 (chap. 20).

566) Miller, Peter; Bradley, John B.; Gross, Richard S.;
and Wood, Gene. "Review of Homosexuality Research
(1960-66) and Some Implications for Treatment," in
Anne M. Duhasz (ed.), Sexual Development and Behavior: Selected Readings (Homewood, Ill.: Dorsey
Press, 1973), pp. 311-17 (chap. 24). (Reprinted in
Ruitenbeek, no. 127, pp. 148-53.) (Reprinted from
Psychotherapy: Theory, Research and Practice, 5:
3-6, Winter 1968)

567) Millett, Kate. "Norman Mailer" and "Jean Genet,"
in Sexual Politics (Garden City, N.Y.: Doubleday
and Co., 1970), pp. 314-35 and 336-61 (chaps. 7 and
8). (Paperback ed.: Avon Equinox)

568) Millon, Theodore and Renee. "Homosexuality," in
Abnormal Behavior and Personality: A Biosocial
Learning Approach (Philadelphia: Saunders Co.,
1974), pp. 194-98.

569) Mintz, Elizabeth. "Overt Male Homosexuals in Combined Group and Individual Treatment," in Ruitenbeek,
no. 127, pp. 181-90. (Reprinted from Journal of
Consulting Psychology, 30:193-98, 1966)

570) Mitzel, John. "Lucifer with a Book," in John Horne
Burns: An Appreciative Autobiography (Dorchester,
Mass.: Manifest Destiny Books, 1975), pp. 77-89.

571) Monahan, Jim. "Facing Up," in Lehman, no. 88,
p. 19.

572) Money, John. "Sexual Dimorphism and Homosexual
Gender Identity" and "Pubertal Hormones and Homosexuality, Bisexuality, and Heterosexuality," in Livingood, no. 92, pp. 42-54 and 73-77.

573) _____. "The Therapeutic Use of Androgen-deplet-
ing Hormone," in H. L. P. Resnik and Martin E.
Wolfgang (eds.), Sexual Behaviors: Social, Clinical,
and Legal Aspects (Boston: Little, Brown and Co.,
1972), pp. 351-60.

574)     Murphy, John.  "Queer Books," in Jay and Young, no. 77, pp. 72-93.  (Reprinted from Murphy, no. 105, pp. 42-70)

575)     Nappy, Pierre-Claude.  "An Open Letter on Homosexuality," translated from the French by Violet Neville, in Michael J. Taylor (ed. ), Sex Thoughts for Contemporary Christians (Garden City, N. Y. : Doubleday and Co. , 1972), pp. 222-43; and in Ruitenbeek no. 127, pp. 116-36 (chap. 9).  (Reprinted from Cross Currents, 20:221-37, Fall 1970)

576)     Nash, Richard.  "Power to Gay People: A Los Angeles Experiment in Community Action [Gay Community Services Center]," in Jay and Young, no. 76, pp. 248-55.

577)     National Gay Task Force.  "Famous Gays: Renowned Homosexuals--Past and Present," in David Wallechinsky and Irving Wallace (eds. ), The People's Almanac (Garden City, N. Y. : Doubleday and Co. , 1975), pp. 1005-06.

578)     Nicol, C. S.  "Sexually Transmitted Diseases," in Ronald B. Scott and R. Milnes Walker (eds. ), The Medical Annual: 1973 (Bristol, Eng. : Wright, 1973), pp. 422-27.

579)     Nicolson, Nigel.  "Part IV," in Portrait of a Marriage (New York: Atheneum, 1973), pp. 135-85. (Paperback ed. : Bantam) (Biography)

580)     Noll, Dolores.  "A Gay Feminist in Academia," in Lehman, no. 88, pp. 57-59.

581)     Norse, Harold.  "I'm Not a Man," in Richmond and Noguerra, no. 122, pp. 169-70.

582)     Norton, Rictor.  "Ganymede Raped: Gay Literature--The Critic as Censor," in Ian Young, The Male Homosexual in Literature: A Bibliography (Metuchen, N. J. : Scarecrow Press, 1975), pp. 192-205.

583)     Nossa, Catherine.  "Hookers: Queer Fish," in Jay and Young, no. 76, pp. 13-16.

584)     Nouwen, Henri J. M.  "The Self-availability of the

Homosexual," in Oberholtzer, no. 112, pp. 204-12 (chap. 10).

585)  Oberholtzer, W. Dwight.  "Subduing the Cyclops--A Giant Step toward Ethics," in Oberholtzer, no. 112, pp. 11-73.

586)  Page, James D.  "Sex Deviance," in Psychopathology: The Science of Understanding (Chicago: Aldine-Atherton, 1971), pp. 367-81 (chap. 14).

587)  Panky, Ted.  "Gay Lib," in McCaffrey, no. 101, pp. 172-74.

588)  Parisex (Henry Gerber).  "In Defense of Homosexuality," in Homosexual Emancipation Miscellany, no. 65, 12 pp.  (Reprinted from The Modern Thinker, 1932, pp. 286-97)

589)  Parker, William.  "Bibliography," in Oberholtzer, no. 112, pp. 261-87.  (300 items)

590)  _____.  "Homosexuality: Selected Abstracts and Bibliography," in A Gay Bibliography, no. 52, pp. 365-479.  (102 abstracts and 188 bibliographical items)  (Reprint of work published in 1966)

591)  Parman, Leah and Bat-Lena, Hannah.  "The Women's Caucus," in Universities and the Gay Experience, no. 51, pp. 91-95.

592)  Perreault, Jeanne.  "Lesbian Mother," in Jay and Young, no. 76, pp. 125-27.

593)  Perry, Troy.  "God Loves Me Too," in Oberholtzer, no. 112, pp. 116-22 (chap. 4).

594)  Perutz, Kathrin.  "Homosexual Marriage," in Marriage is Hell (New York:  Morrow and Co. , 1972), pp. 117-25.

595)  Phelps, Robert.  "Le Livre Blanc: Notes on Homosexuality," in Professional Secrets: An Autobiography of Jean Cocteau, Drawn from his Lifetime Writings, translated from the French by Richard Howard (New York:  Farrar, Straus, and Giroux, 1970), pp. 117-24.

596)    Phillips, William.   "The New Immoralists [Jean
        Genet and William Burroughs]," in Irving Buchen
        (ed.), The Perverse Imagination:  Sexuality and Lit-
        erary Culture (New York:  New York University
        Press, 1970), pp. 139-46.

597)    Pittenger, W. Norman.   "The Homosexual Expression
        of Love," in Oberholtzer, no. 112, pp. 221-38
        (chap. 12).

598)    _____.  "The Homosexual Expression of Sexuality,"
        in Making Sexuality Human (Philadelphia:  Pilgrim
        Press, 1970), pp. 59-68 (chap. 6).

598a)   _____.  "Making a 'Case' for Gays in the Church
        and in the Ministry," in Wickliff, no. 159a, pp. 15-51.

599)    Poland, Jefferson F. and Alison, Valerie.   "Interview
        with Sophia," in The Records of the San Francisco
        Sexual Freedom League (New York:  Olympia Press,
        1971), pp. 155-78 (chap. 10).

600)    Poltergeist, Jaye V.  "Happy Birthday, Baby Butch,"
        in Jay and Young, no. 77, pp. 96-99.

601)    Purple September Staff.   "The Normative Status of
        Heterosexuality," in Myron and Bunch, no. 106,
        pp. 79-83.

602)    Radicalesbians.   "Woman-identified Woman," in Deb-
        orah Babcox and Madeline Belkin (eds.), Liberation
        Now:  Writings from the Women's Liberation Move-
        ment (New York:  Dell Publishing Co., 1971), pp.
        287-91; and in Jay and Young, no. 77, pp. 172-77.

603)    Radicalesbians Health Collective.   "Lesbians and the
        Health Care System," in Jay and Young, no. 77, pp.
        122-41.

604)    Radicalesbians, New York City.   "Leaving the Gay
        Men Behind," in Jay and Young, no. 77, pp. 290-93.

605)    Raimone, Nanette; Shelley, Martha; and Hart, Lois.
        "Lesbians are Sisters," in Leslie B. Tanner (ed.),
        Voices from Women's Liberation (New York:  New
        American Library, 1971), pp. 349-61.   (Paperback
        ed.:  Signet)

606)   Ramer, Leonard V.   "Basic Facts Concerning Homo-
        sexuality," Your Sexual Bill of Rights (New York:
        Exposition Press, 1973), pp. 61-74 (chap. 5).

607)   Ramsey, Ronald W.; Heringa, P. M.; and Boorsma,
        I.   "A Case Study:  Homosexuality in the Nether-
        lands," in Loraine, no. 95, pp. 121-39 (chap. 5).

608)   "Rapping with a Street Transvestite Revolutionary--
        An Interview with Marcia Johnson," in Jay and Young,
        no. 77, pp. 112-20.

609)   Realesbians and Politicalesbians.   "Gay Revolution
        Party Women's Caucus," in Jay and Young, no. 77,
        pp. 177-81.

610)   The Red Butterfly.   "The Anthropological Perspec-
        tive," in Jay and Young, no. 77, pp. 157-65.

611)   Reiche, Reimut.   "Latent Homosexuality and the 'Con-
        vergence' of the Sexes," in Sexuality and Class Strug-
        gle, translated from the German by Susan Bennett
        (Bristol, Eng.:  Western Printing Services, 1970),
        pp. 115-20.

612)   Reid, Coletta.   "Coming Out in the Women's Move-
        ment," in Myron and Bunch, no. 106, pp. 89-108.

613)   Reik, Theodor.   "The Same Sex," in Psychology of
        Sex Relations (Westport, Ct.:  Greenwood Press,
        1973), pp. 44-55.   (Reprint of work published in 1945)

614)   "Resolution of Lesbians International," in Birkby and
        Others, no. 16, p. 93.

615)   Richardson, Frank.   "Napoleon and the Male Sex,"
        in Napoleon:  Bisexual Emperor (New York:  Horizon
        Press, 1973), pp. 148-77 (chap. 8).

616)   Richmond, Len.   "Gay Liberation Presents 2001, A
        Sex Odyssey," in Richmond and Noguerra, no. 122,
        pp. 196-99.

617)   Riess, Bernard F.   'New Viewpoints on the Female
        Homosexual," in Violet Franks and Vasanti Burtle
        (eds.), Women in Therapy:  New Psychotherapies for
        a Changing Society (New York:  Brunner-Mazel, 1974),
        pp. 191-214.

618)     Riki. "Aging," in Jay and Young, no. 76, pp. 215-17.

619)     Rogers, Martin.   "Critical Incidents in the Evolution
         of a Gay Liberation Group," in Lehman, no. 88,
         pp. 25-28.

620)     Rook, June.   "Preserving the Past for the Future,"
         in Jay and Young, no. 76, pp. 232-35.

621)     Rosenthal, David.   "Homosexuality," in Genetic The-
         ory and Abnormal Behavior (New York:   McGraw-
         Hill Book Co., 1970), pp. 250-55.

622)     _____. "Homosexuality," in Genetics of Psycho-
         pathology (New York:   McGraw-Hill Book Co., 1971),
         pp. 144-49.

623)     Rosenzweig, Saul.   "Human Sexual Autonomy as an
         Evolutionary Attainment, Anticipating Proceptive Sex
         Choice and Idiodynamic Bisexuality," in Joseph Zubin
         and John Money (eds.), Contemporary Sexual Behav-
         ior:   Critical Issues in the 1970s (Baltimore:   Johns
         Hopkins University Press, 1973), pp. 189-230
         (chap. 10).

624)     Rubin, Isadore.   "Coping with Homosexual Fears,"
         in James P. Semmens and Kermit E. Krantz (eds.),
         The Adolescent Experience:   A Counseling Guide to
         Social and Sexual Behavior (New York:   Macmillan,
         1970), pp. 98-114.

625)     Rugoff, Milton.   "Deviations and Diversions," in
         Prudery and Passion:   Sexuality in Victorian America
         (New York:   Putnam's Sons, 1971), pp. 263-70 and
         365-69.

626)     Ruitenbeek, Hendrik M.   "Homosexuality:   An Evolu-
         tion," "The Dutch Situation," and "The Myth of Bi-
         sexuality," in Ruitenbeek, no. 127, pp. 13-15, 32-
         36, and 199-204.

627)     Rule, Janet.   "With All Due Respect:   In Defense of
         Lesbian Lifestyles," in Jay and Young, no. 76, pp.
         22-26.

628)     Sabaroff, Nina.   "Lesbian Sexuality," in Jay and
         Young, no. 76, pp. 5-15.

629)     San Francisco Committee on Crime. "Sexual Con-
         duct: Homosexuality," in A Report on Non-Victim
         Crime in San Francisco (San Francisco: San Fran-
         cisco Committee on Crime, 1971), pp. 4-11.

630)     Schaffer, Ralph S. "Will You Still Need Me When
         I'm 64?" in Jay and Young, no. 77, pp. 278-79; and
         in Richmond and Noguerra, no. 122, pp. 177-79.

631)     Schreiber, Ron. "Giving a Gay Course," in Lehman,
         no. 88, pp. 53-57.

632)     Schur, Edwin M. "Sociocultural Factors in Homo-
         sexual Behavior," in Livingood, no. 92, pp. 30-41.

633)     Schwartz, Karen M. "Struggle to Be 'The Way I
         Am,'" in Lehman, no. 88, pp. 11-13.

634)     "A Selected Gay Bibliography," in Jay and Young,
         no. 77, pp. 369-73. (62 items)

635)     Serban, George. "The Existential Therapeutic Ap-
         proach to Homosexuality," in Louis Diamant (ed.),
         Case Studies in Psychopathology (Columbus, O.:
         Merrill Publishing Co., 1971), pp. 195-207. (Re-
         printed from American Journal of Psychotherapy,
         22:491-501, 1968)

636)     Sex Information and Education Council of the U.S.
         "Homosexuality," in Sexuality and Man (New York:
         Scribner's, 1970), pp. 73-82 (chap. 6).

637)     Shelley, Martha. "Gay Is Good," in Jay and Young,
         no. 77, pp. 31-34.

638)     _____. "I Am a Lesbian--I Am Beautiful," in
         Joann S. and Jack R. DeLora (eds.), Intimate Life
         Styles: Marriage and Its Alternatives (Pacific Pali-
         sades, Ca.: Goodyear Publishing Co., 1970), pp.
         265-68.

639)     _____. "Lesbians and the Women's Liberation
         Movement," in Sookie Stambler (ed.), Women's Lib-
         eration: Blueprint for the Future (New York: Ace
         Books, 1970), pp. 123-29. (Paperback)

640)     Shively, Charley. "Getting It Together Journalism:

A View of 'Fag Rag,'" in Jay and Young, no. 76, pp. 236-47. (Includes list of 40 gay periodicals)

641) Silverstein, Mike. "An Open Letter to Tennessee Williams," "Gay Bureaucrats: What Are They Doing to You?" and "The Politics of My Sex Life," in Jay and Young, no. 77, pp. 69-72, 165-69, and 270-75.

642) Sim, Myre. "Homosexuality," in Guide to Psychiatry (3rd ed.; Edinburgh: Churchill Livingstone, 1974), pp. 414-27.

643) Simon, William and Gagnon, John H. "Femininity in the Lesbian Community," in Goode and Troiden, no. 55, pp. 256-67. (Reprinted from Social Problems, 15:212-21, Fall 1967)

644) _____ and _____. "Homosexuality: The Formulation of a Sociological Perspective," in Ruitenbeek, no. 127, pp. 20-31. (Reprinted from Journal of Health and Social Behavior, 8:177-85, 1967)

645) _____ and _____. "The Lesbians: A Preliminary Overview," in John H. Edwards (ed.), Sex and Society (Chicago: Markham Publishing Co., 1972), pp. 81-108 (chap. 7). (Abridged from Gagnon and Simon [eds.], Sexual Deviance [New York: Harper and Row, 1967], pp. 247-82)

646) _____ and _____. "On Becoming a Lesbian," in Jack D. Douglas (ed.), Observations of Deviance (New York: Random House, 1970), pp. 107-11 (chap. 7). (Excerpt from Gagnon and Simon [eds.], Sexual Deviance [New York: Harper and Row, 1967], pp. 251-55)

647) "Sissy in Prison--an Interview with Ron Veron," in Jay and Young, no. 77, pp. 99-112.

648) Skeist, Robbie. "The Orderly," in Jay and Young, no. 77, pp. 153-57.

649) Slater, Eliot. "Birth Order and Maternal Age of Homosexuals," in James Shields and Irving Gottesman (eds.), Man and Heredity: Selected Papers of Eliot Slater on Psychiatry and Genetics (Baltimore: Johns Hopkins University Press, 1971), pp. 261-65. (Reprinted from Lancet, 1:69-71, 1962)

650)    Small, Margaret. "Lesbians and the Class Position
        of Women," in Myron and Bunch, no. 106, pp. 49-61.

651)    Socarides, Charles W. "Homosexuality," in Beyond
        Sexual Freedom (New York: Quadrangle Books,
        1975), pp. 81-112 (chap. 7).

652)    _____. "Homosexuality," in Silvano Arieti (ed. ),
        American Handbook of Psychiatry (2nd ed.; New
        York: Basic Books, 1974), v. 3, pp. 291-315
        (chap. 14).

653)    Solomon, Barbara. "Taking the Bullshit by the
        Horns," in Myron and Bunch, no. 106, pp. 39-47.

654)    Sonnenschein, David. "The Ethnography of Male Ho-
        mosexuality," in Ruitenbeek, no. 127, pp. 83-96
        (chap. 6). (Reprinted from Journal of Sex Research,
        4:69-83, 1968)

655)    Sorenson, Robert C. "Adolescent Homosexuality,"
        in Adolescent Sexuality in Contemporary America
        (New York: World Publishing Co., 1973), pp. 283-
        95 (chap. 11).

656)    Southard, Helen F. "Homosexuality," in Sex Before
        Twenty: New Answers for Young People (Rev. ed.;
        New York: Dutton and Co., 1971), pp. 32-34.

657)    Spock, Benjamin. "Homosexuality," in A Teenager's
        Guide to Life and Love (New York: Simon and Schus-
        ter, 1970), pp. 121-25.

658)    Spring, Marjorie P. "A Contribution to the Study of
        Homosexuality in Adolescence," in Marjorie Harley
        (ed. ), The Analyst and the Adolescent at Work (New
        York: Quadrangle, 1974), pp. 68-109.

659)    "Statutory Provisions Affecting Licensing of Gays,"
        in ACLU Handbook, no. 18, pp. 211-35.

660)    Stoller, Robert J. "Homosexuality," in Splitting:
        A Case of Female Masculinity (New York: Quadran-
        gle, 1973), pp. 271-301 (chap. 14).

661)    Stone, Walter; Schengber, John; and Seifried, F.
        Stanley. "The Treatment of a Homosexual Woman

in a Mixed Group," in Harold I. Kaplan and Benjamin J. Sadock (eds. ), Group Treatment of Mental Disease (New York:  Dutton and Co. , 1972), pp. 41-46 (chap.  3).

662)    Strachey, Lytton.  "Curious Manuscript" and "An Arabian Night, " in The Really Interesting Question and Other Papers, edited by Paul Levy (London: Weidenfeld and Nicolson, 1972), pp. 151-55 and 156-65.

663)    Student Committee on Human Sexuality, Yale University.  "Homosexuality, " in Student Guide to Sex on Campus (New York:  New American Library, 1970), pp. 127-34 and 139-40.   (Paperback ed. :  Signet)

664)    Suggs, Robert C. and Marshall, Donald S.  "Normality and Deviance, " in Robert C. Suggs and Donald S. Marshall (eds. ), Human Sexual Behavior:  Variations in the Ethnographic Spectrum (New York:  Basic Books, 1971), pp. 229-36.

665)    "Supermen in G-Strings, " in Richmond and Noguerra, no. 122, pp. 187-89.

666)    Szasz, Thomas S.   "The Product Conversion--from Heresy to Illness" and "The Model Psychiatric Scapegoat--the Homosexual, " in The Manufacture of Madness:  A Comparative Study of the Inquisition and the Mental Health Movement (New York:  Harper and Row, 1970), pp. 160-67 (chap. 10) and 242-59 (chap. 13).   (Chapter 10 is reprinted in McCaffrey, no. 101, pp. 101-20)

667)    Terry, Megan.  "Dorothy Brewster, " in Couplings and Groupings (New York:  Pantheon Books, 1972), pp. 5-15.

668)    Thin, R. N. T.  "Sexually Transmitted Diseases, " in Ronald B. Scott and R. Milnes Walker (eds. ), The Medical Annual:  1974 (Bristol, Eng. :  Wright, 1974), pp. 380-81.

669)    Third World Gay Revolution (New York City).  "What We Want, What We Believe, " in Jay and Young, no. 77, pp. 363-67.

670)     Third World Gay Revolution and Gay Liberation Front
         (Chicago). "Gay Revolution and Sex Roles," in Jay
         and Young, no. 77, pp. 252-59.

671)     Thorp, Charles P. "I.D., Leadership and Violence,"
         in Jay and Young, no. 77, pp. 352-63.

672)     Trimmer, E. J. "Female Homosexuality," in Nor-
         man Norris (ed.), Psychosomatic Medicine in Obste-
         trics and Gynaecology (Basel: Karger, 1972), pp.
         382-84.

673)     Troiden, Richard R. "Homosexual Encounters in a
         Highway Rest Stop," in Goode and Troiden, no. 55,
         pp. 211-28.

674)     Ulmschneider, Loretta. "Bisexuality," in Myron and
         Bunch, no. 106, pp. 85-88.

675)     Van Buren, Abigail. "Dear Abby: Odd Couple," in
         Richmond and Noguerra, no. 122, p. 133.

676)     Vassi, Marco. "The Trucks" and "Bisexuality, The-
         rapy, and Revolution," in MetaSex, Mirth, and Mad-
         ness (New York: Penthouse Press, 1975).

677)     Vidal, Gore. "Bisexual Politics," in Richmond and
         Noguerra, no. 122, pp. 134-37. (Reprinted from Vi-
         dal, The City and the Pillar Revised [New York:
         Dutton and Co., 1965], pp. 245-49)

678)     _____. "Notes on Pornography" in Irving Buchen
         (ed.), The Perverse Imagination: Sexuality and Lit-
         erary Culture (New York: New York University Press,
         1970), pp. 125-38.

679)     von Rohr, John. "Toward a Theology of Homosexu-
         ality" and "A Response to the Responses," in Ober-
         holtzer, no. 112, pp. 75-97 (chap. 1) and 239-51
         (chap. 13).

680)     Ward, David and Kassebaum, Gene G. "The Dyna-
         mics of Prison Homosexuality: The Character of a
         Love Affair," in Jack D. Douglas (ed.), Observations
         of Deviance (New York: Random House, 1970), pp.
         89-106 (chap. 6). (Reprinted from Ward and Kasse-
         baum, Women's Prison: Sex and Social Structures
         [Chicago: Aldine Publishing Co., 1965])

681)     _____ and _____ . "The Jailhouse Turnout: Homosexuality among Women in Prison," in David Dressler (ed.), Readings in Criminology and Penology (2nd ed.; New York: Columbia University Press, 1972), pp. 625-35.

682)     _____ and _____ . "Lesbian Liaisons," in John H. Gagnon and William Simon (eds.), The Sexual Scene (Chicago: Aldine Publishing Co., 1970), pp. 125-36.

683)     Warren, Carol A. B. "Observing the Gay Community," in Jack D. Douglas (ed.), Research in Deviance (New York: Random House, 1972), pp. 139-63.

684)     Watts, Alan. "No More Armed Clergymen," in Richmond and Noguerra, no. 122, pp. 87-89.

685)     Weightman, John. "Gide and Sexual Liberation," in The Concept of the Avant-Garde: Explorations in Modernism (LaSalle, Ill.: Library Press, 1973), pp. 98-112.

686)     Weiner, Melvin L. "Homosexuality," in Personality: The Human Potential (New York: Pergamon Press, 1973), pp. 85-98 (chap. 8).

687)     Werner, Steve. "The Gay Student Group," in Yates, Werner, and Rosen, no. 296, pp. 239-67. (Reprinted in abbreviated form in Lehman, no. 58, pp. 29-33)

688)     West, Donald J. "Homosexuality in Various Communities" in John N. Edwards (ed.), Sex and Society (Chicago: Markham Publishing Co., 1972), pp. 69-78 (chap. 5). (Reprinted from West, Homosexuality [Chicago: Aldine Publishing Co., 1967], pp. 17-29)

689)     Whan, Del. "Elitism," in Jay and Young, no. 77, pp. 318-23.

690)     Whitmore, George. "Living Alone," in Jay and Young, no. 76, pp. 52-61.

691)     Williams, Lewis (pseud.). "Walls of Ice--Theology and Social Policy," in Oberholtzer, no. 112, pp. 163-84 (chap. 7).

692)     Wilson, Paul. "Homosexuality," in Sexual Dilemma
         (St. Lucia, Queensland, Australia: University of
         Queensland Press, 1971), pp. 60-64 (chap. 31).

693)     Winant, Fran. "Christopher Street Liberation Day,
         June 28, 1970" and "Looking at Women," in Jay and
         Young, no. 77, pp. 4-6 and 284-90.

694)     _____ and Ulmschneider, Loretta. "Gertrude Stein
         and Alice Toklas," in Myron and Bunch, no. 107, pp.
         63-76.

695)     Winick, Charles and Kinsie, Paul M. "Male Homo-
         sexual Prostitution," in The Lively Commerce: Pros-
         titution in the United States (Chicago: Quadrangle
         Books, 1971, pp. 89-96 (chap. 2). (Paperback ed.:
         Signet)

696)     Winslow, Robert W. and Virginia. "Homosexuality,"
         in Deviant Reality: Alternative World Views (Boston:
         Allyn and Bacon, 1974).

697)     Wittman, Carl. "Refugees from Amerika: A Gay
         Manifesto," in Jay and Young, no. 77, pp. 330-42;
         in McCaffrey, no. 101, pp. 157-71; and in Joann S.
         and Jack R. DeLora (eds.), Intimate Life Styles:
         Marriage and its Alternatives (Pacific Palisades, Ca.:
         Goodyear Publishing Co., 1970), pp. 255-65. (Re-
         printed from San Francisco Free Press, Dec. 22,
         1969, pp. 3-5)

698)     Wolf, Steve. "Sex and the Single Cataloguer," in
         Celeste West and Elizabeth Katz (eds.), Revolting
         Librarians (San Francisco: Booklegger Press, 1972),
         pp. 39-44.

699)     The Wolfenden Report. "The Gay Minority," in Ro-
         bert W. Winslow (ed.), The Emergence of Deviant
         Minorities: Social Problems and Social Change (New
         Brunswick, N.J.: Transaction Books, 1972), pp.
         143-61. (Excerpts from Report of the Committee on
         Homosexual Offenses and Prostitution [London: Her
         Majesty's Stationery Office, 1957])

700)     Wolman, Benjamin B. "Tragedies and Diseases ...
         Homosexuality," in Call No Man Normal (New York:
         International Universities Press, 1973), pp. 281-87.

701)     Woodruff, Robert A.; Goodwin, Donald W.; and Guze,
         Samuel B.   "Sexual Problems," in Psychiatric Diag-
         nosis (New York:  Oxford University Press, 1974),
         pp.  173-81 (chap.  12).

702)     Yates, Aubrey J.   "Sexual Disorders," in Behavior
         Therapy (New York:  Wiley and Sons, 1970), pp. 224-
         45 (chap.  12).

703)     Young, Allen.   "Gay Gringo in Brazil," in Richmond
         and Noguerra, no.  122, pp.  60-67.

704)     _____.  "On Human Identity and Gay Identity:  A
         Liberationist Dilemma,"  "Survival in a Hostile
         World," and "Some Thoughts on how Gay Men Relate
         to Women," in Jay and Young, no.  76, pp.  27-34,
         85-88 and 195-204.

705)     _____.  "Out of the Closets and Into the Streets,"
         "The Cuban Revolution and Gay Liberation," and "On
         the Venceremos Brigade:  A Forum," in Jay and
         Young, no.  77, pp.  6-31,  206-28, and 228-44.

706)     Young, Ian.   "The Flower Beneath the Foot:  A Short
         History of the Gay Novel" and "The Poetry of Male
         Love," in Ian Young, The Male Homosexual in Liter-
         ature:  A Bibliography (Metuchen, N.J.:  Scarecrow
         Press, 1975), pp.  149-61 and 175-92.

707)     Young, Perry D.   "Questions We Never Asked," in
         Two of the Missing:  A Reminiscence of Some Friends
         in the War (New York:  Coward, McCann and Geog-
         hegan, 1975), pp.  197-201.   (Autobiographical)

NEWSPAPER ARTICLES

708)    Advertisement Sponsored by Uniformed Fire Officers
        Association (New York City) Opposing Gay Rights Bill
        before City Council, New York Daily News, Apr. 26,
        1974, p. 25.

709)    American Baptist Churches Deny Admission of Gay
        Church, Los Angeles Times, Sep. 18, 1973, sec. 1,
        p. 3.

710)    American Civil Liberties Union Seeks to Prevent U.S.
        Civil Service Commission from Dismissing or Not
        Hiring Homosexuals, New York Times, Dec. 21,
        1971, p. 26.

711)    American Psychiatric Association, After Debate, De-
        cides Homosexuality Is Not a Mental Illness, New
        York Times, Feb. 9, 1973, p. 24; Dec. 16, 1973,
        p. 1 and sec. 4, p. 8; Dec. 23, 1973, sec. 4, p. 5;
        Jan. 6, 1974, sec. 4, p. 5; Apr. 9, 1974, p. 12;
        Apr. 14, 1974, sec. 4, p. 7; May 26, 1974, p. 39;
        Jun. 1, 1975, p. 42.

712)    American Telephone and Telegraph Co. Bans Bias in
        Employment of Homosexuals, Wall Street Journal,
        Aug. 8, 1974, p. 17.

713)    Anderson, Jack.   "Washington Merry-Go-Round: ...
        Homosexual Hunt," Washington Post, May 16, 1970,
        p. C11.

714)    Arrest of 8 Men Alleged to Be Part of a Homosexual
        Ring Operating in Suffolk County (N.Y.), New York
        Times, May 4, 1973, p. 44; May 6, 1974, p. 62.

715)    Arrest of 5 Men Allegedly Paying Money to Rogue
        Cops in Return for Protection of Gay Bars, New York
        Times, May 21, 1975, p. 47.

74

716)   Arrest of 17 Gays at Demonstration against Mayor
       John Lindsay of New York City, New York Times,
       Jan. 27, 1972, p. 50.

717)   Arrest of 10 Men after Gay Demonstration, New York
       Times, Aug. 30, 1970, p. 49.

718)   Arrest of 2 Men Charged with Training Young Boys
       to be Homosexual Prostitutes, New York Times,
       May 23, 1972, p. 31.

719)   Australian Parliament Votes to Decriminalize Consen-
       sual Homosexual Acts, New York Times, Nov. 4,
       1973, p. 13.

720)   Austria Legalizes Homosexual Acts between Consent-
       ing Adults, New York Times, Jul. 11, 1971, p. 9.

721)   Barnes, Clyde.   Review of Stage Play:  "Nightride,"
       New York Times, Dec. 10, 1971, p. 54.

722)   Barton, Lee (pseud.).   "Why Do Homosexual Play-
       wrights Hide their Homosexuality?" New York Times,
       Jan. 23, 1972, sec. 2, p. 1.

723)   Baseball Game between New York City Police and
       Homosexual Group, New York Times, Aug. 28, 1973,
       p. 70.

724)   Bell, Arthur.   Criticism of Movies Which Treat Ho-
       mosexuals in Mocking Fashion, New York Times,
       Apr. 8, 1973, sec. 2, p. 15.

725)   _____.  "Gay Is Sweeping the Country," Village
       Voice, Apr. 4, 1974, pp. 24-25.

726)   _____.  "Has the Gay Movement Gone Establish-
       ment?" Village Voice, Mar. 28, 1974, pp. 10-11.

727)   _____.  "Little John [Wojtowicz] and the Mob:
       Saga of a Heist," Village Voice, Aug. 31, 1972, pp.
       1, 30, 32-33.

728)   _____.  "Mayhem on the Gay Waterfront [Violence
       against Homosexuals]," Village Voice, Jan. 13, 1975,
       p. 5 and Jan. 20, 1975, p. 42.

729)    _____. "Meeting Two Hustlers: The Doorway
and the Sofa," Village Voice, Mar. 2, 1972, pp. 1,
52.    (Reprinted in Ruitenbeek, no. 127, pp. 137-43)

730)    _____. Murders of Gays in Greenwich Village,
Village Voice, Jan. 25, 1973, pp. 22, 24.

731)    _____. "The Swell Guy Murderer [Dean Corll]--
Deep in the Dark of Texas," Village Voice, Aug. 30,
1973, pp. 5-6.

732)    (Dr.) Benjamin Spock Supports Gay Rights Struggle,
New York Times, Jul. 3, 1972, p. 16; Jul. 30,
1972, p. 27; Jun. 26, 1973, p. 21.

733)    Berkeley (Ca.) Gay Liberation Front Rejects Alpine
Proposal, New York Times, Nov. 5, 1970, p. 58.

734)    Bierman, Bill. "Homosexuals: Struggle for Acceptance," Akron Beacon Journal--Sunday Magazine, Sep.
15, 1974, 9 pp.

735)    Bill to Ban Discrimination against Homosexuals Introduced in U.S. House of Representatives, New York
Times, Mar. 26, 1975, p. 6.

736)    Bill to Protect Homosexuals from Employment Discrimination Introduced in New York State Assembly,
New York Times, Feb. 17, 1973, p. 1; Feb. 21,
1973, p. 31.

737)    Black, Jonathan. "A Happy Birthday for Gay Liberation," Village Voice, Jul. 2, 1970, pp. 1, 58.    (Reprinted in Ruitenbeek, no. 127, pp. 97-103.)

738)    Blum, Howard. "The Gay Underworld: Boys for
Sale," Village Voice, Feb. 3, 1973, pp. 1, 84.

739)    _____. "Gays Take on the Cops: From Rage to
Madness," Village Voice, Sep. 3, 1970, pp. 1, 42,
44.

740)    _____. "The Mafia and Gay Bars," Village Voice,
Feb. 22, 1973, pp. 1, 76; Mar. 22, 1973, pp. 3, 15.

741)    Boulder (Colo.) Councilman Who Pushed for City Ordinance Barring Discrimination against Homosexuals

Recalled from Office, New York Times, Sep. 12, 1974, p. 35.

742) British Government Releases Information on Homosexual Brothel Scandal (Cleveland Street, London, 1900), New York Times, Mar. 12, 1975, p. 7.

743) Brody, Jane E. 'Homosexuality: Parents Aren't Always to Blame," New York Times, Feb. 10, 1971, p. 48.

744) _____. Homosexuals Aided to Become Heterosexuals, New York Times, Feb. 28, 1971, p. 1.

745) Brooklyn Bank Robbery: Arrest, Conviction, and Sentence of John Wojtowicz. New York Times, Aug. 23, 1972, pp. 1, 45; Aug. 24, 1972, pp. 1, 37, 40; Aug. 25, 1972, p. 1; Aug. 26, 1972, p. 52; Aug. 27, 1972, sec. 4, p. 2; Apr. 24, 1973, p. 81. (See no. 3001, and Appendix I)

746) Brukenfeld, Dick. Review of Stage Play: 'Naomi Court," Village Voice, Oct. 3, 1974, p. 80.

747) _____. Review of Stage Play: "The Ritz," Village Voice, Feb. 3, 1975, p. 85.

748) Buckley, Tom. "Cherry Grove Stays Aloof from Gay Activists' Cause," New York Times, Jul. 14, 1972, pp. 33, 62.

749) Burch, Charles. "Gay Lib and the Police: Bad Day at Hauppage," Village Voice, May 11, 1972, pp. 12, 76.

750) Byron, Stuart. "Gay News and the [New York] Times: An Indelicate Balance," Village Voice, Apr. 1, 1971, pp. 13-14.

751) _____. 'Hazards for Homosexuals--Trick or Thief: My Six Rip-Offs," Village Voice, Sep. 21, 1972, pp. 1, 24, 26.

752) _____. Movie Review: 'Death in Venice" and "Fortune and Men's Eyes," New York Times, Jul. 18, 1971, sec. 2, pp. 11-12.

753)     California Court Holds Threat of Homosexual Rape
         May Justify Escape from Jail, New York Times,
         Jan. 20, 1975, p. 25.

754)     California Homosexuals Fight Repeal of Consensual
         Sex Law, New York Times, Jun. 19, 1975, p. 28;
         Jun. 29, 1975, sec. 4, p. 5.

755)     California Legalizes Consensual Homosexual Acts,
         New York Times, May 2, 1975, p. 12; May 14,
         1975, p. 42.

756)     California Peace Officers Want to Retain Anti-Homo-
         sexual Laws, San Francisco Chronicle, Jun. 4, 1971,
         pp. 1, 4.

757)     California Religious Group Fails in Drive to Repeal
         New Consenting Adult Sex Acts Law, Los Angeles
         Times, Jul. 22, 1975, sec. 1, p. 16.

758)     Calls for Repeal of Criminal Laws against Homosex-
         ual Acts, New York Times, Jan. 8, 1971, pp. 1, 29.

759)     Canby, Vincent. Movie Review: "Sunday, Bloody
         Sunday," New York Times, Sep. 22, 1971, p. 56;
         Oct. 3, 1971, sec. 2, p. 1.

760)     Candidates for District of Columbia Council Address
         Gay Group, Washington Post, Aug. 22, 1974, p. A22.

761)     Catholic Group ["Dignity"] Seeks Rights for Homo-
         sexuals, Washington Post, Apr. 5, 1974, p. D19.

762)     Champlin, Charles. Movie Review: "The Boys in
         the Band," Los Angeles Times, Calendar Section,
         Mar. 29, 1970, pp. 1, 14.

763)     Changing Church Attitudes toward Homosexuality, Los
         Angeles Times, Jul. 7, 1975, sec. 1, p. 3.

764)     Charges against 167 Men Dismissed--New York City
         Police Deny Harassment, New York Times, Mar. 26,
         1970, p. 30.

765)     Charges of Discrimination against Homosexuals in
         Employment, New York Times, Jan. 1, 1971, p. 43.

766)   Chatfield-Taylor, Joan.   "Bisexuality--Is It a Chic
       Fad or a Way of Life?" San Francisco Chronicle,
       Jul. 3, 1974, p. 14; Jul. 4, 1974, p. 23.

767)   Chicago Church for Homosexuals, Chicago Tribune,
       Feb. 24, 1974, sec. 1, p. 30.

768)   Christopher Isherwood Discusses his Homosexuality
       and the Gay Movement, New York Times, Mar. 25,
       1973, sec. 7, p. 10.

769)   Church Leaders View Current Attitudes on Homosex-
       uality, Los Angeles Times, Aug. 30, 1975, sec. 1,
       p. 27.

770)   Church of Beloved Apostle in New York City Minis-
       ters to Homosexuals, New York Times, Jul. 19,
       1971, p. 32; Oct. 8, 1973, p. 37; Oct. 30, 1973,
       p. 39.

771)   Church of Christ Refuses to Endorse Ordaining of
       Homosexuals, Washington Post, May 5, 1972, p. A13.

772)   Church of Nazarene Asks California to Outlaw Homo-
       sexual Acts, Los Angeles Times, May 24, 1975,
       sec. 1, p. 29.

773)   Churches Assailed as Foes of Homosexuals, New
       York Times, Mar. 25, 1971, p. 30.

774)   "Clergy Hits Homosexual Job Bias," San Francisco
       Chronicle, Oct. 19, 1971, p. 6.

775)   Colombia Reduces Homosexual Acts to Misdemeanors,
       New York Times, Sep. 6, 1970, p. 34.

776)   Columbia University Approves, After Long Debate,
       Lounge for Homosexual Students, New York Times,
       Sep. 26, 1970, p. 30; Dec. 10, 1971, p. 34; Sep.
       19, 1972, p. 66; Oct. 4, 1972, p. 51.

777)   Comito, Terry.   Police Raid 9 After-hours Bars,
       Village Voice, Jul. 29, 1971, pp. 3, 12, 33.

778)   Connecticut's Law Legalizing Homosexual Acts be-
       tween Consenting Adults Goes into Effect, New York
       Times, Oct. 2, 1971, p. 35.

779)     Connor, J. J.; Miller, Merle; and Others.   TV Re-
         view:  "That Certain Summer," New York Times,
         Oct. 29, 1972, sec. 2, p. 21; Nov. 3, 1972, p. 79;
         Nov. 5, 1972, sec. 2, p. 19; Nov. 19, 1972, sec.
         2, p. 17.

780)     The Continental Baths: New York's Newest "In" Spot,
         San Francisco Chronicle, Mar. 1, 1972, p. 18.

781)     Corporal [J. A. Dunbar] Challenges Armed Services'
         Discharge of Homosexuals, New York Times, Mar.
         22, 1972, p. 19.

782)     Court Awards Custody of Children to California Ho-
         mosexual Mother, Los Angeles Times, May 21, 1975,
         sec. 2, p. 2.

783)     Court Orders Back Pay Given to Discharged Homo-
         sexual, New York Times, Jan. 21, 1973, p. 52.

784)     Court Tells Oklahoma University to Confer Equal
         Status on Gay Groups, Washington Post, Sep. 1,
         1972, p. A12.

785)     Dallas Police May Have Uncovered Homosexual Ring,
         New York Times, Aug. 16, 1973, p. 16.

786)     Dance at Princeton University Sponsored by Gay Or-
         ganization, New York Times, May 21, 1973, p. 70.

787)     Democratic Platform Committee and Democratic Party
         Vote against Gay Rights Plank, New York Times,
         Jun. 26, 1972, p. 1; Jun. 28, 1972, p. 34; Jul. 13,
         1972, p. 1.

788)     Difficult Life of Homosexuals in the Military, Wash-
         ington Post, May 29, 1975, p. B4.

789)     "Dignity" [a Catholic Group of Homosexuals] Holds
         Conference in Boston, New York Times, Sep. 30,
         1975, p. 50.

790)     District of Columbia Appeals Court Overturns Dis-
         trict's Lewdness Law, Washington Post, May 10,
         1974, p. B1.

791)     District of Columbia Corporation Counsel Reverses

Stand and Says Homosexual Acts Are Illegal, Washington Post, Aug. 10, 1973, p. C3.

792) District of Columbia "Immoral Soliciting" Law Overturned, Washington Post, Jun. 2, 1972, p. A20.

793) District of Columbia School Board Adopts Unbiased Policy toward Homosexuals, Washington Post, May 24, 1972, p. B3.

794) District of Columbia Survey on Abortion and Homosexuality, Washington Post, Aug. 8, 1975, p. C1.

795) District of Columbia to End Prosecution of Adult Private Homosexual Acts, Washington Post, May 31, 1972, p. A1.

796) Donald Segretti's Dirty Tricks Include Charges of Homosexual Conduct against a U.S. Senator, New York Times, May 3, 1973, p. 1; May 5, 1973, p. 1; May 11, 1973, p. 21; May 12, 1973, p. 14; May 13, 1973, p. 48; May 18, 1973, p. 20; Jun. 1, 1973, p. 17; Jun. 16, 1973, p. 12; Jul. 1, 1973, p. 1; Oct. 4, 1973, p. 1; Nov. 6, 1973, p. 1.

797) Drummond, William J. "State Tries to Offset Prison Homosexuality," Los Angeles Times, Feb. 7, 1971, sec. H, pp. 1, 3.

798) Duberman, Martin. Review of Stage Plays: "Coming Out" and "The Faggot," New York Times, Jul. 22, 1973, sec. 2, p. 1.

799) _____. Review of 12 books on Homosexuality Written by Scientists and Gay Liberationists, New York Times, Dec. 10, 1972, sec. 7, pp. 6-7, 28-29.

800) Dyer, Richard. Review of Opera: "Death in Venice," Los Angeles Times, Calendar Sec., Nov. 10, 1975, p. 50.

801) Edelman, Maurice. Book Review: H. Montgomery Hyde, The Love That Dared Not Speak Its Name, New York Times, Jul. 5, 1970, sec. 7, p. 6.

802) Editorial Calling on Government Officials to Stop Persecuting Homosexuals and to Stop Denying Them Employment, Washington Post, Feb. 2, 1971, p. A14.

803)     Editorial Criticizing Dismissal of Gay Teacher, Hack-
         ensack Record, Sep. 24, 1973.

804)     Editorial Criticizing New York City Council for Not
         Passing Gay Rights Bill, New York Times, May 25,
         1975, p. 28.

805)     Editorial Criticizing Physical Attack on a Gay Rally,
         Connecticut Sunday Herald, Jun. 13, 1971.

806)     Editorial Criticizing U. S. Marine Corps for Discharge
         of Homosexual Corporal, Washington Post, Mar. 26,
         1972, p. B6.

807)     Editorial Supporting Homosexual Marriage, San Fran-
         cisco Chronicle, Jun. 16, 1970, p. 40.

808)     Editorial Supporting New York City Gay Rights Bill,
         Village Voice, Sep. 15, 1975, p. 4.

809)     Editorial Supporting U. S. Civil Service Commission's
         Guidelines Forbidding Employment Discrimination
         against Homosexuals, New York Times, Jul. 16,
         1975, p. 36.

810)     Editorial Urging New York City Council to Pass Gay
         Rights Bill, New York Times, Apr. 19, 1974, p. 36;
         May 3, 1974, p. 38.

811)     Editorial Urging U. S. Air Force to Permit Qualified
         Homosexuals to Remain in Military Service, New
         York Times, Oct. 13, 1975, p. 28.

812)     Elaine Noble (Lesbian) Elected to Massachusetts Leg-
         islature, New York Times, Nov. 6, 1974, p. 34;
         Nov. 14, 1974, p. 60.

813)     Employers Ease Curbs on Hiring of Homosexuals,
         Wall Street Journal, Nov. 2, 1971, p. 3.

814)     Employment Service for Homosexuals, Los Angeles
         Times, Nov. 4, 1973, sec. 1, p. 18.

815)     Episcopal Homosexual Group Faces Dispute at Chica-
         go Convention, Chicago Tribune, Aug. 2, 1975, sec.
         N2, p. 11.

816) Experiment Shows Stress Predisposes Rats to Homosexual Behavior, New York Times, Jan. 13, 1972, p. 35.

817) Feingold, Michael. Review of Stage Play: "Lovers," Village Voice, Feb. 25, 1975, p. 76.

818) _____. Review of Stage Play: "P.S. Your Cat Is Dead," Village Voice, Apr. 28, 1975, p. 91.

819) Firms Now Hiring Homosexual Employees, Wall Street Journal, July 1, 1974, pp. 1, 15.

820) First Congregational Church, District of Columbia, to Oust Homosexual Group, Washington Post, May 20, 1974, p. C1.

821) First Homosexual Social Service Agency Operates in Los Angeles, Los Angeles Times, Jul. 6, 1973, sec. 4, p. 1.

822) Florida Legislature Fails to Enact Law against Sodomy, Washington Post, Apr. 20, 1972, p. E2.

823) Four Homosexuals Dismissed from Federal Employment Sue for Reinstatement, New York Times, Dec. 21, 1971, p. 26.

824) Fredonia (New York) Parents Angered over Lecture by Homosexual, Buffalo Evening News, Mar. 15, 1972, p. 29.

825) Frymer, Murry. Interview of Jim Owles, Gay Activist, San Francisco Chronicle, Sunday Punch Sec., Aug. 15, 1971, p. 1.

826) Garrett, Thomas B. and Wright, Richard. New Homosexuality Laws Have Made Little Impact, Los Angeles Times, Oct. 16, 1975, sec. 2, p. 7.

827) Gay Academic Union Holds Conference, New York Times, Dec. 1, 1974, p. 74; Nov. 29, 1975, p. 20.

828) Gay Activists Alliance (New York City) Charge Mickey Maye with Assault; Trial and Acquittal of Maye, New York Times, Feb. 28, 1972, p. 83; Mar. 4, 1972,

p. 25; Apr. 16, 1972, p. 42; Apr. 19, 1972, p. 23;
Apr. 20, 1972, p. 38; Apr. 22, 1972, p. 19; Apr.
25, 1972, p. 11; May 2, 1972, p. 86; May 5, 1972,
p. 22; May 12, 1972, p. 45; May 23, 1972, p. 30;
May 24, 1972, p. 51; Jun. 8, 1972, p. 35; Jun. 24,
1972, p. 36; Jun. 27, 1972, p. 42; Jun. 28, 1972,
p. 46, Jul. 6, 1972, p. 38.

829)    Gay Activists Alliance Granted Incorporation after
        Court Battle, New York Times, Feb. 22, 1971, p.
        32; May 22, 1971, p. 25; Mar. 4, 1972, p. 28; Jan.
        13, 1973, p. 28; May 22, 1973, p. 45.

830)    Gay Activists Alliance Holds Rally in City Hall Park
        Urging Passage of Gay Rights Bill before New York
        City Council, New York Times, May 6, 1975, p. 33.

831)    Gay Activists Alliance Picket Senator Edmund Muskie,
        New York Times, Jan. 6, 1972, p. 22.

832)    Gay Activists Alliance's Community Center Burns,
        New York Times, Oct. 16, 1974, p. 19.

833)    Gay Activists Claim Syndicate Control of Many New
        York Gay Bars, New York Times, Jul. 26, 1971,
        p. 27.

834)    Gay Activists Demonstrate Against Abe Beam, Can-
        didate for Mayor of New York, New York Times,
        Oct. 27, 1973, p. 17.

835)    Gay Activists Demonstrate against Mayor John Lind-
        say of New York, New York Times, Jan. 26, 1972,
        p. 18; Jan 27, 1972, p. 50.

836)    Gay Activists Press Presidential Candidate George
        McGovern, New York Times, Aug. 22, 1972, p. 37;
        Oct. 21, 1972, p. 16.

837)    Gay Activists Protest American Medical Association's
        Failure to Meet the Needs of Homosexuals, New York
        Times, Jun. 22, 1970, p. 1.

838)    Gay Activists Protest Ouster of Homosexual from
        U.S. Marine Corps, Washington Post, Mar. 22,
        1972, p. C1.

839) Gay Bars Are Found in Small Towns Like Saugatuck, Mich., Chicago Tribune, Mar. 18, 1972, sec. 1, p. 7.

840) Gay Conspiracy to Take over Alpine County, Ca., San Francisco Examiner, Oct. 18, 1970, pp. 1, 25.

841) Gay Foster Homes for Gay Boys, New York Times, May 7, 1974, p. 47.

842) "Gay Ghettos Seen as Police Targets," New York Times, Aug. 31, 1970, p. 28.

843) Gay Groups Protest Los Angeles Police Harassment, Los Angeles Times, Jan. 22, 1974, sec. 1, p. 2; Mar. 3, 1974, sec. 1, p. 2; Sep. 6, 1974, sec. 3, p. 14.

844) "Gay Jewish Women," Village Voice, May 31, 1973, p. 25.

845) Gay Journalist, Brian McNaught, Files Bias Suit against "Michigan Catholic," Chicago Tribune, Aug. 12, 1974, sec. 3, p. 12.

846) Gay Liberation Front and Black Panthers Participate in Revolutionary People's Constitutional Convention, New York Times, Sep. 8, 1970, p. 57.

847) Gay Liberation Front Protests at American Psychiatric Association Meeting against the Use of Electric Shock Treatment, New York Times, May 15, 1970, p. 38.

848) Gay Liberation Proponents Meet Near White House, Washington Post, May 6, 1972, p. B2.

849) Gay Pride Parade in Chicago, Chicago Tribune, Jun. 25, 1973, sec. 1, p. 4; Jul. 1, 1974, sec. 1A, p. 1; Jun. 30, 1975, sec. 4, p. 11.

850) Gay Pride Parade in Hackensack, N.J., New York Times, Jun. 29, 1974, p. 63.

851) Gay Pride Parade in New York City, New York Times, Jun. 29, 1970, p. 1; Jul. 5, 1970, sec. 4, p. 12; Jun. 27, 1971, p. 30; Jun. 28, 1971, p. 23; Jun. 26,

1972, p. 21; Jun. 25, 1973, p. 21; Jul. 1, 1974,
p. 33.

852)   Gay Pride Parade in New York City, Village Voice,
       Jul. 1, 1971, pp. 7-8; Jul. 6, 1972, pp. 17, 24;
       Jun. 28, 1973, pp. 16-18, Jun. 7, 1975, p. 26.

853)   Gay Pride Parade in Philadelphia, New York Times,
       Jun. 12, 1972, p. 39.

854)   Gay Pride Parade in San Francisco, San Francisco
       Chronicle, Jun. 25, 1973, p. 3; Jul. 1, 1974, p. 3;
       Jun. 30, 1975, p. 3.

855)   Gay Raider Mark Segal Interrupts CBS News Pro-
       gram, New York Times, Dec. 12, 1973, p. 94.

856)   Gay Rights Bill Defeated by Worcester, Mass. City
       Council, New York Times, Jul. 18, 1974, p. 7.

857)   Gay Rights Bill Repeatedly Introduced and Defeated
       in New York City Council, New York Times, May 17,
       1971, p. 25; Oct. 3, 1971, p. 66; Oct. 8, 1971, p.
       31; Oct. 19, 1971, p. 39; Nov. 16, 1971, p. 49; Nov.
       29, 1971, p. 34; Dec. 18, 1971, p. 23; Jan. 28,
       1972, p. 1; Feb. 7, 1972, p. 21; Feb. 16, 1972, p.
       38; Apr. 3, 1972, p. 23; Apr. 24, 1972, p. 23; Jul.
       20, 1972, p. 35; Jan. 15, 1973, p. 26; Feb. 11,
       1973, p. 62; Apr. 20, 1973, p. 38; Apr. 27, 1973,
       p. 44; Apr. 28, 1973, p. 37; Apr. 29, 1973, p. 49;
       May 1, 1973, p. 53; Dec. 21, 1973, p. 1; Dec. 23,
       1973, sec. 4, p. 5; Jan. 1, 1974, p. 23; Jan. 4,
       1974, p. 28; Jan. 19, 1974, p. 63; Apr. 12, 1974,
       p. 35; Apr. 18, 1974, p. 45; Apr. 19, 1974, pp. 1,
       36, 44; Apr. 21, 1974, p. 52; Apr. 24, 1974, p. 45;
       Apr. 28, 1974, p. 41; Apr. 30, 1974, pp. 6, 38, 49,
       70, 81; May 3, 1974, p. 38; May 5, 1974, sec. 4,
       p. 6; May 6, 1974, p. 39; May 9, 1974, p. 42; May
       12, 1974, p. 50; May 18, 1974, p. 67; May 21, 1974,
       p. 40; May 22, 1974, p. 47; May 23, 1974, p. 1;
       May 24, 1974, p. 1; May 25, 1974, p. 28; May 26,
       1974, pp. 4, 32, 39; May 31, 1974, p. 32; Jun. 4,
       1974, pp. 36, 40; Jun. 24, 1974, p. 33.

858)   Gay Student Organizations Found at Many Colleges and
       Universities, New York Times, Dec. 15, 1971, p. 1;
       Jan. 28, 1973, p. 46; Jun. 5, 1974, p. 1.

859)    Gay Student Sit-in at New York University, New York
        Times, Sep. 21, 1970, p. 26.

860)    Gay Student Union Sues Tulane University over Recog-
        nition, New Orleans Times Picayune, Jan. 18, 1975,
        sec. 1, p. 12.

861)    Gay Students protest at Columbia University, New
        York Times, Sep. 21, 1970, p. 26; Dec. 10, 1971,
        p. 34; Sep. 19, 1972, p. 66; Oct. 4, 1972, p. 51.

862)    Gay Teachers Caucus at National Education Associa-
        tion Convention, New York Times, Jul. 2, 1972, sec.
        4, p. 5.

863)    Gays Come Out of Closet, New York Times, Aug.
        24, 1970, p. 1; Mar. 1, 1974, p. 27; Mar. 4, 1974,
        p. 29.

864)    Gays Demonstrate Against New York City Police Raid
        on Gay Bar, New York Times, Mar. 9, 1970, p. 29.

865)    Gays Demonstrate outside St. Patrick's Cathedral in
        New York City in Protest against Roman Catholic
        Church's Oppression of Homosexuals and Oppostion to
        Gay Rights Bill, New York Times, Mar. 23, 1971,
        p. 46; Jul. 13, 1975, p. 17; Sep. 22, 1975, p. 37.

866)    Gays Denied Permission to Place Wreath in Arlington
        Cemetery in Honor of Homosexual Soldiers Who Died
        in Action, New York Times, May 28, 1973, p. 35.

867)    Gays Interrupt Dr. David Reubin's Speech in Phila-
        delphia, New York Times, Jun. 19, 1974, p. 51.

868)    Gays Involved in Presidential Politics, New York
        Times, Jun. 16, 1972, p. 24.

869)    Gays Meet to Plan for National Political Conventions,
        Washington Post, May 8, 1972, p. C4.

870)    Gays Protest Lesbian Episode in NBC's TV Show
        "Police Woman," New York Times, Oct. 11, 1974,
        p. 75, Nov. 24, 1974, sec. 2, p. 23; Nov. 30,
        1974, p. 61.

871)    Gays Protest Treatment by New York City Police,

New York Times, Nov. 12, 1972, p. 48.

872)     Gays Protest Treatment by Psychiatrists and Thera-
         pists, New York Times, May 15, 1970, p. 38; Oct.
         9, 1972, p. 32.

873)     Gays Protest TV Program "Marcus Welby" for Its
         Treatment of Homosexuality, New York Times, Sep.
         28, 1974, p. 59; Oct. 6, 1974, sec. 2, p. 19; Oct.
         8, 1974, p. 82; Oct. 27, 1974, sec. 2, p. 31.

874)     Germany Reduces Age of Consent from 21 to 18 for
         Homosexual Acts, New York Times, Jun. 10, 1973,
         p. 11.

875)     Glasser, Ira.   Nazi Execution of 250,000 Homosex-
         uals, New York Times, Sep. 10, 1975, p. 45.

876)     Glassner, Barry.   "The World of the Homosexual"
         and "What Parents Can Do to Prevent Homosexuality,"
         Tucson Daily Citizen, Ole Section, Jul. 1, 1972, pp.
         4-7.

877)     Gold, Joe and Nathanson, Elaine.   "Homosexual Sub-
         Culture Flourishing in Tucson?" Arizona Daily Star,
         Nov. 5, 1971, p. B6; "Gay Lib Movement Seeks
         Wider Acceptance," Nov. 6, 1971, p. B2; and "Dis-
         criminatory Policy against Gays Challenged," Nov.
         7, 1971, p. A17.

878)     Goldstein, Richard.   "S and M: The Dark Side of
         Gay Liberation," Village Voice, Jul. 7, 1975, pp.
         10-13.

879)     Gornick, Vivian.   "Lesbians and Women's Lib," Vil-
         lage Voice, Mar. 18, 1971, pp. 5, 8.

880)     Grand Jury Clears Man Accused of Assault on Homo-
         sexual, New York Times, Jul. 7, 1972, p. 15; Jul.
         8, 1972, p. 30.

881)     Greene, Daniel S.   "They're Gay, and Happy," Na-
         tional Observer, Apr. 14, 1973, pp. 1, 18.

882)     Gribbin, August.   "The YMCA: It's Also YMC-Gay,"
         National Observer, Sep. 7, 1974, pp. 1, 14.

883)    Grieg, Michael.  "The Boom in Gay Marriages,"
        San Francisco Chronicle, Jul. 14, 1970, p. 1.

884)    _____.  "Gay Married Life--Lesbian Partners,"
        San Francisco Chronicle, Jul. 15, 1970, pp. 1, 30.

885)    _____.  "The Patterns of Homosexual Life," San
        Francisco Chronicle, Apr. 6, 1970, p. 3.

886)    Harmetz, Aljean.  Movie Review: "Sunday, Bloody
        Sunday," New York Times, Nov. 28, 1971, sec. 2,
        p. 13.

887)    (Dr.) Harold Brown of New York City Announces His
        Homosexuality and Involvement in the Gay Liberation
        Movement, New York Times, Oct. 3, 1973, p. 1;
        Oct. 4, 1973, p. 49; Oct. 7, 1973, sec. 4, p. 4;
        Oct. 12, 1973, p. 42; Oct. 16, 1973, p. 37.

888)    Harrington, Stephanie.  "TV: An American Family--
        The Louds Refuse to Acknowledge Son Lance's Homo-
        sexuality," New York Times, Jan. 7, 1973, sec. 2,
        p. 19.

889)    Hebrew Synagogue for Homosexuals Set up in New
        York City and Los Angeles, New York Times, Dec.
        23, 1973, p. 21.

890)    Hendin, Herbert.  Book Review: C. A. Tripp, Ho-
        mosexual Matrix, New York Times, Oct. 26, 1975,
        sec. 7, p. 35.

891)    _____.  "Homosexuality and the Family," New
        York Times, Aug. 22, 1975, p. 31.

892)    Hendrix, Kathleen.  "Lesbian Alcoholics," Los An-
        geles Times, Jul. 16, 1975, sec. 4, pp. 1, 6-7 and
        Jul. 17, 1975, sec. 4, pp. 1, 13-15.

893)    High School Teacher and Gay Activist [John Gish] Is
        Ordered to Undergo Psychiatric Examination, New
        York Times, Oct. 21, 1973, p. 92; Dec. 4, 1974,
        p. 91; Dec. 8, 1974, p. 100.

894)    High School Teacher in Novato, Ca. Warned for In-
        viting Homosexual to Speak to Class, Los Angeles
        Times, Jun. 22, 1972, sec. 1, p. 2.

895)   High School Teacher in Phoenix Who Invited Homo-
       sexual to Speak to Class Resigns, New York Times,
       May 10, 1970, p. 54.

896)   Hollywood Discotheque for Teenage Homosexuals, New
       York Times, Jun. 19, 1975, p. 28.

897)   Homosexual Churches and Church Attitudes toward
       Homosexuals, New York Times, Mar. 28, 1971, sec.
       4, p. 7.

898)   Homosexual Clerk Loses Job Suit against FBI, Wash-
       ington Post, Dec. 23, 1975, p. B8.

899)   Homosexual Fighting Dishonorable Discharge Declared
       AWOL, Washington Post, May 13, 1972, p. A9.

900)   Homosexual Group Seeks to Meet with Governor of
       New Hampshire, Washington Post, May 13, 1974,
       p. A4.

901)   Homosexual Lawyer [Harris Kimball] Denied Admis-
       sion to New York State Bar--Decision Overruled,
       New York Times, Jan. 10, 1973, p. 16; Jul. 10,
       1973, p. 82.

902)   Homosexual Lawyer [Jack Baker] Permitted to Take
       Minnesota Bar Examination, New York Times, Jan.
       7, 1973, p. 55.

903)   Homosexual Loses Fight against Discharge from U.S.
       Marine Corps, Washington Post, Jun. 2, 1972, p.
       A19.

904)   Homosexual Marriage Forbidden by Bill Passed by
       Louisiana House, New Orleans Times Picayune, Jun.
       1, 1975, sec. 1, p. 5.

905)   Homosexual Marriage in Colorado Stirs up Contro-
       versy, New York Times, Apr. 27, 1975, p. 49.

906)   Homosexual Marriages Condemned by Vatican Aide,
       New York Times, Jul. 26, 1970, p. 8.

907)   Homosexual Marriages Defended by United Nations
       Aide, New York Times, Aug. 11, 1970, p. 23.

908)    Homosexual Movement in Portugal, New York Times,
        May 19, 1974, p. 13.

909)    Homosexual Rape in Mississippi Prison, New York
        Times, Sep. 18, 1972, p. 39.

910)    Homosexual Teacher [Joseph Acanfora] Files Suit for
        Removal from Classroom in Maryland Junior High
        School, New York Times, Nov. 12, 1972, p. 49.

911)    Homosexual Tie Noted in Ten District of Columbia
        Slayings in 1970, Washington Post, Mar 3, 1972,
        p. A25.

912)    Homosexuality in Prison, New York Times, Apr. 25,
        1971, p. 40.

913)    Homosexuality in Women's Prisons, Washington Post,
        Feb. 2, 1972, p. A1.

914)    Homosexuality: One of the Top Religious Issues of
        1975, Chicago Tribune, Dec. 27, 1975, sec. 1B,
        p. 10.

915)    Homosexuals and Hormones, New York Times, Nov.
        18, 1971, p. 30.

916)    Homosexuals and Venereal Diseases, New York
        Times, Jun. 11, 1972, p. 9.

917)    Homosexuals Are Not Sick Says San Francisco Men-
        tal Health Association, San Francisco Chronicle,
        Jun. 5, 1971, p. 2.

918)    Homosexuals Declare Their Right to Teach, New York
        Times, May 20, 1974, p. 63.

919)    Homosexuals Demonstrate before Philadelphia City
        Council over Stalled Civil Rights Measure, New York
        Times, Dec. 5, 1975, p. 83.

920)    Homosexuals Eligible for Public Welfare, New York
        Times, Jun. 27, 1973, p. 57.

921)    "Homosexuals in Revolt," New York Times, Aug. 24,
        1970, pp. 1, 28.

922)    Homosexuals Isolated in Manhattan House of Deten-
        tion, New York Times, Oct. 23, 1971, p. 68.

923)    Homosexuals Not Permitted to Work for FBI, New
        York Times, Apr. 29, 1972, p. 17.

924)    Homosexuals Protest Federal Job Discrimination, San
        Francisco Chronicle, Jun. 8, 1971, p. 17.

925)    Homosexuals Seek to Improve Image in Media, Los
        Angeles Times, Dec. 10, 1973, sec. 4, p. 1.

926)    Homosexuals Take Civil Rights Plea to United Nations,
        San Francisco Chronicle, Jul. 29, 1970, p. 10

927)    "How Can You Be Sure He's Straight, Single?" San
        Francisco Chronicle, Jul. 12, 1975, p. 13.

928)    How Police Interpret Indecent Acts Related in Hear-
        ing, Washington Post, Jan. 21, 1972, p. A13.

929)    Illo, John. "Against Homosexuality," New York
        Times, Jul. 18, 1974, p. 35.

930)    Internal Revenue Service Refuses Joint Return Sub-
        mitted by Minneapolis Homosexual Couple, New York
        Times, Jan. 5, 1975, p. 91.

931)    Interview with Laura Hobson Regarding a Mother's
        Experience with Homosexual Son, New York Times,
        Sep. 22, 1975, p. 38.

932)    Jahr, Cliff. "The All-Gay Cruise: Prejudice and
        Pride," New York Times, Apr. 6, 1975, sec. 10,
        pp. 1, 16.

933)    _____. "Gay Movies for Straight People," Village
        Voice, Jun. 30, 1975, pp. 12-13.

934)    _____. "Littlejohn, the 'Dog Day' Bank Robber,
        Learns that Moviemaking, Like Crime, Does Not
        Pay," Village Voice, Sep. 29, 1975, pp. 124-25.

935)    Jesuit John McNeill Receives Permission to Publish
        his Book on Roman Catholic Church and Homosexu-
        ality, New York Times, Dec. 28, 1975, p. 32.

936)    Jim Owles, a Homosexual, Runs for New York City
       Council, New York Times, Jan. 28, 1973, p. 14.

937)    Johnston, Jill.   Book Reviews: Dennis Altman, Ho-
       mosexual Oppression; Arthur Bell, Dancing the Gay
       Lib Blues; and George Weinberg, Society and the
       Healthy Homosexual, New York Times, Feb. 20,
       1972, sec. 7, p. 5.

938)    _____.  "Hordes of Dykes and Faggots [Gay Lib-
       eration March]," Village Voice, Jun. 29, 1972, pp.
       29-30, 38.

939)    _____.  "The Making of a Lesbian Chauvinist,"
       Village Voice, Jun. 17, 1972, pp. 45, 58.

940)    _____.  "The Myth of Bonnies without Clydes:
       Lesbian Feminism and the Male Left," Village Voice,
       Apr. 28, 1975, p. 14.

941)    Jones, Cecil, "Police and Homosexuals:  A Confron-
       tation," Rocky Mountain News, Apr. 23, 1973.

942)    Judge Bars Firing of Oregon Teacher for Homosex-
       uality, Los Angeles Times, Feb. 4, 1973, sec. 1,
       p. 2.

943)    "Judge Rules Gay Slogans Disturbed Peace," San
       Francisco Chronicle, Apr. 23, 1970, p. 22.

944)    Kantrowicz, Arnie.   "A Gay Struggles with the New
       Acceptance," Village Voice, Nov. 17, 1975, pp. 36,
       39-41.

945)    _____.  "We Are Already Your Children," New
       York Times, Sep. 1, 1973, p. 21.

946)    Kerner, Leighton.   "'Death in Venice' Vivifies the
       Met," Village Voice, Oct. 24, 1974, pp. 57-58.

947)    Kirp, David.   Book Review:  Walter Barnett, Sexual
       Freedom and the Constitution, San Francisco Sunday
       Examiner and Chronicle, Jul. 8, 1972, Magazine Sec.,
       p. 36.

948)    Klemesrud, Judy.   "The Lesbian Issue and Women's

Lib," New York Times, Dec. 18, 1970, p. 47.

949)     Kotis, Michael.   "Homosexual Militance," New York
         Times, Feb. 19, 1971, p. 37.

950)     Lamb, Myrna.   Book Review: Sidney Abbott and Bar-
         bara Lane, Sappho was a Right-on Woman, New York
         Times, Feb. 25, 1973, sec. 7, pp. 39-40.

951)     Lambda Legal Defense Fund to Aid Homosexuals Set
         up, New York Times, Nov. 7, 1973, p. 51.

952)     Lehmann-Haupt, Christopher.   Book Review: Arno
         Karlen, Sexuality and Homosexuality, New York
         Times, Oct. 25, 1971, p. 31.

953)     _____.   Book Review: C. A. Tripp, Homosexual
         Matrix, New York Times, Dec. 19, 1975, p. 37.

954)     Lesbian Mother Given Custody of Children after Court
         Battle, Los Angeles Times, Jul. 13, 1972, sec. 1,
         p. 32.

955)     Lesbian Mother Loses Case for Custody of Her 9
         Year Old Son, New York Times, Dec. 21, 1975, p.
         35; Dec. 24, 1975, p. 42.

956)     Lesbian Mothers Discuss Their Lives, New York
         Times, Jan. 31, 1973, p. 46

957)     Lesbians and the Women's Movement, New York
         Times, Oct. 2, 1972, p. 46.

958)     Lesbians in Centers for Delinquent Girls, New York
         Times, May 18, 1971, p. 21.

959)     Lesbians Questioned by FBI about Radical Women's
         Movement, New York Times, Apr. 9, 1975, p. 56.

960)     Levin, Bernard.   "One Area of the Law Where the
         Principle of Sexual Equality Is Sadly Neglected,"
         London Times, Oct. 17, 1975, p. 12.

961)     Life for Homosexuals Becoming Less Difficult, New
         York Times, Sep. 1, 1972, p. 32.

962)     Lilleston, Lynn.   "Lesbians," Los Angeles Times,

Jun. 21, 1970, sec. D, pp. 2, 15 ("A Minority with New Visibility"); Jun. 22, 1970, sec. 4, pp. 1, 10 ("Lesbians Want to Lose 'Freak' Image"); Jun. 23, 1970, sec. 4, pp. 1, 6, ("Twosome's Relationship Rivals Normal Marriage"); Jun. 24, 1970, sec. 4, pp. 1, 6 ("Child-rearing Tasks Become Part of the Lesbian Household"); Jun. 25, 1970, sec. 4, pp. 1, 6 ("Causes Sought through Research with Children").

963)   Loeb, William. "Sodom and Gomorrah at Durham [University of New Hampshire], " Manchester Union Leader, Dec. 18, 1973, p. 1.

964)   Lombardi, John.   "Selling Gay to the Masses, " Village Voice, Jun. 30, 1975, pp. 10-11.

965)   Los Angeles Church and Synagogue for Homosexuals Report Gains, Los Angeles Times, Feb. 14, 1973, sec. 1, p. 24.

966)   Los Angeles City Attorney Issues Opinion on Police Department Hiring of Homosexuals, Los Angeles Times, May 10, 1975, sec. 1, p. 1.

967)   Los Angeles City Attorney to Curb Gay Bar Prosecutions, Los Angeles Times, Apr. 23, 1974, sec. 2, pp. 1, 8.

968)   Los Angeles City Council, Mayor, and Police Commission Discuss the Hiring of Homosexuals, Los Angeles Times, Oct. 17, 1975, sec. 1, p. 1.

969)   Los Angeles Gay Community Demands Liberalized Morals Laws, Los Angeles Times, Jan. 24, 1972, sec. 1, p. 1.

970)   Los Angeles Gays Picket Los Angeles Times Because of Its Inadequate Coverage of Gay News, New York Times, Oct. 23, 1974, p. 34.

971)   Los Angeles Refuses to Hire Homosexuals as Police Officers, Washington Post, Sep. 28, 1975, p. A2.

972)   "Lunching with S. I. R. [Gays Host Old Folks], " San Francisco Chronicle, Mar. 4, 1971, p. 4.

973)   Lutheran Church in America Urges Understanding and

Justice for Homosexuals, New York Times, Jul. 3, 1970, p. 16.

974) Man Sentenced for Distributing Obscene Materials Appealing to Homosexuals, New York Times, Aug. 29, 1971, p. 53.

975) Marriage Licence Denied to Two Minneapolis Men, New York Times, Jan. 10, 1971, p. 65.

976) Mass Murders in Houston Texas: Trial and Conviction of Elmer W. Henley, Jr. and David G. Brooks, New York Times, Jan. 23, 1973, p. 72; Jan. 25, 1973, p. 14; Jan. 26, 1973, p. 34; Jan. 28, 1973, p. 12; Jan. 30, 1973, p. 69; Jan. 31, 1973, p. 23; Feb. 2, 1973, p. 58; Apr. 8, 1973, p. 30; Apr. 10, 1973, p. 22; Apr. 20, 1973, p. 8; Aug. 9, 1973, p. 24; Aug. 10, 1973, p. 1; Aug. 11, 1973, pp. 1, 17; Aug. 12, 1973, sec. 4, pp. 7, 51; Aug. 13, 1973, p. 57; Aug. 14, 1973, pp. 1, 18; Aug. 15, 1973, p. 34; Aug. 16, 1973, pp. 1, 17; Aug. 17, 1973, p. 18; Aug. 21, 1973, p. 16; Aug. 24, 1973, p. 31; Sep. 18, 1973, p. 27; Oct. 9, 1973, p. 28; Oct. 13, 1973, p. 70; Oct. 24, 1973, p. 38; Jan 15, 1974, p. 10; Jan. 23, 1974, p. 72; Jan. 25, 1974, p. 14; Jan. 26, 1974, p. 34; Jan. 28, 1974, p. 12; Jan. 30, 1974, p. 69; Jan. 31, 1974, p. 23; Feb. 2, 1974, p. 58; Apr. 8, 1974, p. 30; Apr. 10, 1974, p. 22; Apr. 20, 1974, p. 8; Jul. 1, 1974, p. 21; Jul. 2, 1974, p. 18; Jul. 9, 1974, p. 16; Jul. 10, 1974, p. 14; Jul. 11, 1974, p. 12; Jul. 12, 1974, p. 32; Jul. 13, 1974, p. 11; Jul. 15, 1974, p. 10; Jul. 16, 1974, p. 9; Jul. 17, 1974, p. 75; Jul. 21, 1974, p. 41 and sec. 4, p. 16; Aug. 9, 1974, p. 34; Aug. 11, 1974, p. 27; Nov. 6, 1974, p. 24; Mar. 4, 1975, p. 65; Mar. 9, 1975, sec. 4, p. 9; Mar. 15, 1975, p. 65. (See nos. 59, 113 and 120)

977) Massachusetts Red Cross Blood Program Recognizes Homosexual Couples as Family Units, New York Times, Jul. 30, 1973, p. 54.

978) Mayor John Lindsay of New York City Issues Executive Order Prohibiting Discrimination against Homosexuals in City Employment, New York Times, Feb. 8, 1972, p. 35; Feb. 13, 1972, sec. 4, p. 4.

979)     Mayor John Lindsay of New York City Supports Gay
         Rights Bill before City Council, New York Times,
         May 17, 1972, p. 25.

980)     McAllister, William. "A California Community [Al-
         pine County] Fumes as Homosexuals Talk of a Take-
         Over, " Wall Street Journal, Oct. 27, 1970, p. 1.

981)     McCabe, Charles. "The Fearless Spectator: Gay
         Is Good?" San Francisco Chronicle, Oct. 1, 1970,
         p. 53.

982)     McGuinness, Richard.   Review of Stage Play: "For-
         tune and Men's Eyes, " Village Voice, Jul. 1, 1971,
         p. 55.

983)     Member of Homosexual Ring Preying on Boys Sen-
         tenced to Prison, New York Times, Nov. 18, 1972,
         p. 41.

984)     Methodist Minister in Texas [Gene Leggett] Suspended,
         New York Times, Jun. 3, 1971, sec. 4, p. 3; Apr.
         28, 1974, p. 71.

985)     Metropolitan Community Church Accepted by Brooklyn
         Division of the Council of Churches of New York
         City, New York Times, Oct. 27, 1974, p. 115.

986)     Metropolitan Community Church Admitted to Santa
         Clara County Council of Churches, Los Angeles
         Times, Dec. 27, 1975, sec. 1, p. 19.

987)     Metropolitan Community Church Expands and Plans to
         Apply for Membership in National Council of Churches,
         New York Times, Apr. 1, 1973, p. 27.

988)     Metropolitan Community Church Has Right to Hold
         Services for Homosexual Prison Inmates, Los An-
         geles Times, May 22, 1975, sec. 1, p. 30.

989)     Metropolitan Community Church--Los Angeles Homo-
         sexuals Establish Their Own Church, New York
         Times, Feb. 15, 1970, p. 58.

990)     Metropolitan Community Church of Providence Ac-
         cepted by Rhode Island Council of Churches, New
         York Times, Mar. 28, 1974, p. 25.

991)     Michaelson, Judith.   "Family's Son [Lance Loud]
         Digs His TV Image," New York Post, Jan. 19,
         1973, p. 2.

992)     Miller, Merle.   "What It Means to Be a Homosex-
         ual," San Francisco Chronicle, Jan. 25, 1971, pp.
         1, 12 and Jan. 26, 1971, p. 1.   (Reprint of no.
         1266.   See also no. 102)

993)     _____.   "Homosexual's Story:  No More Quiet
         Desperation," Los Angeles Times, Jan. 31, 1971,
         sec. F, p. 2.   (Abbreviated version of preceding
         entry)

994)     Minneapolis Judge Allows One Homosexual to Adopt
         Another Homosexual, New York Times, Aug. 26,
         1971, p. 34.

995)     Minneapolis Passes Gay Rights Ordinance, Washing-
         ton Post, Mar. 31, 1974, p. A6.

996)     Minnesota State Senator Allan Spear Announces his
         Homosexuality, New York Times, Dec. 10, 1974,
         p. 53.

997)     Miss America Contestant Criticized for Supporting
         Gay Liberation Movement, New York Times, Sep.
         8, 1973, p. 68.

998)     Moskowitz, Ron.   "The Homosexual Pupil," San
         Francisco Chronicle, Nov. 12, 1970, p. 6.

999)     Murders of Homosexuals Concern Gay Community,
         New York Times, Jan. 18, 1973, p. 41; Jan. 19,
         1973, p. 20; Jan. 28, 1973, p. 36.

1000)    National Advisory Commission on Criminal Justice
         to Recommend Decriminalization of Consensual Adult
         Homosexual Acts, New York Times, Oct. 1, 1972,
         p. 64.

1001)    National Broadcasting Co. Officials Agree TV has
         at Times Dealt Unfairly with Homosexuals in Its
         Programs, New York Times, Oct. 27, 1973, p. 63.

1002)    National Commission on Reform of Federal Criminal
         Laws Recommends Decriminalization of Consensual

Adult Homosexual Acts, New York Times, Jul. 18, 1970, p. 33; Jan. 8, 1971, p. 1.

1003)     National Council of Churches Unit Backs Civil Rights for Homosexuals, Chicago Tribune, Mar. 7, 1975, sec. 1, p. 4.

1004)     National Organization of Women Says Lesbian Rights Are Important, New York Times, Feb. 19, 1973, p. 12; Oct. 28, 1975, p. 15.

1005)     National Priests' Council of Catholic Church Calls for Christian Ministry to Homosexuals, New York Times, Mar. 17, 1972, p. 20.

1006)     New Hampshire Governor Angered at Gay Student Organization at University of New Hampshire, New York Times, May 22, 1973, p. 37; Dec. 19, 1973, p. 53; Jan. 18, 1974, p. 38; Jan. 30, 1974, p. 8; Jun. 21, 1974, p. 21.

1007)     New York Attorney General Seeks to Close Gay Clubs in Greenwich Village, New York Times, Jan. 9, 1971, p. 52.

1008)     New York Candidates for Governor and Senator Support Gay Civil Rights, New York Times, Oct. 27, 1970, pp. 18, 36.

1009)     New York City Board of Education and Police and Fire Departments Reluctant to Permit Employment of Homosexuals, New York Times, Nov. 16, 1971, p. 49.

1010)     New York City Board of Education, IBM, and CBS Accused of Employment Bias against Homosexuals, New York Times, Jan. 7, 1971, p. 43.

1011)     New York City Gays Protest Oppression by Roman Catholic Church, New York Times, Mar. 23, 1971, p. 46; May 6, 1974, p. 39; May 25, 1974, p. 58; Jun. 24, 1974, p. 33.

1012)     New York City Gays Protest Police Harassment, New York Times, Aug. 31, 1970, p. 28; Nov. 12, 1972, p. 48; Aug. 10, 1973, p. 35.

1013)    New York City Police Crack down on Homosexual
         Prostitution Involving Minor Boys, New York Times,
         Mar. 30, 1973, p. 43.

1014)    New York State Assembly Defeats Gay Rights Bill,
         New York Times, May 27, 1971, p. 26.

1015)    New York State Legislature Urged to Repeal Con-
         sensual Sodomy Laws, New York Times, Jan. 8,
         1971, p. 29; Sep. 14, 1971, p. 35.

1016)    New York State Liquor Authority Says Some Gay
         Bars Are Operating After Hours without a License,
         New York Times, Mar. 23, 1970, p. 33.

1017)    New York University Offering Peer Group Counsel-
         ing Service to Students with Homosexual and Drug
         Problems, New York Times, Oct. 11, 1971, p. 24.

1018)    New York Women's Lobby Urges Removal of Res-
         trictions on Sex Relations between Consenting Adults,
         New York Times, Feb. 19, 1975, p. 39.

1019)    O'Connor, John J.   Review of Pat Collins' TV In-
         terviews with Homosexual Clients at Continental
         Baths, New York Times, Feb. 20, 1974, p. 75.

1020)    _____ .  Review of TV Episode in "The Bold
         Ones," New York Times, Nov. 3, 1972, p. 79.

1021)    _____ .  Review of TV Episode in "Hotel Balti-
         more," New York Times, Mar. 2, 1975, sec. 2,
         p. 29.

1022)    Office of Gay Concerns Wins Unitarian Support,
         Washington Post, Jun. 27, 1975, p. D15.

1023)    Offutt Air Base Case Sparks Wide Homosexuality
         Probe, Omaha World Herald, Feb. 6, 1970, p. 2.

1024)    Oliver Sipple, Former Marine, Deflects Pistol
         Aimed at President Gerald Ford and Files Suit for
         Invasion of Privacy by News Media, New York
         Times, Sep. 26, 1975, p. 16; Oct. 1, 1975, p. 20.

1025)    Pastor of Homosexual Church Discusses New Growth
         Phase, New Orleans Times Picayune, Feb. 16,
         1974, sec. 2, p. 4.

1026)    Pennsylvania Lobbyist Seeking Homosexual Rights,
         New York Times, Sep. 20, 1970, p. 56.

1027)    Pentagon Issues First Security Clearance to Homo-
         sexual, Washington Post, Feb. 2, 1975, p. A3.

1028)    Police Raid on 8 New York City After Hours Gay
         Clubs, New York Times, Jul. 19, 1971, p. 32.

1029)    Policeman and Lawyer Attempt to Extort Money
         from Businessman Arrested on Morals Charge, New
         York Times, Apr. 21, 1970, p. 45.

1030)    Political Power of California Homosexuals, Wash-
         ington Post, Jun. 1, 1975, p. A4.

1031)    Power of Homosexuals as Voting Group in San
         Francisco, Los Angeles Times, Sep. 30, 1975,
         sec. 1, p. 1.

1032)    President of Lutheran Church in America Opposes
         Homosexual Ministers, San Francisco Chronicle,
         Jun. 6, 1972, p. 38.

1033)    Prison Guards Allegedly Involved in Homosexual
         Acts with Prisoners, New York Times, Apr. 10,
         1975, p. 1; Apr. 29, 1975, p. 29; May 9, 1975,
         p. 1.

1034)    Prisons and Homosexuality, New York Times, Apr.
         25, 1971, p. 40; Apr. 13, 1972, p. 45; Dec. 14,
         1973, p. 51.

1035)    Proposal to Repeal Regulations Forbidding Homo-
         sexuals from Frequenting or Working in Cabarets
         and Dance Halls, New York Times, Oct. 12, 1971,
         p. 35.

1036)    Public Attitudes Toward Homosexuality Held by Re-
         ligious Groups, New York Times, Nov. 14, 1973,
         p. 22.

1037)    Rader, Dotson.  Book Reviews: Donn Teal, Gay
         Militants; Arno Karlen, Sexuality and Homosexuality;
         Colin Williams and Martin Weinberg, Homosexuals
         and the Military; and Gordon Merrick, One for the
         Gods, New York Times, Oct. 3, 1971, sec. 7, pp.
         5, 43.

1038)     Raspberry, William.  "Matlovich and Punch-in-the
          Nose Prejudice [Military Prejudice against Homo-
          sexuals]," Washington Post, Oct. 31, 1975, p. A27.

1039)     _____.  "A Reputation, A Career, A Fight [Dis-
          missal of a Black Homosexual Teacher at Univer-
          sity of Florida]," Washington Post, Oct. 28, 1974,
          p. A27.

1040)     Review of Gay Civil Rights Legislation in Washing-
          ton, D.C., Minneapolis, Detroit, Ann Arbor, and
          San Francisco, New York Times, May 19, 1974,
          sec. 4, p. 7.

1041)     Robinson, Marty.  "Gay Rights Bill," Village Voice,
          Feb 17, 1972, pp. 18-19; Feb. 24, 1972, pp. 23,
          26.

1042)     _____.  "Homosexuals and Society:  The 'Cure'
          is Rebellion," Village Voice, Apr. 29, 1971, pp.
          29, 41, 82.

1043)     Rockwell, John.  Review of Program of Homosex-
          ual Songs of Steven Grossman at New York City
          Nightclub, New York Times, May 7, 1974, p. 52.

1044)     Roman Catholic Archdiocese of New York Opposes
          Gay Rights Bill, New York Times, Apr. 28, 1974,
          p. 41.

1045)     Rosselini, Lynn.  "Gay Athletes."  Washington Star,
          Dec. 12, 1975, Sports Sec., p. 1 ("Gay Athletes
          Still in Closets"); Dec. 13, 1975, Sports Sec., p.
          1 ("Female Professional Athletes Carry 'Gay' Stig-
          ma"); Dec. 14, 1975, Sports Sec., p. 1 ('Discov-
          ery Can Ruin Gay Athletes"); Dec. 15, 1975, Sports
          Sec., p. 1 ("Coaches May Help Cause Homosexu-
          ality").

1046)     Safire, William.  "Big Week for Gays [Government
          Should Not Interfere in Sex Acts of Consenting
          Adults]," New York Times, Sep. 29, 1975, p. 31.

1047)     _____.  "Don't Slam the Closet Door [Support
          of Gay Rights Bill before New York City Council],"
          New York Times, Apr. 18, 1974, p. 41.

1048)    San Francisco Commission on Crime Recommends
         Decriminalization of Consensual Adult Homosexual
         Acts, San Francisco Chronicle, Jun. 4, 1971, pp.
         1, 4.

1049)    San Francisco Homosexuals' Political Machine, San
         Francisco Chronicle, Oct. 18, 1971, pp. 1, 22.

1050)    "San Francisco Police Assess Male Prostitution,"
         San Francisco Chronicle, Aug. 27, 1971, p. 4.

1051)    Sarris, Andrew W.   "Enduring Summer Camp [Ho-
         mosexuality in Films]," Village Voice, Jul. 21,
         1975, pp. 67-69.

1052)    _____.  Movie Review:  "Dog Day Afternoon,"
         Village Voice, Sep. 29, 1975, p. 111.

1053)    Senator Ted Kennedy Says Homosexuals Are Not
         Security Risks, New York Times, Nov. 17, 1971,
         p. 30.

1054)    Six Arrested at Gay Activist Protest in Arlington,
         Va., Washington Post, Jan. 6, 1972, p. D2.

1055)    Six Hundred Homosexuals 'Hold Hands' across
         George Washington Bridge, New York Times, May
         7, 1973, p. 43.

1056)    Special Travel Tours for Homosexuals, New York
         Times, Mar. 11, 1973, sec. 10, p. 21.

1057)    Stewart, P. J.   "Gay Couples:  A Look at their
         Lives Together," Arizona Daily Star, Aug. 10,
         1975, p. B1.

1058)    Store Picketed for Arresting Homosexuals, San
         Francisco Chronicle, Jul. 28, 1970, p. 4.

1059)    "Stupid Spy [John Vassall]," Parade, Mar. 9, 1975,
         p. 7.

1060)    Suffolk County (New York) District Judge Rules Ho-
         mosexuals and Other Unmarried Persons May En-
         gage in Consensual Sodomy, New York Times, Feb.
         3, 1975, p. 29.

1061)       Suffolk County (New York) Police Commissioner
            Charges District Attorney with Sodomy, New York
            Times, Sep. 4, 1975, p. 39; Sep. 5, 1975, pp. 28,
            33; Sep. 6, 1975, p. 23; Sep. 7, 1975, sec. 4, p.
            6; Sep. 10, 1975, p. 88; Sep. 11, 1975, p. 47;
            Sep. 12, 1975, p. 37; Sep. 13, 1975, p. 12; Sep.
            16, 1975, p. 82; Sep. 17, 1975, p. 49; Sep. 18,
            1975, p. 45; Sep. 19, 1975, p. 41; Sep. 23, 1975,
            p. 41; Sep. 29, 1975, p. 35; Oct. 4, 1975, p. 31;
            Oct. 12, 1975, p. 127; Oct. 17, 1975, p. 39; Oct.
            20, 1975, p. 37; Nov. 1, 1975, p. 33; Nov. 17,
            1975, p. 34; Nov. 22, 1975, p. 31.

1062)       Superintendent Denies Homosexuality Is Widespread
            in New York State Prisons, New York Times, Feb.
            14, 1975, p. 34; Feb. 15, 1975, p. 45.

1063)       Survey of 21 Cities on Hiring Homosexuals, Los
            Angeles Times, Oct. 12, 1975, sec. 1, p. 3.

1064)       Thomas, Kevin. Movie Review: "A Very Natural
            Thing," Los Angeles Times, Sep. 20, 1974, sec.
            4, p. 8.

1065)       Three Hundred Persons Demonstrate for Gay Rights
            at Albany, N. Y., New York Times, Apr. 16, 1972,
            p. 16.

1066)       Three Persons in Jersey City Charged with Homo-
            sexual Activity with Teenage Boys, New York
            Times, Nov. 18, 1973, p. 18.

1067)       Tipmore, David. "Homosexual Cult Figures [In En-
            tertainment]," Village Voice, Jan. 27, 1975, pp.
            120, 72-76.

1068)       Townley, Rod. "Gay Philadelphia," Philadelphia
            Inquirer, May 12, 1974, Magazine Sec., pp. 10-18,
            22-30.

1069)       Trecker, Barbara. "Homosexuals in New York:
            The Gay World," New York Post, Mar. 25, 1975,
            p. 39 ("Moving Out of the Closet"); Mar. 26, 1975,
            p. 39 ("Where Did We go Wrong?"); Mar. 27, 1975,
            p. 41 ("Coming Out"); Mar. 28, 1975, p. 41 ("Les-
            bians in Harmony"); Mar. 29, 1975, p. 49 ("Is It
            Normal?"); Mar. 30, 1975, p. 25 ("The Job Mar-
            ket").

1070)   Tucker, Carll.   Review of Stage Play:   "Boy Meets Boy," Village Voice, Sep. 29, 1975, p. 105.

1071)   "Twenty-five Men Arrested in Police Raid," Tampa Times, Sep. 6, 1972, p. 1.

1072)   Two High School Girls Pose as Homosexuals to Test Peers, Los Angeles Times, May 16, 1973, sec. 1, p. 3.

1073)   Two Lesbians Fight Ouster from Women's Army Corps, Washington Post, Jun. 5, 1975, p. B17.

1074)   Two Male Homosexuals Marry in District of Columbia Church, Washington Post, Jul. 9, 1972, p. D3.

1075)   Two Male Homosexuals Marry in Phoenix, Arizona Daily Star, Nov. 1, 1975, p. C2.

1076)   "Unitarians OK Ministry to Homosexuals," Los Angeles Times, Apr. 1, 1973, sec. 5, p. 16.

1077)   United Church of Christ General Synod Supports Civil Rights Legislation for Homosexuals, New York Times, Jul. 2, 1975, p. 30.

1078)   United Church of Christ in California Ordains Homosexual as Minister, Los Angeles Times, May 2, 1972, sec. 2, p. 1.

1079)   United Methodist Church General Conference Takes Stand on Homosexuals and Homosexuality, New York Times, Apr. 27, 1972, p. 16.

1080)   United Methodist Church in Wisconsin Refuses Homosexual's Ordination, Washington Post, Dec. 13, 1974, p. D14.

1081)   United Nations Representative from Ghana calls Homosexual Issue Frivolous, New York Times, Jul. 19, 1970, p. 33.

1082)   United Presbyterian Church's General Assembly Refuses to Recognize Presbyterian Gay Caucus, New York Times, May 19, 1975, p. 30.

1083)   United States Air Force Discharges Another Homosexual, Washington Post, Dec. 21, 1975, p. B6.

1084)     United States Air Force Discharges Sgt. Leonard
          Matlovich for Homosexuality, New York Times,
          May 26, 1975, p. 1; Jun. 3, 1975, p. 32; Jun. 7,
          1975, p. 26; Jul. 1, 1975, sec. 4, p. 8; Jul. 7,
          1975, p. 26; Sep. 17, 1975, p. 14; Sep. 18, 1975,
          p. 12; Sep. 19, 1975, p. 14; Sep. 20, 1975, pp.
          1, 15; Oct. 3, 1975, p. 31; Nov. 9, 1975, sec. 6,
          p. 16; Nov. 22, 1975, p. 62.

1085)     United States Air Force Discharges Sgt. Rudolph
          Keith for Homosexuality, New York Times, Sep.
          25, 1975, p. 14.

1086)     United States Armed Services Cite Number of Dis-
          charges for Homosexuality and Other Reasons, New
          York Times, Oct. 10, 1971, p. 35; Mar. 24, 1974,
          p. 46.

1087)     United States Army Discharges Two Lesbians, New
          York Times, Feb. 24, 1973, p. 35.

1088)     United States Army Discharges Two WACs for Ho-
          mosexuality, New York Times, Jul. 5, 1975, p. 15.

1089)     United States Citizenship Ordered Granted to Homo-
          sexual Immigrant, New York Times, Mar. 25, 1971,
          p. 30.

1090)     United States Civil Service Commission Sets New
          Guidelines on Homosexuals and Federal Employment,
          New York Times, Jul. 4, 1975, p. 45; Jul. 10,
          1975, p. 8.

1091)     United States Defense Department Ordered to Restore
          Security Clearance to Homosexual [Bennington Went-
          worth], Washington Post, May 27, 1972, p. A26.

1092)     United States Immigration Service's Use of Word
          "Faggots" Criticized, Los Angeles Times, Dec. 4,
          1975, sec. 2, p. 2.

1093)     United States Navy Board Recommends Discharge of
          Bisexual Officer, Los Angeles Times, Jun. 27, 1975,
          p. 30.

1094)     United States Navy Reports American Sailors are
          Pleading Drug Usage Rather than Homosexuality as

Quick Way out of the Service, New York Times, Oct. 10, 1971, p. 35.

1095)  United States Park Police Stage Raids on District of Columbia Homosexual Haunts, Washington Post, Jan. 3, 1972, p. B1.

1096)  United States Supreme Court Dismisses Challenge to Arkansas Sodomy Statute, New York Times, Nov. 6, 1973, p. 8.

1097)  United States Supreme Court Rejects Case of Homosexual's Job Loss [Michael McConnell], Washington Post, Oct. 16, 1974, p. B14.

1098)  United States Supreme Court Upholds Decision of School Board to Refuse to Rehire Probationary Teacher Acquitted of Criminal Charge of Homosexual Activity, New York Times, Dec. 10, 1974, p. 26.

1099)  United States Supreme Court Upholds Dismissal of Maryland Teacher [Joseph Acanfora] for Not Listing Membership in Homosexual Organization, New York Times, Oct. 16, 1974, p. 25.

1100)  University of Maine Gay Student Organization Arouses Anger, Washington Post, May 7, 1974, p. A28.

1101)  University of New Hampshire Gay Student Organization's Right to Exist Is Guaranteed by State and Federal Courts, New York Times, Dec. 19, 1973, p. 53; Jan. 18, 1974, p. 38; Jan. 30, 1974, p. 8; Nov. 1, 1975, p. 34.

1102)  Valente, Michael F.  "On Homosexuality, " New York Times, Jan. 14, 1975, p. 33.

1103)  Van Gelder, Lawrence.  New Kinsey Study Assails Armed Forces Policy toward Homosexuals, New York Times, Jul. 19, 1971, p. 32.

1104)  Van Hoffman, Nicholas.  "Of Gayety in a Democracy [Civil Rights for Homosexuals], " Washington Post, May 6, 1974, p. B1.

1105)         _____ . "Out of the Closet into the Class [Homosexual Teachers]," Washington Post, Jul. 3, 1972, p. C1.

1106)    Washington Court Orders Boy taken from Homosexual Foster Home, Washington Post, Oct. 29, 1975, p. A2.

1107)    Westchester County Theater Group Puts on "Boys in the Band," New York Times, Dec. 10, 1972, p. 108.

1108)    Wicker, Tom. "Is Gay a Security Risk?" New York Times, Jun. 27, 1972, p. 41.

1109)         _____ . "New Fight on an Old Front [Gay Rights Bill before New York City Council]," New York Times, May 14, 1974, p. 37.

1110)    Wiedrich, Bob. "Cops, Pols, Mob in Gay-Bar Payoffs," Chicago Tribune, Oct. 4, 1973, sec. 1, p. 18.

1111)    Will, George F. "Legislating Homosexual Rights," Washington Post, May 31, 1974, p. A27.

1112)    Wilson, William. Review of Anthony E. Friedkin's Photo Show of Homosexuals in California, Los Angeles Times, Jul. 12, 1973, sec. 4, p. 8.

1113)    Women's Liberation Leaders Support Gay Movement, New York Times, Dec. 18, 1970, p. 47.

1114)    Workers Admit Homosexuality to Keep Security Clearances, Washington Post, Dec. 25, 1975, p. D7.

## ARTICLES IN POPULAR MAGAZINES

1115)  "Across the Frontiers of Sex [Transsexuals],"
       Newsweek, 83:73-75, Apr. 8, 1974.

1116)  Adam, Corinna. "Cruelty in the Camp [Self-degrad-
       ing Humor among Homosexuals]," New Statesman,
       87:759 May 31, 1974.

1117)  _____. "A Special House in Hamburg [Male
       Prostitution]," New Statesman, 85:521-22, Apr. 13,
       1973.

1118)  "Adopting a Lover," Time, 98:50, Sep. 6, 1971.

1119)  Alexander, Dolores. "Rita Mae Brown: The Issue
       for the Future is Power," Ms., 3:110-13, Sep. 1974.

1120)  Amory, Mark. "The Exhibitionist: The Naked Civil
       Servant," Sunday Times Magazine, Nov. 9, 1975,
       p. 79.

1121)  Angly, Patricia. "Australian Television--Almost
       Anything Goes," Parade, Apr. 21, 1974, p. 34.

1122)  "Are Homosexuals Sick?" Newsweek, 81:71, May
       21, 1973.

1123)  (Lord) Arran. "Sexual Offences Act: A Personal
       Memoir," Encounter, 38:3-8, Mar. 1972.

1124)  Atcheson, Richard. "God, Gurus, and Gay Guer-
       rillas," Holiday, 47:50-54, 90-91, Mar. 1970.

1125)  "Austerity on Campus [Liberation of Women and Ho-
       mosexuals]," Time, 97:51, 53, Jun. 14, 1971.

1126)  Bailey, Paul. "Hilarious and Gay," Listener, 91:
       633-34, May 16, 1974.

1127)     Baker, A. T.   Book Review: Dennis Altman, Ho-
          mosexual: Oppression and Liberation, Time, 99:
          81-82, Feb. 28, 1972.

1128)     Baker, Robb.   "Al Carmines' 'The Faggot':  The
          First Musical-Comic Look at Gay Liberation,"
          After Dark, 6:36-39, Jul. 1973.

1129)     Bell, Arthur.   "The Fate of the Boys Next Door
          [the Houston Mass Murders]," Esquire, 81:96-99,
          174, 176, Mar. 1974.

1130)     "Better than Lying [Case of a Homosexual Minister-
          ial Candidate]," Time, 99:88, May 15, 1972.

1131)     "Bisexual Chic:  Anyone Goes," Newsweek, 89:90-
          91, May 27, 1974.

1132)     Boeth, Richard.   "The Assault on Privacy [Some
          Relaxation of Concern over Sexual Lives of Adult
          Homosexuals]," Newsweek, 76:15-20, Jul. 27, 1970.

1133)     Boucher, Sandy.   "Mountain Radio," Ms., 3:82-87,
          Apr. 1975.

1134)     Bowers, Faubion.   "Homosex:  Living the Life,"
          Saturday Review, 55:23-28, Feb. 12, 1972.   (Re-
          printed in Ruitenbeek, no. 127, pp. 104-15.)

1135)     "Boys in the Band:  Gay Students' Organizations at
          Universities of Maine and New Hampshire," News-
          week, 83:108, Mar. 25, 1974.

1136)     Brennan, John.   "Gay Libb," American Opinion,
          14:37-40, Mar. 1971.

1137)     Brogan, Colin.   "Notes from London:  Voyage au-
          tour de ma Chambre [Homosexuals among the
          Bloomsbury Set]," National Review, 22:897, Aug.
          25, 1970.

1138)     Brudnoy, David.   "Reflections on the Issue of Gay
          Rights," National Review, 26:802-03, Jul. 19, 1974.

1139)     "Bulldozer Rapist," Harper's, 251:6-7, Jul. 1975.

1140)     Burke, Tom.   "Violet Millennium or the Invert

Comes of Age," Rolling Stone, Aug. 30, 1973, pp. 53-56, 58, 60.

1141)   Burks, John and Link, Geoffrey. "The Gay Mecca: But San Francisco Is Still No Utopia for Homosexuals," San Francisco, Apr. 1970, pp. 30-34, 42-45.

1142)   Burns, Skip. "Bobby Seale's Gay Problem," Oui, 2:57, 86, 96, 112-114, Nov. 1973.

1143)   Calder-Marshall, Arthur. "Havelock Ellis and Company [Controversy over Homosexuality in 1890s]," Encounter, 37:8-23, Dec. 1971.

1144)   "California: Gay Mecca No. 1 [Proposed Alpine Take-over]," Time, 96:12, Nov. 2, 1970.

1145)   "Chickenhawks [Young Male Prostitutes]," Newsweek, 81:42, Apr. 30, 1973.

1146)   Christmas, Linda. "Erogenous Zone [Homosexuality in Germany]," Guardian, May 23, 1975, p. 11.

1147)   Cocks, Jay. Movie Review: "Butley," Time, 103: 76-77, Apr. 29, 1974.

1148)   _____ . Movie Review: "The Conformist," Time, 97:86, Apr. 5, 1971.

1149)   "Conservative Anarchist [Paul Goodman]," Time, 100:43-44, Aug. 14, 1972.

1150)   Cunningham, Laura. "Up Front with Gay Liberation," Cosmopolitan, Apr. 1972, pp. 194-98.

1151)   Deford, Frank. "Hero with a Tragic Flaw [Bill Tilden]," Sports Illustrated, 42:50-58, Jan. 13, 1975 and 42:30-36, 41, Jan. 20, 1975. (Biography)

1152)   DeJongh, Nicholas. "Lib and let live," Guardian, Jul. 12, 1974, p. 13.

1153)   De la Noy, Michael. "Contact Advertisements for Male Homosexuals," Guardian, Aug. 22, 1975, p. 9.

1154)   Duberman, Martin. "Case of the Gay Sergeant [Leonard Matlovich]," New York Times Magazine,

Nov. 9, 1975, pp. 16-17, 58.

1155)        _____. "Is Bisexuality Normal?" New Times, 2:34-41, Jun. 28, 1974.

1156)    Duncan, Ben. "Unlucky in Love," New Society, Feb. 22, 1973, pp. 424-25.

1157)    Durham, Michael. "Homosexuals in Revolt," Life, 71:62-72, Dec. 31, 1971.

1158)    Epstein, Joseph. "Homo/Hetero: The Struggle for Sexual Identity," Harper's, 241:37-44, 49-51, Sep. 1970. Discussion: 241:6, Nov. 1970.

1159)    Evans, Medford. "Sex Denied: Perversion and the Hatred of God," American Opinion, 14:39-48, Nov. 1971.

1160)    Forbes, Dennis. "Creating Peter Berlin," After Dark, 7:44-51, Feb. 1975.

1161)    Freehof, S. B. "Homosexuality and Jewish Tradition," Jewish Digest, 18:30-32, Aug. 1973.

1162)    "The Fruits of Misbelief--Study of American Lutherans," Time, 100:71, Jul. 10, 1972.

1163)    Furbank, P. N. "The Personality of E. M. Forster," Encounter, 35:61-68, Nov. 1970.

1164)    "The Gay Church," Time, 98:38-39, Aug. 23, 1971.

1165)    "Gay GIs?" Economist, 256:63, Jul. 12, 1975.

1166)    "Gay Manifesto [Special Issue of Trends]," Time, 101:80, Jun. 25, 1973.

1167)    "Gay Power," Newsweek, 81:32, Feb. 26, 1973.

1168)    "Gay Pride [Parades in New York City and Los Angeles]," Time, 96:6, Jul. 13, 1970.

1169)    "Gay Rights," National Review, 26:635-36, Jun. 7, 1974.

1170)    "The Gay Vote," New Republic, 166:10, Feb. 19, 1972.

1171)   Gaynor, Janie. "Men of Vassar," Esquire, 82:100, 179-80, Sep. 1974.

1172)   "Gays on the March," Time, 106:32-43, Sep. 8, 1975.

1173)   Gelman, David. "Gays and the Press," Newsweek, 86:93, Oct. 20, 1975.

1174)   Geng, Veronica. Book Review: Dolores Klaich, Woman plus Woman and Bettie Wysor, The Lesbian Myth, Ms., 3:45, 80-81, Dec. 1974.

1175)   "German [Criminal Law] Reforms [Lowering of Age of Consent]," Time, 102:134, Nov. 26, 1973.

1176)   "Girlish Boys: Gender Identity Research and Treatment Program at University of California at Los Angeles," Time, 102:133-34, Nov. 26, 1973.

1177)   Goldstein, Richard. "A Night at the Continental Baths," New York, 6:51-55, Jan. 8, 1973.

1178)   Gould, Robert E. "What We Don't Know about Homosexuality," New York Times Magazine, Feb. 24, 1974, pp. 12-13, 51-63. Discussion: Mar. 17, 1974, sec. 6, pp. 73, 76.

1179)   Graham, Billy. "What the Bible Says about Sex," Readers Digest. 96:117-20, May 1970.

1180)   Greene, Johnny. "Decadence by Invitation Only-- Bisexuality," New Times, 2:36-41, Apr. 19, 1974.

1181)   Gross, Amy. "We're the Thorn in Everyone's Side ... An Inquiry into Bisexuality," Mademoiselle, 77:138-39, 189-90, Sep. 1973.

1182)   Harris, Mervyn. "The Dilly Boys [Male Prostitution]," New Society, Apr. 6, 1972, pp. 6-8.

1183)   _____ "Hustling for Bread: On the Dilly [Male Prostitution]," Spectator, no. 7588, Dec. 1, 1973, p. 700.

1184)   _____ . "The Marginal Person [Male Prostitution]," Spectator, no. 7589, Dec. 8, 1973, p. 741.

1185)            . "A Walk on the Wild Side [Male Prosti-
tution]," Spectator, no. 7587, Nov. 24, 1973, p. 669.

1186)    Harrison, Barbara G.  "Sexual Chic, Sexual Fas-
cism, and Sexual Confusion" and "Lesbians, Bisexuals, and the Struggle for Power in the Women's
Movement," New York, 7:31-36 and 36, Apr. 1, 1974.

1187)    Harvey, Ian.  "The Homosexual Stigma," Spectator,
no. 7612, May 18, 1974, p. 606.

1188)            . "Homosexuals: Evolution or Revolution,"
Spectator, no. 7558, May 1973, pp. 566-67.

1189)            . "Homosexuals' Plight," New Statesman,
81:489-90, Apr. 9, 1971.

1190)            . "Reform and Reaction," Guardian, Jan.
24, 1972, p. 10.

1191)    Harvey, Veronica.  "Sons and Lovers," Guardian,
May 25, 1973, p. 11.

1192)    Hatterer, Lawrence J.  "How to Spot Homosexuality
in Children," Harper's Bazaar, 108:56-57, Jul. 1975.

1193)            . "What Makes a Homosexual?" McCalls,
98:32, 34-35, 37, Jul. 1971. (Summary in Readers
Digest, 99:71-74, Sep. 1971.)

1194)            and Hatterer, Myra.  "What Parents Should
Know about Homosexuality," PTA Magazine, 65:6-9,
Jun. 1971.

1195)    Hayman, Jane.  Book Review: Jill Johnston, Lesbian Nation; Sidney Abbott and Barbara Love, Sappho Was a Right-on Woman; and Ingrid Bengis, Combat in the Erogenous Zone, Nation, 217:506-08, Nov.
12, 1973.

1196)    Haynes, Muriel.  Book Review: Kate Millett, Flying, New Republic, 171:28-29, Jul. 6, 1974.

1197)    "Healthy Homosexuals," Economist, 250:45-46, Jan.
12, 1974.

1198)    Heilbrun, Carolyn.  Book Review: Nigel Nicolson,

Portrait of a Marriage, Ms., 2:39-42, Feb. 1974.

1199)    Hess, Thomas B. "Come Back to the Raft Ag'in, Winslow Homer, Honey," New York, 6:75-76, Jun. 11, 1973.

1200)    "Homosexual Chemistry [Hormones and Homosexuality]," Newsweek, 77:54-55, Apr. 26, 1971.

1201)    "Homosexual Church," Newsweek, 76:107, Oct. 12, 1970.

1202)    "Homosexual Minister [in Texas Suspended]," Newsweek, 77:114, Jun. 14, 1971.

1203)    "Homosexual Rights," Newsweek, 83:76-77, May 20, 1974.

1204)    "Homosexual Sergeant: Case of Leonard Matlovich," Time, 105:18-19, Jun. 9, 1975.

1205)    "Hope for the Homosexual [Church for Homosexuals]," Time, 96:46, 49, Jul. 13, 1970.

1206)    Hopkins, John. Review of Stage Play: "Find Your Way Home," Time, 103:42, 44, Jan. 14, 1974.

1207)    "Horror Story [Homosexual Murders in Houston]," Newsweek, 83:23-24, Feb. 4, 1974.

1208)    "The Houston Horrors [Homosexual Murders]," Time, 102:24, Aug. 20, 1973.

1209)    "How George Did It [Political Use of Charges of Homosexuality]," Newsweek, 75:27, Jun. 15, 1970.

1210)    Hunt, Morton. "Sexual Behavior in the 1970s: VI: Deviant Sexuality," Playboy, 21:54-55, 183-84, Mar. 1974.

1211)    Hurwood, Bernhardt J. "One Woman Gives her Answer to the Question of Bisexuality," Vogue, 163:162-63, 197-98, May 1974.

1212)    "I Am a Homosexual: The Gay Drive for Acceptance," Time, 106:32-43, Sep. 8, 1975.

1213)     "Instant Cure [Psychiatrists Drop Sickness Label],"
          Time, 103:45, Apr. 1, 1974.

1214)     James, Clive.   "Auden's Achievement," Commen-
          tary, 56:53-58, Dec. 1973.

1215)     Johnston, Jill.   Book Review:  Karla Jay and Allen
          Young, Out of the Closet, Ms., 3:85-86, Jun. 1975.

1216)     Jordan, Philip.   "Fears Behind a Minor Problem,"
          Guardian, Jan. 9, 1975, p. 11.

1217)     Kalem, T. E.   Book Review:  C. P. Cavafy, Col-
          lected Poems and Robert Liddell, Cavafy, Time,
          106:63-64, Aug. 25, 1975.

1218)     _____.   Book Review:  Tennessee Williams,
          Memoirs, Time, 106:83-K11, Dec. 1, 1975.

1219)     _____.   Review of Stage Play:  "Butley," Time,
          100:82, Nov. 13, 1972.

1220)     _____.   Review of Stage Play:  "The Dirtiest
          Show in Town," Time, 96:63, Jul. 13, 1970.

1221)     _____.   Review of Stage Play:  "The Ritz,"
          Time, 105:59, Feb. 3, 1975.

1222)     Kanfer, Stefan.   Movie Review:  "Death in Venice,"
          Time, 98:66, Jul. 5, 1971.

1223)     _____.   Movie Review:  "The Music Lovers,"
          Time, 97:82-83, Feb. 8, 1971.

1224)     _____.   Movie Review:  "Sunday, Bloody Sunday,"
          Time, 98:82, Sep. 27, 1971.

1225)     _____.   Movie Review:  "Trash," Time, 96:79,
          Nov. 9, 1970.

1226)     _____.   Movie Review:  "The Villain," Time,
          97:83, Jun. 14, 1971.

1227)     Katz, Jonathan.   Book Review:  Karla Jay and Al-
          len Young, Out of the Closets and Dennis Altman,
          Homosexual:  Oppression and Liberation, Nation,
          217:25-26, Jul. 2, 1973.

1228)    Klemesrud, Judy.  "The Bisexuals," New York,
         7:37-38: Apr. 1, 1974.

1229)    _____.  "Lesbians:  The Disciples of Sappho,
         Updated," New York Times Magazine, Mar. 28,
         1971, pp. 38-39, 41-52.  Discussion:  Apr. 11,
         1971, sec. 6, pp. 5, 55 and May 9, 1971, sec. 6,
         pp. 79-80.

1230)    Kluge, P. F. and Moore, Thomas.  "Boys in the
         Bank [Brooklyn Bank Robbery]," Life, 73:64-65, 68-
         70, 72, 74, Sep. 22, 1972.

1231)    Knox, Louise.  "The Bisexual Phenomenon," Viva,
         Jun. 1974, pp. 42-45, 88, 94.

1232)    Kome, Penney.  "Couples:  Portrait of Homophiles
         as Just Plain Folks," Maclean's, 85:44-45, 62, 64,
         Dec. 1972.

1233)    Kopkind, Andrew.  "The Boys in the Barracks [Ho-
         mosexuals and the Military]," New Times, 5:19-27,
         Aug. 8, 1975.

1234)    _____.  "Gay Rock:  The Boys in the Band,"
         Ramparts, 11:49-51, Mar. 1973.

1235)    Kroll, Jack.  Review of Stage Play:  "Butley,"
         Newsweek, 80:96, Nov. 13, 1972.

1236)    Kunen, James S.  "Are Fire Fighters Sexist Re-
         actionaries? [Homosexuals and Employment]," New
         Times, 3:6, Jul. 12, 1974.

1237)    LaGuardia, Robert.  "Diary of Three Motley Days
         in a Quebec Jailhouse:  Filming 'Fortune and Men's
         Eyes,'" After Dark, 4:35-40, May 1971.

1238)    "Lavender Panthers [Preventing Muggings of Homo-
         sexuals in San Francisco]," Time, 102:73, Oct. 8,
         1973.

1239)    Lawrenson, Helen.  "Bisexuality:  A New Look at
         an Old Story," Playgirl, Jul. 1974, pp. 40-41, 46,
         128.

1240)    Leech, Michael T.  "Benjamen Britten's 'Death in

Venice,'" After Dark, 6:48-53, Dec. 1973.

1241)    "Lesbian as Mother," Newsweek, 82:75-76, Sep.
         24, 1973.

1242)    "Lesbian Mothers: Robin and Joyce and Family,"
         Ms., 2:81-82, Oct. 1973.

1243)    Lessard, Suzannah. "Gay Is Good for Us All,"
         Washington Monthly, 2:39-49, Dec. 1970. (Re-
         printed in McCaffrey, no. 101, pp. 205-18)

1244)    "Life to Come [Homosexuality in Short Stories of
         E. M. Forster]," Time, 102:67-68, Jul. 2, 1973.

1245)    Loney, Glenn. "The Royal Shakespeare Company's
         'Section Nine,'" After Dark, 7:58-61, Jun. 1974.

1246)    Lumsden, Andrew. "Gay Liberation," Spectator,
         no. 7436, Jan. 2, 1971, pp. 11-12.

1247)    MacInnes, Colin. "Sexual Freedoms," New Society,
         Oct. 23, 1975, p. 224.

1248)    Maclean, Una. "A Society of Friends," New So-
         ciety, Jan. 9, 1975, pp. 76-77.

1249)    Mailer, Norman. "The Prisoner of Sex," Harper's,
         242:41-92 at 79-82, Mar. 1971.

1250)    "Male and Female [Homosexuals Challenge Army
         and Air Force]," Time, 105:73, Jun. 16, 1975.

1251)    "The Man Who Grabbed the Gun [Oliver Sipple Who
         Blocked Gun Pointed at President Gerald Ford],"
         Time, 106:20, Oct. 6, 1975.

1252)    Mano, D. Keith. "Coming Out at Columbia [Gay
         People at Columbia University]," National Review,
         24:463-64, Apr. 28, 1972.

1253)    Marchand, Philip. "Send No Psychiatrists to Leo
         [Gay Liberation]," Saturday Night, 87:24-26, Aug.
         1972.

1254)    Marmor, Judd. "Straight Talk on Homosexuals,"
         People, 2:43-45, Jul. 8, 1974.

1255)    Martin, Del and Lyon, Phyllis. "Lesbian Mothers,"
         Ms., 2:78-82, Oct. 1973.

1256)    Martin, Robert K. "Whitman's Song of Myself: Ho-
         mosexual Dream and Vision," Partisan Review, 42:
         80-96, 1975.

1257)    Mason, Clifford. "The Abominable Crime," Hu-
         manist, 85:210-12, Jul. 1970.

1258)    "The McConnell Decision [Refusal to Employ Homo-
         sexual Librarian]," New Republic, 166:9-10, May
         13, 1972.

1259)    Mead, Margaret. "Bisexuality: What Is It All
         About?" Redbook, 144:29, 31, Jan. 1975.

1260)    "Methodist Malaise [What to Do about Homosexuals],"
         Time, 99:67, May 8, 1972.

1261)    "Militant Homosexuals [Gay Liberation Movement],"
         Newsweek, 78:45-48, Aug. 23, 1971.

1262)    Miller, Henry. "Homosexuality," Listener, 87:273-
         74, Mar. 2, 1972.

1263)    Miller, Merle. "Homosexual Husbands: What Wives
         Must Know," Redbook, 144:74-76, 178-82, Apr. 1975.

1264)    _____. "New York Gay Rights Defeat: It Isn't
         Chic to Support Pansies," Rolling Stone, no. 167,
         Aug. 15, 1974, pp. 8-9.

1265)    _____. "The Torment of a Homosexual Gentle-
         man," Pageant, 26:98-106, May 1971. (Abbreviated
         version of article following immediately below)

1266)    _____. "What It Means to Be a Homosexual,"
         New York Times Magazine, Jan. 17, 1971, pp. 9-
         11, 48-49, 57, 60. Discussion: Feb. 21, 1971,
         sec. 6, pp. 14, 59. (See no. 102)

1267)    _____. "What It Means to Be a Homosexual
         (Continued)," New York Times Magazine, Oct. 10,
         1971, pp. 67, 69, 72, 74, 81. (See no. 102)

1268)    Millett, Kate. "Balance of Power," Partisan Re-
         view, 37:199-218, 1970.

1269)    Morgenstern, Joseph.  "Eight Desperate Men--The
         Boys in the Band," Newsweek, 75:91, Mar. 30,
         1970.

1270)    "Murder in Philadelphia [John S. Knight]," Time,
         106:22, 24, Dec. 22, 1975.

1271)    "Murder of Pier Paolo Pasolini," Time, 106:73,
         Nov. 17, 1975.

1272)    Nemy, Enid.  "The Heart of a Lesbian," Pageant,
         25:54-61, Mar. 1970.

1273)    "Neurosis:  Just a Bad Habit [Behavior Therapy],"
         Time, 98:41, Aug. 2, 1971.

1274)    "New Bisexuals," Time, 103:79, May 13, 1974.

1275)    "New Commandment:  Thou Shalt Not--Maybe
         [Churches and Sex]," Time, 98:73-74, Dec. 13, 1971.

1276)    Newman, David and Benton, Robert.  "Who's Afraid
         of Virginia Wolf [Attitudes about Lesbianism, Homo-
         sexuality, and Bisexuality]," Madamoiselle, 76:52-
         54, Apr. 1973.

1277)    "The Nicest Person [Homosexual Murders in Hous-
         ton]," Newsweek, 82:32, Aug. 20, 1973.

1278)    Nies, Judith.  "Elaine Noble:  Not Just Another
         Gay Legislator," Ms., 4:58-61, 79, 108, Aug. 1975.

1279)    Nightfyrd, Jeff.  "They'd Rather Die than Go Home:
         Runaway Murder in Texas," Crawdaddy, Dec. 1973,
         p. 38.

1280)    "Nightride," After Dark, 4:65-66, Feb. 1972.

1281)    "No to Matlovich [Discharge from Air Force for
         Homosexuality]," Time, 106:32, Sep. 29, 1975.

1282)    Nolan, James.  "Third Sex," Ramparts, 12:21-26,
         56-59, Dec. 1973.

1283)    "Ornament of the Third Sex," Times Literary Sup-
         plement, 72:1329-30, Nov. 2, 1973.

1284)    "Out of the Closet [Depicting Homosexuality on TV]," Time, 101:80, Mar. 5, 1973.

1285)    "Out of the Closets and into the Subceller [Gay Lounge at New York University]," Rat, Oct. 6-27, 1970, p. 25.

1286)    "Pain of Public Scrutiny," Ms., 2:76-79, Jun. 1974. (Excerpt from Kate Millett's Flying.)

1287)    Panati, Charles. Book Review: Clarence A. Tripp, The Homosexual Matrix, Newsweek, 86:108, 111, Oct. 20, 1975.

1288)    "Parade: First Anniversary Celebration of the Gay Liberation Movement," New Yorker, 46:19-20, Jul. 11, 1970.

1289)    Pinkus, Susan. "If Your Child Is Queer," Observer, May 6, 1973, p. 30.

1290)    "Playboy Forum," Playboy, 17:58, 72, Jan. 1970 ("Homosexuals Seek Civil Service," "Psychosexual Disturbance," "Homosexuals' Right to Work," and "Homosexuals and the Law").

1291)    _____, Playboy, 17:41-43, 46-48, Feb. 1970 ("Dissent, Disruption, Destruction," "Doctors Examined," "Sex Law Revision," "Help for Homosexuals," and "Are Homosexuals Sick?")

1292)    _____, Playboy, 17:54, 56, 59, Mar. 1970 ("Homosexual Teachers," "Half a Loaf for Homosexuals," "Homosexuals and the Army," and "Homosexual Police.")

1293)    _____, Playboy, 17:56-57, Jun. 1970 ("Homosexuality as Disorder," "Gay Liberation," and "Homosexual Informer.")

1294)    _____, Playboy, 17:44-46, Jul. 1970 ("Transsexualism" and "Texas Sodomy Law.")

1295)    _____, Playboy, 17:46-47, Aug. 1970 ("An American Tragedy," "On Tolerating Homosexuals," "Holding the Line," and "Good Book or Hate Book.")

1296)        _____, Playboy, 17:63, 204, Oct. 1970 ("Homosexual Persecution," "Gay Generation Gap," and
"The Freaking Fag Revolution.")

1297)        _____, Playboy, 17:68, 70, Nov. 1970 ("Intoler-
able Intolerance" and "Men's Men.")

1298)        _____, Playboy, 17:80-81, 90, 93, Dec. 1970
("Buggering the Draft," "Deviation Potion," "Gay
Revolutionaries," "Homosexual Tragedy," "Trans-
sexualism," and "Lesbians and Long-Hairs.")

1299)        _____, Playboy, 18:46-47, Feb. 1971 ("Gay Lib-
erators.")

1300)        _____, Playboy, 18:54-55, Mar. 1971 ("Alpine
County Revisited.")

1301)        _____, Playboy, 18:48-49, 52, Apr. 1971 ("Florida Sex Crimes," "Unsafe at any Speed," and
"Crosstianity and Christianity.")

1302)        _____, Playboy, 18:63, 69, 70, 183, May 1971
("Death by Slow Torture," "Blowing Hardhats'
Minds," and "Women's Lib and Lesbians.")

1303)        _____, Playboy, 18:57, Jun. 1971 ("Presto!
Change-O!")

1304)        _____, Playboy, 18:45, 52, Jul. 1971 ("Revolutionary Repression," "Out of the Closets," and "Let
Me Be.")

1305)        _____, Playboy, 18:44-45, Aug. 1971 ("Women's
Lib and Lesbians," "The Gay President," and "Homosexual Hormones.")

1306)        _____, Playboy, 18:70-71, Sep. 1971 ("Sex Laws
Reformed," "Campus Press Problems," and "One
Step at a Time.")

1307)        _____, Playboy, 18:68-69, Oct. 1971 ("Challenge
to Sex Laws" and "Sin in San Francisco.")

1308)        _____, Playboy, 18:79, 86, Nov. 1971 ("Bell Gets
Wrung" and "Y.A.F. Not Involved.")

1309)        _____, Playboy, 18:78-79, Dec. 1971 ("Rotten to the Corps" and "Teenager on Death Row. ")

1310)        _____, Playboy, 19:46-47, Jan. 1972 ("Good News for Gays. ")

1311)        _____, Playboy, 19:49-51, Feb. 1972 ("Sex Law Reform Defeated" and "Homosexual Hormones. ")

1312)        _____, Playboy, 19:55-56, Mar. 1972 ("No Funny Stuff in Miami Bars" and "Queer-Killing License. ")

1313)        _____, Playboy, 19:189, Apr. 1972 ("Masculine Homosexuals. ")

1314)        _____, Playboy, 19:70, May 1972 ("View from Austria. ")

1315)        _____, Playboy, 19:74, Jun. 1972 ("Challenging Sodomy Laws" and "Balancing Terms. ")

1316)        _____, Playboy, 19:50, Jul. 1972 ("Sex Backlash in Idaho. ")

1317)        _____, Playboy, 19:57, 60, Sep. 1972 ("Good News for Gays" and "Homosexuality and Normality. ")

1318)        _____, Playboy, 19:59, Oct. 1972 ("Disgusting Abnormality--Homosexuals at University of New Hampshire. ")

1319)        _____, Playboy, 20:45, Feb. 1973 ("Knot Tied through Loophole--Homosexual Marriage in Texas.")

1320)        _____, Playboy, 20:51, Mar. 1973 ("Changing Homosexuality. ")

1321)        _____, Playboy, 20:56-57, 64, Jun. 1973 ("Homosexuality Reconsidered by American Psychiatric Association" and "Gay Rights. ")

1322)        _____, Playboy, 20:62, Oct. 1973 ("Freud and Homosexuality. ")

1323)        _____, Playboy, 20:87, Dec. 1973 ("Lavender Panthers. ")

1324)          _____, Playboy, 21:57, 60-62, Apr. 1974 ("Good
News for Gays--American Psychiatric Association
Decision" and "The Unquiet Grave--Gay Rights at
University of New Hampshire. ")

1325)          _____, Playboy, 21:60-62, Mar. 1974 ("Better
Break for Vets" and "Out of the Closets. ")

1326)          _____, Playboy, 21:56-61, Jun. 1974 ("Cop-
Outs, " "Illness by Edict, " "What's in a Handicap, "
"Immoral Deviations, " and "Survival Threat. ")

1327)          _____, Playboy, 21:62, 64, 66, Sep. 1974
("Priests with Guns, " "Texas Sex Laws, " "The Law
Is Queer, " and "Gay Rights Effort at Boulder,
Colo. ")

1328)          _____, Playboy, 21:59, Oct. 1974 ("Long Way to
Go--Public Attitudes. ")

1329)          _____, Playboy, 21:60, Nov. 1974 ("Out of the
Closet. ")

1330)          _____, Playboy, 21:72, Dec. 1974 ("Lesbian
Mothers. ")

1331)          _____, Playboy, 22:41, Feb. 1975 ("Compromis-
ing Cops" and "Young and Gay. ")

1332)          _____, Playboy, 22:56, Apr. 1975 ("Odd Squad.")

1333)          _____, Playboy, 22:54-55, May 1975 ("Fondling
the Suspects, " "Scholarship for Gays, " "Sex Law
Revised, " and "Homosexual Parents. ")

1334)          _____, Playboy, 22:49, Jul. 1975 ("Sexual Security. ")

1335)          _____, Playboy, 22:50, Sep. 1975 ("California
Sex Laws Reformed. ")

1336)          _____, Playboy, 22:51, Oct. 1975 ("Recrimina-
lizing Sex. ")

1337)          _____, Playboy, 22:52-53, Nov. 1975 ("Homosexual Rights and Civil Service" and "VD and
Privacy. ")

1338)  "Playboy Interview: Tennessee Williams," Playboy,
       20:69-84, Apr. 1973.

1339)  "Playboy Panel: Homosexuality," Playboy, 18:61-
       92, 164, 178-91, Apr. 1971.  Discussion:  18:9-
       10, Jul. 1971.

1340)  "Playboy Panel: New Sexual Life Styles," Playboy,
       20:73-98, 192-96, Sep. 1973.

1341)  "Prisoners of Sex [Transsexuals]," Time, 103:63-64,
       Jan. 21, 1974.

1342)  "A Puritanical Government [U.S. Civil Service Com-
       mission Investigates Male Homosexuality]," Time,
       95:60, Apr. 27, 1970.

1343)  "Quartet of Soloists [Movie Review: 'Women in
       Love']," Time, 95:103, 106, Apr. 30, 1970.

1344)  Raab, E.  "Homosexuals and the Jews," Jewish Di-
       gest, 18:25-26, Apr. 1973.

1345)  Rader, Dotson.  "An American Son [Lance Loud],"
       Rolling Stone, Apr. 27, 1973, pp. 44-46.

1346)  _____.  "Gay Liberation: All the Sad Young
       Men," Evergreen, 84:18, 20, 74-75, 78-79, Nov.
       1970.

1347)  _____ and Cleaver, Wilhelmina.  Letters on El-
       dridge Cleaver and Homosexuality, Playboy, 20:12,
       Aug. 1973.

1348)  Reid, John.  "Best Little Boy in the World Has a
       Secret," New York, 6:57-62, May 7, 1973.  (Re-
       printed in Goode and Troiden, no. 55, pp. 161-73)
       (Autobiographical)

1349)  _____.  "How 'Gay' Is New York?" New York,
       6:72-79, Sep. 24, 1973.

1350)  Review of Stage Play: "Let My People Come,"
       Playboy, 21:145-47, Jul. 1974.

1351)  Sabin, Louis.  "Homosexuality Today: What Parents
       Want to Know," Parents Magazine, 49:46-47, 60, 62,
       Mar. 1974.

1352)    Sagarin, Edward.  "Behind the Gay Liberation
         Front," The Realist, no. 87, May-Jun. 1970, pp.
         1, 17-23.

1353)    Sayre, Nora.  "New York's Gay-In," New States-
         man, 80:53-54, Jul. 17, 1971.

1354)    Schickel, Richard.  Movie Review:  "The Boys in
         the Band," Life, 68:12, Apr. 10, 1970.

1355)            .  Movie Review:  "Dog Day Afternoon,"
         Time, 106:69-70, Oct. 16, 1975.

1356)            .  Movie Review:  "Sunday, Bloody Sun-
         day," Life, 71:16, Oct. 8, 1971.

1357)    Seabrook, Jeremy.  "The Gay Consumers," New
         Society, Sep. 26, 1974, pp. 818-20.

1358)    "Sex and How to Read All about It," Newsweek, 76:
         38-42, Aug. 24, 1970.

1359)    "A Sex Poll [Playboy], 1973," Time, 102:63-64,
         Oct. 1, 1973.

1360)    "Sexploitation," Newsweek, 81:78, Feb. 12, 1973.

1361)    "Shades of Lavender [Movie Review:  'The Boys in
         the Band']," Time, 95:97, 100, Mar. 30, 1970.

1362)    Shestack, Melvin.  "Sex on Campus," Penthouse,
         Oct. 1972, pp. 36-40, 124, 128, 130.

1363)    Simon, John.  "Homosexuals in Life and the Arts,"
         New Leader, 57:14-16, Oct. 28, 1974.

1364)            .  Movie Review:  "Dog Day Afternoon,"
         New York, 8:85, Sep. 29, 1975.

1365)            .  Review of Stage Play:  "Equus," Hudson
         Review, 28:97-106, Spr. 1975.

1366)            .  Review of Stage Play:  "The Faggot,"
         New York, 6:64, Jul. 9, 1973.

1367)            .  Review of Stage Play:  "Lovers," New
         York, 8:75, Feb. 17, 1975.

1368)    _____. Review of Stage Play: "The Ritz," New
         York, 8:65, Feb. 3, 1975.

1369)    Skir, Leo. "The Road that Is Known," Evergreen,
         84:16, Sep. 1970.

1370)    _____. "We're Freakin' on in: A Look at Gay
         Power," Mademoiselle, 71:150-51, 195-98, Sep.
         1970.

1371)    Sobran, M. J. Jr. "Mr. Brudnoy's Argument,"
         National Review, 26:925, Aug. 16, 1974.

1372)    Starr, Jack. "Homosexual Couple: Jack Baker and
         Michael McConnell," Look, 35:69-71, Jan. 26, 1971.

1373)    _____. "The Presbyterian Debate over Sex,"
         Look, 34:54, 59-60 at 59, Aug. 11, 1970.

1374)    "State Penalties for Consensual Sex Offenses," Play-
         boy, 19:188-89, Aug. 1972.

1375)    Steiner, George. Book Review: E. M. Forster,
         Maurice, New Yorker, 47:158-69, Oct. 9, 1971.

1376)    Stoop, Norma M. "Christopher Isherwood: A Meet-
         ing by Another River," After Dark, 7:60-65, Apr.
         1975.

1377)    Storey, Peter. "Christianity and Homosexuality--
         An Interview with Lord Soper," Spectator, no. 7561,
         May 26, 1973, pp. 646, 648.

1378)    Sutcliffe, Tom. "Husbands of Christ [Homosexual
         Ministers]," Spectator, no. 7558, May 5, 1973,
         p. 553.

1379)    "Teen-Age Sex: Letting the Pendulum Swing,"
         Time, 100:34-36, Aug. 21, 1972.

1380)    Thorpe, Edward. "Gay's the Word," New States-
         man, 80:779-800, Dec. 11, 1970.

1381)    "Transvestites," Guardian, Sep. 13, 1973, p. 13.

1382)    Trillin, Calvin. "U.S. Journal: Manhattan--Ac-
         tivities of the Gay Activists Alliance," New Yorker
         48:64-69, Jul. 15, 1972.

1383)   Tweedie, Jill.  "Desperate Straights, " Guardian,
        Jul. 7, 1975, p. 9.

1384)   "Uncommon Apprentice [Review of Stage Play: 'Find
        Your Way Home'], " Time, 103:64, Feb. 25, 1974.

1385)   Van den Haag, Ernest.   "Reflections on the Issue
        of Gay Rights, " National Review, 26:804-06, Jul.
        19, 1974.

1386)   Van Maanen, James.  "Deviant Sex in the Movies?"
        After Dark, 7:48-53, Mar. 1975.

1387)   "VD:  A National Emergency, " Time, 96:36, Jul.
        27, 1970.

1388)   Veitch, Andrew.  "The Right to Be Gay, " Guardian,
        Feb. 28, 1974, p. 11.

1389)   Waugh, Auberon.  "Le Vice anglais [Homosexuality
        and the Church of England], " New Statesman, 89:
        109, Jan. 24, 1975.

1390)   Weintraub, Stanley.   Book Review:  Brian Reade,
        Sexual Heretics, New Republic, 164:30-31, Feb. 27,
        1971.

1391)   "We're Not Gay, We're Angry, " Rat, Sep. 11-25,
        1970, p. 27.

1392)   "What They Think Now [Yankelovich Poll], " Time,
        103:46, Jun. 3, 1974.

1393)   "When Women Love Other Women:  A Frank Dis-
        cussion of Female Homosexuality [with Mary Cal-
        derone, Wardell Pomeroy, and Barbara Gittings], "
        Redbook, 138:84-85, 186-95, Nov. 1971.

1394)   "White Slavery, 1972 [Young Male Prostitutes], "
        Time, 99:24, Jun. 5, 1972.

1395)   Wickes, George (ed. ).   "A Natalie Barney Garland,"
        Paris Review, 16:84-134, Spring 1975.

1396)   Weiner, Joan.   "The Cockettes, " Rags, Aug. 1970,
        pp. 40-43.

1397)   Williamson, Chilton Jr.   "West Village Town Meet-
        ing [Problem of Homosexual Bars]," National Re-
        view, 27:944, Aug. 29, 1975.

1398)   "Wonderful Tchaikovsky," Time, 95:56-57, Apr. 27,
        1970.

1399)   Wood, Abigail.   "How Should You Feel About a Ho-
        mosexual?" Seventeen, 30:160-62, Jun. 1971.

1400)   Young, Allen.   "Out of the Closet: A Gay Manifes-
        to," Ramparts, 10:52-59, Nov. 1971.

1401)   Young, Perry D.   "Some Things I've Wanted to Say
        [Letter of a Homosexual to His Mother]," Ms., 3:
        115-16, 120, Mar. 1975.

1402)   Zimmerman, Paul D.   Movie Review: "Butley,"
        Newsweek, 83:106, May 20, 1974.

1403)   _____.   Movie Review: "The Conformist," News-
        week, 77:92, Apr. 5, 1971.

1404)   _____.   Movie Review: "Death in Venice,"
        Newsweek, 79:92, Jun. 28, 1971.

1405)   Zohar, Danah.   "Gay Misery," New Statesman, 82:
        267, Aug. 27, 1971.

# ARTICLES IN RELIGIOUS JOURNALS

1406)    Adair, Nancy. "My Thinking with Gertrude Stein with my Thinking," <u>Motive</u>, v. 32, issue 1, pp. 38-39, 1972.

1407)    Aikin, David L. "Dethroning the King [the White Heterosexual Male]," <u>Motive</u>, v. 32, issue 2, pp. 46-48, 1972.

1408)    Alderson, Ortez. "On Being Black, Gay, and in Prison ... ," <u>Motive</u>, v. 32, issue 2, pp. 26-27, 1972.

1409)    Alston, Jon P. "Attitudes toward Extramarital and Homosexual Relations," <u>Journal for the Scientific Study of Religion</u>, 13:479-81, Dec. 1974.

1410)    Anonymous. "A Letter to the Church of Jesus Christ," <u>Crux</u>, 10:6-8, 1973.

1411)    Austin, Charles M. Movie Review: "Sunday, Bloody Sunday," <u>Christian Century</u>, 88:1529-30, Dec. 29, 1971.

1412)    Baum, Gregory. "Catholic Homosexuals: Views of Dignity," <u>Commonweal</u>, 99:479-82, Feb. 15, 1974. Discussion: 100:51, Mar. 22, 1974 and 100:141, Apr. 12, 1974.

1413)    Berson, Ginny. "Reformism [within the Gay Liberation Movement]: The Politics of Ostriches," <u>Motive</u>, v. 32, issue 1, pp. 48-49, 1972.

1414)    Bexell, Monica. "Homosexuality and the Church," <u>New Blackfriars</u>, 56:459-82, 1975.

1415)    Blackburn, Elizabeth K. "From the Inside," <u>Friends Quarterly</u>, 18:108-10, Jul. 1973.

1416)     Blumenfeld, Warren.  "Gays on Campus," Motive,
          v. 32, issue 2, pp. 22-24, 1972.

1417)     Bockmühl, Klaus.  "Homosexuality in Biblical Per-
          spective--an Interview," Christianity Today, 17:12-
          18, Feb. 16, 1973.

1418)     Boyd, Malcolm.  "Gay Rights," Christian Century,
          92:474, May 7, 1975.

1419)     Boyle, John H.  "Understanding Homosexual Behav-
          ior and Homosexuality," Review and Expositor, 68:
          217-26, Spring 1971.

1420)     Brass, Perry.  "In America, All Men Were Created
          Straight," Motive, v. 32, issue 2, pp. 39-42, 1972.

1421)     "Bringing up Children in the Gay Community," Mo-
          tive, v. 32, issue 1, pp. 54-55, 1972.

1422)     Brown, Rita M.  "The Last Straw [Lesbianism],"
          Motive, v. 32, issue 1, pp. 56-59, 1972.

1423)     Bryant, Florence V.  "The Church and the Homo-
          sexual," Trends, 5:10-18, Jul.-Aug. 1973.

1424)     _____ and Shoemaker, Dennis E.  "The Begin-
          ning is at Hand," Trends, 5:39-40, Jul.-Aug. 1973.

1425)     Bunch, Charlotte and Brown, Rita M.  "What Every
          Lesbian Should Know," Motive, v. 32, issue 1, pp.
          4-8, 1972.

1426)     "Cardinal Retells Church Stand on Homosexuality,"
          National Catholic Reporter, 10:24, Sep. 6, 1974.

1427)     "A Case for Sexual Restraint," Christianity Today,
          14:31-32, Mar. 13, 1970.

1428)     Castelli, Jim.  "Bishops Issue Homosexual Guide-
          lines for Confessors," National Catholic Reporter,
          10:1, 20, Mar. 8, 1974.

1429)     "Catholic University Seminar Hears Homosexual
          Pleas, Charges," National Catholic Reporter, 7:2,
          Nov. 27, 1970.

1430)     "Catholics Cited for Gay Rights Bill Defeat," Na-
          tional Catholic Reporter, 10:3, Jun. 7, 1974.

1431)     Chamberlain, Gary. "Homosexuality," The Critic:
          A Catholic Review of Books and Articles, 33:16-17
          and 74-80, Mar.-Apr. 1975.

1432)     Charles, Guy. "Gay Liberation Confronts the
          Church," Christianity Today, 19:14-17, Sep. 12,
          1975.

1433)     Cleath, Robert L. "Gays Go Radical," Christianity
          Today, 15:40-41, Dec. 4, 1970.

1434)     _____. "The Homosexual Church," Christianity
          Today, 14:48-50, Sep. 11, 1970.

1435)     Coleman, James. "Surviving Psychotherapy," Mo-
          tive, v. 32, issue 2, pp. 54-58, 1972.

1436)     Coleman, John A. "Churches and the Homosexual:
          San Francisco's Gay Community," America, 124:
          113-17, Feb. 6, 1971. Discussion: 124: Inside
          cover, Feb. 6, 1971, 124:161, Feb. 20, 1971, and
          124:273, Mar. 20, 1971.

1437)     Curran, Charles E. "Homosexuality and Moral The-
          ology: Methodological and Substantive Considera-
          tions," Thomist, 35:447-81, Jul. 1971.

1438)     Dedek, John F. "Two Moral Cases: Invalid Mar-
          riage and Homosexuality," Chicago Studies, 13:20-
          33, Spring 1974.

1439)     Deedy, John. "Managing Literary History: Reflect-
          ing on a Request by W. H. Auden," Commonweal,
          101:38-41, Oct. 11, 1974.

1440)     _____. "That Detroit Canning: Case of Colum-
          nist Brian McNaught," Commonweal, 101:26, Oct.
          11, 1974.

1441)     Devor, Richard C. "Homosexuality and St. Paul,"
          Pastoral Psychology, 23:50-58, May 1972.

1442)     "Dollars for Disobedience [Grant to Lutherans Con-
          cerned for Gay People]," Christianity Today, 19:
          46, May 23, 1975.

Religious Articles

1443)     Dominian, Jacob. "Helping the Homosexual," St.
          Anthony Messenger, 81:12-19, Jun. 1973.

1444)     Douglass, Chris. "Letters: A Family Portrait,"
          Motive, v. 32, issue 2, pp. 20-21, 1972.

1445)     Driver, Tom F. "Contemporary and Christian Con-
          texts," Commonweal, 98:103-06, Apr. 6, 1973.
          Discussion: 98:311-13, Jun. 1, 1973.

1446)     Duque, A. "Homosexuality: A Theological Evalu-
          ation," Priest, 31:30-33, Mar. 1975; 31:19-25,
          Apr. 1975; and 31:26-31, May 1975.

1447)     Durning, P. "Homosexuality," Linacre Quarterly,
          40:63-66, Feb. 1973.

1448)     Eddey, Roy and Ferri, Michael. "Approaching Lav-
          ender," Motive, v. 32, issue 2, pp. 2-3, 1972.

1449)     Edson, Cynthia J. "Pastoral Counseling Conference
          Discusses Women's Liberation and Homosexuality,"
          Christian Century, 88:1473-74, Dec. 15, 1971.

1450)     Enroth, Ronald M. "Homosexual Church; an Ec-
          clesiastical Extension of a Subculture," Social Com-
          pass, no. 3, pp. 355-60, 1974.

1451)     "Episcopal Bishop Bans Homosexual Wedding,"
          Christian Century, 88:278, Mar. 3, 1971.

1452)     Evans, Ted D. "Homosexuality: Christian Ethics
          and Psychological Research," Journal of Psychology
          and Theology, 3:94-98, 1975.

1453)     Fager, Charles. "Preacher Opens 32d Gay Church,"
          National Catholic Reporter, 9:1, 16, Feb. 23, 1973.

1454)     Fehren, Henry. "A Christian Response to Homo-
          sexuals," United States Catholic, 37:6-11, Sep. 1972.

1455)     "Finding Ourselves--Coming Out," Motive, v. 32,
          issue 2, pp. 29-31, 1972.

1456)     Fink, Peter E. "Pastoral Hypothesis; Gay Pride
          Week and the Church Stayed Home," Commonweal,
          98:107-12, Apr. 6, 1973. Discussion: 98:311-13,
          Jun. 1, 1973.

1457)  Flaherty, Daniel L.   "Of Many Things," America, 124: Inside front cover, Feb. 6, 1971.

1458)  Gastonguay, Paul R.   "Homosexuality: Order or Disorder?" America, 131:117-18, Sep. 14, 1974 and 131:264-65, Nov. 2, 1974.

1459)  _____.  "Psychosurgery: Call for a Moratorium," America, 130:329-30, Apr. 27, 1974.

1460)  "Gay Catholics Ask Apostolate," National Catholic Reporter, 10:5, Nov. 30, 1973.

1461)  "Gay Catholics Focus on Civil, Not Moral Rights; 2d National Convention of Dignity," National Catholic Reporter, 11:18, Sep. 12, 1975.

1462)  "Gay Church Grows," National Catholic Reporter, 7:2, Jul. 30, 1971.

1463)  "Gay Church Meetings; United Methodist Gay Caucus," Christian Century, 92:784, Sep. 17, 1975.

1464)  "Gay Demands" and "Militant Homosexuals," Christianity Today, 15:234 and 248, Dec. 4, 1970.

1465)  "Gay Ground Gaining," Christianity Today, 16:27-28, Jun. 23, 1972.

1466)  "Gay Guerrillas?  National Task Force on Gay People in the Church," Christianity Today, 18:68, Oct. 26, 1973.

1467)  "Gay Newsman Goes on Fast," National Catholic Reporter, 10:18, Sep. 27, 1974.

1468)  "Gay Student Requests Church Reparations for Homosexuals," Christian Century, 88:1489, Dec. 22, 1971.

1469)  Gearhart, Sally.   "Lesbians and God-the-Father," Radical Religion, 1:19-21, Spring 1974.

1470)  Golder, W. Evan.   "Ordaining a Homosexual Minister [Rev. William Johnson]," Christian Century, 89:713-16, Jun. 28, 1972.

1471)   Grahn, Judy.   "Edward the Dyke," Motive, v. 32,
        issue 1, pp. 10-11, 1972.

1472)   Grange, A.   "The Mystery of Homosexuality," New-
        Church Magazine, 92:129-33, Oct.-Dec. 1973.

1473)   Griffo, Michela.   "Romaine Brooks:  Thief of
        Souls," Motive, v. 32, issue 1, pp. 21-24, 1972.

1474)   Gross, Alfred A.   "Thesis, Antithesis, and Syn-
        thesis," Pastoral Psychology, 22:41-44, Dec. 1971.

1475)   Hadden, Samuel.   "Group Psychotherapy in the
        Treatment of Homosexuality," Linacre Quarterly,
        38:149-56, Aug. 1971.

1476)   Harris, Helaine.   "Baby Don't Live Here Anymore,"
        Motive, v. 32, issue 1, pp. 14-15, 1972.

1477)   Harvey, John F.   "The Controversy Concerning No-
        menclature vis-à-vis Homosexuality," Linacre Quart-
        erly, 41:187-92, Aug. 1974.

1478)   _____.   "Homosexual Marriages," Marriage,
        56:18-23, Jan. 1974.

1479)   _____.   "Homosexuality and Vocations," Ameri-
        can Ecclesiastical Review, 164:42-55, Jan. 1971.

1480)   _____.   "The Pastoral Implications of Church
        Teaching on Homosexuality," Linacre Quarterly,
        38:157-64, Aug. 1971.

1481)   Hiltner, Seward.   "The Neglected Phenomenon of
        Female Homosexuality," Christian Century, 91:591-
        93, May 29, 1974.

1482)   Hinand, Gail.   "One in Christ in His Church Today?"
        Trends, 5:36-38, Jul.-Aug. 1973.

1483)   Holmes, W.   "America's Saddest Minority," Sign,
        50:19-22, Apr. 1971.

1484)   Holton, Robert R.   "Church Criticized for View on
        Gays," National Catholic Reporter, 10:6, Jun. 21,
        1974.

1485)     "The Homosexual and the Church," Commonweal,
          98:99-100, Apr. 6, 1973.   (Editorial)

1486)     "Homosexual Methodist Cleric Expelled from Min-
          istry," Christian Century 88:770, Jun. 23, 1971.

1487)     "Homosexual Rights," Commonweal, 100:275-76,
          May 24, 1974.

1488)     "Homosexuality in the Service," America, 133:179-
          80, Oct. 4, 1975.

1489)     "Homosexuality May Not Be Unnatural," National
          Catholic Reporter, 10:6, Mar. 1, 1974.

1490)     "Homosexuality: No Longer Off Limits," Eternity,
          Feb. 1970, p. 8.

1491)     "Homosexuality No Mental Disorder," National Ca-
          tholic Reporter, 10:11, Dec. 28, 1973.

1492)     "Homosexuality: Personality Structure or Person-
          ality Disorder?" Christian Century, 88:497-500,
          Apr. 21, 1971.

1493)     "Homosexuals Meet with Church Executives, Ask
          for Equity and Acceptance," Christian Century, 88:
          489, Apr. 21, 1971.

1494)     Hull, A.   "A Christian Response to Homosexuality,"
          Herald of Holiness, Nov. 7, 1973, p. 17.

1495)     Hyer, Marjorie.   "Gays Explore Relationship of
          Faith to Their Life Style," National Catholic Re-
          porter, 7:8-9, Apr. 16, 1971.

1496)     "International List of Gay Groups, Places, and
          Things," Motive, v. 32, issue 2, pp. 60-64, 1972.
          (314 items)

1497)     Jack, Homer A.   "Homosexuals' Presence Felt [at
          Unitarian Universalist Convention]," Christian Cen-
          tury, 88:860, Jul. 14, 1971.

1498)     Johnson, Dick.   "Ordination of Homosexuals," En-
          gage/Social Action, 3:53-54, May 1975.

1499) Johnson, William R. "The Saga of Bill Johnson [Homosexual Minister]," Trends, 5:3-9, Jul.-Aug. 1973.

1500) Jones, W. Paul. "Homosexuality and Marriage: Exploring on the Theological Edge," Pastoral Psychology, 21:29-37, Dec. 1970.

1501) Katz. " ... At Least You Could Act Like Ladies," Motive, v. 32, issue 1, pp. 25-28, 1972.

1502) Kay, Barry. "A World of Make-believe," Observer Magazine, Aug. 17, 1975, pp. 24-27. (Transvestites)

1503) Kelly, G. "The Political Struggle of Active Homosexuals to Gain Social Acceptance," Homiletic and Pastoral Review, 75:8-23, Feb. 1975 and 75:22-32, Mar. 1975.

1504) Knotts, Mary. "Dear Church, Will You Miss Us When We're Gone?" Christian Century, 89:660-61, Jun. 7, 1972.

1505) Langston, Maxine M. "A United Church of Christ Struggles toward a Ministry to Gay Christians," Engage/Social Action, 3:36-37, May 1975.

1506) Lerrigo, Charles. "Priest Says Alienated Youths Sexually Confused," National Catholic Reporter, 9: 2, Feb. 16, 1973.

1507) Lindsell, Harold. "Homosexuals and the Church," Christianity Today, 17:8-12, Sep. 28, 1973.

1508) Link, Terry. "Homosexual Minister Wants to Be Accepted," National Catholic Reporter, 7:8, Apr. 16, 1971.

1509) Lyon, Phyllis and Maurer, Tom. "Homosexuals Are Persons," Spectrum: International Journal of Religious Education, 47:14-17, 47, Nov. 1971.

1510) Mace, David R. "The Sexual Revolution: Its Impact on Pastoral Care and Counseling," Journal of Pastoral Care, 25:220-32, Dec. 1971.

1511) Martin, Del. "If That's All There Is," Motive, v. 32, issue 1, pp. 45-46, 1972.

1512)        _____ and Lyon, Phyllis. "Lesbians--the Key to Women's Liberation," Trends, 5:33-35, Jul.-Aug. 1973.

1513)        Martin, Peter. "The Gospel and the Homosexual according to Rev. Troy Perry," Nova, Mar. 1971, pp. 74-76.

1514)        "Mass Set to Support Homosexual Newsman [Brian McNaught]," National Catholic Reporter, 10:3, Aug. 30, 1974.

1515)        McCabe, H. "Homosexuality," New Blackfriars, 56:98-99, Mar. 1975.

1516)        McCaffrey, Joseph A. "Homosexuality, Aquinas, and the Church," Catholic World, 212:183-86, Jul. 1971.

1517)        _____. "Homosexuality in the Seventies," Catholic World, 213:121-25, Jun. 1971.

1518)        McConnell, Nancy F. "Is the Church Ready?" Engage, 3:4-8, Apr. 15, 1971.

1519)        McCormick, Richard A. "Notes on Moral Theology ... of Theology and Liberation," Theological Studies, 33:100-19, Mar. 1972.

1520)        McGraw, James R. "The Scandal of Peculiarity," Christianity and Crisis, 33:63-68, Apr. 16, 1973.

1521)        McGuire, B. P. "Love, Friendship, and Sex in the Eleventh Century: The Experience of Anselm," Studia Theologica, v. 28, issue 2, pp. 111-52, 1974.

1522)        McNaught, Brian. "The Sad Dilemma of the Gay Catholic," United States Catholic, 40:6-11, Aug. 1975.

1523)        McNeill, John. "The Christian Male Homosexual," Homiletic and Pastoral Review, 70:667-77, Jun. 1970; 70:747-58, Jul. 1970; and 70:828-36, Aug. 1970.

1524)        _____. "The Homosexual and the Church," National Catholic Reporter, 9:7-8, 13-14, Oct. 5, 1973.

1525)    Meeks, John E.  "Should Homosexuals Lead Youth
         Groups?" Engage/Social Action, 3:32-33, May 1975.

1526)    "Metropolitan Community Church: Deception Dis-
         covered," Christianity Today, 18:13-14, Apr. 26,
         1974.

1527)    Meyers, Jeffrey.  Book Review: E. M. Forster's
         Life to Come, Commonweal, 98:506-08, Sep. 21,
         1973.

1528)    "The Mission of the Gay Church," Trends, 5:30-32,
         Jul.-Aug. 1973.

1529)    Moody, Howard R.  "Rationing Our Rights," Chris-
         tianity and Crisis, 34:147-49, Jul. 8, 1974.

1530)    Myron, Nancy.  "Lace Curtains and a Plastic
         Jesus," Motive, v. 32, issue 1, pp. 34-37, 1972.

1531)    Nappey, Pierre-Claude.  "An Open Letter on Homo-
         sexuality," Cross Currents, 20:221-37, 1970.
         (Translated from the French by Violet Neville)

1532)    "Newark Paper Backs Gay Rights," National Catho-
         lic Reporter, 10:3, May 31, 1974.

1533)    "Not Because They Are Gay," Christianity Today,
         16:23, Jul. 28, 1972.

1534)    "Notes of an Old Gay," Motive, v. 32, issue 1, pp.
         16-18, 1972.

1535)    Novak, Michael.  "Brother McNaught, Brother
         O'Rourke," Commonweal, 101:56, 70, Oct. 18,
         1974.  Discussion:  101:203, 222, Nov. 29, 1974.

1536)    _____.  "Gay Is Not Liberation," Commonweal,
         100:304, 318-19, May 31, 1974.  Discussion: 100:
         381-83, Jul. 12, 1974.

1537)    "On Our Own:  Gay Men in Consciousness-raising
         Groups," Motive, v. 32, issue 1, pp. 49-51, 1972.

1538)    Patrinos, Dan.  "An Integrated Stance," National
         Catholic Reporter, 7:91, Apr. 16, 1971.

1539)    Pattison, E. Mansell. "Defrocking the Stereotypes,"
         Christianity Today, 16:20-21, May 12, 1972.

1540)    Phillips, Gene D. "Homosexual Revolution," Amer-
         ica, 123:406-07, Nov. 14, 1970. Discussion: 123:
         504, Dec. 12, 1970.

1541)    Pitchford, Kenneth. "Who Are the Flaming Fag-
         gots?" Motive, v. 32, issue 2, pp. 16-19, 1972.

1542)    Pittenger, Norman. "E. M. Forster, Homosexual-
         ity, and Christian Morality," Christian Century,
         88:1468-71, Dec. 15, 1971. Discussion: 89:171-72,
         Feb. 9, 1972 and 89:963-64, Sep. 27, 1972.

1543)    _____. "Homosexuality and the Christian Tra-
         dition," Christianity and Crisis, 34:178-81, Aug.
         5, 1974.

1544)    _____. "A Theological Approach to Understand-
         ing Homosexuality," Religion in Life, 43:436-44,
         Winter 1974.

1545)    Plowman, Edward E. "The Metropolitan Community
         Church: Equal Rights for All Homosexuals," Chris-
         tianity Today, 19:38-39, Mar. 28, 1975.

1546)    _____. "Sexuality and Ministry: United Metho-
         dist Controversy," Christianity Today, 19:28-30,
         Jan. 31, 1975.

1547)    Poole, Lee. "The Catholic Homosexual," New
         Blackfriars, 56:500-05, 1975.

1548)    Powell, John R. "Understanding Male Homosexua-
         lity: Developmental Recapitulation in a Christian
         Perspective," Journal of Psychology and Theology,
         2:163-73, 1974.

1549)    Preston, John. "Beyond Rhetoric," Motive, v. 32,
         issue 2, pp. 11-14, 1972.

1550)    "Priests' Guidelines Back Eucharist for Homosex-
         uals," National Catholic Reporter, 10:1, 20, Apr.
         5, 1974.

1551)    Rash, John P. "Reforming Pastoral Attitudes

toward Homosexuality," Union Seminary Quarterly Review, 25:439-55, Summer 1970.

1552)   Rashke, Richard. "Writing Gag Lifted on Theologian [John McNeill]," National Catholic Reporter, 12:3, 6, Nov. 14, 1975.

1553)   Reid, Coletta. "Motherhood Is Powerless," Motive, v. 32, issue 1, pp. 52-53, 1972.

1554)   "Retreat Center for 'Gay' Clergy, Religious Sought," National Catholic Reporter, 9:1-2, Apr. 13, 1973.

1555)   Rowe, James. "Up from the Underground; But Still Security Risks," National Catholic Reporter, 7:8-9, Apr. 16, 1971.

1556)   "St. Paul Passes Gay Rights Law," National Catholic Reporter, 10:16, Aug. 2, 1974.

1557)   Sandmire, James E. "Accepting my Uniqueness," Trends, 5:27-29, Jul.-Aug. 1973.

1558)   Scanzoni, Letha. "On Friendship and Homosexuality," Christianity Today, 18:11-14, Sep. 27, 1974.

1559)   "Seminar on Hedonistic Sex, Mutual Affection Sex, and Bible Sex," Religious Education, 65:170-76, 1970.

1560)   Shaunessey, Daniel. "St. Tarcissus Was a Sissy," Motive, v. 32, issue 2, pp. 4-6, 1972.

1561)   Shoemaker, Dennis E. "Getting Straight about Gays," Trends, 5:20-26, Jul.-Aug. 1973.

1562)   Skeist, Robbie. "The Orderly," Motive, v. 32, issue 2, pp. 34-35, 1972.

1563)   Spaulding, Jack. "Catholic Homosexuals Hold First Convention," National Catholic Reporter, 9:1, 16, Sep. 14, 1973.

1564)   Stemper, W. "Church Must Act to End Its Oppression of Homosexuals," Engage-Social Action, 1:21-24, Dec. 1973.

1565)    Tibe, R.    "Homosexuality in Light of the Scrip-
         tures," Good News Broadcaster, Mar. 1974, p. 4.

1566)    "To Accept Homosexuals," Christian Century, 88:
         275, Mar. 3, 1971.   (Editorial)  Discussion:  88:
         497-500, Apr. 21, 1971; 88:804, Jun. 30, 1971; and
         89:172, Feb. 9, 1972.

1567)    Touchet, F.    "A View from the Other Side of the
         Garden; New York's New Homophile Groups,"
         Listening, 6:42-48, Winter 1971.

1568)    "Twenty-eight Jesuits Back Bill on Gay Rights,"
         National Catholic Reporter, 10:1-2, May 17, 1974.

1569)    Van der Ploeg, J.    "Death of Decency," Banner,
         Aug. 28, 1970, p. 8.

1570)    "Vatican Inquires into Jesuit's Work on Homosexu-
         ality [John McNeill]," National Catholic Reporter,
         10:1-2, Jan. 25, 1974.

1571)    Vincent, M.    "A Christian View of Homosexuality,"
         Eternity, Aug. 1972, p. 23.

1572)    Wall, James M.    "Methodists Face the Homosexual
         Issue," Christian Century, 92:243-44, Mar. 12,
         1975.    Discussion:  92:474-75, May 7, 1975.

1573)    _____.    "Unreal World of a National Council of
         Churches Meeting," Christian Century, 92:275-76,
         Mar. 19, 1975.    Discussion:  92:474, May 7, 1975.

1574)    Weber, Joseph C.    "Does the Bible Condemn Homo-
         sexual Acts," Engage/Social Action, 3:28-31, May
         1975.

1575)    Whitman, Charles.    "Book Review: R. M. Enroth
         and G. E. Jamison, The Gay Church," Christian
         Century, 91:542-43, May 15, 1974.

1576)    "Worcester Diocese Hits Gay Rights Bill," National
         Catholic Reporter, 10:3, Jul. 5, 1974.

1577)    Wright, Elliott.    "The Church and Gay Liberation,"
         Christian Century, 88:281-85, Mar. 3, 1971.

ARTICLES IN LEGAL JOURNALS

1578)     Armanno, Benna F.   "Lesbian Mother:  Her Right
          to Child Custody," Golden Gate Law Review, 4:1-
          18, 1973.

1579)     Benedict, James N.   "Homosexuality and the Law--
          A Right to Be Different," Albany Law Review, 38:
          84-104, 1973.

1580)     Berendt, Gerald E.   "Criminal Law--Laws Which
          Prohibit Consenting Adults from Participating in Ho-
          mosexual Activities in Private," South Carolina Law
          Review, 23:816-25, 1971.

1581)     Berger, Richard S.   "Criminal Law--Escape from
          Prison, Defenses--Duress--Homosexual Attacks:
          People v. Harmon ... 220 N.W. 2d 212," Akron
          Law Review, 8:352-59, 1974/75.

1582)     Bragg, Morgan S.   "Victimless Sex Crimes:  To
          the Devil, Not the Dungeon," University of Florida
          Law Review, 25:139-59, 1972.

1583)     Calvani, Terry.  Book Review: Walter Barnett, Sexual
          Freedom and the Constitution, Stanford Law Re-
          view, 26:965-79, 1973/74.

1584)     _____.     "Homosexuality and the Law--An
          Overview," New York Law Forum, 17:273-303, 1971.

1585)     Chaitlin, Ellen and Lefcourt, V. Roy.   "Is Gay Sus-
          pect?" Lincoln Law Review, 8:24-54, 1973.

1586)     Chappell, Duncan and Wilson, Paul R.   "Changing
          Attitudes toward Homosexual Law Reform," Aus-
          tralian Law Journal, 46:22-29, 1972.

1587)     "Constitutionality of Laws Forbidding Private

Homosexual Conduct," Michigan Law Review, 72: 1613-37, 1974.

1588)   Convissar, Shelley T.   "Concept of Attorney-fitness in New York: New Perspectives [Harris L. Kimball]," Buffalo Law Review, 24:553-66, 1975.

1589)   Couris, Thomas T.   "Sexual Freedom for Consenting Adults--Why Not?" Pacific Law Journal, 2:206-25, 1971.

1590)   "Criminal Law--Unreasonable Visual Observation Held to Violate Fourth Amendment [State v. Bryant, 177 N.W. 2d 800]," Minnesota Law Review, 55: 1255-65, 1970/71.

1591)   Crumpler, William B.   "Administrative Law--Constitutional Law--Is Government Policy Affecting the Employment of Homosexuals Rational?" North Carolina Law Review, 48:912-24, 1970.

1592)   Davis, Elaine.   "Homosexuals in Government Employment: The Boys in the Bureau," Seton Hall Law Review, 3:89-107, 1971/72.

1593)   "Dismissal of Homosexuals from Government Employment: The Developing Role of Due Process in Administrative Adjudications--Norton v. Macy," Georgetown Law Journal, 58:632-45, 1970.

1594)   Fadeley, Edward N.   "Sex Crime in the New Code," Oregon Law Review, 51:515-24, 1971/72.

1595)   "Family Law: Statute Governing Marriage Does Not Authorize Same Sex Marriage," Minnesota Law Review, 56:959-60, 1972.

1596)   Fisher, Robert G.   "Sex Offender Provisions of the Proposed New Maryland Criminal Code: Should Private, Consenting, Homosexual Behavior Be Excluded?" Maryland Law Journal, 30:91-113, 1970.

1597)   Freimann, Arlene.   "Acanfora v. Board of Education (491 F. 2d 498): New Interpretations on Standing; Section 1983 and Judicial Review of an Administrative Determination," Temple Law Quarterly, 48:384-96, 1975.

1598)     Galyon, L. Anderson.  "Criminal Law--Sodomy--
          Requirements for Corroboration of Testimony of an
          Accomplice [Davis v. State, 442 S.W. 2d 283], "
          Tennessee Law Review, 38:286-89, 1970/71.

1599)     "Gay Students Organization v. Bonner (367 F. Supp.
          1088):  Expressive Conduct and First Amendment
          Protection, " Maine Law Review, 26:397-414, 1974.

1600)     "Gays on Campus:  Rights at Tulane, " Civil Liber-
          ties, May 1974, pp. 2-3.

1601)     "Government Employment and the Homosexual, " St.
          John's Law Review, 45:303-23, 1970/71.

1602)     Graham, Kathleen M.  "Security Clearances for Ho-
          mosexuals, " Stanford Law Review, 25:403-29, 1972/
          73.

1603)     Grey, Antony.  "Civilizing Our Sex Laws, " Journal
          of the Society of Public Teachers of Law, 13:106-12,
          July 1974.

1604)     _____.  "Sexual Law Reform Society Working
          Party Report, " Criminal Law Review, June 1975,
          pp. 323-35.

1605)     Hansen, Ted L.  "Domestic Relations--Minnesota
          Marriage Statute Does Not Permit Marriage between
          Two Persons of the Same Sex, " Drake Law Review,
          22:206-12, 1972.

1606)     Hirschhorn, James M.  "Due Process in Undesirable
          Discharge Proceedings, " University of Chicago Law
          Review, 41:164-89, 1973/74.

1607)     Iglow, Robert A.  "Oral Copulation:  A Constitution-
          al Curtain Must Be Drawn, " San Diego Law Review,
          11:523-34, 1974.

1608)     Itzkowitz, Theodore D.  "Constitutional Law--Corpor-
          ations--First Amendment Rights:  State ex rel. Grant
          v. Brown ... 313 N.E. 2d 847 (1974), " Akron Law
          Review, 8:375-82, 1974/75.

1609)     Johanns, Michael.  "Constitutional Law--Freedom
          of Speech--Maryland Federal District Court Upholds

Transfer and Dismissal of Teacher Because of 'Repeated' and 'Unnecessary' Public Appearances Made to Explain Plight as Homosexual Teacher," Creighton Law Review, 7:92-104, 1973.

1610)   Johnson, H. A.   "Homosexual Propensity and Corroboration," New Law Journal, 125:189-91 and 203-04, Feb. 20-27, 1974.

1611)   Joplin, Larry E.   "Criminal Law--Examination of Oklahoma Laws concerning Sexual Behavior," Oklahoma Law Review, 23:459-72 at 466-72, 1970.

1612)   Katchadourian, Herant A. and Lunde, Donald T. "Sex and the Law--a Look at Our Legal Anachronisms," Student Lawyer, 2:27-40, Sep. 1973.

1613)   Kenny, Walter F.   "Homosexuality and Nullity: Developing Jurisprudence," Catholic Lawyer, 17: 110-22, Sep. 1971.

1614)   Ketcham, Carleton P.   Jr.   "Criminal Law--Sodomy Statute Not Describing Prohibited Conduct But Referring Only to Crime against Nature Held Unconstitutionally Overbroad," Cumberland-Sanford Law Review, 3:525-31, 1972.

1615)   Kovarsky, Irving.   "The Law and the Homosexual," Student Lawyer, 1:27-32 and 70-71, Oct. 1972 and 1:12-16, Nov. 1972.

1616)   Lauritsen, John and Thorstad, David.   "Forerunners of Gay Liberation," Civil Liberties Review, 2:81-102, Summer 1975.   (Excerpts from no. 87)

1617)   "The Legality of Homosexual Marriage," Yale Law Review, 82:573-89, 1972/73.

1618)   Lentz, William D.   "Constitutional Law--Marriage Rights--Homosexuals and Transsexuals [B. v. B ... 355 N.Y.S. 2d 712 (1974)," Akron Law Review, 8: 369-74, 1974/75.

1619)   Ludwig, Frederick J.   "Case for Repeal of the Sex Corroboration Requirement in New York," Brooklyn Law Review, 36:378-86, 1970.

1620) Lynch, Norman B. "The Administrative Discharge: Changes Needed," Maine Law Review, 22:141-69, 1970.

1621) Neier, Aryeh. "Protest Movements among the Disfranchised," Civil Liberties Review, 1:49-74 at 60-62, 1973/74.

1622) Olivieri, Antonio and Finkelstein, Irwin. "Report on 'Victimless Crime' in New York State," New York Law Forum, 18:77-120 at 114-20, 1972.

1623) Pakalka, William R. "Sodomy--Constitutional Law--Texas Statute Prohibiting Sodomy Is Unconstitutionally Overbroad in Proscribing Private, Consensual Acts of Married Couples, Buchanan v. Batchelor," Texas Law Review, 49:400-06, 1971.

1624) Parker, William. "The Emerging Homosexual Minority," Civil Liberties Review, 2:136-44, Summer 1975.

1625) _____. "The Homosexual in American Society Today: The Homophile--Gay Liberation Movement," Criminal Law Bulletin, 8:692-99, 1972.

1626) _____. "Homosexuality--A Bibliographic Essay," Criminal Law Bulletin, 8:716-24, 1972.

1627) Punzo, Vincent C. "Morality and the Law: The Search for Privacy in Community," St. Louis University Law Journal, 18:175-96 at 184-85, 1973.

1628) Ragan, James A. "Duress-Defense to Escape--Substantial Threats of Homosexual Attack May Support the Defense of Duress in a Prosecution for Prison Escape. People v. Harmon ... 220 N.W. 2d 212 (1974)," American Journal of Criminal Law, 3:331-40, 1975.

1629) Reese, Susan E. "Forgotten Sex: Lesbians, Liberation, and the Law," Willamette Law Journal, 11:354-77, 1975.

1630) Riley, Marilyn. "Avowed Lesbian Mother and Her Right to Child Custody: A Constitutional Challenge that Can No Longer Be Denied," San Diego Law Review, 12:799-864, 1974/75.

1631)   Schmidt, John R.   "Homosexuality and Validity of Marriage--A Study in Homopsychosexual Inversion," Jurist, 32:381-99 and 494-530, 1972.   Reprinted in Catholic Lawyer, 19:84-101 and 169-99, 1973 and 21:85-121, 1975.

1632)   Schmidt, Paul W.   "Special Review Board [Wisconsin Sex Crimes Law]," Wisconsin Law Review, 1973: 172-209 at 192-93 and 199-200.

1633)   "Sexual Assaults and Forced Homosexual Relationships in Prison; Cruel and Unusual Punishment," Albany Law Review, 36:428-38, 1971/72.

1634)   Silverman, Hugh.   "Counselling and the Sex Offence," Criminal Law Quarterly, 14:23-67, 1971/72.

1635)   Silverstein, Arthur J.   "Constitutional Aspects of the Homosexual's Right to a Marriage License," Journal of Family Law, 12:607-34, 1972/73.

1636)   Simmons, John F.   "Constitutional Law--Sodomy Statutes:   The Question of Constitutionality [Buchanan Case]," Nebraska Law Review, 50:567-75, 1970/71.

1637)   Sparks, Ty M.   "Constitutional Law--Right of Marital Privacy--Unconstitutional Overbreadth of the Texas Sodomy Statute--Buchanan v. Batchelor," Texas Law Review, 2:115-20, 1970/71.

1638)   Steinhauer, Bennett C.   "Corporation Law--Discretionary Granting of Non-profit Charters," University of Toledo Law Review, 6:237-52, 1974.

1639)   Stodola, Mark A.   "Homosexual's Legal Dilemma," Arkansas Law Review, 27:687-721, 1973.

1640)   Vacek, Albert E. Jr.   "Constitutionality of the Texas Sodomy Statute--Buchanan v. Batchelor," Baylor Law Review, 22:300-03, 1970.

1641)   West, Donald J. Book Review:  Walter Barnett, Sexual Freedom and the Constitution, South Carolina Law Review, 47:683-87, 1974.

# COURT CASES INVOLVING CONSENTING ADULTS

1642)    A. v. A.   514 P. 2d 358 (Ore. , 1973) - homosexual father and child custody.

1643)    Acanfora v. Board of Education.   359 F. Supp. 843
(Md. , 1973).   Affirmed 491 F. 2d 498 (4th Cir. ,
1974.) Certiorari denied 419 U. S.  836 (1974) -
employment as a teacher.

1644)    Anon. v. Anon.   325 N. Y. S. 2d 499 (N. Y. , 1971) -
marriage of two men.

1645)    Associated Students of Sacramento State College v.
Butz.   No. 200795, Superior Court, Sacramento
(Calif. , 1971) - gay student organization.

1646)    Baker v. Nelson.   191 N. W. 2d 185 (Minn. , 1971).
Appeal dismissed 409 U. S. 800 (1972) - homosexual
marriage license.

1647)    Ballew, State v.   532 P. 2d 407 (Mont. , 1975) -
clarity of deviate sexual conduct statute.

1648)    Becker v. State Liquor Authority.   353 N. Y. S. 2d
511 (N. Y. , 1974) - conduct in gay bar.

1649)    Bennett v. Clemens.   196 S. E. 2d 842 (Ga. , 1973)
- lesbian mother and child custody.

1650)    Board of Education v. Calderon.   110 Cal. Rptr.
916 (Calif. , 1973).   Certiorari denied 419 U. S.
807 (1974) - employment as teacher.

1651)    Brodie, In re Petition for Naturalization of.   394 F.
Supp. 1208 (Ore. , 1975) - naturalization of homosexual alien.

1652)    Brown, People v.   212 N. W. 2d 55 (Mich. , 1973)

- lesbian mother and child custody.

1653)    Bryant, State v.    177 N.W. 2d 800 (Minn., 1970) -
         consensual sodomy and clandestine police observa-
         tion.

1654)    Buchanan v. Batchelor.    308 F. Supp. 729 (Tex.,
         1970).    Vacated and remanded for reconsideration
         on jurisdictional grounds sub nom. Wade v. Buchan-
         an.    401 U.S. 989 (1971) - constitutionality of so-
         domy statute.

1655)    Buchanan, State v.    471 S.W. 2d 401 (Tex., 1971)
         - clandestine police observation.

1656)    Burton v. Cascade School District.    353 F. Supp.
         254 (Ore., 1973).    Affirmed 512 F. 2d 850 (9th
         Cir., 1975) - employment as teacher.

1657)    Carson, U.S. v.    319 A. 2d 329 (D.C., 1974) -
         constitutionality of solicitation statute.

1658)    Cason v. U.S. Navy.    471 F. 2d 1225 (Ct. Cl.,
         1973) - military discharge and back pay.

1659)    Chaffin v. Frye.    119 Cal. Rptr. 22 (Calif., 1975)
         - lesbian mother and child custody.

1660)    Cozart, U.S. v. 321 A. 2d 342 (D.C., 1974) -
         constitutionality of solicitation statute.

1661)    Crafts, People v.    91 Cal. Rptr.    563 (Calif.,
         1970) - clandestine police observation.

1662)    Dayter, People v.    307 N.Y.S. 2d 244 (N.Y., 1970)
         - threat of revealing defendant's homosexual condi-
         tion.

1663)    Enslin v. North Carolina.    214 S.E. 2d 381 (N. Car.,
         1975) Affirmed 425 U.S. 901 (Mar. 29, 1976) -
         constitutionality of sodomy statute.

1664)    Florida Bar v. Kay.    232 So. 2d 378 (Flda., 1970).
         Certiorari denied 400 U.S. 956 (1970) - disbarment
         of homosexual lawyer.

1665)    Franklin v. State.    257 So. 2d 21 (Flda., 1971) -
         constitutionality of sodomy statute.

1666)      Gay Activists Alliance v. Lomenzo.   320 N. Y. S.
           2d 994 (N. Y. , 1971).   Reversed 341 N. Y. S. 2d
           108 (N. Y. , 1973) - incorporation of gay organiza-
           tion.

1667)      Gay Students' Organization of University of New
           Hampshire v. Bonner.   367 F. Supp. 1088 (N.
           Hamp. , 1974).   Affirmed 509 F. 2d 652 (1st Cir. ,
           1974) - gay student organization.

1668)      Gayer v. Laird.   332 F. Supp. 169 (D. C. , 1971).
           (Retitled Gayer v. Schlesinger. )  Remanded for
           further action 490 F. 2d 740 (D. C. Cir. , 1973) and
           amended 494 F. 2d 1135 (D. C. Cir. , 1973) - se-
           curity clearance.

1669)      Harmon, People v.   220 N. W. 2d 212 (Mich. ,
           1974).   Affirmed 232 N. W. 2d 187 (Mich. , 1975) -
           homosexuality and escape from prison.

1670)      Harris v. U. S.   293 A. 2d 851 (D. C. , 1972).  Re-
           versed 315 A. 2d 569 (D. C. Cir. , 1973) - keeping
           a bawdy house for homosexuals.

1671)      J. , S. , and C. , In re.   324 A. 2d 90 (N. J. , 1974)
           - visitation rights of a homosexual father.

1672)      Jarrell, State v.   211 S. E. 2d 837 (N. Car. , 1975)
           - clandestine police observation.

1673)      Jones v. Hallahan.   501 S. W. 2d 588 (Ky. , 1973) -
           homosexual marriage license.

1674)      Jones v. State.   200 N. W. 2d 587 (Wis. , 1972) -
           homosexual acts in jail.

1675)      Kimball, Application of, for Admission to Practice
           as an Attorney.   339 N. Y. S. 2d 302 (N. Y. , 1973).
           Modified 342 N. Y. S. 2d 373 (N. Y. , 1973).  Re-
           versed 347 N. Y. S. 2d 453 (N. Y. , 1973) - admis-
           sion of homosexual to the practice of law.

1676)      Kovacs v. U. S.   476 F. 2d 843 (2d Cir. , 1973) -
           homosexual acts and naturalization.

1677)      Kroehler v. Scott.   391 F. Supp. 1114 (Pa. , 1975)
           - clandestine police observation.

1678)    Labady, In re Petition for Naturalization.  326 F.
         Supp.  924 (N.Y. , 1971) - naturalization of homo-
         sexual alien.

1679)    Marks v. Schlesinger.  384 F. Supp. 1373 (Calif. ,
         1974) - security clearance.

1680)    McConnell v. Anderson.  316 F. Supp. 809 (Minn. ,
         1970).  Reversed 451 F. 2d 193 (8th Cir. , 1971).
         Certiorari denied 405 U.S. 1046 (1972) - employment
         as librarian.

1681)    McKeand v. Laird.  Civil No. 70-873-JWC (Calif. ,
         1971).  Affirmed 490 F. 2d 1262 (9th Cir. , 1973) -
         security clearance.

1682)    McLaughlin v. Board of Medical Examiners.  111
         Cal. Rptr. 353 (Calif. , 1973) - homosexual pro-
         position and doctor's fitness to practice medicine.

1683)    Metcalf, People v.  98 Cal. Rptr. 925 (Calif. ,
         1971) - solicitation and clandestine police observa-
         tion.

1684)    Moles, State v.  195 S.E. 2d 352 (N. Car. , 1973)
         - constitutionality of crime against nature statute.

1685)    Mortimer, State v.  467 P. 2d 60 (Az. , 1970) -
         public acts.

1686)    Owles v. Lomenzo.  329 N.Y.S. 2d 181 (N.Y. ,
         1972).  Affirmed 341 N.Y.S. 2d 108 (N.Y. , 1973) -
         incorporation of gay organization.

1687)    Parker, People v.  109 Cal. Rptr. 354 (Calif. ,
         1973) - constitutionality of oral copulation statute.

1688)    Pruett v. State.  463 S.W. 2d 191 (Tex. , 1970).
         Appeal dismissed 402 U.S. 902 (1971) - constitu-
         tionality of sodomy statute.

1689)    Purifoy v. State Board of Education.  106 Cal.
         Rptr. 201 (Calif. , 1973) - employment and teaching
         credential.

1690)    Rice, People v.  363 N.Y.S. 2d 484 (N.Y. , 1974) -
         constitutionality of sodomy statute.

1691)    Richardson v. Hampton.   345 F. Supp. 600 (D. C.,
         1972) - federal employment.

1692)    Riley v. U. S.   298 A. 2d 228 (D. C., 1972).   Cer-
         tiorari denied 414 U. S. 840 (1973) - solicitation of
         police decoy.

1693)    Safransky v. State Personnel Board.   215 N. W. 2d
         385 (Wis., 1974) - state employment.

1694)    Segal, People v.   358 N. Y. S. 2d 866 (N. Y., 1974) -
         non-criminality of advocating homosexuality.

1695)    Shad, State v.   470 P. 2d 246 (Utah, 1970) - death
         from consensual act.

1696)    Silva v. Municipal Court.   115 Cal. Rptr. 479
         (Calif., 1974) - constitutionality of solicitation for
         lewd acts statute.

1697)    Singer v. Hara.   522 P. 2d 1187 (Wash., 1974) -
         homosexual marriage license.

1698)    Society for Individual Rights v. Hampton.   528 F.
         2d 905 (9th Cir., 1975) - federal employment.

1699)    Spence v. Durham.   198 S. E. 2d 537 (N. Car.,
         1973) - lesbian mother and child custody.

1700)    State ex rel. Grant v. Brown.   313 N. E. 2d 847
         (Ohio, 1974).   Certiorari denied 420 U. S. 916 (1975)
         - incorporation of gay organization.

1701)    Thom, Application of.   337 N. Y. S. 2d 588 (N. Y.,
         1972).   Reversed 347 N. Y. S. 2d 571 (N. Y., 1973) -
         gay rights organization.

1702)    Triggs, People v.   102 Cal. Rptr. 725 (Calif.,
         1972).   Vacated 106 Cal. Rptr. 408 (Calif., 1973) -
         clandestine police observation.

1703)    Ulrich v. Laird.   Civil No. 203-71 (D. C., 1971).
         (Retitled Ulrich v. Schlesinger.)  Affirmed 490 F.
         2d 740 (D. C. Cir., 1973) and amended 494 F. 2d
         1135 (D. C. Cir., 1973) - security clearance.

1704)    Velez-Lozano v. Immigration and Naturalization

Service.   463 F.  2d 1305 (D.C.  Cir. ,  1972) - de-
portation of homosexual alien.

1705)      Washington v.  Rodriguez.   483 P.  2d 309 (N. Mex.,
1971) - homosexual acts in prison.

1706)      Wentworth v.  Laird.   348 F.  Supp.   1153 (D.C.,
1972).   (Retitled Wentworth v.  Schlesinger. )  Re-
manded for reconsideration 490 F.  2d 740 (D.C.
Cir. ,  1973) and amended 494 F.  2d 1135 (D.C.
Cir. ,  1973) - security clearance.

1707)      Wier v.  U.S.   474 F.  2d 617 (Ct.  Cl. ,  1973) -
discharge from military service.

1708)      Wilhelmi v.  Beto.   426 F.  2d 795 (5th Cir. ,  1970)
- homosexual act.

1709)      Wood v.  Davison.   351 F.  Supp.  543 (Ga. ,  1972) -
gay student organization.

# ARTICLES IN MEDICAL AND SCIENTIFIC JOURNALS

1710)     Abel, Gene G.; Barlow, David H.; Blanchard, Edward B.; and Mavissakalian, Matig. "Measurement of Sexual Arousal in Male Homosexuals: Effects of Instruction and Stimulus Modality," Archives of Sexual Behavior, 4:623-29, 1975.

1711)     Abel, T. M. "Treatment of a Male Homopaedophile," Newsletter of International Mental Health Research, 14:10-16, 1972.

1712)     Abernethy, Virginia. "Dominance and Sexual Behavior: A Hypothesis," American Journal of Psychiatry, 131:813-17, 1974.

1713)     Acosta, Frank X. "Etiology and Treatment of Homosexuality: A Review," Archives of Sexual Behavior, 4:9-29, 1975.

1714)     Alexander, G. L. "Homosexuality: The Psychoanalytic Point of View," Psychiatric Communications, 16:19-23, Apr. 1975.

1715)     Allen, John A. and Boice, Robert. "Effects of Rearing on Homosexual Behavior in the Male Laboratory Rat," Psychonomic Science, 23:321-22, 1971.

1716)     Altman, Harold; Sletten, Ivan W.; Eaton, Mary E.; and Ulett, George A. "Demographic and Mental Status Profiles: Patients with Homicidal, Assaultive, Suicidal, Persecutory, and Homosexual Ideation," Psychiatric Quarterly, 45:57-64, 1971.

1717)     Anderson, Elizabeth A. "The Elusive Homosexual: A Reply to Stone and Schneider," Journal of Personality Assessment, 39:580-82, 1975.

1718)     Andress, Vern R.; Franzini, Louis R.; and Linton,

Marigold. "A Comparison of Homosexual and Heterosexual Responses to the Menninger Wald Association Test," Journal of Clinical Psychology, 30: 205-07, 1974.

1719) Anonymous. "I Am a Homosexual Physician," Medical Opinion, 2:49-58, Jan. 1973.

1720) "Are Homosexuals Different? Nay and Yea," Psychology Today, Feb. 1972, pp. 19-20.

1721) Baker, Howard J. "Homosexuality, Transvestism, and Transsexualism," Medical Aspects of Human Sexuality, 4:64, Aug. 1970.

1722) Baker, Jack. "Homosexuality and Testosterone," New England Journal of Medicine, 286:380, Feb. 17, 1972.

1723) Bancroft, John. "Aversion Therapy of Homosexuality," British Journal of Psychiatry, 116:676-77, 1970.

1724) _____. "Homosexuality in the Male," British Journal of Psychiatry, special issue no. 9, pp. 173-84, 1975.

1725) Barker, G. B. "The Female Homosexual in Hospital," British Journal of Projective Psychology and Personality Study, 15:2-6, Dec. 1970.

1726) Barlow, David H. "Increasing Heterosexual Responsiveness in the Treatment of Sexual Deviation: A Review of the Clinical and Experimental Evidence," Behavior Therapy, 4:655-71, 1973. (Reprinted in Cyril M. Franks and G. Terence Wilson [eds.], Annual Review of Behavior Therapy, Theory and Practice [New York: Brunner/Mazel Publishers, 1974], pp. 637-54 [chap. 33])

1727) _____; Abel, Gene G.; Blanchard, Edward B.; and Mavissakalian, Matig. "Plasma Testosterone Level and Male Homosexuality: A Failure to Replicate," Archives of Sexual Behavior, 3:571-75, 1974.

1728) _____ and Agras, W. Stewart. "Fading to

Increase Heterosexual Responsiveness in Homosexuals," Journal of Applied Behavior Analysis, 6:355-66, 1973.

1729)    _____; _____; Abel, Gene G.; Blanchard, Edward B.; and Young, Larry D.  "Biofeedback and Reinforcement to Increase Heterosexual Arousal in Homosexuals," Behaviour Research and Therapy, 13:45-50, 1975.

1730)    _____; _____; Leitenberg, Harold; Callahan, Edward J.; and Moore, Robert C.  "The Contribution of Therapeutic Instruction of Covert Sensitization," Behaviour Research and Therapy, 10:411-15, 1972.

1731)    Barr, R. F.  "Responses to Erotic Stimuli of Transsexual and Homosexual Males," British Journal of Psychiatry, 123:579-85, 1973.

1732)    _____ and Greenberg, H. P.  "Homosexuality and Psychological Adjustment," Medical Journal of Australia, 1:187-89, 1974.

1733)    _____ and McConaghy, N.  "Penile Volume Responses to Appetitive and Aversive Stimuli in Relation to Sexual Orientation and Conditioning Performance," British Journal of Psychiatry, 169:377-83, 1971.

1734)    _____; Raphael, B.; and Hennessey, Norma.  "Apparent Heterosexuality in Two Male Patients Requesting Change-of-sex Operations," Archives of Sexual Behavior, 3:325-30, 1974.

1735)    Barry, Herbert.  "Homosexuality and Testosterone," New England Journal of Medicine, 286:380-81, Feb. 17, 1972.

1736)    Bell, Alan P.  "Human Sexuality: A Response," International Journal of Psychiatry, 10:99-102, 1972.

1737)    _____.  "Research in Homosexuality: Back to the Drawing Board," Archives of Sexual Behavior, 4: 421-31, 1975.

1738)    Berc, Kenneth M.  "Wives of Homosexual Men,"

American Journal of Psychiatry, 131:832-33, 1974.

1739)     Berent, Irving.   "Original Sin:  'I Didn't Mean to
          Hurt You, Mother':  A Basic Fantasy Epitomized
          by a Male Homosexual," Journal of the American
          Psychoanalytic Association, 21:262-84, 1973.

1740)     Besdine, Matthew.   "Michelangelo:  The Homosex-
          ual Element in the Life and Work of a Genius,"
          Medical Aspects of Human Sexuality, 3:127-40, May
          1970.

1741)     _____.  "Shakespeare:  The Homosexual Element
          in the Life of a Genius," Medical Aspects of Human
          Sexuality, 5:158-83, Feb. 1971.

1742)     Bhatia, R. P.   "A Case of Manifest Homosexuality
          with Acute Paranoid Trends Accompanied by Depres-
          sions and Suicidal Tendencies," Samiksa, 28:94-
          125, 1974.

1743)     Bieber, Irving.   "Homosexual Dynamics in Psychia-
          tric Crisis," American Journal of Psychiatry, 128:
          1268-72, 1972.

1744)     _____.  "Recognizing Homosexual Tendencies in
          Children," Medical Aspects of Human Sexuality, 4:
          71, Dec. 1970.

1745)     _____ and Bieber, Toby.   "Heterosexuals Who
          are Preoccupied with Homosexual Thoughts," Medi-
          cal Aspects of Human Sexuality, 9:152-68, Apr. 1975.

1746)     Bieber, Toby.   "Group and Individual Psychotherapy
          with Male Homosexuals," Journal of the American
          Academy of Psychoanalysis, 2:255-60, 1974.

1747)     Birk, Lee; Huddleston, William; Miller, Elizabeth;
          and Cohler, Bertram.   "Avoidance Conditioning for
          Homosexuality," Archives of General Psychiatry,
          25:314-23, 1971.

1748)     _____; Miller, Elizabeth; and Cohler, Bertram.
          "Group Psychotherapy for Homosexual Men by Male-
          Female Co-therapists," Acta Psychiatrica Scandin-
          avica, Supplement, 218:9-38, 1970.

1749)        _____; Weinberg, George; Hatterer, Lawrence;
            Hoffman, Martin; Gritter, Gordon; Bieber, Irving;
            nad Haynes, Stephen.   "Can Homosexuals Become
            Heterosexuals?"  Medical Aspects of Human Sexu-
            ality, 8:148-55, Nov. 1974.

1750)        _____; Williams, Gordon H.; Chasin, Marcia;
            and Rose, Leslie I.   "Serum Testosterone Levels
            in Homosexual Men," New England Journal of Med-
            icine, 289:1236-38, Dec. 6, 1973.

1751)       Blitch, Joseph W. and Haynes, Stephen N.   "Multi-
            ple Behavioral Techniques in a Case of Female Ho-
            mosexuality," Journal of Behavior Therapy and Ex-
            perimental Psychiatry, 3:319-22, 1972.

1752)       Brass, Alister.   "Gay Is What?"  New England
            Journal of Medicine, 283:817, Oct. 8, 1970.

1753)       Brengersma, E.   "Sexuality and the Law," Journal
            of the American Institute of Hypnosis, 14:210-25,
            Sep. 1973.

1754)       British Cooperative Clinical Group.   "Homosexual-
            ity and Venereal Disease in the United Kingdom,"
            British Journal of Venereal Diseases, 49:329-34,
            1973.

1755)       Brodie, H. Keith; Gartrell, Nanette; Doering,
            Charles; and Rhue, Thomas.   "Plasma Testosterone
            Levels in Heterosexual and Homosexual Men,"
            American Journal of Psychiatry, 131:82-83, 1974.

1756)       Brown, Howard J.   "The Gay Physician; a Homo-
            sexual after Hours," Medical Opinion, 2:49-58,
            Jan. 1973.

1757)       _____.   "Problems in Homosexuality," Journal
            of the American Medical Association, 228:978,
            May 20, 1974.

1758)       Brown, Marvin and Amoroso, Donald M.   "Attitudes
            toward Homosexuality among West Indian Male and
            Female College Students," Journal of Social Psycho-
            logy, 97:163-68, 1975.

1759)       Bucknam, Frank G.   "Do Homosexuals Want to Be

Women?" Medical Aspects of Human Sexuality, 8:
53, Aug. 1974.

1760)      Buda, B. "Homosexuality," Therapia Hungarica,
           21:11-22, 1973.

1761)      Bullough, Vern L. "Attitudes toward Deviant Sex
           in Ancient Mesopotamia," Journal of Sex Research,
           7:184-203, 1971.

1762)      _____. "Homosexuality as Submissive Behavior:
           Example from Mythology," Journal of Sex Research,
           9:283-88, 1973.

1763)      _____. "Sex and the Medical Model," Journal
           of Sex Research, 11:291-303, 1975.

1764)      Burdick, J. Alan and Stewart, D. Yvette. "Differ-
           ences Between 'Show' and 'No Show' Volunteers in
           a Homosexual Population," Journal of Social Psy-
           chology, 92:159-60, 1974.

1765)      _____; _____; and Adamson, J. D. "Cardiac
           Activity and Verbal Report on Homosexuals and Het-
           erosexuals," Journal of Psychosomatic Research,
           18:377-85, 1974.

1766)      Burnham, John. "Early References to Homosexual
           Communities in American Medical Writings," Med-
           ical Aspects of Human Sexuality, 7:34-49, Aug. 1973.

1767)      Call, Hal. Review of Colin Williams and Martin
           Weinberg, Homosexuals and the Military, Psycho-
           logy Today, Feb. 1972, p. 96.

1768)      Callahan, Edward J. and Leitenberg, Harold.
           "Aversion Therapy for Sexual Deviation: Contingent
           Shock and Covert Sensitization," Journal of Abnor-
           mal Psychology, 8:60-73, 1973.

1769)      Cameron, J. Malcolm. "The Bible and Legal Med-
           icine," Medicine, Science and the Law, 10:7-13,
           1970.

1770)      Canton-Dutari, Alejandro. "Combined Intervention
           for Controlling Unwanted Homosexual Behavior,"
           Archives of Sexual Behavior, 3:367-71, 1974.

1771)    Carrier, J. M.  "Comments on a Neuroendocrine
         Predisposition for Homosexuality in Men," Archives
         of Sexual Behavior, 4:667, 1975.

1772)    _____.  "Participants in Urban Medical Male Ho-
         mosexual Encounters," Archives of Sexual Behavior,
         1:279-91, 1971.

1773)    Cautela, Joseph R.  "Covert Reinforcement," Be-
         haviour Therapy, 1:33-50, 1970.

1774)    _____ and Wisocki, Patricia A.  "Covert Sensi-
         tization for Treatment of Sexual Deviations," Psy-
         chological Record, 21:37-48, 1971.

1775)    Chevalier-Skolnikoff, Suzanne.  "Male-female, Fe-
         male-female, and Male-male Sexual Behavior in the
         Stumptail Monkey, with Special Attention to the Fe-
         male Orgasm," Archives of Sexual Behavior, 3:95-
         116, 1974.

1776)    Chiles, John A.  "Homosexuality in the United
         States Air Force," Comprehensive Psychiatry, 13:
         529-32, 1972.

1777)    Chyatte, Conrad.  "Official Status of Homosexuality,"
         Journal of the American Medical Association, 227:
         1262, Mar. 18, 1974.

1778)    Clark, Thomas R.  "Homosexuality and Psychopa-
         thology in Nonpatient Males," American Journal of
         Psychoanalysis, 35:163-68, 1975.

1779)    _____.  "Homosexuality as a Criterion Predictor
         of Psychopathology in Nonpatient Males," Proceed-
         ings of the 81st Annual Convention of the American
         Psychological Association, 8:407-08, 1973.

1780)    _____ and Epstein, Ralph.  "Self-concepts and
         Expectancy for Social Reinforcement in Non-institu-
         tionalized Male Homosexuals," Journal of Consulting
         and Clinical Psychology, 38:174-80, 1972.

1781)    Clippinger, John A.  "Homosexuality Can Be Cured,"
         Corrective and Social Psychiatry and Journal of Be-
         havior Technology, Methods, and Therapy, 20:15-
         28, 1974.

1782)        _____. "Homosexuality:  Give up the Ship, Paul
             Jones," Corrective Psychiatry and Journal of So-
             cial Therapy, 17:46-57, 1971.

1783)        _____. "Homosexuals Are Different!" Correc-
             tive Psychiatry and Journal of Applied and Behavior
             Therapy, 19:24-32, 1973.

1784)        Cochrane, Raymond.  "Values as Correlates of De-
             viancy," British Journal of Social and Clinical Psy-
             chology, 13:257-67, 1974.

1785)        Colson, Charles E.  "Olfactory Aversion Therapy
             for Homosexual Behavior," Journal of Behavior
             Therapy and Experimental Psychiatry, 3:185-87,
             1972.

1786)        Coombs, Neil R.  "Male Prostitution: A Psycho-
             social View of Behavior," American Journal of Or-
             thopsychiatry, 44:782-89, 1974.  (Summary in Psy-
             chiatry Digest, 36:51, Jun. 1975.)

1787)        Cooper, Alan J.; Ismail, A. A.; Phanjoo, A. L.;
             and Love, D. L.  "Antiandrogen (Cyproterone Ace-
             tate) Therapy in Deviant Hypersexuality," British
             Journal of Psychiatry, 120:59-63, 1972.

1788)        Cotton, Wayne L.  "Role-playing Substitutions among
             Homosexuals," Journal of Sex Research, 8:310-23,
             1972.

1789)        _____. "Social and Sexual Relationships of Les-
             bians," Journal of Sex Research, 11:139-48, 1975.

1790)        Covi, L.  "A Group Psychotherapy Approach to the
             Treatment of Neurotic Symptoms in Male and Fe-
             male Patients of Homosexual Preference," Psycho-
             therapy and Psychosomatics, 20:176-80, 1972.

1791)        Cowden, James E. and Morse, Edwin L.  "The Re-
             lationship of Defensiveness to Responses on the Sex
             Inventory," Journal of Clinical Psychology, 26:505-
             09, 1970.

1792)        Cubitt, G. H. and Gendreau, Paul.  "Assessing the
             Diagnostic Utility of MMPI and 16 PF Indexes of
             Homosexuality in a Prison Sample," Journal of Con-
             sulting and Clinical Psychology, 39:342, 1972.

1793)    Curtis, R. H. and Presly, A. S.  "The Extinction
         of Homosexual Behavior by Covert Sensitization:
         A Case Study," Behaviour Research and Therapy,
         10:81-83, 1972.

1794)    Dank, Barry M.  "Coming Out in the Gay World,"
         Psychiatry, 34:180-97, 1971.

1795)    _____.  "Six Homosexual Siblings," Archives of
         Sexual Behavior, 1:193-204, 1971.

1796)    _____.  "Why Homosexuals Marry Women,"
         Medical Aspects of Human Sexuality, 6:14-23, Aug.
         1972.

1797)    Dannels, Joann C.  "Homosexual Panic," Perspec-
         tives in Psychiatric Care, 10:106-11, 1972.

1798)    Davenport, Charles W.  "Homosexuality--Its Ori-
         gins, Early Recognition, and Prevention," Clinical
         Pediatrics, 11:7-10, Jan. 1972.

1799)    Davies, T. S.  "Cyproterone Acetate for Male Hy-
         persexuality," Journal of International Medical Re-
         search, 2:159-63, 1974.

1800)    Davison, Gerald C. and Wilson, G. Terence.  "At-
         titudes of Behavior Therapists toward Homosexual-
         ity," Behavior Therapy, 4:686-96, 1973.

1801)    _____.  "Goals and Strategies in Behavioral
         Treatment of Homosexual Pedophilia:  Comments on
         a Case Study," Journal of Abnormal Psychology,
         83:196-98, 1974.

1802)    Davison, Kenneth; Brierley, Harry; and Smith, Col-
         in.  "A Male Monozygotic Twinship Discordant for
         Homosexuality:  A Repertory Grid Study," British
         Journal of Psychiatry, 118:675-82, 1971.

1803)    DeBetz, Barbara.  "Gender Disorders:  Homosex-
         uality, Transsexualism, and Hermaphroditism,"
         Medical Aspects of Human Sexuality, 9:87-88, Apr.
         1975.

1804)    Dengrove, Edward.  "Treating Homosexuals,"
         American Journal of Psychiatry, 128:494-95, 1971.

1805)        Denholtz, Myron S.   "An Extension of Covert Pro-
             cedures in the Treatment of Male Homosexuals,"
             Journal of Behavior Therapy and Experimental Psy-
             chiatry, 4:305, 1973.

1806)        Doerner, Guenter.   "Neuro-endocrine Pathogenesis,
             Prevention, and Treatment of Congenital Sexual De-
             viations," German Medical Monthly, 15:108-13, Feb.
             1970.

1807)        _____ and Others.   "A Neuro-endocrine Predis-
             position for Homosexuality in Men," Archives of
             Sexual Behavior, 4:1-8, 1975.

1808)        Doerr, Peter and Others.   "Plasma Testosterone,
             Estradial, and Semen Analysis in Male Homosex-
             uals," Archives of General Psychiatry, 29:829-33,
             1973.

1809)        Domino, George.   "Homosexuality and Creativity,"
             Proceedings of the 81st Annual Convention of the
             American Psychological Association, 8:409-10, 1973.

1810)        Dreyfus, Edward G.   "Homosexuality and Medicine:
             A Reply," Journal of the American Medical Associa-
             tion, 213:1494-96, Aug. 31, 1970.

1811)        Dunbar, John; Brown, Marvin; and Amoroso, Donald
             M.   "Some Correlates of Attitudes toward Homosex-
             uality," Journal of Social Psychology, 89:271-79,
             1973.

1812)        _____; _____; and Vuorinen, Sophie.   "Attitu-
             des toward Homosexuality among Brazilian and Ca-
             nadian College Students," Journal of Social Psycho-
             logy, 90:173-83, 1973.

1813)        Edwards, Neil B.   "Case Conference: Assertive
             Training in a Case of Homosexual Pedophilia,"
             Journal of Behavior Therapy and Experimental Psy-
             chiatry, 3:55-63, 1972.

1814)        Eisinger, A. J. and Others.   "Female Homosexual-
             ity," Nature, 238:106, Jul. 14, 1972.

1815)        Evans, Ray B.   "Adjective Check List Scores of
             Homosexual Men," Journal of Personality Assess-
             ment, 35:344-49, 1971.

1816)        _____ . "Biological Factors in Male Homosexuality," Medical Aspects of Human Sexuality, 7:12-
33, Jul. 1973.

1817)        _____ . "Parental Relations and Homosexuality,"
Medical Aspects of Human Sexuality, 5:164-77, Apr.
1971.

1818)        _____ . "Physical and Biochemical Characteristics of Homosexual Men," Journal of Consulting and
Clinical Psychology, 39:140-47, 1972.

1819)        _____ . "16 Personality Factor Questionnaire
Score of Homosexual Men," Journal of Consulting
and Clinical Psychology, 34:212-15, 1970.

1820)    Farrell, Ronald A. and Morrione, Thomas J. "Social Interaction and Stereotypic Responses to Homosexuals," Archives of Sexual Behavior, 3:425-42,
1974.

1821)    Federman, Daniel D. "A New Look at Homosexuality," New England Journal of Medicine, 285:1197-
98, Nov. 18, 1971.

1822)    Feldman, M. P. "Homosexual Behaviour: Therapy
and Assessment," British Journal of Psychiatry,
121:456-57, 1972.

1823)        _____ and MacCulloch, M. J. "Avoidance Conditioning for Homosexuals: A Reply to MacDonough's
Critique," Behaviour Therapy, 3:430-36, 1972.

1824)    Ferlemann, Mimi. "Homosexuality," Menninger
Perspective, 5:24-27, Summer 1974.

1825)    Fisher, Gary and Howell, Leisla M. "Psychological Needs of Homosexual Pedophiliacs," Diseases
of the Nervous System, 31:623-25, 1970.

1826)    Fiumara, N. J. "Primary Syphilis in the Oral
Cavity," British Journal of Venereal Diseases,
50:463-64, 1974.

1827)    Fleming, Joyce D. Book Review: Clarence A.
Tripp, The Homosexual Matrix, Psychology Today,
Nov. 1975, pp. 105-06.

1828)    Forgey, Donald G.  "The Institution of the Berdache
         among the North American Plains Indians," Journal
         of Sex Research, 11:1-15, 1975.

1829)    Fort, Joel; Steiner, Claude; and Conrad, Florence.
         "Attitudes of Mental Health Professionals toward
         Homosexuality and Its Treatment," Psychological
         Reports, 29:347-50, 1971.   (Reprinted in Ruitenbeek,
         no. 127, pp. 154-58)

1830)    Fraas, Louis A.  "Sex Figure Drawing in Identify-
         ing Practicing Male Homosexuals," Psychological
         Reports, 27:172-74, 1970.

1831)    Francher, J. Scott and Henkin, Janet.  "The Meno-
         pausal Queen:  Adjustment to Aging and the Male
         Homosexual," American Journal of Orthopsychiatry,
         43:670-74, 1973.

1832)    Freedman, Mark.  "Homosexuals May Be Healthier
         than Straights," Psychology Today, Mar. 1975, pp.
         28-32.

1833)    Freeman, William and Meyer, Robert C.  "A Be-
         havioral Alteration of Sexual Preferences in the Hu-
         man Male," Behavior Therapy, 6:206-12, 1975.

1834)    Freemon, Frank R.  "Oscar Wilde:  Poet, Novelist,
         Playwright, Homosexual," Medical Aspects of Human
         Sexuality, 5:112-24, Jun. 1971.

1835)    Friedberg, R. L.  "Early Recollections of Homo-
         sexuals as Indicators of Their Life Styles," Jour-
         nal of Individual Psychology, 31:196-204, 1975.

1836)    Frenkel, Richard E.  "Homosexuality:  A Psycho-
         logical Addiction," Medical Counterpoint, 6:17,
         Aug. -Sep. 1974.

1837)    Freund, Kurt.  "The Present State of the Phallo-
         metric Test of Erotic Preference," European Jour-
         nal of Behavioural Analysis and Modification, 1:27-
         28, Apr. 1975.

1838)    _____ and Others.  "Femininity and Preferred
         Partner Age in Homosexual and Heterosexual Males,"
         British Journal of Psychiatry, 125:442-46, 1974.

1839)           . "Heterosexual Aversion in Homosexual Males," British Journal of Psychiatry, 122:163-69, 1973.

1840)           . "Heterosexual Aversion in Homosexual Males: A Second Experiment," British Journal of Psychiatry, 125:177-80, 1974.

1841)           . "Heterosexual Interest in Homosexual Males," Archives of Sexual Behavior, 4:509-18, 1975.

1842)           . "Measuring Feminine Gender Identity in Homosexual Males," Archives of Sexual Behavior, 3:249-60, 1974.

1843)           . "Parent-Child Relations in Transsexual and Non-Transsexual Homosexual Males," British Journal of Psychiatry, 124:22-23, 1974.

1844)           . "The Phobic Theory of Male Homosexuality," Archives of General Psychiatry, 31:495-99, 1974.

1845)           . "The Trans-sexual Syndrome in Homosexual Males," Journal of Nervous and Mental Disease, 158:145-53, 1974.

1846) Gadpaille, Warren. "Brief Guide to Office Counseling: Adolescent Concern about Homosexuality," Medical Aspects of Human Sexuality, 7:105-09, Nov. 1973.

1847)           . "Homosexuality in Adolescent Males," Journal of the American Academy of Psychoanalysis, 3:361-71, 1975.

1848)           . "Male 'Physique' Magazines," Medical Aspects of Human Sexuality, 5:45, 48, 51, 54-57, 60-61, Apr. 1971.

1849)           . "More Frequent Male Homosexuality," Medical Aspects of Human Sexuality, 5:75-78, Oct. 1971.

1850)           . "Research into the Physiology of Maleness and Femaleness: Its Contributions to the

Etiology and Psychodynamics of Homosexuality,"
Archives of General Psychiatry, 26:193-206, 1972.

1851)          _____ . "What Is Acceptable Sexual Behavior?"
Sexual Behavior, 2:36-41, Jul. 1972.

1852)          Gandy, Patrick and Deisher, Robert.    "Young Male
Prostitutes:  The Physician's Role in Social Reha-
bilitation," Journal of the American Medical Association, 212:1661-66, Jun. 8, 1970.

1853)          Garfield, Sol L.    "Values:  An Issue in Psychotherapy:  Comments on a Case Study," Journal of Ab-
normal Psychology, 83:202-03, 1974.

1854)          Gartrell, Nanette; Kraemer, Helena; and Brodie, H.
Keith.    "Psychiatrists' Attitudes toward Female Homosexuality," Journal of Nervous and Mental Disease, 159:141-44, 1974.

1855)          Gaughan, Edward J. and Gaynor, Michael W.    "College Student Ratings of Arousal Value of Pornograph-
ic Photographs," Proceedings of the 81st Annual
Convention of the American Psychological Association, 8:409-10, 1973.

1856)          Gawienowski, Anthony M. and Hodges, Gary D.
"Homosexual Activity in Male Rats after P. Chloro-
phenylolanine:  Effect of Hypophysectomy and Testosterone," Physiology and Behavior, 7:551-55, 1971.

1857)          "Gay Liberation at the American Psychiatric Association," Science Newsletter, 104:389, Dec. 22,
1973.

1858)          Gershman, Harry.    "The Effect of Group Therapy
on Compulsive Homosexuality in Men and Women,"
American Journal of Psychoanalysis, 35:303-16,
1975.

1859)          _____ . "The Role of Core Gender Identity--the
Genesis of Perversions," American Journal of Psychoanalysis, 30:58-67, 1970.

1860)          _____ . "The Use of the Dream in the Therapy
of Homosexuality," American Journal of Psychoanalysis, 31:80-94, 1971.

1861)    Gillette, Paul J.   "How to Counsel and Treat Gay
         Patients:  Clinical Sequelae of Homosexuality," Mo-
         dern Medicine, 43:60-73, Apr. 15, 1975.

1862)    Gluckman, Jeffrey B.; Kleinman, Martin S.; and
         May, Allyn G.   "Primary Syphilis of the Rectum,"
         New York State Journal of Medicine, 74:2210-11,
         1974.

1863)    Gluckman, Laurie K.   "Transcultural Consideration
         of Homosexuality with Special Reference to the New
         Zealand Maori," Australian and New Zealand Jour-
         nal of Psychiatry, 8:121-25, 1974.

1864)    Gnepp, E. H.   "Biology, Mental Illness and Homo-
         sexuality:  A Comment on Public Affairs," Psycho-
         logy:  A Journal of Human Behavior, 12:60-61, Nov.
         1975.

1865)    Goldberg, Steven.   "What Is 'Normal'?   Logical As-
         pects of the Question of Homosexual Behavior,"
         Psychiatry, 38:227-43, 1975.

1866)    Golding, Stephen L. and Rorer, Leonard G.   "Il-
         lusory Correlation and Subjective Judgment [in Ror-
         schach Signs]," Journal of Abnormal Psychology,
         80:249-60, 1972.

1867)    Goldstein, Michael; Kant, Harold; Judd, Lewis;
         Rice, Clinton; and Green, Richard.   "Experience
         with Pornography:  Rapists, Pedophiles, Homosex-
         uals, Transsexuals, and Controls," Archives of
         Sexual Behavior, 1:1-15, 1971.

1868)    Gonen, Jay Y.   "Negative Identity in Homosexuals,"
         Psychoanalytic Review, 58:345-52, 1971.

1869)    Goodall, Kenneth.   "Homosexuality:  No Target for
         Behavior Modification," Psychology Today, Oct.
         1975, p. 59.

1870)    Goodhart, C. B.   "Female Homosexuality," Nature,
         239:174, Sep. 15, 1972.

1871)    Gottheil, Edward and Freedman, Abraham.   "Sexual
         Beliefs and Behavior of Single, Male Medical Stu-
         dents," Journal of the American Medical Association,
         212:1327-32, May 25, 1970.

1872)      Gould, Robert E.  "Homosexuality on Television,"
           Medical Aspects of Human Sexuality, 7:116-27, Oct.
           1973.

1873)      Gray, James J.  "Case Conference:  Behavior The-
           rapy in a Patient with Homosexual Fantasies and
           Heterosexual Anxiety," Journal of Behavior Therapy
           and Experimental Psychiatry, 1:225-32, 1970.

1874)      Green, Richard.  "Homosexuality as a Mental Ill-
           ness," International Journal of Psychiatry, 10:77-
           98 and 126-28, 1972.

1875)      Greenberg, Jerrold S.  "A Study of the Self-esteem
           and Alienation of Male Homosexuals," Journal of
           Psychology, 83:137-43, 1973.

1876)      Greenblatt, Robert B.; Jungck, Edwin C.; and Blum,
           Henry.  "Endocrinology of Sexual Behavior," Medi-
           cal Aspects of Human Sexuality, 6:110-31 at 124-29,
           Jan.  1972.

1877)      Greenspan, Barney.  "Some Reasons Why Most Ho-
           mosexual Relations Don't Last," Journal of Contem-
           porary Psychotherapy, 4:34-36, 1971.

1878)      Greenspan, Stanley I.  "Homosexual Fears in Ado-
           lescent Boys," Medical Aspects of Human Sexuality,
           8:158, 163, Nov. 1974.

1879)      Greenwald, Harold.  "Fashion Models and Sex,"
           Medical Aspects of Human Sexuality, 4:83-95, Jun.
           1970.

1880)      Griffiths, P. D. and Others.  "Homosexual Women:
           An Endocrine and Psychological Study," Journal of
           Endocrinology, 63:549-56, 1974.

1881)      Gundlach, Ralph H.  "Data on the Relation of Birth
           Order and Sex of Sibling of Lesbians Oppose the
           Hypothesis that Homosexuality Is Genetic," Annals
           of the New York Academy of Science, 197:179-81,
           1972.

1882)      Hadden, Samuel B.  "Group Therapy for Homosex-
           uals," Medical Aspects of Human Sexuality, 5:116-
           26, Jan. 1971.

1883)  _____.  "Group Psychotherapy with Homosexual Men," International Psychiatric Clinics, 8:81-94, 1971.

1884)  Haist, Mark and Hewitt, Jay.  "The Butch-Fem Dichotomy in Homosexual Behavior," Journal of Sex Research, 10:68-75, 1974.

1885)  Hanson, Richard W. and Adesso, Vincent J.  "A Multiple Behavioral Approach to Male Homosexual Behavior:  A Case Study," Journal of Behavior Therapy and Experimental Psychiatry, 3:323-25, 1972.

1886)  Harris, J. R. W.; Mahony, J. D. H.; Holland, J.; and McCann, J. S.  "Sexually Transmitted Diseases in Homosexual Relationships," Journal of the Irish Medical Association, 65:62-64, Feb. 5, 1972.

1887)  Harry, Joseph.  "Urbanization and the Gay Life [Gay Bars]," Journal of Sex Research, 10:238-47, 1974.

1888)  Hart, Roy H.  "Homosexuality:  A Sexual-object Distortion," Medical Counterpoint, 6:16, Aug.-Sep. 1974.

1889)  Hartman, John J.; Gibbard, Graham S.; and Issacharoff, Amnon.  "Bi-sexual Fantasy and Group Process," Contemporary Psychoanalysis, 9:302-26, 1973.

1890)  Hassell, Julie and Smith, Edward W.  "Female Homosexuals' Concepts of Self, Men, and Women," Journal of Personality Assessment, 39:154-59, 1975.

1891)  Hatterer, Lawrence J.  "A Critique of Green's 'Homosexuality as Mental Illness,'" International Journal of Psychiatry, 10:103-04, 1972.

1892)  _____.  "The Homosexual Dilemma," Psychiatric Opinion, 8:15-17, Feb. 1971.

1893)  _____.  "Nine Medical Myths about Homosexuality," Medical Opinion, 2:38-46, Jan. 1973.

1894)  Hatterer, Myra.  "The Problems of Women Married to Homosexual Men," American Journal of

Psychiatry, 131:275-78, 1974. (Summary in Psychiatry Digest, 35:24-26, Nov. 1974.)

1895)     Haynes, Stephen N. "Learning Theory and the Treatment of Homosexuality," Psychotherapy: Theory, Research and Practice, 7:91-94, 1970.

1896)     Hedblom, Jack H. "Dimensions of Lesbian Sexual Experience," Archives of Sexual Behavior, 2:329-41, 1973.

1897)     Herman, Steven H.; Barlow, David H.; and Agras, W. Stewart. "An Experimental Analysis of Exposure to 'Explicit' Heterosexual Stimuli as an Effective Variable in Changing Arousal Patterns of Homosexuals," Behavior Research Therapy, 12:335-45, 1974.

1898)     _____ ; _____ ; and _____ . "Exposure to Heterosexual Stimuli: An Effective Variable in Treating Homosexuality," Proceedings of the 79th Annual Convention of the American Psychological Association, 6:699-700, 1971.

1899)     _____ and Prewett, Michael. "An Experimental Analysis of Feedback to increase Sexual Arousal in Case of Homo- and Heterosexual Impotence: A Preliminary Report," Journal of Behavior Therapy and Experimental Psychology, 5:271-74, 1974.

1900)     Hoenig, J. and Duggan, Elaine. "Sexual and Other Abnormalities in the Family of a Transsexual," Psychiatria Clinica, 7:334-46, 1974.

1901)     Hoffman, Martin. "Homosexuality as a Mental Illness: Philosophic, Empirical, and Ecologic Remarks," International Journal of Psychiatry, 10:105-07, 1972.

1902)     _____ . "Homosexuality: A Reply to Socarides," Journal of the American Medical Association, 213:1495-96, Aug. 31, 1970.

1903)     _____ . "The Male Prostitute," Sexual Behavior, 2:16-21, Aug. 1972.

1904)     _____ ; Hadden, Samuel B.; Lazarus, Arnold A.;

Lamberd, W. G.; and Larson, Donald E. "View-points: What Outcome Can Be Expected in the Psychotherapy of Homosexuals?" Medical Aspects of Human Sexuality, 5:90-101, Dec. 1971.

1905)     Holder, W. R.; Roberts, D. P.; Duncan, W. C.; and Knox, J. M. "Preliminary Report on Spectinomycin H C1 in the Treatment of Gonorrhea in Homosexual Men," British Journal of Venereal Diseases, 48:274-76, 1972.

1906)     "Homosexual Doctors: Their Place and Influence in Medicine Today," Medical World News, 15:41-51, Jan. 4, 1974.

1907)     "The Homosexual Husband," Sexual Medicine Today, 15:25-28, 1974.

1908)     "Homosexuality and Testosterone," New England Journal of Medicine, 286:380-81, Feb. 17, 1972.

1909)     "Homosexuality--Opposing Camps," Medical World News, 14:5-6, Mar. 2, 1973.

1910)     "Homosexuals in Medicine," New England Journal of Medicine," 283:1295, Dec. 3, 1970.

1911)     "Homosexuals--To Cure, Not to Convert," Medical Dimensions, 1:48-50, Mar, 1972.

1912)     Hood, Ralph W. "Dogmatism and Opinion about Mental Illness," Psychological Reports, 32:1283-90, 1973.

1913)     Hooker, Evelyn and Chance, Paul. "Facts that Liberated the Gay Community," Psychology Today, Dec. 1975, pp. 52-55, 101.

1914)     Hopkins, June H. "Lesbian Signs on the Rorschach," British Journal of Projective Psychology and Personality Study, 15:7-14, Dec. 1970.

1915)     Hori, A. and Akimoto, T. "Two Cases of Fetishism," Kurume Medical Journal, 20:57-66, 1973.

1916)     Horn, Jack. "Problems of a Not So Gay Old Age," Psychology Today, Oct. 1974, p. 35.

1917)    Huff, Frederick W.   "The Desensitization of a Ho-
         mosexual," Behaviour Research and Therapy, 8:99-
         102, 1970.

1918)    Ince, Laurence P.   "Behavior Modification of Sex-
         ual Disorders," American Journal of Psychotherapy,
         17:446-51, 1973.

1919)    Ismail, A. A.; Adamopoulos, D. A.; Loraine, John
         A.; and Dove, G. A.   "Endocrine Function in Male
         and Female Homosexuals," Journal of Endocrinology,
         48:xxxvi-vii, 1970.

1920)    Jacobs, Sydney.   "Homosexuality, Gonorrhea, Jaun-
         dice," Journal of the Louisiana State Medical So-
         ciety, 125:133-37, Apr. 1973.

1921)    James, William H.   "Sex Ratios of Half-sibs of
         Male Homosexuals," British Journal of Psychiatry,
         118:93-94, 1971.

1922)    Janzen, William and Coe, William C.   "Clinical and
         Sign Prediction:  The Draw-A-Person and Female
         Homosexuality," Journal of Clinical Psychology, 31:
         757-65, 1975.

1923)    Jeffries, D. J.; James, W. H.; Jefferis, F. J. G.;
         MacLeod, K. G.; and Willcox, R. R.   "Australia
         (Hepatitis-associated) Antigen in Patients Attending
         a Venereal Disease Clinic," British Medical Jour-
         nal, 2:455-56, 1973.

1924)    Johnsgard, Keith W. and Schumacher, Ray M.   "The
         Experience of Intimacy in Group Psychotherapy with
         Male Homosexuals," Psychotherapy:  Theory, Re-
         search and Practice, 7:173-76, 1970.   (Reprinted
         in Ruitenbeek, no. 127, pp. 169-75)

1925)    Johnson, Josephine and O'Brien, Charles R.   "Mul-
         tiple Therapy with the Homosexual," Psychology:
         A Journal of Human Behavior, 12:23-26, Nov. 1975.

1926)    Johnson, William G.   "Some Applications of Homme's
         Coverant Control Therapy:  Two Case Reports," Be-
         haviour Therapy, 2:240-48, 1971.

1927)    Jones, Ivor H.   "Australian Students with Psychiatric

Illness," Medical Journal of Australia, 59:459-64, 1972.

1928)   Kahn, Michael H.; Mahrer, Alvin R.; and Bornstein, Robert.  "Male Psychosexual Development:  Role of Sibling Sex and Ordinal Position," Journal of Genetic Psychology, 121:187-96, 1972.

1929)   Kameny, Franklin E.  "Gay Liberation and Psychiatry," Psychiatric Opinion, 8:18-27, Feb. 1971. (Reprinted in McCaffrey, no. 101, pp. 182-94; and in Ruitenbeek, no. 127, pp. 70-82)

1930)   Kant, Harold.  "Exposure to Pornography and Sexual Behavior in Deviant and Normal Groups," Corrective Psychiatry and Journal of Social Therapy, 17:5-17, 1971.

1931)   Kanzer, Mark.  "Freud's Views on Bisexuality and Therapy:  Clinical Notes," International Journal of Psychiatry, 10:66-69, 1972.

1932)   Karlen, Arno.  "A Discussion of 'Homosexuality as Mental Illness,'" International Journal of Psychiatry, 10:108-13, 1972.

1933)   Kendrick, Sherril R. and McCullough, James P. "Sequential Phases of Covert Reinforcement and Covert Sensitization in the Treatment of Homosexuality," Journal of Behavior Therapy and Experimental Psychiatry, 3:229-31, 1972.

1934)   Kenyon, F. Edward.  "Homosexuality in the Female," British Journal of Hospital Medicine, 3:183-206, 1970.

1935)   _____.  "Homosexuality in the Female," British Journal of Psychiatry, special issue no. 9, pp. 185-200, 1975.

1936)   Kestenbaum, Clarice J.  "Adolescent Homosexual Experiences," Medical Aspects of Human Sexuality, 9:99-100, Jan. 1975.

1937)   Kestenberg, Judith S.  "A Developmental Approach to Disturbances of Sex-specific Identity," International Journal of Psychoanalysis, 52:99-102, 1971.

1938)    Ketterer, Warren A.   "Homosexuality and Venereal
         Disease," Medical Aspects of Human Sexuality, 5:
         114-29, Mar. 1971.

1939)    Khan, M. Masud.   "Ego-orgasm in Bisexual Love,"
         International Journal of Psychoanalysis, 1:143-49,
         1974.

1940)    Kiefer, C. Raymond.   "Evaluating Homosexual Man
         as Adoptive Father," Medical Aspects of Human
         Sexuality, 5:33, 102, Dec. 1971.

1941)    Kirkpatrick, Martha J.   "Homosexuality in Relation
         to Societal Restrictions," Medical Aspects of Human
         Sexuality, 5:220, Feb. 1971.

1942)    Kohlenberg, Robert J.   "Treatment of a Homosexual
         Pedophiliac Using in vivo Desensitization:   A Case
         Study," Journal of Abnormal Psychology, 83:192-
         203, 1974.

1943)    Kolodny, Robert C.   "Hormones and Homosexuality,"
         Annals of Internal Medicine, 79:897, 1973.

1944)    _____; Masters, William H.; Hendryx, Julie; and
         Toro, Gelson.   "Plasma Testosterone and Semen An-
         alysis in Male Homosexuals," New England Journal
         of Medicine, 285:1170-74, Nov. 18, 1971.

1945)    _____; _____; Jacobs, Laurence S.; Toro,
         Gelson; and Daughaday, William H.   "Plasma Gona-
         dotropins and Prolactin in Male Homosexuals,"
         Lancet, 2:18-20, July 1, 1972.

1946)    Koptagel, Günsel.   "The Pictorial Expressions Ser-
         ving as a Means of Self-satisfaction for a Young
         Man with Homosexual and Transvestite Tendencies,"
         Confinia Psychiartica, 15:71-76, 1972.

1947)    Kraft, Tom.   "A Case of Homosexuality Treated by
         Combined Behaviour Therapy and Psychotherapy:   A
         Total Assessment," Psychotherapy and Psychosoma-
         tics, 19:342-58, 1971.

1948)    _____.   "Systematic Desensitization in the Treat-
         ment of Homosexuality," Behaviour Research and
         Therapy, 8:319, 1970.

1949)    Kremer, Malvina W.   "Lesbian Patients," Medical
         Aspects of Human Sexuality, 8:219-21, Oct. 1974.

1950)    Kuethe, James L.   "Children's Schemata of Man
         and Woman: A Comparison with the Schemata of
         Heterosexual and Homosexual Populations," Journal
         of Psychology, 90:249-58, 1975.

1951)    Lachmann, Frank M.   "Homosexuality: Some Diag-
         nostic Perspectives and Dynamic Considerations,"
         American Journal of Psychotherapy, 29:254-60, 1975.

1952)    Langevin, Ron; Stanford, A.; and Block, R.   "The
         Effect of Relaxation Instructions on Erotic Arousal
         in Homosexual and Heterosexual Males," Behavior
         Therapy, 6:453-58, 1975.

1953)    Larson, Donald E.   "An Adaptation of the Feldman
         and MacCulloch Approach to Treatment of Homosex-
         uality by the Application of Anticipatory Avoidance
         Learning," Behaviour Research and Therapy, 8:209-
         10, 1970.

1954)    Latorre, Ronald A. and Borgeson, Amy L.   "Body-
         parts Satisfaction and Sexual Preferences," Psycho-
         logical Reports, 36:430, 1975.

1955)    Lebovitz, Phil S.   "Feminine Behavior in Boys:
         Aspects of Its Outcome," American Journal of Psy-
         chiatry, 128:1283-89, 1972.

1956)    Lee-Evans, M. and Others.   "Penile Plethymsmo-
         graphic Assessment of Sexual Orientation," European
         Journal of Behavioural Analysis and Modification,
         1:20-26, Apr. 1975.

1957)    _____.   "Reply to K. Freund's Observations on
         Penile Plethymsmographic Assessment of Sexual
         Orientation," European Journal of Behavioural An-
         alysis and Modification, 1:29, Apr. 1975.

1958)    Lesse, Stanley.   "The Current Confusion over Ho-
         mosexuality," American Journal of Psychotherapy,
         27:151-54, 1973.

1959)    _____.   "To Be or Not to Be an Illness?   That
         Is the Question--or, the Status of Homosexuality,"

American Journal of Psychotherapy, 28:1-3, 1974.

1960)    Lester, David. "The Relationship between Paranoid Delusions and Homosexuality," Archives of Sexual Behavior, 4:285-94, 1975.

1961)    Levin, Max. "The Lesbians--Bright Dream, Sad End," Current Medical Dialog, 42:43-44, Jan. 1975.

1962)    Lewis, Mary A. and Schoenfeldt, Lyle F. "Developmental-interest Factors Associated with Homosexuality," Journal of Consulting and Clinical Psychology, 41:291-93, 1973.

1963)    Lewis, Thomas H. "Oglala (Sioux) Concepts of Homosexuality and the Determinants of Sexual Identification," Journal of the American Medical Association, 225, 312-13, Jul. 16, 1973.

1964)    Liss, Jay L. and Weltner, Amos. "Change in Homosexual Orientation," American Journal of Psychotherapy, 27:102-04, 1973.

1965)    Lockwood, Ronald. "Gay on Gay," Journal of Clinical Child Psychology, 3:16-17, 1974.

1966)    Loney, Jan. "Background Factors, Sexual Experiences, and Attitudes toward Treatment in Two 'Normal' Homosexual Samples," Journal of Consulting and Clinical Psychology, 38:57-65, 1972.

1967)    _____. "Family Dynamics in Homosexual Women," Archives of Sexual Behavior, 2:343-50, 1973.

1968)    _____. "An MMPI Measure of Maladjustment in a Sample of 'Normal' Homosexual Men," Journal of Clinical Psychology, 27:486-88, 1971.

1969)    LoPiccolo, Joseph. "Case Study: Systematic Desensitization of Homosexuality," Behavior Therapy, 2:394-99, 1971.

1970)    _____; Stewart, Rita; and Watkins, Bruce. "Treatment of Erectile Failure and Ejaculatory Incompetence of Homosexual Etiology," Journal of Behavior Therapy and Experimental Psychiatry, 3:233-36, 1972.

1971)    Loraine, John A.  "Hormones and Homosexuality,"
         New Scientist, 53,270-71, Feb. 3, 1972.

1972)    _____; Adamopoulos, D. A.; Kirkham, K. E.;
         Ismail, A. A.; and Dove, G. O.  "Patterns of Hor-
         mone Excretion in Male and Female Homosexuals,"
         Nature, 234:552-55, Dec. 3, 1971.

1973)    _____; _____; Ismail, A. A.; and Dove, G.
         A.  "Endocrine Function in Male and Female Ho-
         mosexuals," British Medical Journal, 4:406-09, 1970.

1974)    Lynch, Vincent P.  "Parasite Transmission," Jour-
         nal of the American Medical Association, 222:1309-
         10, Dec. 4, 1972.

1975)    MacCulloch, M. J.; Birtles, C. J.; and Feldman,
         M. P.  "Anticipatory Avoidance Learning for the
         Treatment of Homosexuality:  Recent Developments
         and an Automatic Aversion Therapy System," Be-
         havior Therapy, 2:151-69, 1971.  (Reprinted in
         Cyril M.  Franks and C. Terence Wilson [eds.],
         Annual Review of Behavior Therapy, Theory and
         Practice [New York:  Brunner-Mazel, Publishers,
         1973], pp. 203-17)

1976)    _____; Feldman, M. P.; and Bancroft, John H.
         "Aversion Therapy of Homosexuality," British Jour-
         nal of Psychiatry, 116:673-77, 1970.

1977)    _____ and Sambrooks, J. E.  "Sexual Interest
         Latencies in Aversion Therapy:  A Preliminary Re-
         port," Archives of Sexual Behavior, 3:289-99, 1974.

1978)    MacDonald, A. P.; Huggins, Jim; Young, Susan;
         and Swanson, Richard A.  "Attitudes toward Homo-
         sexuality:  Preservation of Sex Morality or the
         Double Standard?" Journal of Consulting and Clini-
         cal Psychology, 40:161, 1973.

1979)    MacDonough, Tomi S.  "A Critique of the First
         Feldman and MacCulloch Avoidance Conditioning
         Treatment of Homosexuals," Behavior Therapy, 3:
         104-11, 1972.

1980)    Mackay, John W.  "The Doctor and the Homosex-
         ual," Medical Journal of Australia, 1:1015 and 1316,
         1973.

1981)    Maletzky, Barry M.   "'Assisted' Covert Sensitiza-
         tion:  A Preliminary Report," Behavior Therapy,
         4:117-19, 1973.

1982)    _____ and George, Frederick S.   "The Treatment
         of Homosexuality by 'Assisted' Covert Sensitization,"
         Behavior Research and Therapy, 11:655-57, 1973.

1983)    Malkin, Edward E.   "Stoicism and Paranoia," Psy-
         chiatry, 38:186-92, 1975.

1984)    Malmquist, Carl P.   "Premonitory Signs of Homi-
         cidal Aggression in Juveniles--[Homosexual Threats],"
         American Journal of Psychiatry, 128:461-65, 1971.

1985)    Manaster, Guy J. and King, Marc.   "Early Recol-
         lections of Male Homosexuals," Journal of Individual
         Psychology, 29:26-33, 1973.

1986)    Mandel, Karl H.   "Preliminary Report on a New
         Aversion Therapy for Male Homosexuals," Behav-
         iour Research and Therapy, 8:93-95, 1970.

1987)    Manosevitz, Martin.   "The Development of Male Ho-
         mosexuality," Journal of Sex Research, 8:31-40,
         1972.

1988)    _____ .   "Early Sexual Behavior in Adult Homo-
         sexual and Adult Heterosexual Males," Journal of
         Abnormal Psychology, 76:396-402, 1970.

1989)    _____ .   "Education and MMPI MF Scores in Ho-
         mosexual and Heterosexual Males," Journal of Con-
         sulting and Clinical Psychology, 36:395-99, 1971.

1990)    _____ .   "Item Analyses of the MMPI MF Scale
         using Homosexual and Heterosexual Males," Journal
         of Consulting and Clinical Psychology, 35:395-99,
         1970.

1991)    Marberg, Hilde M.   "Fragmentary Psychoanalytic
         Treatment of Acute Homosexual Panic," Psychoan-
         alytic Review, 59:295-304, 1972.

1992)    Margolese, M. Sydney.   "The Homosexual:  Is It
         Chemistry?"  Medical World News, 12:4-5, Apr.
         23, 1971.

1993)          . "Homosexuality: A New Endocrine Cor-
relate," Hormones and Behavior, 1:151-55, 1970.

1994)          and Janiger, Oscar. "Androsterone-
etiocholanolone Ratios in Male Homosexuals," British Medical Journal, 3:207-10, 1973.

1995) Marmor, Judd. "Dynamic Psychotherapy and Behavior Therapy: Are They Irreconcilable?" Archives of General Psychiatry, 24:22-28, 1971.

1996)          . "Homosexuality and Cultural Value Systems," American Journal of Psychiatry, 130:1208-
09, 1973.

1997)          . "Homosexuality in Males," Psychiatric
Annals, 1:44-59, Dec. 1971.

1998)          . "Homosexuality--Mental Illness or Moral
Dilemma?" International Journal of Psychiatry, 10:
114-17, 1972.

1999)          . "'Normal' and 'Deviant' Sexual Behavior,"
Journal of the American Medical Association, 217:
165-70, Jul. 12, 1971.  (Reprinted in Anne M. Ju-
hasz [ed.], Sexual Development and Behavior: Selected Readings [Homewood, Ill.: Dorsey Press,
1973], pp. 89-107 [chap. 8]; in Judd Marmor, Psychiatry in Transition [New York: Brunner-Mazel,
Publishers, 1974], pp. 77-89 [chap. 7]; and in Goode
and Troiden, no. 55, pp. 45-57)

2000)          ; Voth, Harold M.; Thompson, Norman L.;
Bieber, Toby; Hooker, Evelyn; Drakeford, John W.;
and Socarides, Charles W. "Viewpoints: Is Homosexuality Pathologic or a Normal Variant of Sexuality?" Medical Aspects of Human Sexuality, 7:10-29,
Dec. 1973.

2001) Marquis, John N. "Orgasmic Reconditioning:
Changing Sexual Choice through Controlling Mastur-
bation Fantasies," Journal of Behavior Therapy and
Experimental Psychiatry, 1:263-71, 1970.

2002) Mastellone, Max. "Aversion Therapy: A New Use
for the Old Rubber Band," Journal of Behavior Therapy and Experimental Psychiatry, 5:311-12, 1974.

2003)     Mathews, Andrew; Bancroft, John H.; and Slater,
          Patrick.   "The Principal Components of Sexual Pre-
          ference," Journal of Social and Clinical Psychology,
          11:35-43, 1972.

2004)     Maurer, R. B.   "Health Care and the Gay Commu-
          nity," Postgraduate Medicine, 58:127-30, 1975.

2005)     Mavissakalian, Matig; Blanchard, Edward B.; Abel,
          Gene C.; and Barlow, David H.   "Responses to
          Complex Erotic Stimuli in Homosexual and Hetero-
          sexual Males," British Journal of Psychiatry, 126:
          252-57, 1975.

2006)     May, Robert.   "Further Studies on Deprivation/En-
          hancement Patterns," Journal of Personality Asses-
          ment, 39:116-22, 1975.

2007)     McCawley, Austin.   "Paranoia and Homosexuality:
          Schreber Reconsidered," New York State Journal of
          Medicine, 71:1506-13, 1971.

2008)     McConaghy, N.   "Aversion Therapy," Seminars in
          Psychiatry, 4:139-44, 1972.

2009)     _____.   "Aversion Therapy of Homosexuality,"
          Current Psychiatric Therapies, 12:38-47, 1972.

2010)     _____.   "Aversive and Positive Conditioning
          Treatments of Homosexuality," Behaviour Research
          and Therapy, 13:309-19, 1975.

2011)     _____.   "Aversive Therapy of Homosexuality:
          Measures of Efficacy," American Journal of Psy-
          chiatry, 127:1221-24, 1971.

2012)     _____.   "The Doctor and Homosexuality," Medi-
          cal Journal of Australia, 1:68-70 and 1015-16, 1973.

2013)     _____.   "Measurement of Change in Penile Di-
          mensions," Archives of Sexual Behavior, 3:381-88,
          1974.

2014)     _____.   "Penile Response Conditioning and Its
          Relationship to Aversion Therapy in Homosexuals,"
          Behaviour Therapy, 1:213-21, 1970.

2015)        _____. "Subjective and Penile Plethysmograph
             Responses to Aversion Therapy for Homosexuality:
             A Follow-up Study," British Journal of Psychiatry,
             117:555-60, 1970.

2016)        _____ and Barr, R. F. "Classical Avoidance
             and Backward Conditioning Treatments of Homosex-
             uality," British Journal of Psychiatry, 122:151-62,
             1973.

2017)        _____; Proctor, N.; and Barr, R. F. "Subjec-
             tive and Penile Plethysmography Responses to
             Aversion Therapy for Homosexuality: A Partial Re-
             plication," Archives of Sexual Behavior, 2:65-78,
             1972.

2018)        McCrady, Richard E. "A Forward-fading Techni-
             que for Increasing Heterosexual Responsiveness in
             Male Homosexuals," Journal of Behavior Therapy
             and Experimental Psychiatry, 4:257-61, 1973.

2019)        McDougall, Joyce. "Primal Scene and Sexual Per-
             version," International Journal of Psychoanalysis,
             53:371-84, 1972.

2020)        "Medical Advice for Homosexuals," Lancet, 2:218,
             Jul. 25, 1970.

2021)        Meyer, Jon K. "Clinical Variants among Applicants
             for Sex Re-assignment," Archives of Sexual Behav-
             ior, 3:527-58, 1974.

2022)        Meyer, Robert G. and Freeman, William. "The
             Alteration of Sexual Preferences via Conditioning
             Therapies," Proceedings of the 81st Annual Conven-
             tion of the American Psychological Association, 8:
             923-24, 1973.

2023)        Meyer, V. and Levy, R. "Behavioral Treatment
             of a Homosexual with Compulsive Rituals," British
             Journal of Medical Psychology, 42:63-67, 1970.

2024)        Miller, Derek. "The Treatment of Adolescent Sex-
             ual Disturbances," International Journal of Child
             Psychotherapy, 2:93-126, 1973.

2025)        Miller, Michael M.; Shainess, Natalie; Bieber, Toby;

Sagarin, Edward; and Willis, Stanley. "Viewpoints: Why Are the Women's Fashion and Hair-styling Industries Dominated by Homosexual Males?" Medical Aspects of Human Sexuality, 5:60-67, May 1971.

2026)   Miller, Milton L. and Monroe, John T. "Psychoanalytic Therapy of Homosexuality," Psychiatric Forum, 3:15-21, 1973.

2027)   Mitler, Merrill M.; Morden, Bruce; Levine, Seymour; and Dement, William. "The Effects of Parachorophenylalanine on the Mating Behavior of Male Rats," Physiological Behavior, 8:1147-50, 1972.

2028)   Moan, Charles E. and Heath, Robert G. "Septal Stimulation for the Initiation of Heterosexual Behavior in a Homosexual Male," Journal of Behavior Therapy and Experimental Psychiatry, 3:23-30, 1972.

2029)   Money, John. "Sexual Dimorphism and Homosexual Gender Identity," Psychological Bulletin, 74:425-40, 1970.

2030)   _____. "Strategy, Ethics, Behavior Modification and Homosexuality," Archives of Sexual Behavior, 2:79-81, 1972.

2031)   _____ and Brennan, John G. "Heterosexual versus Homosexual Attitudes: Male Partners' Perception of the Feminine Image of Male Transsexuals," Journal of Sex Research, 6:193-209, 1970.

2032)   Moore, Peter. "'Homosexual': The Label that Damns," Canadian Medical Association Journal, 106:1071-74, 1972.

2033)   Moran, P. A. P. "Familial Effects in Schizophrenia and Homosexuality," Australian and New Zealand Journal of Psychiatry, 6:116-19, 1972.

2034)   Morgenthaler, Fritz. "Panel: Disturbances of Male and Female Identity as Met with in Psychoanalytic Practice," International Journal of Psychoanalysis, 51:251-54, 1970.

2035)   Morris, Philip A. "Doctors' Attitudes to Homosexuality," British Journal of Psychiatry, 122:435-36, 1973.

2036)    Muller, D.; Roeder, F.; and Orthner, H.    "Further
         Results of Stereotaxis in the Human Hypothalmus in
         Sexual Deviations," Neurochirurgia, 16:113-26, 1973.

2037)    Myrick, Fred L.    "Attitudinal Differences between
         Heterosexually and Homosexually Oriented Males and
         between Covert and Overt Male Homosexuals," Jour-
         nal of Abnormal Psychology, 83:81-86, 1974.

2038)    _____." "Homosexual Types: An Empirical In-
         vestigation," Journal of Sex Research, 10:226-37,
         1974.

2039)    Nazemi, Malek M.; Musher, Daniel M.; Schell,
         Ronald F.; and Milo, Simcha.    "Syphilitic Proctitis
         in a Homosexual," Journal of the American Medical
         Association, 231:389, Jan. 27, 1975.

2040)    Neumarkt, Paul A.    "Kafka's 'A Hunger Artist':
         The Ego in Isolation," American Imago, 27:109-21,
         1970.

2041)    "Neurosurgery for the Paedophilic Homosexual,"
         World Medicine, 6:42-45, 1970.

2042)    "New York City's Former Health Chief [Howard
         Brown] Admits He's Homosexual," Medical World
         News, 14:18-19, Oct. 26, 1973.

2043)    Newman, Lawrence E. and Stoller, Robert J.    "The
         Oedipal Situation in Male Transsexualism," British
         Journal of Medical Psychology, 44:295-303, 1971.

2044)    Nicolis, Giorgio and Gabrilove, Lester J.    "Homo-
         sexuals in Boston and St. Louis," New England
         Journal of Medicine, 290:411-12, Feb. 14, 1974.

2045)    Norris, Linda.    "Comparison of Two Groups in a
         Southern State Women's Prison: Homosexual Be-
         havior vs. Non-homosexual Behavior," Psychologi-
         cal Reports, 34:75-78, 1974.

2046)    Nuehring, Elane M.; Fein, Sara B.; and Tyler,
         Mary.    "The Gay College Student: Perspectives
         for Mental Health Professionals," Counseling Psy-
         chologist, 4:64-72, 1974.

2047)    Ohlson, E. LaMonte.    "A Preliminary Investigation

into the Self-disclosing Ability of Male Homosexuals,"
Psychology: A Journal of Human Behavior, 11:21-
25, 1974.

2048)          and Wilson, Marilyn.  "Differentiating Female Homosexuals from Female Heterosexuals by
Use of the MMPI," Journal of Sex Research, 10:
308-15, 1974.

2049)  O'Neal, Thomas P.  "Homosexual Acts Related to
Hospitals," Medicolegal Bulletin, 206:1-5, Jun. 1970.

2050)  Orwin, Arnold; James, Sheelah; and Turner, R.
Keith.  "Sex Chromosome Abnormalities, Homosexuality, and Psychological Treatment," British Journal of Psychiatry, 124:293-95, 1974.

2051)  Ovesey, Lionel and Person, Ethel.  "Gender Identity and Sexual Psychopathology in Men: A Psychodynamic Analysis of Homosexuality, Transsexualism,
and Transvestism," Journal of the American Academy of Psychoanalysis, 1:53-72, 1973.

2052)  Owen, Robert L. and Hill, J. Lawrence.  "Rectal
and Pharyngeal Gonorrhea in Homosexual Men,"
Journal of the American Medical Association, 220:
1315-18, Jun. 5, 1972.

2053)  Pacion, Stanley J.  "Lawrence of Arabia," Medical
Aspects of Human Sexuality, 5:122-39, Apr. 1971.

2054)          .  "Leonardo da Vinci: A Psychosexual
Enigma," Medical Aspects of Human Sexuality, 5:
34-41, Dec. 1971.

2055)          .  "The Life of Nero: Sex and the Fall of
the Roman Empire," Medical Aspects of Human Sexuality, 5:171-85, Mar. 1971.

2056)          .  "Sparta: An Experiment in State-fos-
tered Homosexuality," Medical Aspects of Human
Sexuality, 4:28-32, Apr. 1970.

2057)  Papaevangeliou, George.  "Hepatitis-associated An-
tigen in Venereal Disease Clinic Patients," British
Medical Journal, 3:172, 1973.

2058)  Papatheophilou, R.; James, Sheelah; and Orwin,

Arnold. "Electroencephalographic Findings in Treatment-seeking Homosexuals Compared with Heterosexuals: A Controlled Study," British Journal of Psychiatry, 127:63-66, 1975.

2059) Pariser, Harry and Marino, A. F. "Gonorrhea--Frequently Unrecognized Reservoirs," Southern Medical Journal, 63:198-201, 1970.

2060) Parks, Gary A. and Others. "Variation in Pituitary-gonadal Function in Adolescent Male Homosexuals and Heterosexuals." Journal of Clinical Endocrinology and Metabolism, 39:796-801, 1974.

2061) Pattison, E. Mansell. "Confusing Concepts about the Concept of Homosexuality," Psychiatry, 37:340-49, 1974.

2062) Pauly, Ira B. and Goldstein, Steven G. "Physicians' Attitudes in Treating Male Homosexuals," Medical Aspects of Human Sexuality, 4:26-45, Dec. 1970.

2063) Pedder, J. R. "Psychiatric Referral of Patients in a Venereal Disease Clinic," British Journal of Venereal Diseases, 46:54-57, 1970.

2064) Perkins, Muriel W. "Homosexuality in Female Monozygotic Twins," Behavior Genetics, 3:387-88, 1973.

2065) Person, Ethel and Ovesey, Lionel. "The Transsexual Syndrome in Males: II. Secondary Transsexualism," American Journal of Psychotherapy, 28:174-93, 1974.

2066) Pierce, David M. "MMPI HSX Scale Differences between Active and Situational Homosexuality," Journal of Forensic Psychology, 4:31-38, 1972.

2067) _____. "Test and Nontest Correlates of Active and Situational Homosexuality," Psychology: A Journal of Human Behavior, 10:23-26, 1973.

2068) Pillard, Richard C.; Rose, Robert M.; and Sherwood, Michael. "Plasma Testosterone Levels in Homosexual Men," Archives of Sexual Behavior, 3:453-58, 1974.

2069)    Pittman, Frank S. and DeYoung, Carol D. "The Treatment of Homosexuals in Heterogeneous Groups," International Journal of Group Psychotherapy, 21: 62-73, 1971.

2070)    Poole, Kenneth. "The Etiology of Gender Identity and the Lesbian," Journal of Social Psychology, 87:51-57, 1972.

2071)    Prescott, R. G. W. "Mounting Behavior in the Female Cat," Nature, 228:1106-07, Dec. 12, 1970.

2072)    "Psychosexual Development," British Medical Journal, 1:319-20, 1970.

2073)    Pustel, G.; Sternlicht, M.; and Deutsch, M. "Feminine Tendencies in Figure Drawings," Journal of Clinical Psychology, 27:260-61, 1971.

2074)    Quinn, J. T.; Harbison, J. J. M.; and McAllister, H. "An Attempt to Shape Human Penile Response," Behaviour Research and Therapy, 8:213-16, 1970.

2075)    Raboch, Jan and Sipova, Iva. "Intelligence in Homosexuals, Transsexuals, and Hypogonadropic Eunochoids," Journal of Sex Research, 10:156-61, 1974.

2076)    Racz, I. "Homosexuality among Syphilitic Patients," British Journal of Venereal Diseases, 46:117, 1970.

2077)    Rao, Hari V. "Abnormal Sexual Behavior of Isolated Males of Cimex Lectularius L," Indian Journal of Experimental Biology, 10:295-97, 1972.

2078)    Ratnatunga, C. S. "Gonococcal Pharyngitis," British Journal of Venereal Diseases, 48:184-86, 1972.

2079)    Raychaudhuri, Manas and Mukerji, Kamal. "Rorschach Differentials of Homosexuality in Male Convicts: An Examination of Wheeler and Schafer Signs," Journal of Personality Assessment, 35:22-26, 1970.

2080)    Regenstein, Quentin R.; Williams, Gordon H.; and Rose, Leslie I. "Influence of Perinatal Progesterone on Sexual Activity in the Male Guinea Pig," Journal of Psychiatric Research, 12:149-51, 1975.

2081)     Rehm, Lynn P. and Rozensky, Ronald H.   "Multi-
          ple Behavior Therapy Techniques with a Homosexual
          Client:  A Case Study," Journal of Behavior The-
          rapy and Experimental Psychiatry, 5:53-57, 1974.

2082)     Renik, Owen.   "Awareness of the Back of the Body
          and Homosexual Impulses," Perceptual and Motor
          Skills, 33:1268, 1971.

2083)     Rhodes, Robert J.   "Homosexual Aversion Therapy:
          Electric Shock Technique," Journal of the Kansas
          Medical Society, 74:103-05, Mar. 1973.

2084)     Ritchey, Michael G. and Leff, Arnold M.   "Vene-
          real Disease Control among Homosexuals:  An Out-
          reach Program," Journal of the American Medical
          Association, 232:509-10, May 5, 1975.

2085)     Roback, Howard B.; Langevin, Ron; and Zajac,
          Yaroslaw.   "Sex of Free Choice Figure Drawings
          by Homosexual and Heterosexual Subjects," Journal
          of Personality Assessment, 38:154-55, 1974.

2086)     Robertiello, Richard C.   "A More Positive View of
          Perversions," Psychoanalytic Review, 58:467-71,
          1971.   (Reprinted in Ruitenbeek, no. 127, pp. 176-
          80.)

2087)     _____.   "One Psychiatrist's View of Female Ho-
          mosexuality," Journal of Contemporary Psychothe-
          rapy, 5:31-34, 1972.

2088)     Robertson, Graham.   "Parent-Child Relationships
          and Homosexuality," British Journal of Psychiatry,
          121:525-28, 1972.

2089)     Rodin, P. and Monteiro, G. E.   "Gonococcal Phar-
          yngitis," British Journal of Venereal Diseases, 48:
          182-83, 1972.

2090)     Roeder, Fritz.   "Homosexuality Burned Out," Med-
          ical World News, Sep. 25, 1970.

2091)     Roesler, Thomas and Deisher, Robert W.   "Youth-
          ful Male Homosexuality:  Homosexual Experience
          and the Process of Developing Homosexual Identity
          in Males aged 16 to 22 Years," Journal of the

American Medical Association, 219:1018-23, Feb.
21, 1972.

2092)    Ross, H. Laurence.   'Odd Couples: Homosexuals
         in Heterosexual Marriages," Sexual Behavior, Jul.
         1972, pp. 42-49.

2093)    Ross, Michael W.   "Relationships between Sex Role
         and Sex Orientation in Homosexual Men," New Zea-
         land Psychologist, 4:25-29, Apr. 1975.

2094)    Rossi, R.; Delmonte, P.; and Terracciano, P.
         "The Problem of the Relationship between Homo-
         sexuality and Schizophrenia," Archives of Sexual
         Behavior, 1:357-62, 1971.

2095)    Roth, Loren H.   "Territoriality and Homosexuality
         in a Male Prison Population," American Journal of
         Orthopsychiatry, 41:510-13, 1971.

2096)    Rothenberg, Albert.   'Is There a Relationship be-
         tween Homosexuality and Creativity?" Sexual Behav-
         ior, Feb. 1972, p. 50.

2097)    Roy, David.   "Lytton Strachey and the Masochistic
         Basis of Homosexuality," Psychoanalytic Review,
         59:579-84, 1972.

2098)    Rupp, Joseph C.   "Sudden Death in the Gay World,"
         Medicine, Science, and the Law, 10:189-91, 1971.

2099)    Rutner, Ivan T.   "A Double-Barrel Approach to
         Modification of Homosexual Behavior," Psychological
         Reports, 26:355-58, 1970.

2100)    Ryrie, Christine and Brown, J. Christie.   "Endo-
         crine Function in Homosexuals," British Medical
         Journal, 4:685, 1970.

2101)    Sagarin, Edward.   "Homosexuality as a Social Move-
         ment: First Reports from the Barricades," Jour-
         nal of Sex Research, 9:289-94, 1973.

2102)    _____.   "Language of the Homosexual Subculture,"
         Medical Aspects of Human Sexuality, 4:37-41, Apr.
         1970.

2103)    _____.   "Sex, Law, and the Changing Society,"

*Medical Aspects of Human Sexuality*, 4:103-07, Oct. 1970.

2104) Saghir, Marcel T. "Counseling the Homosexual," *Medical Aspects of Human Sexuality*, 9:149-50, Feb. 1975.

2105) _____ and Robins, Eli. "Male and Female Homosexuality: Natural History," *Comprehensive Psychiatry*, 12:503-10, 1971.

2106) _____; _____; Walbran, Bonnie; and Gentry, Kathye A. "Homosexuality: III. Psychiatric Disorders and Disability in the Male Homosexual," *American Journal of Psychiatry*, 126:1079-86, 1970.

2107) _____; _____; _____; _____. "Homosexuality: IV. Psychiatric Disorders and Disability in the Female Homosexual," *American Journal of Psychiatry*, 127:147-54, 1970.

2108) Salter, Leo G. and Melville, Charles. " A Reeducative Approach to Homosexual Behavior: A Case Study and Treatment Recommendations," *Psychotherapy: Theory, Research and Practice*, 9:166-67, 1972.

2109) Salzman, Leon. "Sexual Problems in Adolescence," *Contemporary Psychoanalysis*, 10:189-207, 1974.

2110) Sambrooks, Jan E. and MacCulloch, M. J. "Sexual Orientation Method Questionnaire and Its Use in the Assessment and Management of Cases of Sexual Dysfunction," *Behavioral Engineering*, 2:1-6, 1974.

2111) Saper, Bernard. "A Report on Behavior Therapy with Outpatient Clinic Patients," *Psychiatric Quarterly*, 45:209-15, 1971.

2112) Schatzberg, Alan; Westfall, Michael; Blumetti, Anthony; and Birk, Lee. "Effeminacy: I. A. Quantitative Rating Scale," *Archives of Sexual Behavior*, 4:31-41, 1975.

2113) Schatzman, Morton. "Paranoia or Persecution: The Case of Schreber," *International Journal of Psychiatry*, 10:53-78, 1972.

2114)    Schiffer, Danella.   "Relation of Inhibition of Curi-
         osity to Homosexuality," Psychological Reports,
         27:771-76, 1970.

2115)    Schimel, John L.   "Homosexual Fantasies in Heter-
         osexual Males," Medical Aspects of Human Sexual-
         ity, 6:138-51, Feb. 1972.

2116)    _____.  "The Patient Who Thinks He Is a 'La-
         tent' Homosexual," Medical Aspects of Human Sex-
         uality, 9:125-26, Sep. 1975.

2117)    Schnelle, John F.; Kennedy, Martha; Rutledge, Al-
         vin W.; and Golden, Stanley B. Jr.   "Pupillary
         Response as Indication of Sexual Preference in a
         Juvenile Correctional Institution," Journal of Clini-
         cal Psychology, 30:146-50, 1974.

2118)    Schwartz, Michael.   "Military Psychiatry--Theory
         and Practice in Noncombat Areas:  The Role Con-
         flicts of the Psychiatrist," Comprehensive Psychi-
         atry, 12:520-25, 1971.

2119)    Schweitzer, Lawrence; Simons, Richard C.; and
         Weidenbacher, Richard.   "Cryptorchism and Homo-
         sexuality," Psychoanalytic Quarterly, 39:251-68,
         1970.

2120)    Schwitzgebel, R. K.   "Learning Theory Approaches
         to the Treatment of Criminal Behavior," Seminars
         in Psychiatry, 3:328-44, 1971.

2121)    Sechrist, L. and Olson, A. K.   "Graffiti in Four
         Types of Institutions of Higher Education," Journal
         of Sex Research, 7:62-71, 1971.

2122)    Segal, Bernard and Sims, Joseph.   "Covert Sensiti-
         zation with a Homosexual:  A Controlled Reply,"
         Journal of Consulting and Clinical Psychology, 39:
         259-63, 1972.

2123)    Seidenberg, Robert.   "The Accursed Race," Psychi-
         atric Opinion, 8:6-14, Feb. 1971.   (Reprinted in
         Ruitenbeek, no. 127, pp. 159-68)

2124)    Seitz, Frank C.; Anderson, Dennis O.; and Braucht,
         George N.   "A Comparative Analysis of Rorschach

Signs of Homosexuality," Psychological Reports, 35:1163-69, 1974.

2125)    Serban, George. "The Phenomenological Concept of Homosexuality," Existential Psychiatry, 7:89-102, 1970.

2126)    Shealy, Allen E. "Combining Behavior Therapy and Cognitive Therapy in Treatment of Homosexuality," Psychotherapy: Theory, Research and Practice, 9: 221-22, 1972.

2127)    Shoemaker, Ted. 'Operation to Relieve Perversion," Science News, 97:50, Jan. 10, 1970.

2128)    Siegelman, Marvin. "Adjustment of Homosexual and Heterosexual Women," British Journal of Psychiatry, 120:477-81, 1972.

2129)    _____. "Adjustment of Male Homosexuals and Heterosexuals," Archives of Sexual Behavior, 1:9-25, 1972.

2130)    _____. "Birth Order and Family Size of Homosexual Men and Women," Journal of Consulting and Clinical Psychology, 41:164, 1973.

2131)    _____. "Parental Background of Homosexual and Heterosexual Women," British Journal of Psychiatry, 124:14-21, 1974.

2132)    _____. "Parental Background of Male Homosexuals and Heterosexuals," Archives of Sexual Behavior, 3:3-18, 1974.

2133)    Sieveking, Nicholas A. "Behavioral Therapy: Bag of Tricks or Point of View? Treatment for Homosexuality," Psychotherapy: Theory, Research and Practice, 9:32-35, 1972.

2134)    Silva, Jorge G. "Two Cases of Female Homosexuality," Contemporary Psychoanalysis, 4:357-76, 1975.

2135)    Silverman, Lloyd H.; Kwawer, Jay S.; Wolitzky, Carol; and Coron, Mark. "An Experimental Study of Aspects of the Psychoanalytic Theory of Male

Homosexuality," Journal of Abnormal Psychology, 82:178-88, 1973.

2136)    Silverstein, Michael.  "The Development of an Iden-
         tity:  Power and Sex Roles in Academia," Journal
         of Applied Behavioral Science, 8:536-63, 1972.

2137)    Singer, Michael I.  "Comparison of Indicators of
         Homosexuality on the MMPI," Journal of Consulting
         and Clinical Psychology, 34:15-18, 1970.

2138)    Skene, R. A.  "Construct Shift in the Treatment of
         a Case of Homosexuality," British Journal of Medi-
         cal Psychology, 46:287-92, 1973.

2139)    Slovenko, Ralph.  "Government Employment of Ho-
         mosexuals," Medical Aspects of Human Sexuality,
         9:108, 142, Oct. 1975.

2140)    Smith, Kenneth T.  "Homophobia: A Tentative Per-
         sonality Profile," Psychological Reports, 29:1091-94,
         1971.

2141)    Smith, Richard W.  "Is Biology Destiny?  Or Is It
         Culture?  A New Look at Transvestism and Homo-
         sexuality," Counseling Psychologist, 5:90-91, 1975.

2142)    Smolenaars, A. J.  "Analysis of Pick 3/8 Data on
         Attitudes towards Homosexuality, by the Compensa-
         tory Distance Model," Nederlands Tijdschrift voor
         Psychologie, 29:631-47, 1974.

2143)    Socarides, Charles W.  "Homosexuality and Medi-
         cine," Journal of the American Medical Association,
         212:1199-1202, May 18, 1970.  (Summary in Psy-
         chiatry Digest, 32:50, Feb. 1971)

2144)    _____.  "Homosexuality--Basic Concepts and Psy-
         chodynamics," International Journal of Psychiatry,
         10:118-25, 1972.

2145)    _____.  "Latent Homosexuality," Medical Aspects
         of Human Sexuality, 8:55, 58, Aug. 1974.

2146)    _____; Bieber, Irving; Bychowski, Gustav; Gersh-
         man, Harry; Jacobs, Theodore J.; Myers, Wayne
         A.; Nackenson, Burton L.; Prescott, Kathryn F.;

Rifkin, Alfred H.; Stein, Stefan; and Terry, Jack. "Homosexuality in the Male: A Report of a Psychiatric Study Group," International Journal of Psychiatry, 11:460-79, 1973.

2147)  Solomon, Joan. "Long Gay's Journey into Light," The Sciences, 12:6-15, Oct. 1972.

2148)  Sonenschein, David. "Homosexual Mannerisms," Medical Aspects of Human Sexuality, 4:135, Sep. 1970.

2149)  Sperber, Michael A. "The 'as if' Personality and Transvestitism," Psychoanalytic Review, 60:605-12, 1973.

2150)  Sreedhar, K. P. and Rao, A. V. "Draw a Person Test in Two Male Homosexuals," Indian Journal of Psychiatry, 15:402-07, 1973.

2151)  Starka, L.; Sipova, Iva; and Hynie, J. "Plasma Testosterone in Male Transsexuals and Homosexuals," Journal of Sex Research, 11:134-38, 1975.

2152)  Steffensmeier, Darrel J. and Renée. "Sex Differences in Reactions to Homosexuals," Journal of Sex Research, 10:52-67, 1974.

2153)  Stephan, Walter G. "Parental Relationships and Early Social Experiences of Activist Male Homosexuals and Male Heterosexuals," Journal of Abnormal Psychology, 82:506-13, 1973.

2154)  "Stereotoxic Surgery Results in 'Cures' of German Sex Offenders," Journal of the American Medical Association, 229:1716, Sep. 23, 1974.

2155)  Stoller, Robert J. "Does Sexual Perversion Exist?" Johns Hopkins Medical Journal, 134:43-57, 1974.

2156)  _____. "Psychotherapy of Extremely Feminine Boys," International Journal of Psychiatry, 9:278-80, 1971.

2157)  _____; Marmor, Judd; Bieber, Irving; Gould, Ronald; Socarides, Charles W.; Green, Richard; and Spitzer, Robert L. "A Symposium: Should

Homosexuality Be in the American Psychiatric Association Nomenclature?" American Journal of Psychiatry, 130:1207-16, 1973.

2158) Stone, Norman M. and Schneider, Robert E. "Concurrent Validity of the Wheeler Signs of Homosexuality in the Rorschach (CI/Rj)," Journal of Personality Assessment, 39:573-79, 1975.

2159) Strupp, Hans H. "Some Observations on the Fallacy of Value-free Psychotherapy and the Empty Organism: Comments on a Case Study," Journal of Abnormal Psychology, 83:199-201, 1974.

2160) Styles, R. A. "A Biblical Study in Homosexuality," Medicine, Science and the Law, 12:71-73. 1972.

2161) Swanson, David W.; Loomis, Dale; Lukesh, Robert; Cronin, Robert; and Smith, Jackson A. "Clinical Features of the Female Homosexual Patient: A Comparison with the Heterosexual Patient," Journal of Nervous and Mental Disease, 155:119-24, 1972.

2162) Swartzburg, Marshall; Schwartz, Arthur H.; Lieb, Julian; and Slaby, Andrew E. "Dual Suicide in Homosexuals," Journal of Nervous and Mental Disease, 155:125-30, 1972.

2163) Szumness, Wolf and Others. "On the Role of Sexual Behavior in the Spread of Hepatitis B Infection," Annals of Internal Medicine, 83:489-95, 1975.

2164) Talmadge-Riggs, G. and Anschel, S. "Homosexual Behavior and Dominance Hierarchy in a Group of Captive Female Squirrel Monkeys (Saimiri Sciureus)," Folia Primatologica, 19:61-72, 1973.

2165) Tanner, Barry. "Aversive Shock Issues," Journal of Behavior Therapy and Experimental Psychiatry, 4:113-15, 1973.

2166) _____. "A Comparison of Automated Aversive Conditioning and a Waiting List Control in the Modification of Homosexual Behavior in Males," Behavior Therapy, 5:29-32, 1974.

2167) _____. "Shock Intensity and Fear of Shock in

the Modification of Homosexual Behavior in Males
by Avoidance Learning," Behaviour Research and
Therapy, 11:213-18, 1973.

2168)    Taylor, Charlotte C. "Identical Twins: Concor-
dance for Homosexuality?" American Journal of
Psychiatry, 129:486-87, 1972.

2169)    Teoh, J. I. "DeClerambault's Syndrome: A Review of Four Cases," Singapore Medical Journal,
13:227-34, 1972.

2170)    Tewflk, G. I. "Homosexuality," Australian and
New Zealand Journal of Psychiatry, 8:207-08, 1974.

2171)    Thompson, Norman L. Jr.; McCandless, Boyd R.;
and Strickland, Bonnie R. "Personal Adjustment
of Male and Female Homosexuals and Heterosexuals," Journal of Abnormal Psychology, 78:237-40,
1971.

2172)    _____; Schwartz, David M.; McCandless, Boyd
R.; and Edwards, David A. "Parent-child Relationships and Sexual Identity in Male and Female
Homosexuals and Heterosexuals," Journal of Consulting and Clinical Psychology, 41:120-27, 1973.

2173)    Thorpe, Geoffrey L. "Learning Paradigms in the
Anticipatory Avoidance Technique: A Comment on
the Controversy between MacDonough and Feldman,"
Behaviour Therapy, 3:614-18, 1972.

2174)    Tourney, Garfield; Buck, Raymond; Hendrix, Hugh;
Petrilli, Anthony; and Schorer, Calvin. "Round-
table: Advising the Homosexual," Medical Aspects
of Human Sexuality, 7:12-33, Jan. 1973. Also
Comments by Lief, Harold I.; Bieber, Irving; and
Gadpaille, Warren J.

2175)    _____ and Hatfield, Lon M. "Androgen Metabolism in Schizophrenics, Homosexuals, and Normal Controls," Biological Psychiatry, 6:23-36, 1973.

2176)    _____; Petrilli, Anthony L.; and Hatfield, Lon
M. "Hormonal Relationships in Homosexual Men,"
American Journal of Psychiatry, 132-288-90, 1975.

2177)   Truax, Richard A.; Moeller, William S.; and Tour-
        ney, Garfield. "Medical Approach to Male Homo-
        sexuality," Journal of the Iowa Medical Association,
        6:397-403, Jun. 1970.

2178)   _____ and Tourney, Garfield. "Male Homosex-
        uals in Group Psychotherapy: A Controlled Study,"
        Diseases of the Nervous System, 32:707-11, 1971.

2179)   Turell, Robert. "Hazards of Homosexual Acts,"
        Medical Aspects of Human Sexuality, 4:116, Jun.
        1970.

2180)   Turner, R. Keith; James, S. R. N.; and Orwin,
        Arnold. "A Note on Internal Consistency of the
        Sexual Orientation Method," Behaviour Research and
        Therapy, 12:273-78, 1974.

2181)   _____; _____; _____; and Pielmaier, H.
        "Personality Characteristics of Male Homosexuals
        Referred for Aversive Therapy: A Comparative
        Study," British Journal of Psychiatry, 125:447-49,
        1974.

2182)   Usdin, Gene L. "Sudden Manifestations of Homo-
        sexuality," Medical Aspects of Human Sexuality,
        4:81, Apr. 1970.

2183)   Vahrman, J. "Atypical Gonorrhea," British Medi-
        cal Journal, 3:579-80, 1971.

2184)   Vaisrub, Samuel. "Cherchez l'Homme? Viral
        Hepatitis Type B," Journal of the American Medical
        Association, 225:1645-46, Sep. 24, 1973.

2185)   Van den Aardweg, Gerald J. "A Grief Theory of
        Homosexuality," American Journal of Psychotherapy,
        26:52-68, 1972.

2186)   "Venereal Disease Reported among Male Homosex-
        uals," Texas Medicine, 70:24, Jan. 1974.

2187)   Walker, Carolyn B. "Psychodrama: An Experi-
        ential Study within the Homosexual Society," Group
        Psychotherapy and Psychodrama, 27:83-97, 1974.

2188)   Ward, Ingebord L. "Prenatal Stress Feminizes and

Demasculinizes the Behavior of Males," Science,
175:82-85, Jan. 7, 1972.

2189)　Warner, Gloria M. and Lahn, Marion. "A Case
of Female Transsexualism," Psychiatric Quarterly,
44:476-87, 1970.

2190)　Waugh, M. A. "Sexual Transmission of Intestinal
Parasites," British Journal of Venereal Diseases,
50:157-58, 1974.

2191)　＿＿＿＿＿. "Threadworm Infestation in Homosexuals," Transactions of the St. John's Hospital Der-
matological Society, 58:224-25, 1972.

2192)　Weeks, Ruth B.; Derdeyn, Andre P.; and Langman,
Margarethe. "Two Cases of Children of Homosexuals," Child Psychiatry and Human Development,
6:26-32, 1975.

2193)　Weinberg, Martin S. "Homosexual Samples: Differences and Similarities," Journal of Sex Research,
6:312-25, 1970.

2194)　Weissbach, Theodore A. and Zagon, Gary. "The
Effect of Deviant Group Membership upon Impres-
sions of Personality," Journal of Social Psychology,
95:263-66, 1975.

2195)　Wells, B. W. P. and Schofield, C. B. S. "Personality Characteristics of Homosexual Men Suffer-
ing from Sexually Transmitted Diseases," British
Journal of Venereal Diseases, 48:75-78, 1972.

2196)　West, Donald J. "Aspects of Homosexuality,"
Journal of Biosocial Science, Supplement, 2:43-50,
May 1970.

2197)　Westfall, Michael P.; Schatzberg, Alan F.; Blumet-
ti, Anthony B.; and Birk, C. Lee. "Effeminacy:
II. Variation with Social Context," Archives of
Sexual Behavior, 4:43-51, 1975.

2198)　White, Emily; Rudikoff, Donald; and Kaufman, Arthur. "Hepatitis as a Venereal Disease in Homosexuals," New England Journal of Medicine, 290:
1384, Jun. 13, 1974.

2199)   Wiedeman, George H. "Homosexuality: A Survey,"
        American Psychoanalytic Association Journal, 22:
        651-96, 1974.

2200)   Williams, A. Hyatt. "Problems of Homosexuality,"
        British Medical Journal, 3:426-28, 1975.

2201)   Williams, Colin and Weinberg, Martin S. "The
        Military: Its Processing of Accused Homosexuals,"
        American Behavioral Scientist, 14:203-17, 1970.

2202)   Wilson, G. Terence and Davison, Gerald C. "Be-
        havior Therapy and Homosexuality: A Critical Per-
        spective," American Psychologist, 29:23-28, Feb.
        1974.

2203)   _____ and _____. "Behavior Therapy and
        Homosexuality: A Critical Perspective," Behavior
        Therapy, 5:16-28, 1974.

2204)   Wilson, Marilyn L. and Greene, Roger L. "Per-
        sonality Characteristics of Female Homosexuals,"
        Psychological Reports, 28:407-12, 1971.

2205)   Wilson, William P.; Zung, William W.; and Lee,
        John C. "Arousal from Sleep of Male Homosexu-
        als," Biological Psychiatry, 6:81-84, 1973.

2206)   Wolfe, Stephen D. and Menninger, W. Walter.
        "Fostering Open Communication about Sexual Con-
        cerns in a Mental Hospital," Hospital and Commu-
        nity Psychiatry, 24:147-50, 1973.

2207)   Wolfgang, Aaron and Joan. "Exploration of Attitudes
        via Physical Interpersonal Distance toward the Obese,
        Drug Users, Homosexuals, Police, and Other Mar-
        ginal Figures," Journal of Clinical Psychology, 27:
        510-12, 1971.

2208)   Wolowitz, Howard M. "The Validity of the Psycho-
        analytic Theory of Paranoid Dynamics: Evaluated
        from the Available Experimental Evidence," Psychi-
        atry, 34:358-77, 1971.

2209)   _____; _____; _____. "Divorce among
        Psychiatric Out-patients," British Journal of Psy-
        chiatry, 121:289-92, 1972.

2210)    Woodruff, Robert A. Jr.; Clayton, Paula J.; and
         Guze, Samuel B. "Suicide Attempts and Psychiatric
         Diagnoses," Diseases of the Nervous System, 33:
         617-21, 1972.

2211)    Woods, Sherwyn M. "Violence: Psychotherapy of
         Pseudohomosexual Panic," Archives of General Psy-
         chiatry, 27:255-58, 1972.

2212)    Woodward, R.; McAllister, H.; Harbison, J. J. M.;
         Quinn, J. T.; and Graham, P. Joan. "A Compari-
         son of Two Scoring Systems for the Sexual Orienta-
         tion Method," British Journal of Social and Clinical
         Psychology, 12:411-14, 1973.

2213)    Zavitzianos, G. "Homeovestism: Perverse Form
         of Behavior Involving Wearing Clothes of the Same
         Sex," International Journal of Psychoanalysis, 53:
         471-77, 1972.

2214)    Zlotlow, Moses. "Religious Rationalization of a
         Homosexual," New York State Journal of Medicine,
         72:2775-78, 1972.

2215)    Zuger, Bernard. "Effeminate Behavior in Boys.
         Parental Age and Other Factors," Archives of Gen-
         eral Psychiatry, 30:173-77, 1974.

2216)    _____. "The Role of Familial Factors in Per-
         sistent Effeminate Behavior in Boys," American
         Journal of Psychiatry, 126:1167-70, 1970.

## ARTICLES IN OTHER SPECIALIZED JOURNALS

2217)   "Aboriginal Naivete [Homosexuality among Austra-
        lian Aborigines]," Human Behavior, 2:32-33, Dec.
        1973.

2218)   "The Air Force and the Primitive 'H' [Homosexual-
        ity]," Human Behavior, 2:42-43, Aug. 1943.

2219)   Akers, Ronald L.; Hayner, Norman S.; and Gruni-
        ger, Werner. "Homosexual and Drug Behavior in
        Prison; A Test of the Functional and Importation
        Models of the Inmate System," Social Problems,
        21:410-22, 1974.

2220)   Allen, Dan. "The Short Stories of Daniel Curzon,"
        Margins, May 1975, pp. 5-9.

2221)   Anonymous. "Some Notes of a Homosexual Teach-
        ing Assistant in His First Semester of Ph.D. Work,"
        College English, 36:331-36, 1974.

2222)   Ashworth, A. E. and Walker, W. M. "Social
        Structure and Homosexuality: A Theoretical Apprais-
        al," British Journal of Sociology, 23:146-58, 1972.

2223)   Athanasiou, Robert and Shaver, Philip. "Correlates
        of Response to Pornography; A Comparison of Male
        Heterosexuals and Homosexuals," Proceedings of the
        78th Annual Convention of the American Psychologi-
        cal Association, 1970, pp. 349-50.

2224)   Austen, Roger. "But for Fate and Ban: Homosex-
        ual Villains and Victims in the Military," College
        English, 36:352-59, 1974.

2225)   Balters, Lorraine. "No Gay Market Yet, Admen,
        Gays Agree," Advertising Age, 43:3, 199, Aug. 28,
        1972.

2226)     Bannon, Barbara A.   "Interview with Merle Miller,"
          Publishers' Weekly, 200:17-18, Oct. 4, 1971.

2227)     Barr, R. F. and Catts, S. V.   "Psychiatric Opin-
          ion and Homosexuality:   A Short Report," Journal
          of Homosexuality, 1:213-15, 1974.

2228)     Bartollas, Clemens; Miller, Stuart J.; and Dinitz,
          Simon.   "The 'Booty Bandit': A Social Role in a
          Juvenile Institution," Journal of Homosexuality, 1:
          203-12, 1974.

2229)     Baym, N.   "Erotic Motif in Melville's 'Clarel,'"
          Texas Studies in Literature and Language, 16:315-
          28, 1974.

2230)     Bell, Alan P.   "Homosexuals: Their Range and
          Character," Nebraska Symposium on Motivation,
          21:1-26, 1973.

2231)     Bentley, Eric; Fulkerson, Richard; Macrobie, Ken;
          Slater, Don; Svoboda, D. T.; and Weintraub, Stan-
          ley.   "Comments on 'The Homosexual Imagination,'"
          College English, 37:73-85, 1975.

2232)     Berenstein, Frederick.   "The Homosexual Retardate
          Theory and Group Work," Journal for Special Edu-
          cators of the Mentally Retarded, 9:74-79, 1973.

2233)     Bieber, Irving.   "Homosexuality; An Adaptive Con-
          sequence of Disorder in Psychosexual Development,"
          Nursing Digest, 3:57, Mar.-Apr. 1975.

2234)     Bingham, Caroline.   "Seventeenth Century Attitudes
          toward Deviant Sex," Journal of Interdisciplinary
          History, 1:447-68, 1971.

2235)     Birk, Lee.   "Group Psychotherapy for Men Who
          Are Homosexual," Journal of Sex and Marital The-
          rapy, 1:29-52, 1974.

2236)     Blair, Ralph.   "Counseling and Homosexuality,"
          Homosexual Counseling Journal, 2:94-106, 1975.

2237)     _____.   "Counseling Concerns and Bisexual Be-
          havior," Homosexual Counseling Journal, 1:26-30,
          1974.

2238)    Bolling, Douglass. "Distanced Heart Artistry in
         E. M. Forster's 'Maurice,'" Modern Fiction Studies,
         20:157-67, 1974.

2239)    Boyette, Purvis E. "Shakespeare's Sonnets: Ho-
         mosexuality and the Critics," Tulane University
         Studies in English, 21:35-46, 1974.

2240)    Braverman, Shirley J. "Homosexuality," American
         Journal of Nursing, 73:652-55, 1973.

2241)    Brown, Carol and Others. "Of This Pure but Ir-
         regular Passion," Synergy, Sep.-Oct. 1970, pp. 9-
         13.   (Annotated Bibliography of 32 items)

2242)    Brown, Donald A. "Counseling the Youthful Homo-
         sexual," School Counselor, 22:325-33, 1975.

2243)    Bulkin, Elly. "The Places We Have Been: The
         Poetry of Susan Griffin," Margins, Aug. 1975, pp.
         31-34.

2244)    Bullough, Vern L. "Heresy, Witchcraft, and Sex-
         uality [in the Middle Ages]," Journal of Homosexu-
         ality, 1:183-201, 1974.

2245)    Cangemi, Joseph P.; Laird, A. W.; and Deeb, Nor-
         man A. "The Philosophy of Existentialism and a
         Psychology of Irreversible Homosexuality," College
         Student Journal Monograph, 8:1-12, Sep.-Oct. 1974.

2246)    Canon, Harry. "Gay Students," Vocational Guidance
         Quarterly, 21:181-85, 1973.

2247)    Carson, Neil. "Sexuality and Identity in 'Fortune
         and Men's Eyes,'" Twentieth Century Literature,
         18:207-18, 1972.

2248)    Chafetz, Janet S.; Sampson, Patricia; Beck, Paula;
         and West, Joyce. "Study of Homosexual Women,"
         Social Work, 19:714-23, 1974.

2249)    "Checklist of Resources," College English, 36:401-
         04, 1974.   (Bibliography of 121 items)

2250)    Chesebro, James W.; Cragan, John F.; and McCul-
         lough, Patricia. "The Small Group Techniques of

the Radical Revolutionary: A Synthetic Study of Consciousness Raising [Gay Liberationists]," Speech Monographs, 40:136-46, 1973.

2251) Clayborne, Jon L. "Modern Black Drama and the Gay Image," College English, 36:381-84, 1974.

2252) "Committee of Gay Historians," American Historical Association Newsletter, 12:4-5, Feb. 1974.

2253) "Coming Out Gay," Human Behavior, 1:34, Jan. - Feb. 1972.

2254) Congdon, Kirby. "Gay Poetry," Margins, May 1975, pp. 12-14.

2255) Conley, John A. and O'Rourke, Thomas W. "Attitudes of College Students toward Selected Issues in Human Sexuality," Journal of School Health, 43: 286-92 at 287-88, 1973.

2256) Coons, Frederick W. "Ambisexuality as an Alternative Adaptation," Journal of the American College Health Association, 21:142-44, Dec. 1972.

2257) Core, Deborah. "Woman-identified," Margins, Aug. 1975, p. 28.

2258) Court, J. H. "Behavioral Sciences in Christian Perspective--Homosexuality," Australian Nurses' Journal, 2:9, 11, Jun. 1973.

2259) Crew, Louie. "Editor Responses to Gay Materials," Margins, May 1975, pp. 5-9.

2260) _____. "The Gay Academic Unmasks," Chronicle of Higher Education, Feb. 25, 1974, p. 20.

2261) _____. "Protest and Community: Gay Male Journalism Now," Margins, May 1975, pp. 14-21.

2262) _____ and Norton, Rictor. "The Homophobic Imagination: An Editorial," College English, 36:272-90, 1974.

2263) Critchfield, Sue. "Gay Is Just a Three Letter Word," Synergy, Sep. -Oct. 1970, pp. 14-19.

2264)    Crowder, John J. "Love that Dares Now Speak Its
         Name: Homosexuality," Choice, 11:209-27, Apr.
         1974. (Annotated Bibliography of 89 items)

2265)    Cruikshank, Cathy. "Lesbian Literature: Random
         Thoughts," Margins, Aug. 1975, pp. 40-45.

2266)    Cruikshank, Peg. "The Sensitive Blue Pencil: One
         Journal's Approach to Feminist Criticism," Margins,
         Aug. 1975, pp. 37-39.

2267)    Cullinan, Robert G. "'Gay' Identity Emerges on
         Campus Amidst a Sea of Prejudice," National Asso-
         ciation of Student Personnel Administrators Journal,
         10:344-77, 1973.

2268)    _____. "One upon a Time--Three Myths about
         Homosexuals," Counseling and Values, 17:55-62,
         1973.

2269)    Curzon, Daniel. "The Problem of Writing Gay Lit-
         erature," Margins, May 1975, pp. 9-12.

2270)    Dailey, Dennis M. "Family Therapy with the Ho-
         mosexual: A Search," Homosexual Counseling Jour-
         nal, 1:7-15, 1974.

2271)    Damon, Gene. "When It Changed, or Growing up
         Gay in America with the Help of Literature," Mar-
         gins, Aug. 1975, pp. 16-18.

2272)    Davis, Edward M. "Victimless Crimes--the Case
         for Continued Enforcement," Journal of Police Sci-
         ence and Administration, 1:11-20 at 13-14, 1973.

2273)    Davis, Patricia C. "Chicken Queen's Delight: D.
         H. Lawrence's 'The Fox,'" Modern Fiction Studies,
         19:565-71, 1973-74.

2274)    "Debunking Gay Stereotypes," Human Behavior, 3:53,
         Oct. 1974.

2275)    "Defining Homosexual," Human Behavior, 1:35, May-
         Jun. 1972.

2276)    Dombroski, R. S. "Undisciplined Eros of Sandro
         Penna," Books Abroad, 47:304-06, 1973.

2277)    Dresser, Norine.  "'The Boys in the Band Is Not
         Another Musical':  Male Homosexuals and Their
         Folklore," Western Folklore, 33:205-18, 1974.

2278)    Driscoll, James P.  "Transsexuals," TransAction,
         8:28-37, 66, Mar.-Apr. 1971.

2279)    Dvosin, Andrew.  "Faggot Culture Quarterlies,"
         Margins, May 1975, pp. 21-23.

2280)    Escoffier, Jeffrey.  "Stigmas, Work Environment,
         and Economic Discrimination against Homosexuals,"
         Homosexual Counseling Journal, 2:8-17, 1975.

2281)    Evans, Dan.  "The Poetry of Ron Schreiber," Mar-
         gins, May 1975, pp. 52-54.

2282)    Evans-Pritchard, E. E.  "Sexual Inversion among
         the Azande," American Anthropologist, 72:1428-34,
         1970.

2283)    Falero, Frank Jr.  "Welfare Implications of Homo-
         sexuality," Journal of Political Economics, 79:1176-
         77, 1971.

2284)    Farrell, Ronald A.  "Class Linkages of Legal Treat-
         ment of Homosexuals," Criminology, 9:49-68, 1971.

2285)    Fields, Sidney J.  "Homosexuality:  A Confused
         Trinity," Group Process, 6:73-82, 1974.

2286)    Fink, Paul J.  "Homosexuality:  Illness or Life
         Style?"  Journal of Sex and Marital Therapy, 1:
         225-33, 1975.

2287)    Fisher, Clarice.  "Character as a Way of Knowing
         in 'A la Recherche du Temps Perdu':  The Baron
         de Charlus," Modern Fiction Studies, 30:407-18, 1974.

2288)    Fone, Byrne R. S.  "The Poetry of Frank O'Hara,"
         Margins, May 1975, pp. 48-50.

2289)    Foster, David E.  "'Cause My House Down:  The
         Theme of the Fall in Baldwin's Novels," Critique:
         Studies in Modern Fiction, v. 13, no. 2, pp. 50-
         62, 1971.

2290)      "The Fourteenth Alexander Meiklejohn Award [Board
           of Trustees, University of Maine]," American As-
           sociation of University Professors Bulletin, 61:114-
           17, Summer 1975.

2291)      Friedkin, Anthony E.   "The Gay World--A Photo
           Essay," Human Behavior, 2:36-43, Dec. 1973.

2292)      Gadpaille, Warren J.   "Myths about Childhood Ho-
           mosexuality," Today's Health, 49:45-47, 65, Jan.
           1971.

2293)      "Gay Academic Union," Intellect, 102:81, Nov. 1973.

2294)      "Gay Activism in Colleges," Intellect, 103:77, Nov.
           1974.

2295)      "Gay Activists and Mental Health," Human Behavior,
           2:44-45, Aug. 1973.

2296)      "Gay Counseling in a Free Clinic; A Group Commu-
           nal Project," Journal of Social Issues, v. 30, no.
           1, pp. 97-104.

2297)      "Gay Couple Counseling:  Proceedings of a Confer-
           ence," Homosexual Counseling Journal, 1:88-139,
           1974.

2298)      "Gay Is:  Social Responsibilities Round Table Task
           Force on Gay Liberation at American Library Asso-
           ciation Conference," Wilson Library Bulletin, 46:
           17, 1971.

2299)      Gibbs, Annette and McFarland, Arthur C.   "Recog-
           nition of Gay Liberation on the State-supported Cam-
           pus," Journal of College Student Personnel, 15:5-7,
           1974.

2300)      Gilbert, Arthur N.   "The 'Africaine' Courts-martial:
           A Study of Buggery and the Royal Navy," Journal of
           Homosexuality, 1:111-22, 1974.

2301)      Giles, James R.   "Religious Alienation and 'Homo-
           sexual Consciousness' in 'City of Night' and 'Go Tell
           It on the Mountain,'" College English, 36:369-80,
           1974.

2302)   Gillette, Paul J.   "What the 1972 Kinsey Report
        Says about You," Sexuality, 1:50-54, 68, 70, Nov.
        1971.

2303)   Ginsberg, Allen.   "Gay Sunshine Interview," College
        English, 36:392-400, 1974.   (Abstract from article
        in Gay Sunshine--see no. 246)

2304)   Gitchoff, G. Thomas and Ellenbogen, Joseph and
        Elsie.   "Victimless Crimes:  The Case against
        Continued Enforcement," Journal of Police Science
        and Administration, 1:401-08 at 403, 1973.

2305)   Gleissner, Robert.   "Hunce Voelcker:  A Beauty,"
        Margins, May 1975, pp. 51-52.

2306)   Glover, William E.   "Homosexuality," American
        Libraries, 2:295, 1971.

2307)   Gochros, Harvey L.   "The Sexually Oppressed,"
        Social Work, 17:16-23, Mar. 1972.

2308)   _____.   "Teaching More or Less Straight Social
        Work Students to Be Helpful to More or Less Gay
        People," Homosexual Counseling Journal, 2:58-67,
        1975.

2309)   Goldberg, Martin.   "Facts and Myths about the Ho-
        mosexual Patient," Consultant, 12:166-69, 1972.

2310)   Gramick, Jeannine.   "Myths of Homosexuality,"
        Intellect, 102:104-07, 1973.

2311)   Greenberg, Jerrold S.   "A Study of Male Homosex-
        uals (predominantly College Students)," Journal of
        the American College Health Association, 22:56-60,
        1973.

2312)   _____.   "A Study of Personality Change Associated
        with the Conducting of a High School Unit on Homo-
        sexuality," Journal of School Health, 45:394-98,
        1975.

2313)   Hammersmith, Sue K. and Weinberg, Martin S.
        "Homosexual Identity:  Commitment, Adjustment,
        and Significant Others," Sociometry, 36:56-79, 1973.

2314)    Hatcher, Duncan.   "To the Air," Margins, May
         1975, pp. 43-45.

2315)    Hawkes, Robert E.   "The Poetry of Ian Young,"
         Margins, May 1975, pp. 54-56.

2316)    "Helping the Homosexual's Family," Behavior To-
         day, Mar. 18, 1974, p. 75.

2317)    Hoffman, Martin.   "Homosexuality," Today's Edu-
         cation, 59:46-48, Nov. 1970.

2318)    Holyoak, William H.   "Playing out Family Conflicts
         in a Female Homosexual 'Family' Group (Chick-vot)
         among Institutional Juveniles:   A Case Presentation,"
         Adolescence, 7:153-68, 1972.

2319)    "Homosexphobia," Human Behavior, 2:44-45, Oct.
         1973.

2320)    "Homosexual Study," Behavior Today, Jun. 3, 1974,
         p. 154.

2321)    "Homosexuals and Love Bonds [No Difference in
         Self-concept of Homosexual and Heterosexual Males],"
         Human Behavior, 3:47, Dec. 1974.

2322)    Hoover, Eleanor L.   "Lesbianism:   Reflections of
         a 'Straight' Woman," Human Behavior, 2:9, Oct.
         1973.

2323)    Horstman, William R.   "MMPI Responses of Ho-
         mosexual and Heterosexual Male College Students,"
         Homosexual Counseling Journal, 2:68-76, 1975.

2324)    Humphreys, Laud.   "New Styles in Homosexual
         Manliness," TransAction, 8:38-46, 64, 66, Mar. -
         Apr. 1971.   (Reprinted in McCaffrey, no. 101,
         pp. 65-83)

2325)    _____.   "Tearoom Trade:   Impersonal Sex in
         Public Places--Excerpts," TransAction, 7:10-14,
         Jan. 1970.

2326)    Hunt, Russell A.   "Whitman's Poetics and the Unity
         of Calamus," American Literature, 46:482-94, 1975.

2327)    Hunter, Jim.  "On Camp:  The Sensibility on Inno-
         cent Frivolity," Journal of the West Virginia Philo-
         sophical Society, 9:28-30, Fall 1975.

2328)    "'I Was Nineteen and I Wanted to Die,'" Nursing
         Times, 69:178, 1973.

2329)    Ibrahim, A. I.  "Deviant Sexual Behavior in Men's
         Prisons," Crime and Delinquency, 20:38-44, 1974.

2330)    "Inhaling Inversion [Behavior Therapy for Homosex-
         uals]," Human Behavior, 2:75, May 1973.

2331)    Ivey, Robert D.  "Consultation with a Male Homo-
         sexual," Personnel and Guidance Journal, 50:749-
         54, 1972.

2332)    Jago, David.  "School and Theater:  Polarities of
         Homosexual Writing in England," College English,
         36:360-68, 1974.

2333)    Jay, Karla.  "A Look at Lesbian Magazines" and
         "Carol Grosberg on Lesbian Theater:  An Inter-
         view," Margins, Aug. 1975, pp. 19-21 and 55-57.

2334)    Jayne, Edward.  "Defense of the Homophobic Im-
         agination," College English, 37:62-67, 1975.  Reply
         by Rictor Norton: 37:67-72, 1974.

2335)    Jensen, Mehri S.  "Role Differentiation in Female
         Homosexual Quasi-Marital Unions," Journal of Mar-
         riage and the Family, 36:360-67, 1974.

2336)    Jim and Janov, Arthur.  "Some Insights on My Ho-
         mosexual Masochism--Postscript," Journal of Pri-
         mal Therapy, 2:111-19, 1974.

2337)    Johnson, Edwin.  "The Homosexual in Prison,"
         Social Theory and Practice, 1:83-95, 1971.

2338)    Johnson, Wendell S.  "Auden, Hopkins, and the Po-
         etry of Reticence," Twentieth Century Literature,
         20:165-71, 1974.

2339)    Johnston, C. D.  "Sexuality and Birth Control:  Im-
         pact of Outreach Programming," Personnel and Guid-
         ance Journal, 52:406-11, 1974.

2340)     Kameny, Franklin. "Is 'Gay' as Good as 'Straight'?"
          Sexology, 36:23-25, Feb. 1970.

2341)     Kantrowitz, Arnie. "Homosexuals and Literature,"
          College English, 36:324-30, 1974.

2342)     Karlen, Arno. "The Homosexual Heresy," Chaucer
          Review, 6:44-63, 1971.

2343)     Kaye, Melanie. "The Female Tribe," Margins,
          Aug. 1975, pp. 27-28.

2344)     Kelly, Gene F. "Bisexuality and the Youth Cul-
          ture," Homosexual Counseling Journal, 1:16-25,
          1974.

2345)     Kelly, Janis. "Sister Love: An Exploration of the
          Need for Homosexual Experience," Family Coodina-
          tor, 21:473-75, 1972.

2346)     Killinger, Raymond R. "The Counselor and Gay
          Liberation," Personnel and Guidance Journal, 49:
          715-19, 1971.

2347)     Kochheiser, Charles. "What Happened When a
          Speaker for Gay Liberation Addressed High School
          Students," Social Education, 39:219-21, 1975.

2348)     Korges, James. "Gide and Mishima: Homosexua-
          lity as Metaphor," Critique: Studies in Modern
          Fiction, v. 12, no. 1, pp. 127-37, 1970.

2349)     Kremer, Ellen B.; Zimpfer, David G.; and Wiggers,
          T. Thorne. "Homosexuality, Counseling, and the
          Adolescent Male," Personnel and Guidance Journal,
          54:94-99, 1975.

2350)     "Landmark American Psychiatric Association Ruling
          on Homosexuality," SIECUS Report, Mar. 1974, p. 3.

2351)     Larkin, Joan. "Nothing Safe: The Poetry of Audre
          Lorde," Margins, Aug. 1975, pp. 23-25.

2352)     Larsen, Knud S. "An Investigation of Sexual Be-
          havior among Norwegian College Students: A Mo-
          tivation Study," Journal of Marriage and the Family,
          33:219-27, 1971.

2353)   Lawrence, John C.   "Homosexuals, Hospitalization, and the Nurse," Nursing Forum, 14:304-17, 1975.

2354)   LeBourgeois, John Y.   "Swinburne and Simeon Solomon," Notes and Queries, 20:91-95, 1973.

2355)   Lerrigo, Charles.   "Metropolitan Community Church:  The Church Comes Out," New World Outlook, New Series, 33:28-32, May 1973.

2356)   "Lesbian Matrimony," Human Behavior, 4:51, Jan. 1975.

2357)   Levitt, Eugene E. and Klassen, Albert D.   "Public Attitudes toward Homosexuality:  Part of the 1970 National Survey by the Institute for Sex Research," Journal of Homosexuality, 1:29-43, 1974.

2358)   Levy, Charles J.   "ARVN as Faggots:  Inverted Warfare in Vietnam," TransAction, 8:18-27, Oct. 1971.

2359)   Libhart, Byron R.   "Julian Green's Troubled American:  A Fictionalized Self-portrait," Publications of the Modern Language Association, 89:341-52, 1974.

2360)   Liebert, Robert.   "The Gay Student:  A Psychopolitical View," Change Magazine, 3:38-44, Oct. 1971.

2361)   Lindley, Peter.   "A Symposium on the Psychiatric Nurse Therapist:  Sexual Deviation in a Young Man," Nursing Mirror, 140:63-64, May 8, 1975.

2362)   Lipschitz, H.   "Deviance:  The Male Homosexual," Australian Nursing Journal, 22:5-8, 1974.

2363)   Lyons, James E.   "Conversation with Gay Liberation:  An Interview," Journal of College Student Personnel, 14:165-70, 1973.

2364)   MacDonald, A. P.   "Identification and Measurement of Multi-dimensional Attitudes toward Equality between the Sexes," Journal of Homosexuality, 1:165-82, 1974.

2365)   _____.   "The Importance of Sex-Role to Gay Liberation," Homosexual Counseling Journal, 1:169-80, 1974.

2366)        _____ and Games, Richard G.  "Some Characteristics of Those Who Hold Positive and Negative
Attitudes toward Homosexuals," Journal of Homosexuality, 1:9-27, 1974.

2367)        Malek, J. S.  "Forster's Albergo Empedocle:  A
Precursor of Maurice," Studies in Short Fiction,
11:427-30, 1974.

2368)        Manford, Jeanne.  "A Mother's Letter," Homosexual Counseling Journal, 2:26-33, 1975.

2369)        Marmor, Judd.  "Homosexuality and Objectivity,"
SIECUS Newsletter, 6:1, 3, Dec. 1970.

2370)        _____.  "Symposium:  Should Homosexuality Be
a Diagnosis?  Homosexuality and Cultural Value
Systems," Nursing Digest, 3:56-57, Mar.-Apr. 1975.

2371)        Martines, Inez.  "The Poetry of Judy Grahn," Margins, Aug. 1975, pp. 48-50.

2372)        May, Eugene P.  "Counselors', Psychologists', and
Homosexuals' Philosophies of Human Nature and At-
titudes toward Homosexual Behavior," Homosexual
Counseling Journal, 1:3-25, 1974.

2373)        McCleary, Roland D.  "Patterns of Homosexuality
in Boys:  Observations from Illinois," International
Journal of Offender Therapy and Comparative Criminology, 16:139-42, 1972.

2374)        McKenney, Mary.  "Gay Liberation," Library Journal, 97:733-34, 1972.

2375)        McNamara, Francis J.  "Are Security Clearances
for Gays in the National Interest?" Human Events,
35:18, Mar. 15, 1975.

2376)        McNamee, Gil.  "Juris-prudence?" Synergy, Sep.-
Oct. 1970, pp. 20-25.

2377)        Meyers, Jeffrey.  "Revisions of Seven Pillars of
Wisdom," Publications of the Modern Language Association, 88:1066-82, 1973.

2378)        Mileski, Maureen and Black, Donald J.  "The Social

Organization of Homosexuality," Urban Life and Culture, 1:187-202, 1972.

2379)   Mills, Ivor H.   "Biology of Sexuality," Nursing Mirror, 135:12-14, Aug. 18, 1972.

2380)   "Minnesota Court Rules Library May Deny Homosexual Post: James M. McConnell Case," Library Journal, 96:4046, 1971.

2381)   Money, John.   "Two Names, Two Wardrobes, Two Personalities," Journal of Homosexuality, 1:65-70, 1974.

2382)   Montag, Tom.   "An Interview with Paul Mariah," Margins, May 1975, pp. 25-32.

2383)   Morin, Stephen.   "Educational Programs as a Means of Changing Attitudes toward Gay People," Homosexual Counseling Journal, 1:160-65, 1974.

2384)   Mundy, Jean.   "Feminist Therapy with Lesbians and Other Women," Homosexual Counseling Journal, 1:154-59, 1974.

2385)   Munter, Preston A.   "Some Observations about Homosexuality and Prejudice," Journal of the American College Health Association, 22:53-55, Oct. 1973.

2386)   Niemi, Judith.   "Jane Rule and the Reviewers," Margins, Aug. 1975, pp. 34-37.

2387)   Nobler, Hindy.   "Group Therapy with Male Homosexuals," Comparative Group Studies, 3:161-78, 1972.

2388)   Noll, Dolores.   "A Gay Feminist in Academia," College English, 36:312-15, 1974.

2389)   Nolte, M. Chester.   "Gay Teachers: The March from Closet to Classroom," American School Board Journal, 160:28-32, Jul. 1973.

2390)   "The Normal Homosexual," Human Behavior, 4:48-49, Dec. 1975.

2391)   Norton, Rictor.   "Homosexual Literary Tradition:

Course Outline and Objectives," College English, 35:674-78, 1974. Reply with Rejoinder: 36:503-04, 1974.

2392) _____. "An Interview with Eric Bentley," College English, 36:291-302, 1974.

2393) Nutt, Roberta L. and Sedlacek, William E. "Freshman Sexual Attitudes and Behavior," Journal of College Student Personnel, 15:345-51, Sep. 1974.

2394) "Opposition to Gay Studies Course at University of Nebraska," Behavior Today, Dec. 7, 1970, p. 1; May 31, 1971, p. 3; and Dec. 17, 1972, p. 4.

2395) Ortleb, Chuck. "Mouth of the Dragon [Gay Poetry]," Margins, May 1975, pp. 23-25.

2396) Osman, Shelomo. "My Stepfather Is a She," Family Process, 11:209-18, 1972.

2397) Ostrander, Kenneth H. "Teacher's Duty to Privacy; Court Rulings in Sexual Deviancy Cases," Phi Delta Kappan, 57:20-22, Sep. 1975.

2398) Parks, Adrienne. "The Lesbian Feminist as Writer as Lesbian Feminist," Margins, Aug. 1975, pp. 67-69.

2399) Phillips, Howard. "Department of Health, Education and Welfare Subsidizes California Homosexuals," Human Events, 35:8-9, Jan. 11, 1975.

2400) Pittman, David J. "The Male House of Prostitution," TransAction, 8:21-27, Mar.-Apr. 1971.

2401) Popenoe, P. "Are Homosexuals Necessary?" Marriage, 53:38-43, May 1971.

2402) "Problems of a Gay Old Age," Behavior Today, Aug. 26, 1974, p. 215.

2403) "'Public' Homosexuals May Not Teach," SIECUS Report, Sep. 1973, pp. 4-5.

2404) "Recommendation of American Bar Association to Repeal Laws Which Criminalize Non-commercial

Sexual Conduct between Consenting Adults in Private," Human Rights, 4:67-73, 1974.

2405)    "Request for Action: Case of [Gay Librarian] J. M. McConnell," American Libraries, 5:43-44, 1974.

2406)    Reuben, David. "Solving Teenagers' Sex Problems-- Homosexuality," Today's Health, 50:28-29, May 1972.

2407)    Rice, Raymond. "The Child Is Father to the Man: A Preliminary Bibliography of the Poetry of Paul Mariah," Margins, May 1975, pp. 36-39.

2408)    Richmond, R. G. O. "The Homosexual in Prison," Canadian Journal of Corrections, 12:553-55, 1970.

2409)    Riess, Bernard F.; Safer, Jeanne; and Yotive, William. "Psychological Test Data on Female Homosexuality: A Review of the Literature," Journal of Homosexuality, 1:71-85, 1974.

2410)    Rising, C. "E. M. Forster's 'Maurice': A Summing Up," Texas Quarterly, 17:84-96, Spring 1974.

2411)    Robins, Peter; Bentley, Eric; Curzon, Daniel; Fee, Dan L.; Penny, Robert L.; and Mariah, Paul. "Poetry," College English, 36:337-49, 1974.

2412)    Rogers, Martin. "Critical Incidents in the Evolution of a Gay Liberation Group," Homosexual Counseling Journal, 2:18-25, 1975.

2413)    Ross, H. Laurence. "Models of Adjustment of Married Homosexuals," Social Problems, 18:385-93, 1971.

2414)    Rossman, Parker. "Pederasts," Society, 10:28-35, Mar. 1973.

2415)    Rubin, Larry. "Homosexual Motif in Willa Cather's 'Paul's Case,'" Studies in Short Fiction, 12:127-31, 1975.

2416)    Russell, Donald H. "On the Psychopathology of Boy Prostitutes," International Journal of Offender Therapy, 15:49-52, 1971.

2417)     Rutledge, Aaron L.   "Treatment of Male Homosex-
          uality through Marriage Counseling:  A Case Pre-
          sentation," Journal of Marriage and Family Coun-
          seling, 1:51-62, 1975.

2418)     Sagarin, Edward.   "Good Guys, Bad Guys, and
          Gay Guys:  Survey Essay," Contemporary Sociology,
          2:3-13, 1973.

2419)     _____.   "Is 'Gay' as Good as 'Straight'?"   Sexo-
          logy, 36:22, 24, Feb. 1970.

2420)     _____.   "Rational Guideposts on Homosexuality,"
          Rational Living, 5:2-7, Fall 1970.

2421)     _____ and MacNamara, Donal E. J.   "The Ho-
          mosexual as a Crime Victim," International Journal
          of Criminology and Penology, 3:13-25, 1975.

2422)     Sage, Wayne.   "The Homosexuality Hangup," Hu-
          man Behavior, 1:56-61, Nov.-Dec. 1972.

2423)     _____.   "Inside the Colossal Closet," Human Be-
          havior, 4:16-23, Aug. 1974.

2424)     Samandari, Jensen M.   "Role Differentiation in Fe-
          male Homosexual Quasimarital Unions," Journal of
          Marriage and the Family, 36:360-67, 1974.

2425)     Schreiber, Ron.   "Giving a Gay Course," College
          English, 36:316-23, 1974.

2426)     Scott, R. L.   "Conservative Voice in Radical Rhet-
          oric:  Gay Liberation, Women's Lib," Speech Mono-
          graphs, 40:123-35, 1973.

2427)     "Search for Gay Genes--The Missing Ketosteroid,"
          Human Behavior, 2:53-54, Mar. 1973.

2428)     Searls, Leslie; Kanton, Daniel; and Sands, Julie.
          "Lesbianism:  Or Did You Hear about the Little
          Girl Who Put Her Finger in the Dike?" Human
          Factor, 10:22-29, 1970.

2429)     Secor, Cynthia.   "Lesbians--the Doors Open,"
          Change Magazine, 7:13-17, Feb. 1975.

2430)      Serber, Michael and Keith, Claudia. "The Atasca-
           dero Project: Model of a Sexual Retraining Pro-
           gram for Incarcerated Homosexual Pedophiles, "
           Journal of Homosexuality, 1:87-97, 1974.

2431)      Shane, Gregory. "I Am [a Homosexual], " Imprint:
           Journal of the Student Nurses Association, 21:20-
           21, Dec. 1974.

2432)      Shively, Charley. "Trapped in an Ashkanazic Ghet-
           to: A Review of Six Washington, D.C. Poets, "
           Margins, May 1975, pp. 56-62.

2433)      Sievert, William. "Out of the Academic Closet, "
           Change Magazine, 6:22-23, Apr. 1974.

2434)      Silverstein, Michael. "Development of an Identity:
           Power and Sex Roles in Academia, " Journal of Ap-
           plied Behavioral Science, 8:536-63, 1972.

2435)      _____. "The History of a Short Unsuccessful
           Academic Career, " Insurgent Sociologist, 1:4-19,
           Fall 1972. (Reprinted as "Power and Sex Roles
           in Academia, " Journal of Applied Behavioral Science,
           8:536-63, 1972. Reprinted also in Joseph H. Pleck
           and Jack Sawyer (eds.), Men and Masculinity [Engle-
           wood Cliffs, N.J.: Prentice-Hall, 1974], pp. 107-
           23)

2436)      "Smiling Faces, " Human Behavior, 1:36-37, Jul.-
           Aug. 1972.

2437)      Socarides, Charles W. "Homosexuality--Findings
           Derived from Fifteen Years of Clinical Research, "
           Nursing Digest, 3:57-58, Mar.-Apr. 1975.

2438)      _____. "Sexual Unreason, " Book Forum, 1:172-
           85, 1974.

2439)      Soldo, John J. "Voice, " Margins, May 1975, pp.
           32-36.

2440)      Spangler, George. "Shadow of a Dream: Howell's
           Homosexual Tragedy, " American Quarterly, 23:110-
           19, 1971.

2441)      Spiegler, Samuel. "Gay Reform, " Journal of

Jewish Communal Service, 49:329-30, 1973.

2442)   Spitzer, Robert L.  "A Proposal about Homosexu-
        ality and the American Psychiatric Association No-
        menclature:  Homosexuality as an Irregular Form
        of Sexual Behavior and Sexual Orientation Distur-
        bance as a Psychiatric Disorder," Nursing Digest,
        3:58-59, Mar.-Apr. 1975.

2443)   Stanley, Julia P.  "Homosexual Slang," American
        Speech, 45:45-59, 1970.

2444)   _____.  "Uninhibited Angels' Metaphors for Love"
        and "Nomads of Revolution," Margins, Aug. 1975,
        pp. 7-9 and 29-30.

2445)   _____.  "When We Say 'Out of the Closets,'"
        College English, 36:385-91, 1974.

2446)   "Staying Gay," Human Behavior, 1:56, Mar.-Apr.
        1972.

2447)   Stencel, Sandra.  "Homosexual Legal Rights,"
        Editorial Research Reports, 1:181-200, 1974.

2448)   Stimpson, Catharine.  "The Androgyne and the Ho-
        mosexual," Women's Studies, 2:237-48, 1974.

2449)   Stockinger, Jacob.  "Toward a Gay Criticism,"
        College English, 36:303-10, 1974.

2450)   Stoller, Richard J.  "Symposium:  Should Homosex-
        uality Be a Diagnosis?" Nursing Digest, 3:55-56,
        Mar.-Apr. 1975.

2451)   Stoltenberg, John.  "Toward Gender Justice," So-
        cial Policy, 6:35-39, May 1975.

2452)   "Strong, Silent, and Gay," Human Behavior, 1:43-
        44, May-Jun. 1972.

2453)   "Substitute Families [Need of Children in Institutions
        for Families to Help Avoid Homosexuality]," Human
        Behavior, 2:55, Feb. 1973.

2454)   Sutherland, Fraser.  "Muy Hombre [The Poetry of
        Edward A. Lacey]," Canadian Literature, Summer
        1975, pp. 104-07.

2455)   Tagett, Richard.  "If Writing a Poem Is a Useless
        Activity ... ," Margins, May 1975, pp. 45-48.

2456)   "Task Force on Gay Liberation Meeting," American
        Libraries, 1:1013, 1970.

2457)   "Teaching Imitations of Daddy [Effeminate Behavior],"
        Human Behavior, 2:56-57, Sep. 1973.

2458)   Thomas, Gordon K.  "To Rictor Norton:  Additions
        to the Course Outline [on Gay Literature] and Some
        Refining of Objectives," College English, 36:503-04,
        1974.

2459)   Thoreen, Bonnie.  "The Androgynous Mystique,"
        Synergy, Sep. -Oct. 1970, pp. 26-28.

2460)   Turnage, John R. and Logan, Daniel L.  "Sexual
        'Variation' without 'Deviation,'" Homosexual Coun-
        seling Journal, 2:117-20, 1975.

2461)   "Two New Journals on Homosexuality," SIECUS Re-
        port, Mar. 1974, p. 4.

2462)   "Uphill Custody Battles for Lesbian Mothers," Hu-
        man Behavior, 4:46-47, Feb. 1975.

2463)   Van Dusen, Wilson and Sherman, Scott L.  "Cul-
        tural Therapy--a New Conception of Treatment,"
        Drug Forum, 4:65-72, 1975.

2464)   Van Dyne, Larry.  "Homosexual Academics Organ-
        ize, Seek End to Discrimination," Chronicle of
        Higher Education, Dec. 10, 1973, p. 7.

2465)   Vierneisel, Karen.  "An Annotated Checklist of Les-
        bian Feminist Resources," Margins, Aug. 1975,
        pp. 11-15.   (69 items)

2466)   Walker, J. L. and Others.  "The Varieties of The-
        rapeutic Experience:  Conjoint Therapy in a Homo-
        sexual Marriage," Canadian Mental Health, 23:3-5,
        Jun. 1975.

2467)   Weinberg, Martin S.  "The Male Homosexual, Age-
        related Variations in Social and Psychological Char-
        acteristics," Social Problems, 17:527-37, 1970.

2468)   Wells, Karen.   "Elsa Gidlow," Margins, Aug. 1975,
        pp. 53-55.

2469)   West, Celeste.   "Body Politic," Synergy, Sep. -Oct.
        1970, pp. 1-4.

2470)   "When the Patient Is Gay," Nursing Update, 5:12-
        15, Feb. 1974.

2471)   "Why Homosexuality?" Journal of Primal Therapy,
        4:353-62, 1975.

2472)   Williams, Colin J. and Weinberg, Martin S.   "Be-
        ing Discovered:  A Study of Homosexuals in the
        Military," Social Problems, 18:217-27, 1970.

2473)   Williams, Gil.  'On Kirby Congdon," Margins, May
        1975, pp. 39-40.

2474)   Willick, Daniel H. ; Gehlker, Gretchen; and Watts,
        Anita M.   "Social Class as a Factor Affecting Ju-
        dicial Disposition:  Defendants Charged with Crim-
        inal Homosexual Acts," Criminology, 13:57-77,
        1975.

2475)   Winant, Fran.   "Lesbian Publish Lesbians:  My
        Life and Times with Violet Press," Margins, Aug.
        1975, pp. 62-66.

2476)   Witty, Kristi.   "When the Patient Is Gay," Patient
        Care, 7:80-87, Nov. 1, 1973.   Reply:  7:17-18,
        Dec. 1, 1973.

2477)   Woodwoman, Libby.   "Pat Parker Talks about Her
        Life and Her Work," Margins, Aug. 1975, pp. 60-61.

2478)   Worsnop, Richard L.   "Sexual Revolution:  Myth or
        Reality?" Editorial Research Reports, 1:239-58 at
        247-51, 1970.

2479)   Zoglin, Richard.   "The Homosexual Executive,"
        MBA, Jul. -Aug. 1975, pp. 26-31.

## ARTICLES IN HOMOPHILE PUBLICATIONS

2480) Aiken, David L. "Protest in the Military [against Discharge of Homosexuals]," Advocate, Dec. 31, 1975, p. 15.

2481) Air Force Sergeant at Nebraska Base Names 200-250 Men and Sets off a Homosexual Witchhunt, Advocate, Apr. 1970, pp. 1, 30.

2482) Alpine California Proposed as Gay Mecca, Advocate, Nov. 11, 1970, pp. 1, 14 and Nov. 25, 1970, p. 2; Gay, Dec. 7, 1970, pp. 5, 16; Vector, Dec. 70, pp. 18-20.

2483) Altman, Dennis. "Young Australian Speaks His Mind about Gay Liberation," Vector, Oct. 1970, pp. 38, 41.

2484) American Bar Association Calls for Consensual Sex Law Reform, Advocate, Aug. 29, 1973, pp. 1, 21.

2485) American Civil Liberties Union Favors Individual Sexual Privacy, Repeal of Restrictive Sex Laws, and Legislation Forbidding Sexual Discrimination, Advocate, Jun. 18, 1975, p. 5.

2486) American Civil Liberties Union Launches Major Gay Rights Project, Advocate, Nov. 21, 1973, p. 18.

2487) American Historians Pass Resolution in Support of Gay Rights, Advocate, Jan. 30, 1974, p. 12.

2488) American Historians Support Research on Homosexuality and the Right of Gay Historians to Teach Gay History, Advocate, May 21, 1975, p. 5.

2489) Amory, Richard. "Somerset Maugham," Vector, Jan. 1971, pp. 10-12.

2490)    Andros, Phil. "André Gide," Vector, Oct. 1970, pp.
         42, 53.

2491)    Angry Gays March on Hollywood Police Station, Ad-
         vocate, Oct. 24, 1973, p. 3.

2492)    "Ann Landers Says Homosexuals Are Sick," Advo-
         cate, Jan. 31, 1973, p. 5.

2493)    Arkansas Sodomy Statute Upheld by U.S. Supreme
         Court, Advocate, Feb. 28, 1973, p. 23.

2494)    Armando, Jerry. "Lenny Bruce on Homosexuality,"
         Vector, Feb. 1972, p. 33 and Mar. 1972, p. 17.

2495)    Arrest of at Least 20 Gays in Protests at Republican
         Conclave, Advocate, Sep. 13, 1972, p. 3.

2496)    Arrest of 54 in Indianapolis Raid, Advocate, Aug.
         15, 1973, pp. 3, 6.

2497)    Arrest of 40 for Hustling in Hollywood Vice Sweep,
         Advocate, Jun. 19, 1974, p. 8.

2498)    Arrest of 43 Men in Galveston, Texas, Advocate,
         Aug. 30, 1972, p. 13.

2499)    Arrest of 46 in San Francisco Tenderloin Sweep,
         Advocate, Dec. 8, 1971, p. 10.

2500)    Arrest of Gay Activists at New York City Hall,
         Gay, Aug. 2, 1971, pp. 1, 3.

2501)    Arrest of 22 in Los Angeles Bar Raid, Advocate,
         Sep. 13, 1972, pp. 1, 8.

2502)    Arsonists Burn San Francisco Gay Centers [SIR
         Headquarters and Metropolitan Community Church],
         Gay, Aug. 21, 1972, pp. 1, 11.

2503)    Baker, Jack. "Don't Count on 'Straight' Politicos,"
         Advocate, Dec. 19, 1973, p. 16.

2504)    Baker, Joe. "Brian McNaught, Gay and Catholic,"
         Advocate, Sep. 24, 1975, p. 17.

2505)    Barnett, Walter. Law Reform in the United States,

Advocate, Apr. 14, 1971, pp. 1, 8-9 and May 12, 1971, pp. 12, 15.

2506)   Bean, Lowell. "Out of the Closets and Into the Textbooks [American Anthropological Association Convention]," Advocate, Mar. 26, 1975, p. 11.

2507)   Becker, Marty. "Gay Singer's Dilemma: Upfront or Commercial?" Advocate, Apr. 11, 1973, p. 27.

2508)   Bell, Arthur. "Gay Activist Looks at Broadway: Despite Liberal Attitudes in Show Business, Few Admit Being Gay," Advocate, Feb. 28, 1973, pp. 32-34.

2509)   Black Panther Party Supports Gay Liberation, Gay, Sep. 14, 1970, pp. 3, 12.

2510)   Bonding Now Available to Known Gays, Gay, Apr. 26, 1971, p. 12.

2511)   Boston Unitarians Approve Gay Office, Advocate, Dec. 19, 1973, p. 11.

2512)   Brigham Young University Mormons Seek to Weed out Homosexuals, Advocate, Jun. 18, 1975, p. 15; Aug. 13, 1975, pp. 14, 16; Oct. 22, 1975, p. 23.

2513)   Brill, David and others. Report on the State of the Gay Movement in the United States in 1975, Advocate, Dec. 31, 1975, pp. 26-31.

2514)   Britton, Jeff. "Primal Therapy: A Gay Viewpoint," Gay Alternative, no. 7, Summer 1975, pp. 30-31.

2515)   Brooklyn Bank Robbery by John Wojtowicz, Gay, Oct. 2, 1972, pp. 8, 16; Oct. 16, 1972, pp. 1, 6-7, 13; Oct. 30, 1972, pp. 10, 12; Advocate, Sep. 13, 1972, p. 1; Vector, Dec. 1972, pp. 26-35 and Jan. 1973, pp. 44-45.

2516)   Busby, Roy M. "The Cleveland Street Scandal: Victorian Conspiracy or Bedroom Farce?" Gay News, no. 74, Jul. 1975, pp. 13-14.

2517)   Buttry, Robert. Historian Martin Duberman, Advocate, Feb. 12, 1975, pp. 13, 36.

2518)    Byron, Stuart.  "The Story of Frank O'Hara [Poet],"
         Gay, Apr. 17, 1972, pp. 5, 16.

2519)    "California Democrats Recognize Homosexual
         Rights," Vector, May 1972, p. 49.

2520)    "California Public Utilities Commission Denies Gay
         Yellow Pages Listing," Advocate, Feb. 1970, p. 5.

2521)    California Teachers Support Gay Rights, Gay, Feb.
         16, 1970, p. 3.

2522)    Canadians Celebrate Gay Pride, Gay, Oct. 2, 1972,
         pp. 1, 17.

2523)    Canadian Gays Protest Discrimination, Advocate,
         Aug. 29, 1973, p. 9.

2524)    Carrier, Joseph M.  "Gay Encounters in Guadala-
         jara," Gay Sunshine, nos. 26-27, Winter 1975, pp.
         8-9.

2525)    Catholic Commission on Social Justice [Archdiocese
         of San Francisco] Recognizes Homosexual Rights,
         Vector, Jun. 1971, p. 20.

2526)    Chapman, David.  "Victorian Closet Couldn't Hold
         [John Addington] Symonds," Advocate, Oct. 24,
         1973, p. 34.

2527)    "Charities Decline Gift from Gays," Advocate, Jun.
         20, 1973, p. 17.

2528)    Citizenship Granted to Gay Alien [Michael Labady],
         Gay, Apr. 26, 1971, p. 12.

2529)    Civil Rights for Homosexuals--Responses of 13 Gov-
         ernors, Advocate, Oct. 22, 1975, pp. 12, 18-19,
         22.

2530)    Cohen, Ira.  "Conversations in Kathmandu:  Charles
         Henri Ford," Gay Sunshine, no. 24, Spring 1975,
         pp. 20-26.

2531)    Cole, Rob.  "Behind Bars:  Lessons on Being Gay,"
         Advocate, Jun. 20, 1973, pp. 1-2.

2532)          _____ . "Military Policies on Gays Make No
          Sense," Advocate, Jul. 8, 1970, pp. 7, 10, 17.

2533)     Coleman, James. "Walt Whitman: Good Gay Poet,"
          Advocate, Mar. 17, 1971, p. 11.

2534)     "College of Sequoias Battles 'Queers,'" Advocate,
          Nov. 22, 1972, p. 10.

2535)     "College Students Tour San Francisco Gay World,"
          Advocate, Jan. 31, 1973, p. 19.

2536)     Colombia Reduces Sodomy from Felony to Misde-
          meanor, Advocate, Oct. 14, 1970, p. 5.

2537)     Compton, Thomas. "Sodomy and Civic Doom" Vec-
          tor, Nov. 1975, pp. 23-27, 57-58.

2538)     Connecticut Gays Celebrate Implementation of New
          Consensual Sex Reform Law, Advocate, Sep. 29,
          1971, p. 1.

2539)     Consensual Sex Law Reform Passed in 11 American
          States, Advocate, Jul. 7, 1971, p. 1 (Colo.); Aug.
          4, 1971, p. 1 (Ore.); Apr. 26, 1972, p. 1 (Haw.);
          Aug. 2, 1972, p. 1 (Del.); Jan. 31, 1973, p. 1
          (Ohio); Mar. 28, 1973, p. 1 (N. Dak.); Jun. 4,
          1975, p. 4 (Calif.); Jul. 2, 1975, p. 4 (N. Mex.);
          Jul. 16, 1975, p. 4 (Maine); Jul. 30, 1975, p. 5
          (Wash.); Sep. 24, 1975, p. 9 (Ark.).

2540)     Consensual Sex Law Reform in Finland, Vector,
          Aug. 1971, p. 43.

2541)     Consensual Sex Law Reform Passed and Repealed
          in Idaho, Advocate, Jun. 9, 1971, p. 1, 13 and
          Mar. 10, 1972, p. 3.

2542)     Consensual Sex Law Reform in Norway, One, 16:4-
          5, Jul.-Aug. 1972.

2543)     Consensual Sex Law Reform in South Australia, Ad-
          vocate, Oct. 22, 1975, p. 9.

2544)     Conviction of 4 Gays for Trespassing against New
          York Daily News, Advocate, Jul. 5, 1972, p. 3.

2545)     Copilow, Barry and Coleman, Tom. "Report and
          Investigation of Enforcement of Section 647(a) of the
          California Penal Code by the Los Angeles Police
          Department," Advocate, Feb. 14, 1973, pp. 2-3, 24.

2546)     Cuba Excludes Gays from Teaching and Work in the
          Arts, Gay, Jul. 5, 1971, p. 5.

2547)     Dallas TV Explores local Gay World, Advocate,
          Oct. 13, 1971, p. 2.

2548)     Damon, Paul. "Author Outlines Plan for Gay
          Writers' Guild," Advocate, Mar. 13, 1973, p. 34.

2549)     D'Arcangelo, Angelo. "The Death of Ramon Novar-
          ro," Gay, Sep. 7, 1970, pp. 4-5.

2550)     "'Dear Abby' Says Gays Are Not Sick," Gay, Jul.
          13, 1970, p. 3.

2551)     Democratic Convention Airs Gay Lib Proposals,
          Gay, Aug. 7, 1972, pp. 1, 10.

2552)     Denmark to Allow Homosexual Prostitution, Gay,
          Jul. 6, 1970, p. 3.

2553)     "Denver Daily Takes Hard Look at Cops' Treatment
          of Gays," Advocate, May 23, 1973, p. 16.

2554)     "Denver Gays Suing over Harassment," Advocate,
          Aug. 29, 1973, p. 22.

2555)     Devlin, Diane. "The Flight of the Gay Student,"
          Gay, May 25, 1970, p. 13.

2556)     Dick Cavett Features Gay Activists Alliance and
          Mattachine Society Spokesmen, Gay, Jan. 18, 1971,
          pp. 1, 16.

2557)     Dignity, Catholic Homosexual Group, Holds Confer-
          ence, Advocate, Sep. 26, 1973, p. 1, 18.

2558)     District of Columbia Gay Activists Alliance Says It
          Has Been Infiltrated and Spied upon by Police and
          FBI, Advocate, Nov. 7, 1973, p. 9.

2559)     District of Columbia School Board Bans Gay Bias,

Advocate, Jun. 21, 1972, p. 3 and Jun. 26, 1972, p. 1.

2560)    Driver, Carl. "Famous Queens of History," Advocate, Sep. 1, 1971, p. 15 (Edward II); Sep. 29, 1971, p. 25 (Alexander); Oct. 27, 1971, p. 26 (Michelangelo); Nov. 24, 1971, p. 17 (Leonardo da Vinci); Jan. 5, 1972, pp. 19, 22 (Oscar Wilde).

2561)    _____. "Gay Fiction May Be Growing Up," Advocate, Dec. 8, 1971, p. 33.

2562)    Dutch Gay Group [C.O.C.] 25 Years Old, Gay, Dec. 20, 1971, p. 10.

2563)    Dutch Gays Protest Military Policy in Holland, Gay, Jan. 29, 1973, p. 18.

2564)    Dynes, Wayne. "Another Gay Genius: Wittgenstein, A Modern Leonardo," Advocate, Nov. 7, 1973, pp. 25, 27.

2565)    Employment Rights Roundup, Advocate, Jun. 29, 1975, pp. 8-9, 14, 42.

2566)    Evans, Arthur. "Are You on the FBI's Sex List?" Advocate, Mar. 13, 1974, p. 37.

2567)    _____. "Besides Gay Power, We Need a Gay Culture," Advocate, Apr. 11, 1973, p. 37.

2568)    _____. "Witchcraft: The Gay Counter Culture. Part V: The Mass Murder of Women and Gays," Fag Rag, Summer, 1975, pp. 13-16.

2569)    Evans, R. Michael. "André Gide," Queens Quarterly, Aug. 1971, pp. 13, 38-39.

2570)    Failure of Consensual Sex Law Reform in Israel, Advocate, Apr. 10, 1974, p. 26.

2571)    Failure of Consensual Sex Law Reform in Minnesota, Advocate, Jun. 18, 1975, p. 5.

2572)    Failure of Consensual Sex Law Reform in New York, Advocate, Jul. 30, 1975, p. 5.

2573)    Federal Grants of Money to Los Angeles Gay Com-
         munity Services Center, Advocate, Jan. 17, 1973,
         pp. 1, 12; Dec. 19, 1973, p. 4; Oct. 22, 1974,
         p. 1.

2574)    Federal Judge Orders U.S. Government to End Ban
         on Hiring Gays, Advocate, Dec. 5, 1973, pp. 3, 7.

2575)    Federal Security Clearance System Challenged by
         Gay Employees, Advocate, Apr. 1970, p. 7; May
         30, 1970, p. 5; Oct. 31, 1971, pp. 1, 26; Feb. 2,
         1972, p. 1; Jun. 21, 1972, p. 1; Oct. 25, 1972,
         p. 5; Sep. 26, 1973, p. 17; Apr. 24, 1974, p. 5;
         Jun. 4, 1974, p. 13; Mar. 25, 1975, p. 4; Apr.
         16, 1975, p. 37; Aug. 27, 1975, p. 4.

2576)    Fifteen New York Political Candidates Pledge Sup-
         port for Gays, Advocate, Mar. 28, 1973, p. 20.

2577)    Findley, Tim and Howe, Charles.  "Nothing Gay
         about Homosexuality in Prison," Advocate, Mar.
         31, 1971, p. 14.

2578)    Five Hundred Homosexuals in New York March for
         Peace, Gay, May 24, 1971, p. 1.

2579)    Floridians Picket Police Charging Gay Harassment,
         Advocate, Oct. 27, 1971, p. 1.

2580)    Forbes, Dennis.   Actor Calvin Culver.  Advocate,
         Jan. 29, 1975, p. 16.

2581)    Freedman, Mark.  "Gays and Public Health," Advo-
         cate, Feb. 13, 1974, p. 37.

2582)    Gay Academics, Organizing, Advocate, Jul. 4, 1973,
         p. 19; Dec. 19, 1973, pp. 2, 10.

2583)    Gay Activists Alliance Wins Incorporation Appeal,
         Advocate, Feb. 14, 1973, p. 19.

2584)    Gay Activists Alliance Zaps Harper's Magazine,
         Advocate, Nov. 25, 1970, p. 1.

2585)    Gay Activists Beaten and Clubbed by Long Island
         Police, Gay, Sep. 27, 1971, pp. 1, 8.

2586)   "Gay Author Banned from Job at Military Teaching
        Center," Advocate, Feb. 27, 1974, p. 12.

2587)   Gay Bar Refused Entertainment License, Advocate,
        Feb. 2, 1972, p. 20.

2588)   "Gay Blades Set Fashion," Gay, Apr. 20, 1970,
        p. 3.

2589)   "Gay Books Displayed at Library Convention," Gay,
        Aug. 7, 1972, pp. 1, 10.

2590)   "Gay Broadcaster [in Minnesota] Fights for Job,"
        Gay, Mar. 15, 1970, p. 20.

2591)   Gay Candidate Elected to Ann Arbor, Michigan, City
        Council, Advocate, May 8, 1974, p. 9.

2592)   "Gay Couple Files Joint Tax Return," Gay, Jun. 1,
        1970, p. 3.

2593)   Gay Courses Offered at American Colleges and Uni-
        versities, Advocate, May 4, 1970, p. 3 (University
        of Nebraska); Sep. 16, 1970, p. 20 (California State
        College at Long Beach); Jan. 20, 1971, p. 2 (New
        York University); Aug. 16, 1972, p. 9 (California
        State College at Sacramento); Aug. 15, 1973, p. 17
        (Yale); May 8, 1974, p. 10 (UCLA); Feb. 12, 1975,
        p. 5 (University of Montana).

2594)   Gay Father Denied Access to Children, Gay, May
        21, 1973, p. 10; Advocate, Nov. 21, 1973, pp. 5,
        15.

2595)   Gay Father Wins Visiting Rights, Advocate, Nov.
        22, 1972, p. 16; Feb. 12, 1975, p. 26.

2596)   "Gay Film Seized in Campus Fuss," Advocate, Apr.
        12, 1972, p. 8.

2597)   Gay High School Teacher in New Jersey (John Gish)
        Fights Adverse School Board Decision, Advocate,
        Oct. 11, 1972, p. 7; Dec. 6, 1972, p. 2; May 8,
        1974, p. 10.

2598)   Gay High School Teacher in Oregon (Peggy Burton)

Cannot Be Dismissed Solely for Homosexuality Says Federal Court, Advocate, Jun. 21, 1972, p. 1; Oct. 11, 1972, p. 18; Dec. 4, 1974, p. 15; Dec. 3, 1975, p. 16.

2599)  Gay High School Teacher in Washington (James Gaylord) Cannot Be Dismissed Solely for Homosexuality Says State Court, Advocate, Jun. 18, 1975. p. 5.

2600)  "Gay Journalists' Caucus Forms at District of Columbia Convention," Advocate, Jul. 4, 1973, p. 18.

2601)  Gay Junior High School Teacher in Maryland (Joseph Acanfora) Removed from Teaching Duties, Advocate, Apr. 3, 1972, p. 1; May 10, 1972, p. 6; Aug. 30, 1972, p. 14; Oct. 11, 1972, p. 1; Oct. 26, 1972, p. 2; Apr. 10, 1974, p. 19; Apr. 24, 1974, p. 8; Nov. 11, 1974, pp. 20-21.

2602)  Gay Law Students Organize, Gay, Oct. 30, 1972, p. 1; Advocate, Oct. 25, 1972, p. 19; Nov. 7, 1973, p. 18.

2603)  Gay Lawyer (Joseph V. Stewart) Admitted to District of Columbia Bar, Advocate, Aug. 27, 1975, p. 6.

2604)  Gay Lawyer ordered Certified in Ohio, Advocate, Jan. 3, 1973, p. 15.

2605)  Gay Lawyer (Harris Kimball) Refused Admission to New York Bar, Advocate, Jan. 31, 1973, p. 17.

2606)  Gay Leadership in Fashion May Be on the Wane, Advocate, Jan. 30, 1974, p. 17.

2607)  Gay Lib Comes to District of Columbia High School, Gay, Apr. 9, 1973, pp. 1, 12.

2608)  Gay Lib Grows in New York City High Schools, Gay, May 7, 1973, p. 10.

2609)  Gay Lib Precursor: Edward Carpenter, Gay Sunshine, no. 7, Jun.-Jul. 1971, p. 3.

2610)  Gay Libbers Help Revise Unitarian Sex Course, Gay, Jun. 26, 1972, pp. 1, 17.

2611)  Gay Liberation Front Spreads to London, Advocate,

Jan. 20, 1971, p. 10; Aug. 18, 1971, p. 7.

2612) Gay Marine Stirs Wide Publicity, Gay, May 1, 1972, pp. 1, 16.

2613) Gay Medical Student Alliance Formed in Brooklyn, Gay, Jun. 4, 1973, p. 9.

2614) "Gay Millionaire Murdered in Los Angeles," Advocate, Mar. 28, 1974, p. 2.

2615) Gay Minister [William Johnson] Ordained in San Francisco, Vector, Jun. 1972, p. 19; Advocate, May 24, 1972, p. 1.

2616) "Gay Mother Wins Custody of Children," Advocate, Jul. 19, 1972, p. 6.

2617) "Gay Named to Atlanta Human Rights Unit," Advocate, Mar. 14, 1973, p. 19.

2618) "Gay People and the Military: A Special Report," Advocate, Jul. 2, 1975, pp. 19-25.

2619) Gay Pride (1974), In Touch, Sep. 1974, pp. 20-27.

2620) Gay Pride Celebration across the Country, Advocate, Jul. 22, 1970, pp. 1, 5, 6; Jul. 21, 1971, pp. 1-5, 8, 11; Jul. 5, 1972, pp. 1, 7; Jul. 19, 1972, pp. 1-3, 5, 15; Jul. 18, 1973, pp. 1, 3, 5, 6; Jul. 3, 1974, p. 8; Jul. 30, 1975, pp. 17-31.

2621) Gay Pride Celebrations on East and West Coasts, Gay, Jun. 29, 1970, pp. 10-11; Jul. 20, 1970, pp. 3-7; Jul. 27, 1970, pp. 4-5; Jul. 5, 1971, pp. 1, 6-7; Jul. 21, 1971, pp. 1-2, 4, 6, 26; Jun. 26, 1972, pp. 12-13, 16.

2622) Gay Professor at California State College at Hayward Released, College Denies Bias, Advocate, May 26, 1971, p. 9.

2623) Gay Professor at University of Florida Dismissed, Advocate, May 22, 1974, p. 18.

2624) Gay Radio Roundup, Advocate, Aug. 27, 1975, p. 8.

2625)      Gay Rights Bill Fails to Pass New York City Coun-
           cil, Advocate, Jun. 10, 1970, p. 2; Feb. 3, 1971,
           p. 1; Jun. 9, 1971, p. 2; Oct. 13, 1971, pp. 1,
           26; Dec. 8, 1971, pp. 3, 16; Feb. 2, 1972, p. 1;
           Feb. 16, 1972, p. 1; Mar. 29, 1972, p. 1; Jun.
           21, 1972, p. 1; Aug. 16, 1972, p. 1; Aug. 30,
           1972, p. 11; Jan. 16, 1973, p. 1; May 23, 1973,
           p. 1; May 8, 1974, p. 3; Jun. 19, 1974, pp. 2, 3.

2626)      Gay Rights Bill Introduced in Congress by Repre-
           sentative Bella Abzug of New York with 23 Other
           Sponsors, Advocate, Apr. 23, 1975, p. 4.

2627)      Gay Rights Employment Ordinances Passed in 1
           Canadian and 19 American Cities, Advocate, May
           10, 1972, p. 1 and Jul. 4, 1973, p. 17 (East Lan-
           sing, Mich.); Apr. 26, 1972, p. 1 (San Francisco);
           Aug. 16, 1972, p. 1 (Ann Arbor, Mich.); Oct. 10,
           1973, p. 1 (Seattle); Nov. 21, 1973, p. 3 (Toronto);
           Dec. 19, 1973, p. 1 (Washington, D.C.); Apr. 24,
           1974, p. 6 (Minneapolis); Oct. 9, 1974, p. 1 (Itha-
           ca, N.Y.); Jan. 15, 1975, p. 1 (Portland, Ore.);
           Mar. 25, 1975, pp. 5-6 (Urbana, Ill.; Cupertino,
           Mountain View, and Sunnyvale, Calif.); Apr. 23,
           1975, p. 6 (Madison, Wis.); Aug. 13, 1975, pp.
           5-6 (Santa Cruz, Calif.; Marshall, Minn.; and Yel-
           low Springs, Ohio); Aug. 27, 1975, p. 5 (Santa Bar-
           bara, Calif. and Austin, Tex.); Oct. 22, 1975, p.
           9 (Chapel Hill, N. Car.).

2628)      Gay Speakers in High Schools Arouse Fuss, Advo-
           cate, Jun. 23, 1971, p. 4; Oct. 25, 1972, p. 9;
           May 9, 1973, p. 4; Feb. 27, 1974, p. 10.

2629)      Gay Student Organizations Formed at Many American
           Colleges and Universities, Gay, Jul. 13, 1970, p.
           3 (Univ. of Mich.); Dec. 21, 1970, pp. 1, 12 (Cor-
           nell); Advocate, Apr. 29, 1970, p. 9 (Harvard and
           Univ. of Chicago); Mar. 17, 1971, pp. 1, 9 (Sacra-
           mento State); Jun. 23, 1971, p. 13 (Univ. of Tenn.);
           Aug. 4, 1971, p. 2 (Univ. of Maine); Sep. 27,
           1972, p. 7 (Univ. of Okla.); Oct. 11, 1972, p. 2
           (Columbia); Jan. 3, 1973, pp. 9, 19 (Univ. of Ga.
           and Univ. of Ky.); Mar. 12, 1973, p. 12 (Penn
           State); Apr. 11, 1973, p. 20 (Univ. of Mo.); Apr.
           25, 1973, p. 23 (Univ. of Kans.); Jul. 4, 1973,
           p. 18 (Univ. of New Hamp.); Apr. 10, 1974, p. 27

(Portland State).   (For fuller list, see nos. 202, 417,  474)

2630)     Gay Summer Travel (1975) Survey of U.S.   Advocate, Jul. 16, 1975, pp. 18-29.

2631)     Gay Symposium Set for Nurses, Advocate, Jan. 19, 1972, p. 9.

2632)     Gay Task Force Recognized by National Council of Churches, Advocate, Nov. 21, 1973, p. 10.

2633)     "Gay Teacher Called Good for Students," Advocate, May 9, 1973, p. 5.

2634)     Gay Teachers Approved by District of Columbia School Board, Gay, Jun. 26, 1972, pp. 1, 17.

2635)     Gay Teachers Organizing, Advocate, Jul. 5, 1972, p. 17.

2636)     "The Gay Vote:  Reality or Illusion," Advocate, Jul. 3, 1974, p. 16.

2637)     "Gays Are Suspect in 'Secret' Oregon Police Files," Advocate, Feb. 27, 1974, p. 18.

2638)     Gays Are Victims of Police Brutality Says Pennsylvania State Report, Gay, Dec. 25, 1972, p. 18.

2639)     "Gays Call for New Nursing Awareness," Advocate, Feb. 27, 1974, p. 14.

2640)     "Gays in Uniform," Advocate, Oct. 13, 1971, pp. 30, 34.

2641)     Gays March, Over 2500 Strong, on New York State Capitol Requesting Basic Rights, Advocate, Apr. 14, 1971, pp. 1, 3; Gay, Apr. 12, 1971, pp. 1, 3, 8.

2642)     "Gays Must Learn How to Use Courts, Lawyer Says," Advocate, Mar. 29, 1972, p. 29.

2643)     "Gays Named to Board of San Francisco Family Agency," Advocate, Mar. 3, 1971, pp. 1, 14.

2644)     "Gays Plunge into Canadian Politics," Advocate,
          Sep. 13, 1972, p. 2.

2645)     Gays Protest "Marcus Welby" TV Show, Advocate,
          Mar. 14, 1973, pp. 1, 21.

2646)     "Gays Snubbed by 'Common Cause' Group," Advo-
          cate, Apr. 12, 1972, p. 17.

2647)     "Gays Still Marked Men in Pentagon," Advocate,
          May 8, 1974, p. 5.

2648)     "Gays Tell It Like It Is in Catholic Seminar," Ad-
          vocate, Dec. 9, 1970, p. 7.

2649)     "Gays Zap CBS Network Center," Advocate, Apr.
          10, 1974, p. 1.

2650)     Gays Zap Dr. David Reubin on Chicago TV Show,
          Gay, Mar. 1, 1971, pp. 3, 12.

2651)     George Raya, Gay Lobbyist in Sacramento, Advo-
          cate, May 21, 1975, pp. 13-15.

2652)     Gibson, Rod. "Insurance Companies Are Biased,
          Have Codes," Advocate, Dec. 23, 1970, p. 24.

2653)     Grant, Celt C. "Faggots in Uniform," Gay Sun-
          shine, no. 16, Jan.-Feb. 1973, p. 18.

2654)     Gregory-Lewis, Sasha. "Building a Gay Politic:
          The San Francisco Model," Advocate, Oct. 8, 1975,
          pp. 27, 32.

2655)     "Groovy Guy" Contest Winners, Advocate, Aug. 16,
          1970, p. 1; Sep. 15, 1971, p. 1; Sep. 13, 1972,
          pp. 1, 5.

2656)     Hallowell, John. "Gore Vidal on Homosexuality,"
          Advocate, Nov. 11, 1970, pp. 16, 19.

2657)     Hampton, Thane. "The Divine Comedy of Pavel
          Tchelitchew [Artist]," Gay, Oct. 11, 1971, pp. 8-
          9, 19.

2658)     _____. "A Visit with W. Dorr Legg of One,
          Inc.," Gay, Dec. 6, 1971, pp. 10, 17.

2659)        _____. "The Wit and Wisdom of Oscar Wilde,"
Gay, Jan. 10, 1972, pp. 10-11.

2660)        Hanson, Craig A. "Gay Liberation without Marx
or Jesus," Fag Rag/Gay Sunshine, Summer, 1974,
p. 26.

2661)        Harbers, Scott and Jackson, Ed. Homosexual Murders in Houston, Advocate, Aug. 29, 1973, pp. 1,
3 and Sep. 12, 1973, pp. 1, 5.

2662)        Harold Brown, Distinguished Doctor and Gay Activist, Advocate, Oct. 24, 1973, p. 1; Nov. 21, 1973,
p. 2; Feb. 26, 1975, p. 4.

2663)        Harrison, Hugh. "The Male Groupie," In Touch,
Dec. 1974, pp. 40-43, 55-56.

2664)        Hernandez, Noel. "The Male Prostitute," Vector,
Oct. 1972, pp. 6-7, 20.

2665)        "Hidden Police Spying in Restroom Outlawed," Advocate, Jan. 19, 1972, p. 9.

2666)        High Schools in New York City allowing Gay Organizations, Advocate, May 9, 1973, p. 11.

2667)        "Historic Hearings [on Gay Rights] Held in New
York City," Gay, Nov. 22, 1971, pp. 1, 8.

2668)        Holt, Mel. "The Hustler's Lot Is Not a Happy
One," Advocate, May 13, 1970, pp. 25, 27.

2669)        "Homophile Poet W. H. Auden Dies," Advocate,
Oct. 24, 1973, p. 11.

2670)        Homosexual Activist Franklin Kameny Runs for Congress in the District of Columbia, Gay, Mar. 15,
1971, pp. 1, 3.

2671)        Homosexual Athlete Bill Tilden Is Voted Number
One, Gay, Feb. 16, 1970, p. 20.

2672)        "A Homosexual Bill of Rights," Vector, Aug. 1972,
p. 10.

2673)        Homosexual Male Found Not Fit to Drive in

Connecticut, Advocate, Jan. 6, 1971, pp. 1, 7.

2674) Homosexual Minister Troy Perry Fasts for Justice for Gays, Gay, Aug. 3, 1970, pp. 4, 12.

2675) "Homosexuality No Yardstick for Witnesses' Honesty, Court Rules," Advocate, Oct. 27, 1971, p. 7.

2676) "Homosexuality Not So Bad, Lutherans and Unitarians Decide," Advocate, Aug. 5, 1970, p. 1.

2677) Hughes, Jeremy. "Grant Tracy Saxon: Encounter with a Happy Hustler," In Touch, Jun. 1975, pp. 50-53, 64.

2678) _____. "Michael Greer--Entertainer," In Touch, Oct. 1975, pp. 26-27.

2679) Hundreds March on Los Angeles Police in Protest, Advocate, Feb. 13, 1974, pp. 1, 14.

2680) Hunter, John F. "If We Can't Come to Your Church, We'll Build Our Own," Gay, Apr. 20, 1970, pp. 4-5, 17.

2681) _____. "Meet Jim Owles, President of the Gay Activists Alliance," Gay, Aug. 31, 1970, pp. 4-5.

2682) "In Catholic Ireland, Priest and Senator Back Gay Rights," Advocate, Apr. 10, 1974, p. 27.

2683) "Inmate [in Oregon Prison] Denied Parole Because He's Gay?" Advocate, Nov. 8, 1972, p. 19.

2684) Interview: Allen Ginsberg, Gay Sunshine, no. 16, Jan.-Feb. 1973, pp. 1, 4-10. (Reprinted in Allen Young, Gay Sunshine Interview with Allen Ginsberg. [Bolinas, Ca.: Grey Fox Press, 1973] 42 pp)

2685) Interview: Bette Midler, Advocate, Apr. 23, 1975, pp. 31-34.

2686) Interview: Chris Robison [Singer and Musician], Fag Rag, Summer 1975, pp. 8-10.

2687) Interview: Christopher Isherwood, Advocate, Dec. 17, 1975, pp. 6-8.

2688)    Interview: Don Slater [Gay Leader], Gay, May 11, 1970, pp. 4-5.

2689)    Interview: Elaine Noble [Lesbian and Member of Massachusetts Assembly]," Advocate, Jun. 4, 1975, pp. 8-9.

2690)    Interview: Gore Vidal, Fag-Rag, Winter-Spring 1974, pp. 1, 3-9.

2691)    Interview: Gore Vidal, Gay Sunshine, no. 26-27, Winter 1975, pp. 20-25.

2692)    Interview: Jack Baker [Gay Leader and Lawyer], Gay, May 11, 1970, p. 13 and May 18, 1970, p. 13.

2693)    Interview: John Damien [Former Jockey and Racing Commissioner], Body Politic, no. 18, May-Jun. 1975, pp. 12-13.

2694)    Interview: John Giorno, Poet, Gay Sunshine, no. 24, Spring 1975, pp. 1-8.

2695)    Interview: John Rechy [Novelist], In Touch, Mar. 1974, pp. 22-29.

2696)    Interview: Mae West, Advocate, Oct. 8, 1975, pp. 33-34.

2697)    Interview: Morris Kight [Gay Leader], Gay, Feb. 1, 1971, pp. 14-16.

2698)    Interview: Ned Rorem [Musician and Writer], Fag Rag/Gay Sunshine, Summer 1974, pp. 6-12.

2699)    Interview: Richard Hongisto [San Francisco County Sheriff], Vector, Mar. 1973, pp. 27-29.

2700)    Interview: Wakefield Poole [Film Maker], Gay, Apr. 3, 1972, pp. 16-17.

2701)    Jack Paar Apologizes for Anti-gay Remarks on TV, Advocate, Feb. 28, 1973, p. 6.

2702)    Jackson, Don. "The Church Is the Oppressor," Vector, Jun. 1972, pp. 24-25.

2703)     Jackson, Ed. "Tax and the Single Gay," Advocate,
          Mar. 17, 1971, pp. 12-13.

2704)     Jacobs, Alan. "Gertrude [Stein] and Alice [Toklas],"
          Vector, Aug. 1971, pp. 10-11.

2705)     _____. "Homosexual Children," Vector, Mar.
          1971, pp. 38-39.

2706)     "Jehovah's Witnesses Say 'Kill Gays,'" Gay, Oct.
          30, 1972, p. 1.

2707)     "Jesus Freaks Stab Boy, Foul Gay Chapel in Holly-
          wood," Advocate, Aug. 2, 1972, p. 6.

2708)     John Damien, Canadian Race Commissioner, Sues
          for His Dismissal for Homosexuality, Advocate,
          Oct. 8, 1975, pp. 16-17.

2709)     "Judge Awards $1100 to Assaulted Gay Man," Ad-
          vocate, Jun. 19, 1974, p. 20.

2710)     "Judge Places Gay Teenage Boy in Lesbian Foster
          Parents' Home," Advocate, May 22, 1974, p. 8.

2711)     Kameny, Franklin. "Action of the Gay Legal
          Front," Vector, Nov. 1972, pp. 7-9.

2712)     _____. "Gays and the U.S. Civil Service," Vec-
          tor, Feb. 1973, pp. 8, 39-41.

2713)     _____. "Homosexuals Challenge U.S. Govern-
          ment--Injustice Continues," Vector, Sep. 1970, pp.
          10-12.

2714)     _____. "My Sex Life Is None of My Govern-
          ment's Goddamned Business," Vector, Oct. 1970,
          pp. 10-12.

2715)     _____. "Security Clearance Granted by Govern-
          ment," Vector, Oct. 1971, pp. 32-33, 53.

2716)     Kantrowitz, Arnie. "Gay Power 1973: Jim Owles,
          Candidate for City Council," Gay, Feb. 12, 1973,
          p. 6.

2717)     _____. "I Am a Gay Jew," Advocate, Jun. 4,
          1975, p. 17.

2718)   Kaput, Arthur. "The Closet in the Classroom:
        The Plight of the Gay Teacher," Gay, Apr. 13,
        1970, pp. 7, 20.

2719)   Kenny, Maurice. "Tinselled Bucks: An Historical
        Study in Indian Homosexuality," Gay Sunshine, no.
        26-27, Winter 1975, pp. 15-17.

2720)   Kepner, Jim. "Another Look at Homosexuality,"
        In Touch, Jan.-Feb. 1975, pp. 30-32.

2721)   _____. "Gays and Religion: The Stew Thickens,"
        Advocate, Aug. 15, 1973, pp. 37, 39.

2722)   _____. "Homophobia Is Not a Straight Disease,"
        In Touch, Feb. 1974, pp. 22-23, 60-63.

2723)   _____. "New Horizons for Catholic Gays," In
        Touch, Nov. 1974, pp. 24-27.

2724)   _____. "Sick No More," In Touch, Mar. 1974,
        pp. 60-61, 70.

2725)   _____. "Those Who Forget History," In Touch,
        Jun. 1974, pp. 50-51, 76-78.

2726)   Kinsey Researcher Urges Gays to Fight Now for
        Their Own Destiny, Advocate, Jul. 3, 1974, p. 29.

2727)   Kyper, John. "Christopher Street Pre-History,"
        Gay Community News, Jul. 5, 1975, p. 10.

2728)   "Largest Bar Raids in New York History," Gay,
        Aug. 16, 1971, pp. 1, 16.

2729)   "Larry Townsend Talks about His Life as a Gay
        Novelist," Vector, Oct. 1971, pp. 40-41 and Nov.
        1971, pp. 34-35.

2730)   Latham, Jack. "A Faggot Father Speaks Out,"
        Gay Sunshine, no. 24, Spring 1975, pp. 10-11.

2731)   Laurence, Leo. "Gays on Campus," Advocate,
        Feb. 2, 1972, pp. 1, 11.

2732)   Legg, W. Dorr. "Homosexuality in Young People:
        For Parents, Teachers, and Youth Workers," One,
        16:3-7, May-Jun. 1972.

2733)      Leitsch, Dick. "Facts Your History Teacher 'Forgot' to Mention," Gay, Jan. 24, 1972, p. 7.

2734)      _____. "Jim Garrison's Homosexual Fantasies," Gay, Feb. 1, 1971, pp. 8-9, 18.

2735)      _____. "The King [James I] Who Was a Queen," Gay, Apr. 17, 1972, p. 7.

2736)      _____. "Mart Crowley: Harriet Beecher Stowe in Drag," Gay, Jun. 21, 1971, p. 11.

2737)      _____. "Poking It to the Pontiff," Gay, Jul. 19, 1971, p. 11.

2738)      _____. "Setting Styles for 'Straights,'" Gay, Jun. 1, 1970, p. 13.

2739)      Leopold, Allan. Actor Calvin Culver, In Touch, Jul. 1974, pp. 16-23.

2740)      _____. David Glasscock, Assistant to Los Angeles County Superviser, In Touch, Apr. 1975, pp. 23-26, 76-80.

2741)      _____. "The Gay War on V. D. [Los Angeles Community Services Center]," In Touch, Dec. 1974, pp. 22-25, 70-71.

2742)      LeRoy, John P. "Gore Vidal: Gay Liberation's Warren G. Harding," Gay, May 7, 1973, p. 8.

2743)      Lesbian Elaine Noble Elected to Massachusetts Assembly, Advocate, Dec. 4, 1974, p. 4.

2744)      Lesbians in Kentucky Apply for Marriage License, Gay, Aug. 10, 1970, p. 3.

2745)      "Lesbians Zap Dick Cavett Show," Advocate, Jan. 2, 1974, p. 5.

2746)      "Liberal Democrats in California Back Gay Rights," Advocate, Dec. 22, 1971, pp. 1, 17.

2747)      "Library Group Forms Gay Lib Task Force," Advocate, Sep. 2, 1970, p. 19.

2748) "Little Gay Liberation in Europe," Advocate, Oct. 25, 1972, p. 15.

2749) Loitering Law Overthrown by Colorado Court, Advocate, May 8, 1974, p. 21.

2750) Loneliness among Gays, Advocate, Dec. 3, 1975, pp. 31-37.

2751) "Looking Back at 1975: A Year to Remember [A Summary of Events]," Advocate, Dec. 31, 1975, pp. 11-13, 23, 26-31.

2752) Los Angeles City Attorney Eases Gay Prosecutions, Advocate, May 22, 1974, pp. 1, 16.

2753) Los Angeles Gay Community Center gets $10,000 in County Aid, Advocate, Nov. 21, 1973, p. 16.

2754) Los Angeles Gays Gain Police Board Ear, Advocate, Oct. 24, 1973, pp. 1, 9.

2755) "Los Angeles Police Chief Lashes out at Gays," Advocate, Oct. 10, 1973, pp. 2, 21.

2756) Los Angeles Police Chief Refuses to Work with Gays, Advocate, Dec. 8, 1971, p. 3.

2757) Los Angeles Police Department Is Target of New Drive for Gay Rights, Advocate, Dec. 22, 1971, p. 3.

2758) "Los Angeles Police Department's Position on Gay People," Advocate, Feb. 26, 1975, p. 8.

2759) "Los Angeles Times Breaks Silence [on Homosexuality]," Advocate, Feb. 16, 1972, p. 6.

2760) "Los Angeles Vice Cops Kill Another Gay," Advocate, Apr. 29, 1970, pp. 1-2.

2761) Lutherans Confront Homosexual Issue, Gay, Apr. 20, 1970, p. 15; Jul. 27, 1970, p. 3; Advocate, Aug. 1, 1973, p. 11; Oct. 10, 1973, p. 11.

2762) Male Prostitution Charges Soar in Seattle, Advocate, Sep. 12, 1973, p. 8.

2763)   Manford, Morty. "Gay America Plans for '72
        Elections," Gay, Mar. 20, 1972, pp. 1, 16.

2764)   _____ and Evans, Arthur. "The Theory and
        Practice of Confrontation Politics," Gay, Feb. 12,
        1973, pp. 18-19; Feb. 26, 1973, pp. 17-18; Mar.
        12, 1973, p. 17.

2765)   Marvin, John. "The Gay Heroes of the Movies,"
        Queens' Quarterly, Aug. 1974, pp. 17-19, 42-46.

2766)   _____. "The Gay Villains [in the Movies],"
        Queens' Quarterly, Aug. 1973, pp. 13-17, 40-41.

2767)   _____. "Homosexuality on Television," Queens'
        Quarterly, Dec. 1972, pp. 13-15.

2768)   _____. "Those TV Fags--Friend or Foe?" Ad-
        vocate, Oct. 25, 1972, p. 28.

2769)   Mayor John Lindsay of New York City Issues Execu-
        tive Order Banning Discrimination against Homosex-
        uals in City Employment, Advocate, Mar. 1, 1972,
        pp. 1, 9.

2770)   "Mayors Reject Hiring Gays," Advocate, Mar. 15,
        1972, p. 16.

2771)   McCullough, Roy L. "Behind Bars," In Touch,
        Dec. 1975, pp. 34-35, 73.

2772)   McNaught, Brian. "My Church Stands Accused,"
        In Touch, Feb. 1975, pp. 22-24, 66-69.

2773)   _____. New Theological Study Challenges Roman
        Catholic Church's Antihomosexual Stand, Advocate,
        Jul. 16, 1975, pp. 10-11.

2774)   Mendenhall, George. "Gay Cops--an Issue Getting
        Attention Nationwide," Advocate, Nov. 19, 1975,
        p. 14.

2775)   _____. "Ma Bell Clings to Anti-gay Policy in
        Liberated San Francisco," Advocate, Jan. 3, 1973,
        p. 6.

2776)   "Metromedia: Gay Programming Gains," Advocate,
        Mar. 13, 1974, p. 19.

2777)     Metropolitan Community Church, Advocate, Aug. 19,
          1970, pp. 1, 5, 16; Sep. 2, 1970, pp. 10-11; Mar.
          3, 1971, pp. 1, 3; Oct. 11, 1971, p. 6; Nov. 24,
          1971, pp. 1, 13; Sep. 27, 1972, pp. 1, 4; Feb. 14,
          1973, pp. 1, 22; Mar. 19, 1973, pp. 1, 21; Aug.
          19, 1973, pp. 1, 9; Sep. 26, 1973, pp. 1, 2, 16;
          Dec. 5, 1973, pp. 1, 3; May 22, 1974, pp. 6, 7;
          Jun. 19, 1974, p. 15; Jan. 29, 1975, p. 15; Feb.
          12, 1975, p. 10; Feb. 26, 1975, p. 15; Apr. 9,
          1975, p. 17; Apr. 23, 1975, p. 18; May 7, 1975,
          p. 19; Jul. 2, 1975, p. 15; Aug. 13, 1975, pp. 17,
          20; Aug. 27, 1975, p. 20; Sep. 10, 1975, p. 4;
          Oct. 22, 1975, p. 23.

2778)     "Mexican Gay Oppression," Gay Sunshine, no. 26-
          27, Winter 1975, p. 5.

2779)     Minnesota Farm-Labor Party Backs Gay Rights,
          Gay, Apr. 23, 1973, p. 21.

2780)     Missouri Legislator Rails against Gay Professors
          at University of Missouri, Advocate, Apr. 25, 1973,
          p. 16.

2781)     Mitzel, John. "The Gay Version of the Warren Re-
          port and Its Critics," Fag-Rag, Summer 1975, pp.
          1-5.

2782)     _____. "John Horne Burns: A Forgotten Fag-
          got," Fag Rag/Gay Sunshine, Summer 1974, pp.
          16-17.

2783)     Monroe, Jack. "Are We Still Pariahs? Surveys
          Disagree," Advocate, Oct. 24, 1973, pp. 1, 4.

2784)     Mullen, Larry. "The U.S. Marines' Fear of Ho-
          mosexuality," Vector, Dec. 1971, pp. 16-17.

2785)     National Council of Churches Supports Gay Rights,
          Advocate, Mar. 26, 1975, p. 5.

2786)     National Gay Task Force Formed, Advocate, Nov.
          7, 1973, pp. 1, 24.

2787)     "National Student Congress Bows to Gay Caucus'
          Goals," Advocate, Sep. 15, 1971, p. 2; Gay, Sep.
          27, 1971, p. 8.

2788)    "National Teachers' Group [National Education Association] Kills Gay Rights Resolution," Advocate, Aug. 1, 1973, p. 14.

2789)    "New Gay Radio Show to Air in Los Angeles," Advocate, May 9, 1973, p. 11.

2790)    "New Kinsey Study Shatters More Myths," Advocate, Jun. 19, 1974, p. 24.

2791)    New Orleans Gay Bar Burns; 32 Die, Advocate, Jul. 18, 1973, p. 2; Aug. 1, 1973, p. 1.

2792)    "New Row over Gay Foster Homes," Advocate, Jul. 3, 1974, p. 6.

2793)    New Study Fails to Verify Hormone Link to Homosexuality, Advocate, Jun. 7, 1972, pp. 1, 12.

2794)    New York City Board of Education Holds Homosexuality Is Not a Bar to Teaching in the Public Schools, Advocate, Feb. 26, 1975, p. 10.

2795)    New York Court Finds Gay Lawyer [Harris Kimball] Fit to Practice Law, Advocate, Aug. 15, 1973, p. 2.

2796)    New York Gay Activists Alliance Center Burns, Advocate, Nov. 6, 1974, p. 1.

2797)    Newton, Huey. "A Letter on the Gay Liberation and Women's Liberation Movements," Vector, Nov. 2, 1972, p. 14. (Reprinted in McCaffrey, no. 101, pp. 195-97.) (Reprinted from Berkeley Barb, Sep. 5, 1970)

2798)    Nichols, Jack. " A Conversation with an Honest Psychologist: Dr. George Weinberg," Gay, Jul. 1973, pp. 7, 14.

2799)    Norton, Rictor. "Edward Carpenter Celebrated Joy of Gay Love in His Poems," Advocate, May 9, 1973, p. 26.

2800)    _____. "Ganymede in Renaissance Literature," Gay Sunshine, no. 19, Fall 1973, p. 16.

2801)    _____. "Gay Genius: Bacon Rose High under

'Queen James,'" Advocate, Aug. 29, 1973, p. 39.

2802)     _____. "Gay London in the 1720's: The Great Raid on Mother Clap's Molly House," Gay Sunshine, no. 24, Spring 1975, pp. 14-15.

2803)     _____. "Gay Tales of Terror," Gay News, no. 34, 1973, p. 10.

2804)     _____. "Hard Gem-like Flame: Walter Pater and his Circle," Gay Sunshine, no. 21, Spring 1974, pp. 14-15.

2805)     _____. "Literature and Obscenity and the Wild Earl of Rochester," California Scene, Jan. 1972, pp. 33-34.

2806)     _____. "The Phoenix of Sodom," Gay News, no. 47, 1974, p. 12.

2807)     _____. "Reflections on the Gay Movement," Fag Rag/Gay Sunshine, Summer 1974, pp. 14-15.

2808)     _____. "Walt Whitman: Prophet of Gay Liberation," Gay News, no. 48, 1974, pp. 10-11.

2809)     One, Inc. Marks 20th Year, Advocate, Mar. 1, 1972, p. 6.

2810)     "Oppression in Cuba--1971," Vector, Aug. 1971, pp. 46-47.

2811)     Parents of Gays Organizing, Gay, Apr. 23, 1973, pp. 1, 10.

2812)     Parker, William. "Employment Discrimination Is Being Confronted," Vector, Nov. 1971, pp. 36-37, 39, 43.

2813)     _____. "Episcopalians Look at Gays," Vector, Feb. 1972, p. 38.

2814)     _____. "Sex Laws--Invasion of Privacy," Vector, Sep. 1970, pp. 36-37, 41.

2815)     Pennsylvania Governor Issues Order Banning Discrimination against Gays in Employment, Advocate, Mar. 26, 1975, p. 4.

2816)   Pennsylvania Governor Vetoes Anti-gay Bill, Advocate, Nov. 19, 1975, p. 9.

2817)   "Pentagon Holds to Anti-gay Stand," Advocate, May 24, 1972, p. 3.

2818)   Perew, T.  "Gays on TV Not the Real Thing," Advocate, May 8, 1974, pp. 32, 39.

2819)   "Playboy Financing Gay Cases," Advocate, Mar. 29, 1972, p. 3.

2820)   Polarization at the Polls--Gays and Politics, Advocate, Dec. 3, 1975, pp. 8-9, 14-15.

2821)   Poll by National Opinion Research Center Shows Public Opposition to Homosexuality, Advocate, Dec. 19, 1973, p. 18.

2822)   "Poll Says Young Adults Back Gay Rights," Advocate, Feb. 16, 1972, p. 4.

2823)   Presidential Candidate George McGovern Includes Gays in "Freedoms," Advocate, Oct. 27, 1971, p. 6.

2824)   Pressman, Kurt.  "The Night They Raided Fire Island," Queens' Quarterly, Summer 1970, pp. 14, 41-42.

2825)   "Principles to Guide Confessors in Questions of Homosexuality," Advocate, Mar. 27, 1974, p. 11.

2826)   "Printers Refuse to Print Gay Articles," Gay, Feb. 7, 1972, p. 3.

2827)   Psychologists Say Homosexuals Aren't Sick, Advocate, Mar. 12, 1975, p. 4.

2828)   Puerto Rico Makes Homosexual Acts Illegal, Advocate, Nov. 6, 1974, p. 12.

2829)   Quaker Convention Passes Gay Lib Resolution, Advocate, Dec. 19, 1973, p. 10.

2830)   Raid on "Call-Boy" Service Nets up to 100,000 Names, Advocate, Sep. 12, 1973, pp. 1, 9.

2831)     "Rebel Catholic Priests Start Ministry for Gays,"
          Advocate, Jan. 20, 1971, p. 3.

2832)     Republicans Avoid Gay Issue, Gay, Oct. 2, 1972,
          pp. 3, 10.

2833)     Richards, Robert. "Government Is the Primary
          Oppressor," Vector, May 1972, p. 41.

2834)     [Rev.] Robert Herrick, Episcopalian Priest and Gay
          Activist, Advocate, Jul. 30, 1975, p. 14.

2835)     Roberts, Paul. "Abel: The First Homosexual,"
          Vector, Nov. 1971, pp. 32-33.

2836)     _____. "Sodomy and St. Paul," Vector, May
          1971, p. 24.

2837)     Rock Group Cuts First Gay Album, Gay, May 11,
          1970, p. 3.

2838)     Rodwell, Craig. "Gay People and the Arts,"
          Queens' Quarterly, Oct. 1972, p. 54.

2839)     _____. "Reflecting on Ten Years of Gay Lib,"
          Queens' Quarterly, Feb. 1972, pp. 27, 41.

2840)     Russo, Vito. Gay Theater Group in New York City,
          Advocate, Oct. 8, 1975, p. 40.

2841)     St. John, Martin. "Liberation Music, Angry and
          Proud, Enters Gay Life," Advocate, Apr. 11, 1973,
          pp. 2, 20.

2842)     _____. "Political Victory--Los Angeles Sweep
          Augurs Gay Power at Polls," Advocate, Jun. 20,
          1973, pp. 1, 6.

2843)     San Francisco Board of Education Says Homosexu-
          als May Teach in Public Schools, Advocate, Jul. 16,
          1975, p. 4.

2844)     San Francisco City Civil Service Formalizes Gay
          Rights, Advocate, Sep. 13, 1972, p. 10.

2845)     San Francisco Gays Picket Macy's over Arrests,
          Advocate, Aug. 19, 1970, p. 1; Sep. 21, 1970, p. 3.

2846)   San Francisco Rites Honor Gays Killed by Vice
        Cops, Advocate, Mar. 29, 1972, p. 3.

2847)   San Mateo County Human Rights Commission Assumes
        Jurisdiction over Gay Employment Discrimination,
        Vector, May 1972, p. 43.

2848)   Sarff, Douglas.  "Cops Keeping Special File on Los
        Angeles Gays?" Advocate, Nov. 20, 1974, p. 1.

2849)   _____.  "Laguna Beach: A Gay Exercise in Civ-
        ics," Advocate, Nov. 7, 1973, pp. 2, 19.

2850)   Sater, Tom.  "Homosexual Parents and Child Cus-
        tody," Advocate, Jul. 16, 1975, p. 5.

2851)   "School Suspends Counselor after Appearance on
        TV," Advocate, Jan. 20, 1971, pp. 1, 11.

2852)   Searles, Baird and Last, Martin.  "W. H. Auden
        Faces Life," Gay, Mar. 15, 1970, p. 17.

2853)   Shaffer, Perrin.  "Gay Alcoholics Reveal Life Styles
        and Attitudes," Gay, Aug. 21, 1972, pp. 1, 11.

2854)   Shilts, Randy.  "Foster Homes for Gay Children--
        Justice or Prejudice?" Advocate, Dec. 17, 1975,
        pp. 11-13.

2855)   _____.  "Future of Gay Rights--Emerging Middle
        Class Group in Seattle," Advocate, Oct. 22, 1975,
        pp. 11-12.

2856)   _____.  "Gay, Jewish, and Proud," Advocate,
        Sep. 10, 1975, pp. 12-13.

2857)   _____.  "What's Happening with Gay Studies
        USA?" Advocate, Jun. 18, 1975, p. 9.

2858)   Shreve, Jack.  "Homosexuality in Renaissance It-
        aly," Gay Literature, no. 2, Spring 1975, pp. 10-14.

2859)   "Sick No More [American Psychiatric Association
        Drops Homosexuality as Sickness]," Advocate, Jan.
        2, 1974, pp. 1, 12; Jan. 16, 1974, pp. 1-2.

2860)   Silva, Larry.  "Fire Island," In Touch, Aug. 1975,
        pp. 30-31.

2861)     Silverstein, Mike.   "The Case for Roger Casement,"
          Gay Sunshine, no. 1, Aug.-Sep. 1970, p. 16.

2862)     Skir, Leo.   "Gay Raps with Lance Loud:  Son of
          an American Family," Gay, Feb. 26, 1973, pp.
          10-11.

2863)     _____ and Nichols, Jack.   "Sing along with [Allen]
          Ginsberg," Gay, Feb. 21, 1972, pp. 4-5.

2864)     "Socialism and Gay Liberation," Gay Sunshine, no.
          8, Sep.-Oct. 1971, p. 7.

2865)     "Sociologists Slam Military Policy on Gays," Advo-
          cate, Aug. 18, 1971, pp. 25-26.

2866)     "Sociologists Vote Yes on Homosexual Rights," Gay,
          Jan. 19, 1970, p. 20.

2867)     Sodomy Reduced from Felony to Misdemeanor in
          Texas, Advocate, Jul. 4, 1973, p. 14; Jul. 18,
          1973, p. 13.

2868)     Solicitation Law Overthrown by Colorado Court, Ad-
          vocate, May 24, 1972, p. 10.

2869)     "Special Detention Camps for Homosexuals in Spain,"
          Gay, Apr. 23, 1973, p. 6.

2870)     "Special Report:  Homosexual Parents," Advocate,
          Oct. 22, 1975, pp. 25-35.

2871)     "Special Report:  Image and Fantasy in the Gay
          World," Advocate, Aug. 27, 1975, pp. 23-46.

2872)     "Special Report:  Parents of Gays," Advocate, Aug.
          13, 1975, pp. 21-35.

2873)     "Special Report:  Sexuality and Gay Sensuality,"
          Advocate, Nov. 5, 1975, pp. 22-35.

2874)     "Special Report:  Work and Gay People," Advocate,
          Sep. 10, 1975, pp. 15-32.

2875)     Stanford University Gay Group Receives $90,000 for
          Pilot Mental Health Study, Advocate, Jun. 19, 1974,
          p. 18.

2876)       Starr, J. P.   "Lot, Sodom, Onan, and Paul," One,
            16:10-15, Jul. -Aug. 1972.

2877)       Starr, Michael.   "Gay Writers Included World's
            Most Famous," Advocate, Jun. 9, 1971, p. 15.

2878)       _____.   "Gays' Impact on Fine Arts Enormous,"
            Advocate, Mar. 3, 1971, pp. 26-27.

2879)       _____.   "Gays' Impact on Theatre Strong," Ad-
            vocate, Jan. 6, 1971, p. 12.

2880)       _____.   "Homosexuality in the Movies," Advo-
            cate, Sep. 1, 1971, p. 20; Sep. 15, 1971, pp. 18-
            19; Oct. 13, 1971, pp. 17-18.

2881)       _____.   "Straight or Not, Many Authors Have
            Made the Stage a Little Gayer," Advocate, Jan. 20,
            1971, p. 10.

2882)       Stoneman, E. Donnell.   "Ballet Dancer Louis Falco,"
            Advocate, Mar. 26, 1975, pp. 25-27.

2883)       "Swede Calls for United Nations Action for Homo-
            sexuals," Advocate, May 23, 1973, p. 14.

2884)       "Switzerland's Homosexuals Discover Liberation,"
            Advocate, Feb. 13, 1974, p. 20.

2885)       Taylor, Clark L. Jr.   "Mexican Gay Life in His-
            torical Perspective," Gay Sunshine, no. 26-27,
            Winter 1975, pp. 1-4.

2886)       Teal, Donn.   "Dennis Altman: Hip Scholar from
            Down Under," Gay, Feb. 7, 1972, pp. 8, 19.

2887)       Teller, Gary.   "The Street Hustler," Vector, Feb.
            1971, pp. 10, 12.

2888)       "Texas Woman Fights 'Pro-gay' Textbooks," Advo-
            cate, Nov. 7, 1973, p. 9.

2889)       Thompson, Mark.   "Gay Liberation in Spain," Ad-
            vocate, Nov. 19, 1975, pp. 17-22.

2890)       Thorpe, Charles.   "A Teen-ager Talks about Being
            Young and Gay," Vector, Nov. 1970, pp. 39, 43-44.

2891) "Toronto's Peter Maloney--a New Kind of Politician: Gay and Proud," Advocate, Oct. 11, 1972, p. 6.

2892) Trial and Conviction of 18 Chicago Policemen for Taking Pay-offs from Gay Bars, Advocate, Jan. 13, 1973, pp. 1, 5; Sep. 12, 1973, p. 3; Oct. 10, 1973, p. 18; Jan. 16, 1974, p. 16.

2893) Twenty-seven Firms Accept Gay Employees, Gay, Sep. 4, 1972, pp. 1, 16.

2894) Two Men in Minneapolis Seek Marriage License, Advocate, Jun. 10, 1970, pp. 1, 4.

2895) United States Attorney Attacks "Chicago 7" as "Faggots," Gay, Mar. 29, 1970, p. 10.

2896) United States Civil Service Commission Ends Its Ban on Employment of Homosexuals, Contact, Mar. 19, 1975, p. 1; Advocate, Jul. 30, 1975, p. 4.

2897) United States Embassy Refuses Visa to Englishman Thought to be Homosexual, Advocate, Feb. 25, 1975, p. 11.

2898) University of Minnesota Refuses to Hire Gay Librarian, Gay, Aug. 30, 1970, pp. 3, 12.

2899) University of Minnesota Students Elect Gay President [Jack Baker], Advocate, Apr. 28, 1971, pp. 1, 7.

2900) "Vatican Says 'No' to Gay Marriages," Gay, Aug. 24, 1970, p. 3.

2901) Vernon, Ron. "Growing up in Chicago Black and Gay," Gay Sunshine, no. 6, Mar. 1971, pp. 14-17.

2902) Von Wiedeman, Donald. Painter Don Bachardy, Advocate, Mar. 12, 1975, pp. 29-30.

2903) Voters in Boulder, Colorado, Reject Gay Rights Law, Advocate, Jun. 19, 1974, p. 6.

2904) Wall Street Purge Causes Job Losses, Gay, Mar. 15, 1970, p. 3.

2905) Warman, Donald; Carrier, Joseph; and Gregory-

Lewis, Sasha. "Behavior Modification: A Preview of 'Clockwork Orange' in 1984," Advocate, Mar. 12, 1975, pp. 8-9.

2906) Warren, Steve. "Director Sidney Lumet Talks about 'Dog Day Afternoon,'" Advocate, Nov. 19, 1975, p. 43.

2907) "We Were There" [Gay Presence at 1972 Democratic National Convention], Advocate, Aug. 2, 1972, pp. 1-2.

2908) Weaver, Neal. "In Search of Gay Heroes: Singers Michael Cohen and Steven Grossman," In Touch, Oct. 1974, pp. 22-27, 75-76.

2909) Whitmore, George. "Gay: A Media Fad," Advocate, Dec. 31, 1975, pp. 20-21.

2910) _____. Jade and Sarsaparilla--Success of Two Lesbian Singers, Advocate, Jun. 18, 1975, p. 31.

2911) _____. "Laura Hobson's Consenting Adult: A Book for Our Parents, Not for Us," Advocate, Aug. 13, 1975, p. 27,

2912) Wicker, Randy. Gay Activists Challenge Syndicate Control of New York City Gay Bars, Gay, Jun. 21, 1971, pp. 1, 13.

2913) _____. "Homicidal Maniac Stalks Greenwich Village," Gay, Feb. 12, 1973, pp. 1, 5; Advocate, Feb. 14, 1973, pp. 1, 18.

2914) _____. "Saddest of All: The Gay Kids Whom No One Wants," Advocate, Jan. 3, 1973, p. 7.

2915) William DuBay, Former Priest, Comes Out, Advocate, Dec. 22, 1971, p. 16.

2916) Williams, Lewis. "The Churches: Lutherans, Presbyterians, Episcopalians, Unitarians--Where They Stand Today," Vector, Aug. 1971, pp. 24-25, 35, 44.

2917) "World Human Rights Group Shuns Gays," Advocate, Aug. 18, 1971, pp. 2, 12.

2918)    YMCA of Greater Boston Dismisses Gay from State
         Youth Service, Gay Community News, Jul. 5, 1975,
         pp. 1, 6.

2919)    Young, Allen. "Gays in Cuba," Body Politic, no.
         19, Jul.-Aug. 1975, pp. 10-11.

2920)    _____. "Heterosexual Press Oppresses Gays,"
         Advocate, No. 7, 1973, pp. 37, 40.

2921)    _____. "On Human and Gay Identity: A Liber-
         ationist Dilemma," Fag Rag/Gay Sunshine, Summer
         1974, pp. 31-32.

2922)    Young, Ian. "Gay Liberation's Great Grandfather:
         Edward Carpenter," Gay, Aug. 30, 1971, pp. 5, 19.

2923)    _____. "The Poetry of Male Love," Gay Sun-
         shine, no. 24, Spring 1975, pp. 12-13, 34.

2924)    "Youths Plead Guilty to Shakedown of Gay," Advo-
         cate, Sep. 1, 1971, p. 10.

2925)    "YWCA Meeting Passes Gay Rights Resolution,"
         Advocate, Jun. 6, 1973, p. 7.

# LITERARY WORKS

## ANTHOLOGIES

2926)      Leyland, Winston (ed.). Angels of the Lyre: A Gay Poetry Anthology. San Francisco: Panjandrum Press and Gay Sunshine Press, 1975. 248 pp. (Paperback) (195 poems by 57 American and Canadian poets)

2927)      Reade, Brian (ed.). Sexual Heretics: Male Homosexuality in English Literature from 1850 to 1900. New York: Coward-McCann Inc., 1970. 459 pp. (89 selections from English prose and poetry)

2928)      Sutherland, Alistair and Anderson, Patrick (eds.). Eros: An Anthology of Friendship. New York: Arno Press, 1975. 433 pp. (Reprint of work published in 1961.)

2929)      Wright, Stephen (ed.). Different: An Anthology of Homosexual Short Stories. New York: Bantam Books, 1974. 394 pp. (Paperback) (24 Stories by 20 authors)

2930)      Young, Ian (ed.). The Male Muse: A Gay [Poetry] Anthology. Trumansburg, N.Y.: Crossing Press, 1973. 127 pp. (Paperback) (101 poems by 40 poets)

## NOVELS

2931)      Aldiss, Brian W. The Hand-Reared Boy. London: Weidenfeld and Nicolson, 1970. 189 pp.

2932)      Aldridge, Sarah. Tottie: A Tale of the Sixties. Reno, Nev.: Naid Press, 1975. 181 pp.

2933)     Allen, David L.  The Light from the Second Story
          Window.  New York:  Exposition Press, 1972.  91
          pp.

2934)     Andrews, Terry.  The Story of Harold.  New York:
          Holt, Rinehart, and Winston, 1974.  388 pp.

2935)     Bailey, Paul.  Trespasses.  New York:  Harper and
          Row, 1970.  189 pp.

2936)     Bannon, Ann.  I Am a Woman.  New York:  Arno
          Press, 1975.  (Reprint of work published in 1959)

2937)     _____ .  Journey to a Woman.  New York:  Arno
          Press, 1975.  (Reprint of work published in 1960)

2938)     _____ .  Odd Girl Out.  New York:  Arno Press,
          1975.  (Reprint of work published in 1957)

2939)     _____ .  Women in the Shadows.  New York:  Ar-
          no Press, 1975.  (Reprint of work published in 1959)

2940)     Bassani, Giorgio.  Behind the Door.  Translated
          from the Italian by William Weaver.  London:  Wei-
          feld and Nicolson, 1973.  150 pp.

2941)     Batchelor, John.  Breathless Hush.  London:  Duck-
          worth, 1975.  167 pp.

2942)     Bennett, Hal.  Lord of Dark Places.  New York:
          Norton, 1970.  310 pp.  (Paperback ed. :  Bantam)

2943)     Bentley, Robert.  Here There Be Dragons.  Chica-
          go:  Ontario Press, 1972.  256 pp.

2944)     Blais, Marie-Claire.  The Wolf.  Translated from
          the French by Sheila Fischman.  Toronto:  McClel-
          land and Stewart, 1974.  142 pp.

2945)     Blumley, Andrew.  Twin.  New York:  Stein and
          Day, 1970.  160 pp.

2946)     Burford, Lolah.  Edward, Edward.  New York:
          Macmillan, 1971.  564 pp.

2947)     Burroughs, William S.  Exterminator.  New York:
          Viking Press, 1973.  168 pp.

2948)        _____.  The Wild Boys: A Book of the Dead.
             New York:  Grove Press, 1971.  184 pp.  (Paper-
             back)

2949)        Carben, Edward.  The Diary of a Catholic Bishop.
             New York:  Crown Publishers, 1974.  314 pp.

2950)        Carney, William.  A Year in the Closet.  New
             York:  Warner Paperback Library, 1974.  285 pp.
             (Paperback)

2951)        Carson, David.  Lament.  New York:  Grove Press,
             1973.  214 pp.

2952)        Chambers, Robert W.  The Gay Rebellion.  New
             York:  Arno Press, 1975.  297 pp.  (Reprint of
             work published in 1913)

2953)        Craigin, Elizabeth.  Either is Love.  New York:
             Arno Press, 1975.  155 pp.  (Reprint of work pub-
             lished in 1937)

2954)        Croft-Cooke, Rupert.  Exiles.  London:  W. H.
             Allen, 1970.  217 pp.

2955)        Crosby, Kip.  Run/Ride.  New York Grossman,
             1972.  342 pp.  (Paperback ed. :  Popular Library)

2956)        Curzon, Daniel.  The Misadventures of Tim McPick.
             Fresno, Cal. :  John Parke Curtis Press, 1975.
             320 pp.  (Paperback)

2957)        _____.  Something You Do in the Dark.  New
             York:  Putnam's, 1971.  352 pp.

2958)        David, Richard (pseud. ).  Ride the Whirlwind.  New
             York:  Vantage Press, 1973.  352 pp.

2959)        Del Castillo, Michel.  The Seminarian.  Translated
             from the Spanish by George Robinson.  New York:
             Holt, Rinehart, and Winston, 1970.  134 pp.

2960)        De Marco, Arlene.  Triangle.  New York:  New
             American Library, 1971.  223 pp.  (Paperback)

2961)        Fitzroy, A. T. (pseud. ).  Despised and Rejected.
             New York:  Arno Press, 1975.  350 pp.  (Reprint
             of work published in 1917)

2962)   Ford, Charles H. and Tyler, Parker. The Young
        and the Evil. New York: Arno Press, 1975. 215
        pp. (Reprint of work published in 1933)

2963)   Forster, E. M. Maurice. New York: Norton,
        1971. 256 pp. (Paperback ed.: Signet)

2964)   Genet, Jean. Querelle. Translated from the French
        by Anselm Hollo. New York: Grove Press, 1974.
        276 pp.

2965)   Gibson, Colin. The Love-Keeper. London: Chatto
        and Windus, 1970. 204 pp.

2966)   Gilbert, Harriett. I Know Where I've Been. New
        York: Harper and Row, 1972. 217 pp.

2967)   Gilliatt, Penelope. Sunday, Bloody Sunday. New
        York: Viking Press, 1972. 135 pp.

2968)   Gordon, Mary. Chase of the Wild Goose. New
        York: Arno Press, 1975. 279 pp. (Reprint of
        work published in 1936)

2969)   Goytisolo, Juan. Count Julian. Translated from
        the Spanish by Helen R. Lane. New York: Viking
        Press, 1974. 204 pp.

2970)   Green, George F. The Power of Sergeant Streeter.
        London: Macmillan, 1972. 224 pp.

2971)   Hall, Lynn. Sticks and Stones. New York: Dell,
        1973. 188 pp.

2972)   Hall, Richard. The Butterscotch Prince. New York:
        Pyramid Books, 1975. 159 pp. (Paperback)

2973)   Hansen, Joseph. Death Claims. New York: Har-
        per and Row, 1973. 166 pp.

2974)   _____. Fadeout. New York: Harper and Row,
        1970. 187 pp.

2975)   _____. Troublemaker. New York: Harper and
        Row, 1975. 155 pp.

2976)   Harris, Bertha. Confessions of Cherubino. New
        York: Harcourt, Brace, and World, 1972. 211 pp.

2977)    Hartley, Leslie P. The Harness Room. London:
         Hamish Hamilton, 1971. 131 pp.

2978)    Hayim, George. Obsession. New York: Grove
         Press, 1970. 187 pp.

2979)    Heath, Avery. The Long Search. New York: Van-
         tage Press, 1971. 416 pp.

2980)    Hilaire, Frank. Thanatos. New York: Dutton,
         1971. 319 pp.

2981)    Hill, Christopher. Scorpion. New York: St. Mar-
         tin's Press, 1974. 224 pp.

2982)    Himes, Chester B. Cast the First Stone. New
         York: New American Library, 1972. 303 pp.
         (Paperback)

2983)    Hobson, Laura Z. Consenting Adult. New York:
         Doubleday, 1975. 256 pp. (Paperback ed.: War-
         ner)

2984)    Hobson, Polly. A Terrible Thing Happened to Miss
         Dupont. New York: McCall, 1970. 189 pp. (Pa-
         perback ed.: Belmont-Tower)

2985)    Holland, Isabelle. The Man without a Face. Phila-
         delphia: Lippincott, 1972. 159 pp. (Paperback ed.:
         Bantam)

2986)    Howard, Elizabeth J. Odd Girl Out. New York:
         Viking Press, 1972. 276 pp. (Paperback ed.:
         Dell)

2987)    Hunter, Alan. Gently with the Ladies. New York:
         Macmillan, 1974. 185 pp.

2988)    Hymola, David and Holton, Michelle. Nevertheless
         I Am: A Documentary Novel. New York: Vantage
         Press, 1974. 167 pp.

2989)    Johnston, Jill. Gullibles Travels. London: Links
         Books, 1974. 283 pp.

2990)    Jones, Rhoda. Left-Handed in Love. London: Pan-
         ther, 1970. 127 pp.

2991)   Kane, Henry. The Moonlighter. New York: Geis
        Associates, 1971. 378 pp.

2992)   King, Francis H. A Domestic Animal. London:
        Longmans, 1970. 211 pp.

2993)   Kirkwood, James. P. S. Your Cat is Dead. New
        York: Stein and Day, 1972. 223 pp. (Paperback
        ed. : Warner Paperback Library)

2994)   Knudson, R. Rozanne. You Are the Rain. New
        York: Delacorte Press, 1974. 134 pp.

2995)   Koch, Stephen. Night Watch. London: Calder and
        Boyars, 1970. 212 pp.

2996)   Lambert, Gavin. The Goodbye People. New York:
        Simon and Schuster, 1971. 191 pp.

2997)   Lauder, Stuart. Camp Commander. London: Har-
        low, Longman, 1971. 213 pp.

2998)   Linden, Geoffrey. Jigsaw. New York: Equinox-
        Avon, 1974. 248 pp. (Paperback)

2999)   Mackay, Shena. An Advent Calendar. London:
        Jonathan Cope, 1971. 158 pp.

3000)   Mallet, Francoise. The Illusionist. Translated
        from the French by Herma Briffault. New York:
        Arno Press, 1975. 250 pp. (Reprint of work pub-
        lished in 1952)

3001)   Mann, Patrick (pseud. ). Dog Day Afternoon. New
        York: Delacorte Press, 1974. 256 pp. (Paperback
        ed. : Dell)

3002)   Maugham, Robin. The Last Encounter. New York:
        McGraw-Hill, 1973. 176 pp.

3003)   _____. The Sign. New York: McGraw-Hill,
        1974. 193 pp.

3004)   _____. The Wrong People. New York: Mc-
        Graw-Hill, 1971. 273 pp.

3005)   Mavor, Elizabeth. A Green Equinox. London:

Michael Joseph, 1973.  191 pp.  (Paperback ed.:
Wilwood House)

3006)    Meacock, Norma.  Thinking Girl.  New York: Dial
Press, 1972.  222 pp.

3007)    Meaker, Marijane.  Shockproof Sydney Skate.  Boston: Little, Brown, 1972.  240 pp.  (Paperback ed.:
Curtis)

3008)    Merrick, Gordon.  Forth into the Night.  New York:
Avon Books, 1974.  348 pp.  (Paperback)

3009)    _____.  The Lord Won't Mind.  New York: Geis
Associates, 1970.  280 pp.  (Paperback ed.: Avon)

3010)    _____.  One for the Gods.  New York: Geis
Associates, 1971.  312 pp.  (Paperback ed.: Avon)

3011)    Miller, Isabel (pseud.).  Patience and Sarah.  New
York: McGraw-Hill, 1971.  215 pp.  (Paperback
ed.: Fawcett Crest)

3012)    Miller, Jimmy.  Some Parts in the Single Life.
New York: Knopf, 1970.  242 pp.

3013)    Miller, Merle.  What Happened.  New York: Harper and Row, 1972.  342 pp.

3014)    Morgan, Claire (pseud.).  The Price of Salt.  New
York: Arno Press, 1975.  276 pp.  (Reprint of
work published in 1952)

3015)    Moyes, Patricia.  Many Deadly Returns.  New York:
Holt, Rinehart, and Winston, 1970.  246 pp.

3016)    Murdoch, Iris.  An Accidental Man.  London: Chatto and Windus, 1971.  377 pp.

3017)    _____.  A Fairly Honorable Defeat.  London:
Chatto and Windus, 1970.  402 pp.

3018)    Newman, Leslie.  Gathering Force.  New York:
Simon and Schuster, 1974.  284 pp.

3019)    Niles, Blair.  Strange Brother.  New York: Arno
Press, 1975.  341 pp.  (Reprint of work published
in 1931)

3020)    Olivia (pseud.).  Olivia.  New York:  Arno Press,
         1975.   135 pp.   (Reprint of work published in 1949)

3021)    Osborn, David.  The Glass Tower.  London:  Hod-
         der and Stoughton, 1971.   254 pp.

3022)    Parker, Robert B.  God Save the Child.  Boston:
         Houghton Mifflin, 1974.   185 pp.

3023)    Porcsa, Michael.  Under the Brightness of Alien
         Stars.  New York:  Vantage Press, 1971.   229 pp.

3024)    Prou, Suzanne.  Mlle Savelli?  Translated from the
         French by Adrienne Foulke.  New York:  Harper
         and Row, 1971.   153 pp.

3025)    Purdy, James.  I am Elijah Thrush.  Garden City,
         N.Y.:  Doubleday, 1972.   120 pp.

3026)    Rader, Dotson.  Government Inspected Meat and
         Other Fun Summer Things.  New York:  Paperback
         Library, 1971.   205 pp.   (Paperback)

3027)    Raven, Simon.  Sound the Retreat.  London:  Blond,
         1971.   224 pp.

3028)    Rechy, John.  The Day's Death.  New York:  Grove
         Press, 1970.   255 pp.

3029)    _____.  The Fourth Angel.  New York:  Viking
         Press, 1972.   157 pp.

3030)    _____.  The Vampires.  New York:  Grove Press,
         1971.   276 pp.

3031)    Redmon, Anne.  Emily Stone.  New York:  Praeger,
         1975.   250 pp.

3032)    Renault, Mary.  The Persian Boy.  New York:
         Pantheon, 1972.   419 pp.   (Paperback ed.:  Bantam)

3033)    Revelli, George.  Resort to War.  New York:
         Grove Press, 1971.   282 pp.   (Paperback ed.:  Dell)

3034)    Rofheart, Martha.  My Name Is Sappho.  New York:
         Putnam's, 1974.   382 pp.

3035)    Rule, Jane.  Against the Season.  New York:

McCall Publishing Co., 1971.  218 pp.

3036)　　　　　　　.  The Desert of the Heart.  New York:
Arno Press, 1975.  224 pp.  (Reprint of work published in 1964)

3037)　　　　　　　.  This Is Not for You.  New York:  Mc-
Call Publishing Co., 1970.  284 pp.  (Paperback
ed.:  Popular Library)

3038)　　Scoppettone, Sandra.  Trying Hard to Hear You.
New York:  Harper and Row, 1974.  264 pp.

3039)　　Sheldon, Deyan.  The Nail Hotel.  New York:  Cro-
well, 1974.  310 pp.

3040)　　Shockley, Ann A.  Loving Her.  Indianapolis:
Bobbs-Merrill, 1975.  187 pp.

3041)　　Skir, Leo.  Boychick.  New York:  Winter House,
Ltd., 1971.  157 pp.

3042)　　Spencer, Colin.  Panic.  London:  Secker and Warburg, 1971.  223 pp.

3043)　　Swicegood, Thomas L. P.  Other Side of the World.
Los Angeles:  Enola Publications, 1975.  207 pp.

3044)　　Underwood, Reginald.  Bachelor's Hall.  2nd ed.
New York:  Arno Press, 1975.  327 pp.  (Reprint
of work published in 1937)

3045)　　Vidal, Gore.  Myron.  New York:  Random House,
1974.  244 pp.  (Paperback ed.:  Ballantine)

3046)　　　　　　　.  Two Sisters:  A Memoir in the Form of
a Novel.  Boston:  Little, Brown, 1970.  256 pp.

3047)　　Walker, Gerald.  Cruising.  New York:  Stein and
Day, 1970.  192 pp.

3048)　　Warren, Patricia N.  The Front Runner.  New York:
William Morrow, 1974.  328 pp.  (Paperback ed.:
Avon and Bantam)

3049)　　Waugh, Alec.  A Spy in the Family.  New York:
Farrar, Straus, and Giroux, 1970.  247 pp.

3050)         Weirauch, Anna E. <u>The Outcast.</u> Translated from the German by Guy Endore. New York: Arno Press, 1975. 242 pp. (Reprint of work published in 1933)

3051)         _____. <u>The Scorpion.</u> Translated from the German by Whittaker Chambers. New York: Arno Press, 1975. 396 pp. (Reprint of work published in 1932)

3052)         Wertenbaker, Lael T. <u>Unbidden Guest.</u> Boston: Little, Brown, 1970. 311 pp.

3053)         Wilhelm, Gale. <u>Torchlight to Valhalla.</u> New York: Arno Press, 1975. 190 pp. (Reprint of work published in 1938)

3054)         _____. <u>We Too Are Drifting.</u> New York: Arno Press, 1975. 305 pp. (Reprint of work published in 1935)

3055)         Williams, Tennessee. <u>Moise and the World of Reason.</u> New York: Simon and Schuster, 1975. 190 pp.

3056)         Wilson, Angus. <u>As if by Magic.</u> London: Secker and Warburg, 1973. 415 pp.

3057)         Winsloe, Christa. <u>The Child Manuela.</u> Translated from the German by Agnes N. Scott. New York: Arno Press, 1975. 310 pp. (Reprint of work published in 1933)

3058)         Winthrop, Joan. <u>Underwater.</u> New York: Putnam's, 1974. 256 pp.

3059)         Wohl, Burton. <u>That Certain Summer.</u> New York: Bantam Books, 1973. 139 pp.

3060)         Wykham, Helen. <u>Ribstone Pippins.</u> London: Figgis-Calder and Boyars, 1974. 226 pp.

## PLAYS

3061)         Barry, Bob. <u>Murder among Friends.</u> 1975.

3062)    Barry, Julian. <u>Lenny: A Play Based on the Life</u>
         <u>and Words of Lenny Bruce.</u>  New York: Grove
         Press, 1972.  118 pp.

3063)    Barton, Lee W.  <u>Nightride.</u>  1971.

3064)    Bateman, Lane.  <u>Kiss the Sky.</u>  1974.

3065)    _____.  <u>Lying in State.</u>  1973.

3066)    Birimisa, George.  <u>Georgie-Porgie.</u>  1971.

3067)    Bradford, Benjamin.  <u>A Public Place.</u>  1973.

3068)    Brown, Walter L.  <u>First Death.</u>  1972.

3069)    Carmines, Al.  <u>The Faggot.</u>  1973.

3070)    Causey, Alan.  <u>Julia Caesar.</u>  1974.

3071)    Clark, Ron and Bobrick, Sam.  <u>Norman, Is That</u>
         <u>You?</u>  1972.

3072)    Dean, Douglas.  <u>Rusty.</u>  1975.

3073)    del Valle, Peter and Sterner, Steven.  <u>Lovers.</u>
         1975.

3074)    Fierstein, Harvey.  <u>In Search of Cobra Jewels.</u>
         1972.

3075)    Friedman, Bruce J.  <u>Steambath.</u>  New York: Knopf,
         1971.  97 pp.

3076)    Glines, John.  <u>Boy on a Lonely Journey.</u>  1975.

3077)    Goodman, Dean.  <u>Special Friends.</u>  1975.

3078)    Gray, Simon.  <u>Butley.</u>  London: Methuen, 1971.
         78 pp.

3079)    Harris, Ted.  <u>Silhouettes.</u>  1970.

3080)    Herlihy, James L.  <u>Stop, You're Killing Me.</u>  New
         York: Simon and Schuster, 1970.  79 pp.

3081)    Hochhauser, Jeff.  <u>The Rainbow Chasers.</u>  1973.

3082)     Hopkins, John R.  Find Your Way Home.  Har-
          mondsworth, Eng. :  Penguin, 1971.  91 pp.

3083)     Jacobs, Ed.  The Evil that Men Do.  1970.

3084)     Katz, Jonathan.  Coming Out!  A Documentary Play
          about Gay Life and Liberation in the U. S. A.  New
          York:  Arno Press, 1975.  105 pp.

3085)     Kemp, Lindsay.  Flowers:  A Pantomime for Jean
          Genet.  1974.

3086)     Kirkwood, James.  P. S. Your Cat Is Dead.  1975.
          (See no. 2993 above)

3087)     _____ and Dante, Nicholas.  A Chorus Line.
          1975.

3088)     Kronengold, A. J.  Hustlers.  1975.

3089)     _____ .  Tub Strip.  1973.

3090)     Kuczewski, Ed and Vitale, Bill.  A Mass Murder
          in the Balcony of the Old Ritz-Rialto.  1975.

3091)     Lane, Robert M.  Foreplay.  1970.

3092)     Laurents, Arthur.  The Enclave.  1973.

3093)     Magdalany, Philip.  Section Nine.  1974.

3094)     McNally, Terrence.  Bad Habits.  1974.

3095)     _____ .  The Ritz.  1975.

3096)     Milligan, Andy.  Cocteau.  1972.

3097)     O'Brien, Richard.  The Rocky Horror Show.  1973.

3098)     Renard, Joseph.  A Boy Named Dog.  1974.

3099)     Santaniello, A. E.  Not to Worry.  1975.

3100)     Sawyer, Michael.  Naomi Court.  1975.

3101)     Scantlin, Ray and Allison, John.  Stand by Your
          Beds, Boys.  1974.

3102)     Silver, Fred. Gay Company. 1974.

3103)     Solly, Bill and Ward, Donald. Boy Meets Boy.
          1975.

3104)     Tremblay, Michel. Hosanna. 1974.

3105)     Weiss, Jeff. Pushover: An Old-Fashioned Homo-
          sexual Mystery Play. 1973.

3106)     Williams, Tennessee. Small Craft Warnings. New
          York: New Directions, 1972. 86 pp.

3107)     Wilson, Doric. Now She Dances. 1975.

3108)     Wilson, Earl Jr. Let My People Come. 1974.

3109)     Wilson, Lanford. The Great Nebula in Orion. 1974.

## SHORT STORIES

3110)     Coriolan, John. Seven Ways from Sunday. New
          York: The Other Traveller, 1972.

3111)     Forster, E. M. The Life to Come. New York:
          Norton, 1972. 240 pp.

3112)     Ihara, Saikaku. Comrade Loves of the Samurai.
          Translated from the Japanese by E. Powys Mathers.
          Rutland, Vt.: Charles E. Tuttle Co., 1972. 134 pp.

## POETRY

3113)     Allen, Donald (ed.). The Collected Poems of Frank
          O'Hara. New York: Knopf, 1972. 586 pp.

3114)     Bifrost, Andrew (ed.) Mouth of the Dragon: A
          Poetry Journal of Male Love. New York: Mouth
          of the Dragon Press. Issued quarterly starting
          May 1974.

3115)     Brown, Rita M. The Hand that Cradles the Rock.
          New York: New York University Press, 1971. 64
          pp. (Paperback ed.: Diana Press)

3116)     _____.  Songs to a Handsome Woman.  Balti-
          more:  Diana Press, 1973.  39 pp.  (Paperback)

3117)     Cavafy, C. P.  Poems.  Translated by John Mav-
          rogordato.  London:  Chatto and Windus, 1971.
          199 pp.  (Paperback)  (Reprint of work published in
          1951)

3118)     _____.  Selected Poems.  Translated by Edmund
          Keeley and Philip Sherrard.  Edited by George Savi-
          dis.  Princeton:  Princeton University Press, 1972.
          97 pp.  (Hardback and paperback)

3119)     Congdon, Kirby.  Black Sun.  Grand Rapids, Mich.:
          Pilot Press, 1973.  46 pp.  (Paperback)

3120)     Ginsberg, Allen.  The Fall of America:  Poems of
          These States, 1965-71.  San Francisco:  City
          Lights, 1973.  188 pp.

3121)     _____.  The Gates of Wrath; Rhymed Poems,
          1948-52.  Bolinas, Cal.:  Grey Fox Press, 1972.
          (Paperback)

3122)     _____.  Howl for Carl Solomon.  San Francisco:
          Grabhorn-Hayem, 1971.  42 pp.  (Paperback)

3123)     _____.  Iron Horse.  Toronto:  Coach House,
          1972.  52 pp.  (Paperback)

3124)     Giorno, John.  Balling Buddha.  New York:  Kulchur
          Foundation, 1970.  174 pp.

3125)     Goodman, Paul.  Homespun of Oatmeal Gray.  New
          York:  Random House, 1970.  120 pp.

3126)     Hill, Brian (transl.).  Ganymede in Rome:  28 Epi-
          grams of Marcus Valerius Martialis.  London:
          Palatine Press, 1971.  32 pp.  (Paperback)

3127)     Hillegas, Don.  We Criminals.  New York:  Adsit
          Graphics, 1974.  64 pp.  (Paperback)

3128)     Lerman, Eleanor.  Armed Love.  Middletown, Ct.:
          Wesleyan University Press, 1973.  64 pp.  (Hard-
          back and paperback)

3129)   Lonidier, Lynn.  Female Freeway.  San Francisco:
        Tenth Muse, 1970.  31 pp.  (Paperback)

3130)   Morgan, Robin.  Monster.  New York:  Random
        House, 1972.  86 pp.  (Hardback and paperback)

3131)   O'Mary, Barbara.  This Woman:  Poetry of Love
        and Change.  Washington, N.J.:  Times Change
        Press, 1973.  61 pp.  (Paperback)

3132)   Pitchford, Kenneth.  Color Photos of the Atrocities.
        Boston:  Little, Brown, 1973.  83 pp.

3133)   Sarton, May.  A Durable Fire:  New Poems.  New
        York:  Norton, 1972.  80 pp.

3134)   Smith, J. Frederick.  Sappho:  The Art of Loving
        Women.  New York:  Chelsea House, Publishers,
        1975.  160 pp.  (Translation of poetry of Sappho)

3135)   Webb, Phyllis.  Selected Poems, 1954-1965.  Van-
        couver:  Talonbooks, 1971.  166 pp.

3136)   Young, Ian.  Some Green Moths.  Scarborough,
        Ontario:  Catalyst Press, 1973.  8 pp.  (Paperback)

## MOVIES

### With a Major Homosexual Theme

"Butley"

"Death in Venice"

"Dog Day Afternoon"

"Entertaining Mr. Sloane"

"Fortune and Men's Eyes"

"Fox and His Friends"

"I Know What I Want"

"Ludwig"

"The Music Lovers"

"Myra Breckenridge"

"The Picture of Dorian Gray"

"The Rocky Horror Show"

"Saturday Night at the Baths"

"Score"

"Some of My Best Friends Are"

"Sunday, Bloody Sunday"

"There Was a Crooked Man"

"A Very Natural Thing"

"Villain"

### With a Minor Homosexual Theme

"The Anderson Tapes"

"Bang the Drum Slowly"

"Battle of the Amazons"

"The Best Man"

"Billy Budd"

"Blazing Saddles"

"Busting"

"Cabaret"

"Cactus in the Snow"

"California Split"

"Charlotte"

"Cleopatra Jones"

"A Clock Work Orange"

"Come Back, Charleston Blue"

"The Conformist"

"Cult of the Diamond"

"The Damned"

"The Day of the Dolphin"

"The Day of the Jackal"

"The Day the Fish Came Out"

"Death Scream"

"Deliverance"

"Diamonds are Forever"

"Dirty Harry"

"The Eiger Sanction"

"Escape from Devil's Island"

"Fellini's Satyricon"

"Four Flies in Gray Velvet"

"Freebie and the Bean"

"The French Connection II"

"Funny Lady"

"Georgia, Georgia"

"Gold"

"Heat"

"Hit"

"In Cold Blood"

"Jesus Christ Superstar"

"Lady Caroline Lamb"

"The Laughing Policeman"

"Lawrence of Arabia"

"The Leather Boys"

"Lenny"

"The Lickerish Quartet"

"Live and Let Live"

"Loot"

"Lord Jim"

"The Love Machine"

"The Magic Garden of Stanley Sweetheart"

"Magnum Force"

"Mahagony"

"Maltese Falcon"

"Marathon Man"

"The McKenzie Break"

"Midnight Cowboy"

"Midnight Man"

"Monte Python and the Holy Grail"

"The New Centurions"

"Night Movies"

"No Way to Treat a Lady"

"Once is not Enough"

"Papillon"

"Performance"

"Pete 'n Tillie"

"Play It as It Lays"

"Private Life of Sherlock Holmes"

"The Producers"

"Psycho"

"The Pyx"

"Riot"

"Save the Tiger"

"Scarecrow"

"The Secret of Dorian Gray"

"Shampoo"

"Sheila Levine Is Dead and Living in New York City"

"Simon, King of Witches"

"Sleeper"

"Something for Everyone"

"The Stone Killer"

"Summer Wishes, Winter Dreams"

"The Tamarind Seed"

"Tell Me that You Love Me, Julie Moon"

"Teorama"

"They Only Kill Their Masters"

"Thunderbolt and Lightning"

"Tommy"

"Touch of Class"

"Trash"

"Wild Party"

"Women in Love"

"X, Y and Zee"

"Z"

"Zachariah"

Appendix II:


TELEVISION PROGRAMS

ABC.        "Barney Miller." Oct. 30, 1975.

ABC.        "Dick Cavett Show." Nov. 27, 1970. (Interview
            with three gay activists)

ABC.        "Dick Cavett Show." Feb. 20, 1973 and Apr. 4,
            1974. (Interview with the Louds of "An American
            Family")

ABC.        "Homosexuals: Out from the Shadows." Feb. 27,
            1975. (Documentary)

ABC.        "Hot l Baltimore." Feb. 21, 1975.

ABC.        "Jack Parr Tonite." Mar. 8, 1973. (Discussion
            with three gay activists)

ABC.        "Marcus Welby, M.D.: The Other Martin Loring."
            Feb. 20, 1973.

ABC.        "Marcus Welby, M.D.: The Outrage." Oct. 8, 1974.

ABC.        "Movie of the Week: That Certain Summer." Nov.
            1, 1972 and Jun. 5, 1973.

ABC.        "On the Rocks." Oct. 9, 1975.

ABC.        "Room 222: What Is a Man?" Dec. 3, 1971.

ABC.        "Wide World Special: Homosexuals: Out from the
            Shadows." Feb. 27, 1975. (Documentary)

CBS.        "All in the Family." Feb. 2, 1971.

CBS.        "Sixty Minutes." Aug. 24, 1973. (Discussion of

proposal to remove sickness label from homosexuality)

CBS.       "Sixty Minutes." Feb. 25, 1975. (Employment difficulties of teacher Joseph Acanfora)

KBSC.      Los Angeles. "David Susskind." Mar. 11, 1973. (Interview with four gay couples)

KEMO.      San Francisco. "The Male Homosexual in America." Jun. 27, 1972. (Documentary)

KERA.      Dallas. "The Other World." Sep. 6, 1971. (Documentary)

KGO.       San Francisco. "The Bay Scene: Female Homosexuality." Mar. 11, 1973. (Interview)

KGO.       San Francisco. "The Bay Scene: Male Homosexuality." Apr. 1, 1973. (Interview)

KHJ.       Los Angeles. "The Morning Show." Apr. 3, 1974. (Interview)

KNBC.      Los Angeles. "Gay Liberation: Out of the Closet." Jul. 1, 1973. (Documentary)

KNBC.      Los Angeles. "Out of the Shadows." Jun. 26, 1970. (Documentary)

KNXT.      Los Angeles. "It Takes All Kinds." Dec. 16, 1973. (Documentary)

KQED.      San Francisco. "The Male Homosexual and the Law." Jan. 7, 1973. (Interview)

KTVM.      Oakland, Cal. "The Homophile Community." Jan. 28, 1973 and Feb. 4, 1973. (Documentary)

NBC.       "The Bob Crane Show: A Case of Misdiagnosis." May 8, 1975.

NBC.       "The Bold Ones: A Very Strange Triangle." Oct. 31, 1972.

NBC.       "Maude." Dec. 2, 1974.

NBC.        "New York Illustrated: Homosexuals: Out of the
            Closet." Feb. 11, 1973. (Documentary)

NBC.        "Police Story: The Ripper." Feb. 12, 1974 and
            Jul. 16, 1974.

NBC.        "Police Woman: Flowers of Evil." Nov. 8, 1974.

NBC.        "Sanford and Son." Oct. 26, 1973.

NBC.        "Today Show." Jan. 13, 1971. (Interview with two
            gay activists)

NBC.        "Tomorrow Show." Oct. 24, 1974. (Metropolitan
            Community Church)

NBC.        "Tomorrow Show." Nov. 7 and 19, 1974. (Dis-
            cussion of boy prostitution)

NBC.        "Tomorrow Show." Feb. 11, 1975. (Interview with
            four lesbians)

NBC.        "Tomorrow Show." Jul. 23, 1975. (Interview with
            three ex-homosexuals)

PBS.        "The Advocates." May 16, 1974. ("Should homo-
            sexuals have the right to marry?")

PBS.        "Masterpiece Theater: Upstairs, Downstairs:
            Rosie's Pigeon." Jun. 8, 1975.

PBS.        "Theater in America: Christopher Marlow's Edward
            II." Sep. 28, 1975.

PBS.        "Theater in America: Feasting with Panthers."
            Mar. 27, 1974 and Jan. 22, 1975. (Play dealing
            with Oscar Wilde's imprisonment)

PBS.        "Women." Jul. 22, 1975. (Discussion of lesbianism)

WCBS.       New York City. "Pat Collins Show." Feb. 19,
            1974. (Interview with homosexual clients of the
            Continental Baths)

## AUDIO-VISUAL AIDS

Christopher Street West--Los Angeles, 1972. 8 mm or super 8 mm film, 200 ft., 1974. Vanowen Enterprises, Sherman Oaks, Cal.

Coming Out. By Berkeley Lesbian-Feminist Film Collective. 16 mm film, black and white, 11 minutes. Women's Film Corporation, Northampton, Mass.

Counseling Parents of Gays. By Rev. Paul R. Shanley. Audio casette, 45 minutes, 1975. Ampro, Inc., Boston, Mass.

Gay and Proud. 16 mm film, black and white, with sound, 11 minutes, 1970. Lilli Vincenz, 5411 S. 8th Place, Arlington, Va. (Christopher Street Parade in New York City)

Gay Liberation: The Minnesota Way. Videotape, casette, color, 26 minutes, 1974. Audio-Visual Library Services, University of Minnesota, Minneapolis, Minn.

Gay People - Straight Health Care. By Jeri Dilno for the Gay Nurses Alliance. Slides, audio casette, color, 15 minutes, 1974. (Problems facing hospitalized gay people)

A Gay View - Male. By Laird Sutton. 16 mm film, color, sound, 17 minutes, 1974. Multi Media Resource Center, San Francisco, Cal. (Discussion by 3 male homosexuals)

Home Movie. By Jan Oxenberg. 16 mm film, color or black and white, sound, 11 minutes, 1973. Multi Media Resource Center, San Francisco, Cal. (Lesbians)

Homosexuality: Thursday's Child. By Naomi Katz, Alan Gelman, and Charles Harrison. Two filmstrips, color, with sound and guide, 36 minutes, 1974. Audio-Visual Narrative Arts, Pleasantville, N.Y. (Interviews with homosexuals)

The Invisible Minority:  The Homosexuals in Our Society.
By Deryck Calderwood and Wasyl Szkodzinsky.  Three filmstrips, color, with records, 20 minutes each, 1972.  Unitarian Universalist Association, Department of Education and
Social Concern, Boston, Mass.  (Gay people, gay movement,
gay issues)

Lavender.  By Colleen Monahan and Elaine Jacobs.  16 mm
and 8 mm film and video casette, color, sound, 13 minutes,
1972.  Perennial Education, Inc., Northfield, Ill.  (Lesbian
couple)

Lesbians and Gay Men:  A New View.  Audio casette, 60
minutes, 1974.  Council for Interdisciplinary Communication
in Medicine, New York, N.Y.  (Discussion by psychiatrist
and 4 gay activists)

On Being Gay.  Audio casette tape, 90 minutes, 1973.  Thesis Creative Educational Resources, Pittsburgh, Pa.  (Discussion by gay males and females, lawyer, psychiatrist, and
seminary president)

A Position of Faith.  By Michael Rhodes.  16 mm film,
color, sound, 18 minutes, 1973.  Contemporary/McGraw-
Hill Films, New York, N.Y.  (Ordination of gay minister)

Sandy and Madeleine's Family.  By Sherrie Farrell and Peter
M. Bruce.  16 mm film, color, sound, 29 minutes, 1973.
Multi Media Resource Center, San Francisco, Cal.  (Lesbian
couple and their children)

Second Largest Minority.  16 mm film, black and white, 8
minutes, 1968.  Lilli Vincenz, 5411 S. 8th Place, Arlington,
Va.  (Gay picketing in Philadelphia)

Some of Your Best Friends.  By Kenneth Robinson and Others.
16 mm film, color, sound, 40 minutes, 1971.  Department
of Cinema, University of Southern California, Los Angeles.
(Gay meetings, parades, demonstrations, and interviews)

Straight Talk about Gays.  By Rev. Paul R. Shanley.  Audio
casette, 60 minutes, 1974.  Ampro, Inc., Boston, Mass.
(A priest discusses homosexuality)

Appendix IV

AMERICAN LAWS APPLICABLE TO CONSENSUAL ADULT HOMOSEXUALS (JANUARY 1, 1976)

| State and Statute | Offense | Penalty imprisonment & fine |
|---|---|---|
| **ALABAMA (Code of Alabama Recompiled)** | | |
| 14.42 & 15.327 | attempt to commit a felony | up to $500 & (optional) up to 6 mos. |
| 14.106 | crime against nature (unnatural carnal copulation) | 2 to 10 yrs. |
| 14.326(1) | indecent exposure | up to 1 yr., up to $500, or both |
| 14.326(a2) | inciting a felony | 1 to 10 yrs. |
| 14.326(a3) | inciting a misdemeanor | up to $500 & (optional) up to 6 mos. |
| 14.437(2) & 14.438 | vagrancy - immoral or profligate life | up to $500 & (optional) up to 6 mos. |
| | (This section was declared unconstitutional by Fed. Dist. Ct.: 298 F. Supp. 260, 1969.) | |
| 15.434-42 | sexual psychopath | commitment to state institution |
| 15.448-58 | failure to register as sex offender | 1 to 5 yrs. & (optional) $1000 |
| **ALASKA (Alaska Statutes 1962 Annotated)** | | |
| 11.10.070(1) | soliciting or inciting a felony | up to $3000, up to 3 yrs., or both |
| 11.10.070(2) | soliciting or inciting a misdemeanor | up to $500, up to 6 mos., or both |
| 11.40.080 | indecent exposure | 3 to 12 mos. or $50 to $500 |
| 11.40.120 | sodomy (anal only) | 1 to 10 yrs. |
| 11.45.030(1) | disorderly conduct | up to $300, up to 10 days, or both |
| 11.60.210 | vagrancy - loitering near a school | $20 to $250, 10 to 25 days, or both |
| **ARIZONA (Arizona Revised Statutes Annotated)** | | |
| 13.371 | disturbing the peace - offensive conduct | up to $200 or up to 2 mos. |
| 13.531 & 13.1645 | lewd exposure | up to 6 mos., up to $300, or both |
| 13.651 | crime against nature, sodomy (anal & oral) | 5 to 20 yrs. |
| 13.652 | unnatural lewd acts | 1 to 5 yrs. |
| 13.992A | vagrancy - loitering near a school | up to $300, up to 6 mos., or both |
| 13.992B | if prior conviction of sex offense | up to 5 yrs. |
| 13.1271-74 & 13.1645 | failure to register as sex offender | up to 6 mos., up to $300, or both |

| State and Statute | Offense | Penalty imprisonment & fine |
|---|---|---|
| **ARKANSAS** (Arkansas Statutes 1947) | (New Criminal Code allowing consensual sex acts at age 16 effective 1-1-76) | |
| 41.1811; 41.901; 41.1101 | public sexual indecency | up to $1000, up to 1 yr. |
| 41.1812; 41.901; 41.1101 | indecent exposure | up to $1000, up to 1 yr. |
| 41.2908(b) & (i); 41.901; 41.1101 | disorderly conduct | up to $100, up to 30 days |
| 41.2914(e); 41.901; 41.1101 | loitering for solicitation to engage in deviate sexual activity | up to $100, up to 30 days |
| 41.3002-03; 41.901; 41.1101 | prostitution | up to $100, up to 30 days |
| 41.3565 | possession of obscene materials | up to $1000, up to 1 yr., or both |
| **CALIFORNIA** (West's Annotated Code) | (New law allowing consensual sex acts at age 18 effective 1-1-76) | |
| 288e | oral copulation in prison | up to 1 yr. or up to 5 yrs. |
| 290 & 19 | failure to register as sex offender | up to 6 mos., up to $500, or both |
| 291 | notification of school authorities re employee failing to register as sex offender | |
| 314(1) & 19 | lewd conduct and indecent exposure for 2nd or subsequent conviction | up to 6 mos., up to $500, or both not less than 1 yr. |
| 314(2) & 19 | procuring or inducing lewd conduct or indecent exposure | up to 6 mos., up to $500, or both |
| 415 | disturbing the peace | up to $200, up to 3 mos., or both |
| 647(a) & 19 | soliciting for or engaging in lewd conduct | up to 6 mos., up to $500, or both |
| 647(b) & 19 | prostitution if previous conviction | up to 6 mos., up to $500, or both mandatory not less than 45 or 90 days |
| 647(c) & 19 | loitering near public toilet with lewd intent | up to 6 mos., up to $500, or both |
| 647b | loitering near adult school | up to 6 mos., up to $500, or both |
| 650 1/2 & 19 | outraging public decency | up to 6 mos., up to $500, or both |
| 653g | loitering near school or public place | up to 6 mos., up to $500, or both |
| **COLORADO** (Colorado Revised Statutes 1973) | (New Criminal Code allowing consensual sex acts at age 16 effective 1-1-72) | |
| 18-7-201 & 18-1-106 | prostitution | $50 to $750, up to 6 mos., or both |
| 18-7-202 & 18-1-106 | soliciting for prostitution | $50 to $750, up to 6 mos., or both |

| | | 3 to 6 mos., $250 to $1000, or both |
|---|---|---|
| 18-7-205 & 18-1-107 | patronizing a prostitute | |
| 18-7-301 & 18-1-107 | public indecency or lewdness | up to $500, up to 6 mos., or both |
| 18-7-302 & 18-1-106 | indecent exposure | $50 to $750, up to 6 mos., or both |
| 18-9-106(a) & 18-1-107 | disorderly conduct - public grossness | up to $500, up to 6 mos., or both |
| 18-9-112(c) & (d) & 18-1-107 | loitering for deviate sexual intercourse, | 3 to 12 mos., $250-$1000, or both |
| | loitering near school | |

CONNECTICUT (General Statutes Annotated 1958) (New Criminal Code allowing consensual sex acts at age 18 effective 8-1-72)

| | | |
|---|---|---|
| 53a-181 & 53a-28, 36, 42 | breach of the peace | up to 6 mos., up to $1000, or both |
| 53a-182 & 53a-28, 36, 42 | disorderly conduct | up to 3 mos., up to $500, or both |
| 53a-185 & 53a-28, 36, 42 | loitering near school | up to 3 mos., up to $500, or both |
| 53a-186 & 53a-28, 36, 42 | public indecency | up to 6 mos., up to $1000, or both |

DELAWARE (Del. Code Annotated Revised 1974) (New Criminal Code allowing consensual sex acts at age 16 effective 7-1-73)

| | | |
|---|---|---|
| 11-768; 11-4206(b) & 4207(b) | indecent exposure | up to 6 mos., up to $500, or both |
| 11-1301(b); 11-4206(b) & 4207(b) | disorderly conduct | up to 6 mos., up to $500, or both |
| 11-1321(2) & (5); 11-4206(b) & 4207(b) | loitering near school; solicitation | up to $250 for 1st offense |
| 11-1341; 11-4206(b) & 4207(b) | public lewdness | up to 6 mos., up to $500, or both |

DISTRICT OF COLUMBIA (District of Columbia Code Encyclopedia completely Annotated)

| | | |
|---|---|---|
| 22.1107 | disorderly conduct - obscene gestures & remarks | up to $250, up to 90 days, or both |
| 22.1112 | indecent exposure; lewd acts | up to $300, up to 90 days, or both |
| 22.1121(1) | disorderly conduct - offensive acts | up to $250, up to 90 days, or both |
| 22.2701 | soliciting prostitution or lewd acts | up to $250, up to 90 days, or both |
| 22.3111 | disorderly conduct in public buildings & grounds | up to $50 |
| 22.3302(3) & (8) & 22.3304 | vagrancy, loitering, immoral life | up to $300, up to 90 days, or both |
| 22.3502 | sodomy (anal and oral) | up to $1000 or up to 10 yrs. |
| 22.3503-3511 | sexual psychopath | commitment to state institution |

FLORIDA (Florida Statutes Annotated)

| | | |
|---|---|---|
| 796.07; 775.082 & .083 | prostitution, lewdness, assignation, solicitation | up to 60 days, up to $500, or both |
| 800.02; 775.082 & .083 | unnatural and lascivious acts | up to 60 days, up to $500, or both |

| State and Statute | Offense | Penalty imprisonment & fine |
|---|---|---|
| **FLORIDA** (Cont'd) | | |
| 800.03; 775.082 & .083 | indecent exposure | up to 1 yr., up to $1000, or both |
| 856.021; 775.082 & .083 | loitering | up to 60 days, up to $500, or both |
| **GEORGIA** (Code of Georgia Annotated) | (New Criminal Code effective 7-1-69) | |
| 26.1001 & 1006 | attempt to commit (sodomy) | 1 to 10 yrs. |
| 26.2002 | sodomy (anal and oral) | 1 to 20 yrs. |
| 26.2003 & 27.2506 | solicitation of (sodomy) | up to $1000, up to 1 yr., or both |
| 26.2011 & 27.2506 | public indecency, lewd exposure | up to $1000, up to 1 yr., or both |
| 26.2610(d) & 27.2506 | indecent or disorderly conduct | up to $1000, up to 1 yr., or both |
| 32.9925-9926 & 27.2506 | loitering on school premises | up to $1000, up to 1 yr., or both |
| **HAWAII** (Hawaii Revised Statutes) | (New Criminal Code allowing consensual sex acts at age 14 effective 1-1-73) | |
| 37.738; 37.640, 641, & 663 | indecent exposure | up to 30 days, up to $500, or both |
| 37.1217; 37.640, 641, & 663 | open lewdness | up to 30 days, up to $500, or both |
| 37.1101; 37.640, 641, & 663 | disorderly conduct - offensive gestures or display | up to 30 days, up to $500, or both |
| **IDAHO** (General Laws of Idaho Annotated 1947) | | |
| 18.4101.1 & 18.113 | indecent exposure and obscenity | up to 6 mos., up to $300, or both |
| 18.4104 & 18.4109 | obscene public conduct - 1st offense | up to 6 mos., up to $300, or both |
| 18.4107 & 18.113 | conspiracy to commit public indecency | up to 6 mos., up to $300, or both |
| 18.5613(1)(b) & 18.113 | loitering for prostitution | up to 6 mos., up to $300, or both |
| 18.6409 & 18.113 | disorderly or offensive conduct | up to 6 mos., up to $300, or both |
| 18.6605 | crime against nature | not less than 5 yrs. |
| **ILLINOIS** (Illinois Annotated Statutes) | (New Criminal Code allowing consensual sex acts at age 18 effective 1-1-62) | |
| 38.8.1 | solicitation to commit an offense | same as for offense itself |
| 38.11.9; 38.1005.8.3 & .9.1 | public indecency, lewd exposure | up to $1000, up to 1 yr., or both |
| 38.11.20(4); 38.1005.8.3 & .9.1 | obscene act or exhibition | up to $1000, up to 1 yr., or both |
| 38.26.1(a)(1); 38.1005.8.3 & .9.1 | disorderly conduct | up to $500, up to 30 days, or both |
| **INDIANA** (Annotated Indiana Statutes) | (New Criminal Code allowing consensual sex acts at age 16 effective 6-1-77) | |

| | | |
|---|---|---|
| 10.1510 | disorderly conduct - offensive behavior | up to $500 & (optional) up to 6 mos. |
| 10.2801 | public indecency - indecent exposure | $100 to $500 & (optional) up to 6 mos. |
| 10.4221 | sodomy, crime against nature | $100 to $1000 & (optional) 2 to 14 yrs. |

**IOWA** (Iowa Code Annotated) (New Criminal Code allowing consensual adult sex acts effective 1-1-77)

| | | |
|---|---|---|
| 705.1 & 2 | sodomy | up to 10 yrs. |
| 724.1 | prostitution and lewdness | up to 5 yrs. |
| 724.2 | solicitation | up to 1 or up to 5 yrs., up to $1000, or both |
| 725.1 | open lewdness, indecent exposure | up to 6 mos., up to $200 |

**KANSAS** (Kansas Statutes Annotated) (New Criminal Code effective 7-1-70)

| | | |
|---|---|---|
| 21.3505 & 21.4502-03 | consensual sodomy (anal and oral) | up to 6 mos., up to $1000, or both |
| 21.3508 & 21.4502-03 | open lewd behavior, indecent exposure | up to 6 mos., up to $1000, or both |
| 21.4101 & 21.4502-03 | disorderly conduct - offensive language | up to 1 mo., up to $500, or both |
| 21.4108(d) & 21.4502-03 | vagrancy - loitering for immoral purpose | up to 1 mo., up to $500, or both |

**KENTUCKY** (Kentucky Revised Statutes Annotated) (New Criminal Code effective 1-1-75)

| | | |
|---|---|---|
| 510.100; 532.090; 534.040 | fourth degree (consensual) sodomy | up to 1 yr., up to $500, or both |
| 510.150; 532.090; 534.040 | indecent exposure | up to 90 days, up to $250, or both |
| 525.060; 532.090; 534.040 | disorderly conduct | up to 90 days, up to $250, or both |
| 525.090(d); 532.090; 534.040 | loitering around a school | up to 90 days, up to $250, or both |

**LOUISIANA** (West's Louisiana Statutes Annotated)

| | | |
|---|---|---|
| 14.27 | attempt to commit (crime against nature) | up to $1000, up to 2 1/2 yrs., or both |
| 14.28 | inciting (crime against nature) | up to $1000, up to 2 yrs., or both |
| 14.89 | crime against nature (anal and oral) | up to $2000, up to 5 yrs., or both |
| 14.103B(e) | disturbing the peace - obscene words & gestures | up to $500, up to 6 mos., or both |
| 14.103.1(2) | disturbing the peace - obscene words & gestures | up to $200, up to 4 mos., or both |
| 14.106(1) | indecent exposure | $100 to $1000, up to 1 yr., or both |
| 14.107(7) | vagrancy - loitering | up to $200, up to 6 mos., or both |

**MAINE** (Maine Revised Statutes Annotated) (New Criminal Code allowing consensual sex acts at age 16 effective 3-1-76)

| | | |
|---|---|---|
| 17A.501; 17A.1152, 1252, 1301 | disorderly conduct - offensive words & gestures | up to 6 mos. or up to $250 |

| State and Statute | Offense | Penalty imprisonment & fine |
|---|---|---|
| **MAINE** (Cont'd) | | |
| 17A.854; 17A.1152, 1252, 1301 | public indecency, indecent exposure | up to 6 mos. or up to $250 |
| **MARYLAND** (Annotated Code of Public Laws of Maryland 1957) | | |
| 27.15g; 27.16 & 17 | lewdness, assignation | up to $500, up to 1 yr., or both |
| 27.122 | disorderly conduct; indecent exposure, obscene language | up to $100, up to 30 days, or both |
| 27.123(c) & (d) | disorderly conduct in public | up to $50, up to 60 days, or both |
| 27.124 | disorderly conduct on private property | $1 to $25 |
| 27.553 | sodomy (anal) | 1 to 10 yrs. |
| 27.554 | unnatural or perverted sexual practices | up to $1000, up to 10 yrs., or both |
| **MASSACHUSETTS** (Annotated Laws of Massachusetts) | | |
| 272.26 | resorting for immoral purposes and acts | $25 to $500, up to 1 yr., or both |
| 272.34 | crime against nature, sodomy, buggery | up to 20 yrs. |
| 272.35 | unnatural and lascivious acts | $100 to $1000 or up to 2 1/2 (or 5) yrs. |
| 272.43 & 272.40 | disorderly conduct - indecent language and behavior | up to 1 mo. or up to $50 |
| 272.53 | lewd behavior, indecent exposure | up to 6 mos., up to $200, or both |
| **MICHIGAN** (Michigan Statutes Annotated) | | |
| 28.355 | sodomy, crime against nature (anal) | up to 15 yrs. |
| | if sexually delinquent person | 1 day to life |
| 28.364-65 & 28.772 | disorderly persons - indecent conduct in public | up to 90 days, up to $100, or both |
| 28.567(1) & 28.200(1) | open or indecent exposure | up to 1 yr. or up to $500 |
| | if sexually delinquent person | 1 day to life |
| 28.570 & 28.200(1) | gross indecency between males, and attempts | up to 5 yrs. or up to $2500 |
| | if sexually delinquent person | 1 day to life |
| 28.570(1) & 28.200(1) | gross indecency between females, and attempts | up to 5 yrs. or up to $2500 |
| | if sexually delinquent person | 1 day to life |
| 28.703 & 28.772 | public solicitation & accosting for lewd acts | up to 90 days, up to $100, or both |

## MINNESOTA (Minnesota Statutes Annotated)

| Statute | Offense | Penalty |
|---|---|---|
| 609.17 | attempt to commit an offense | at least 90 days or at least $100 |
| 609.293, 1 & 5 | consensual sodomy (anal and oral) | up to 1 yr., up to $1000, or both |
| 609.72(3) & 609.025(3) | disorderly conduct - offensive language | up to 90 days, up to $300, or both |
| 609.725 & 609.025(3) | vagrancy - loitering | up to 90 days, up to $300, or both |
| 617.23 | indecent exposure, open lewdness or indecency | at least $5 or at least 10 days for first offense |

## MISSISSIPPI (Mississippi Code 1972 Annotated)

| Statute | Offense | Penalty |
|---|---|---|
| 97-1-7 & 97-29-59 | attempt to commit (crime against nature) | up to 10 yrs. |
| 97-29-31 | indecent exposure in public | up to $500, up to 6 mos., or both |
| 97-29-49 & 97-29-53 | prostitution, assignation, lewdness | up to $200, up to 6 mos., or both |
| 97-29-59 | unnatural intercourse, crime against nature (anal and oral) | up to 10 yrs. |
| 97-35-3(1)(b) | disorderly conduct - indecent remarks & gestures | up to $200, up to 4 mos., or both |
| 97-35-11 & 99-19-31 | indecent exposure, indecent language | up to $500, up to 6 mos., or both |
| 97-35-13 & 15 | disturbing the peace - offensive language or conduct | up to $500, up to 6 mos., or both |
| 97-35-27 | failure to register as a felon | up to 3 mos., up to $100, or both |
| 97-35-37 & 39 | vagrancy - immoral life | 10 to 30 days or bond of at least $201 |

## MISSOURI (Vernon's Annotated Missouri Statutes)

| Statute | Offense | Penalty |
|---|---|---|
| 556.150 | attempt to commit an offense | up to half the penalty of the offense |
| 562.240 & 556.270 | disturbing the peace - indecent language | up to 1 yr., up to $1000, or both |
| 563.150 & 556.270 | open and gross lewdness | up to 1 yr., up to $1000, or both |
| 563.230 | crime against nature (anal and oral) | not less than 2 yrs. |
| 563.340 | vagrancy - loitering | up to 20 days, up to $20, or both |

## MONTANA (Revised Codes of Montana 1947 Annotated) (New Criminal Code effective 1-1-75.)

| Statute | Offense | Penalty |
|---|---|---|
| 94-4-101 | solicitation of an offense | up to the penalty for the offense |
| 94-4-103 | attempt to commit an offense | up to the penalty for the offense |
| 94-5-504 | indecent exposure | up to $500, up to 6 mos., or both |
| 94-5-505 | consensual deviate sexual conduct | up to 10 yrs. |
| 94-8-101(c) | disorderly conduct - profane language | up to $100, up to 10 days, or both |

| State and Statute | Offense | Penalty imprisonment & fine |
|---|---|---|

**NEBRASKA (Revised Statutes of Nebraska)**

| | | |
|---|---|---|
| 28.818 | disturbing the peace | up to $100 or up to 3 mos. |
| 28.919 | sodomy (anal and oral) | up to 20 yrs. |
| 28.920 | indecent exposure, obscene language | up to $100 or up to 90 days |
| 28.920.01 | aiding and counseling indecent exposure | up to 6 mos., $50 to $500, or both |

**NEVADA (Nevada Revised Statutes)**

| | | |
|---|---|---|
| 201.190(b) | crime against nature | 1 to 6 yrs. |
| 201.210 & 193.140 | open or gross lewdness - first offense | up to 1 yr., up to $1000, or both |
| | subsequent offence | 1 to 6 yrs. |
| 201.220 & 193.140 | indecent exposure - first offense | up to 1 yr., up to $1000, or both |
| | subsequent offense | 1 to 6 yrs. |
| 207.030 & 193.150 | vagrancy, soliciting or loitering for lewd conduct | up to 6 mos., up to $500, or both |
| 207.151-57 & 193.150 | failure to register as sex offender | up to 6 mos., up to $500, or both |
| 207.270 & 193.150 | loitering about a school | up to 6 mos., up to $500, or both |
| 208.070 | attempt to commit an offense | half the penalty of the offense |

**NEW HAMPSHIRE (New Hampshire Revised Statutes Annotated 1974) (New Criminal Code effective 11-1-73)**

| | | |
|---|---|---|
| 629.1 & 2 | attempt or solicitation of an offense | same penalty as for the offense |
| 632.2 & 651.2 | deviate sexual relations (excluding husband and wife) | up to 1 yr., up to $1000, or both |
| 645.1 & 651.2 | indecent exposure, lewdness | up to 1 yr., up to $1000, or both |
| 645.2 & 651.2 | prostitution, solicitation | up to 1 yr., up to $1000, or both |

**NEW JERSEY (New Jersey Statutes Annotated 1969)**

| | | |
|---|---|---|
| 2A:85-5 | attempt to commit an offense | up to the penalty for the offense |
| 2A:115-1 & 2A:85-7 | open lewdness, public indecency | up to $1000, up to 3 yrs., or both |
| 2A:133-1 & 2A:85-7 | prostitution, lewdness, assignation | up to $1000, up to 3 yrs., or both |
| 2A:133-2 & 2A:85-7 | aiding prostitution, lewdness, assignation | up to $1000, up to 3 yrs., or both |
| 2A:143-1 | sodomy or crime against nature (anal) | up to $5000, up to 20 yrs., or both |
| 2A:170-1 & 2A:169-4 | disorderly persons with unlawful purpose | up to $500, up to 6 mos., or both |
| 2A:170-5 & 2A:169-4 | lewd solicitation | up to $500, up to 6 mos., or both |

**NEW MEXICO** (New Mexico Statutes Annotated)  (New law allowing consensual sex acts at age 18 effective 7-1-75)

| | | |
|---|---|---|
| 40A-9-24 & 40A-29-4B | indecent exposure | up to 6 mos., up to $100, or both |
| 40A-20-1 & 40A-29-4B | disorderly conduct - indecent conduct | up to 6 mos., up to $100, or both |

**NEW YORK** (Consolidated Laws of New York Annotated)

| | | |
|---|---|---|
| 39,130.38; 39.70.15 & 39.80.5 | consensual sodomy, deviate sexual intercourse | up to 3 mos., up to $500, or both |
| 39,240.20; 39,70.15 & 39.80.5 | disorderly conduct - obscene gestures | up to 15 days, up to $250, or both |
| 39,240.35.3; 39,70.15 & 39,80.5 | loitering & soliciting deviate sex intercourse | up to 15 days, up to $250, or both |
| 39,245.00; 39,70.15 & 39,80.5 | public lewdness, lewd exposure | up to 3 mos., up to $500, or both |

**NORTH CAROLINA** (General Statutes of North Carolina)

| | | |
|---|---|---|
| 14,177; 14.2 | sodomy (anal and oral) | up to 10 yrs., fine, or both |
| 14,190 | indecent exposure | up to $500, up to 6 mos., or both |
| 14,195 & 197 | profane or indecent language | up to $50 or up to 30 days |
| 14,203 & 208; 14.3 | prostitution, assignation - 1st offense | up to 2 yrs., fine, or both |
| 14,275,1 | disorderly conduct, obscene language, loitering | up to $50 or up to 30 days |

**NORTH DAKOTA** (North Dakota Century Code Annotated)  (New Criminal Code allowing consensual sex acts at age 15 eff. 7-1-75)

| | | |
|---|---|---|
| 12,1-06-01; 12,1-32-01 | attempt to commit (sex act in public) | up to 30 days, up to $500, or both |
| 12,1-06-03; 12,1-32-01 | solicitation to commit (sex act in public) | up to $500 |
| 12,1-20-08; 12,1-32-01 | sexual act in public | up to 30 days, up to $500, or both |
| 12,1-31-01(3)&(6); 12,1-32-01 | disorderly conduct, obscene language, gesture, or solicitation of sexual contact | up to 30 days, up to $500, or both |

**OHIO** (Page's Ohio Revised Code Annotated)  (New Criminal Code allowing consensual sex acts at age 16 effective 1-1-74)

| | | |
|---|---|---|
| 2907,07(B); 2929,21-22 | offensive solicitation of person of same sex | up to 6 mos., up to $1000, or both |
| 2907,09; 2929,21-22 | indecent exposure, sexual conduct in public | up to 30 days, up to $250, or both |
| 2917,11A(2) | disorderly conduct--offensive language, gesture | up to $100 |
| | if persisted in after warning | up to 30 days, up to $250, or both |
| | failure to register as sex offender-- | |
| 2950,01-02; 2950,99 | 1st offense | up to 6 mos., up to $1000, or both |
| | subsequent offense | up to 30 days, up to $250, or both |

| State and Statute | Offense | Penalty imprisonment & fine |
|---|---|---|
| **OKLAHOMA** (Oklahoma Statutes Annotated) | | |
| 21.22; 21.10 | outraging public decency | up to 1 yr., up to $500, or both |
| 21.42 | attempt to commit an offense | up to half the penalty for the offense |
| 21.886 | crime against nature (anal and oral) | up to 10 yrs. |
| 21.1021 | lewd and indecent exposure | $100 to $5000, 30 days to 10 yrs., or both |
| 21.1029-31 | prostitution, lewdness, assignation, solicitation | 30 days to 1 yr. |
| **OREGON** (Oregon Revised Statutes) (New Criminal Code allowing consensual sex acts at age 18 effective 1-1-72) | | |
| 163.455; 161.615; 161.635 | public accosting for deviate sex intercourse | up to 30 days or up to $250 |
| 163.465; 161.615; 161.635 | public indecency, indecent exposure, deviate sexual intercourse | up to 1 yr. or up to $1000 |
| 166.025(c) | disorderly conduct, obscene gestures in public | up to 6 mos. or up to $500 |
| 166.045(1) (a) | loitering near school | up to 30 days or up to $250 |
| **PENNSYLVANIA** (Purdon's Consolidated Pennsylvania Statutes Annotated) (New Criminal Code effective 6-6-73) | | |
| 18.901 & 905 | attempt to commit an offense | same penalty as for the offense |
| 18.902 & 905 | solicitation to commit an offense | same penalty as for the offense |
| 18.3124; 18.1101(4); 18.1104(2) | voluntary deviate sexual intercourse | up to 2 yrs., up to $5000, or both |
| 18.3127; 18.1101(4); 18.1104(2) | indecent exposure | up to 2 yrs., up to $5000, or both |
| 18.5503; 18.1101(4); 18.1104(2) | disorderly conduct--obscene language & gestures | up to $300; up to 1 yr., up to $2500, or both |
| 18.5506; 18.1101(4); 18.1104(2) | loitering at night | up to 1 yr., up to $2500, or both |
| 18.5901; 18.1101(4); 18.1104(2) | open lewdness | up to 1 yr., up to $2500, or both |
| **RHODE ISLAND** (General Laws of Rhode Island 1956) | | |
| 11.10.1 | crime against nature (anal) | 7 to 20 yrs. |
| 11.34.1 | prostitution, lewdness, loitering, loitering-- 1st offense | 6 mos. to 5 yrs. |
| | subsequent offense | 1 to 10 yrs |
| 11.45.1 | vagrancy, lewd or indecent behavior | up to 1 yr. or outpatient treatment |

**SOUTH CAROLINA** (Code of Laws of South Carolina 1962 Annotated)

| | | |
|---|---|---|
| 16.409; 16.411 | prostitution, lewdness, assignation--1st offense | up to $100 or up to 30 days |
| 16.412 | buggery | 5 yrs., at least &500, or both |
| 16.413; 17.553 | indecent exposure | discretionary fine, imprisonment, or both |
| 16.558 | disorderly conduct in public, obscene language | up to 30 days or up to $100 |
| 16.565(5) | vagrancy - disorderly life | up to $100 or up to 30 days |

**SOUTH DAKOTA** (South Dakota Compiled Laws 1947 Annotated)   (New Criminal Code allowing consensual sex acts eff. 4-1-77)

| | | |
|---|---|---|
| 22.4.1 | attempt to commit an offense | up to half the penalty for the offense |
| 22.13.7 | disorderly conduct - obscene language | $5 to $50, up to 10 days, or both |
| 22.13.12; 22.13.13(2) | vagrancy - immoral life | up to $100, up to 30 days, or both |
| 22.22.21 | crime against nature (anal and oral) | up to 10 yrs. |
| 22.24.1-2.1 | indecent exposure | up to $2000, up to 1 yr., or both |
| 22.24.6; 22.6.2 | outraging public decency | up to 1 yr., up to $500, or both |

**TENNESSEE** (Tennessee Code Annotated)

| | | |
|---|---|---|
| 39.707 | crime against nature (anal and oral) | 5 to 15 yrs. |
| 39.1209 & 1210 | disorderly conduct - loitering near school | $5 to $50 for 1st offense |
| 39.1211 | disorderly conduct - loitering near school | $20 to $100 for 1st offense |
| 39.1213 | disorderly conduct - offensive language & conduct | $20 to $200 & (optional) up to 30 days |
| 39.3501-3505 | prostitution, assignation, solicitation | $50 for 1st offense |
| 39.4701-4702 | vagrancy | $5 to $25 or 10 days to 1 yr. |

**TEXAS** (Vernon's Texas Code Annotated)   (New Criminal Code effective 1-1-74)

| | | |
|---|---|---|
| 21.06; 21.01; 12.23 | homosexual conduct - deviate sex intercourse | up to $200 |
| 21.07; 12.21 | public lewdness | up to $2000, up to 1 yr., or both |
| 21.08; 12.23 | indecent exposure | up to $200 |
| 42.01; 12.23 | disorderly conduct--indecent language, offensive gesture or display | up to $200 |

**UTAH** (Utah Code Annotated)   (New Criminal Code effective 7-1-73)

| | | |
|---|---|---|
| 76-4-101; 76-3-201, 204, 301 | attempt to commit (consensual) sodomy | up to 90 days, up to $299, or both |

| State and Statute | Offense | Penalty imprisonment & fine |
|---|---|---|
| **UTAH** (Cont'd) | | |
| 76-5-403; 76-3-201, 204, 301 | consensual sodomy | up to 6 mos., up to $299, or both |
| 76-9-102; 76-3-201, 204, 301 | disorderly conduct--obscene language, gestures | up to 90 days, up to $299, or both |
| 76-9-702; 76-3-201, 204, 301 | public lewdness, sex act, indecent exposure | up to 6 mos., up to $299, or both |
| 76-9-703; 76-3-201, 204, 301 | loitering | up to 90 days, up to $299, or both |
| 77-49-1; 77-49-7 | sex offender - mental illness | commitment to state hospital |
| **VERMONT** (Vermont Statutes Annotated) | | |
| 13, 1026 | disorderly conduct - obscene language | up to 60 days, up to $500, or both |
| 13, 2601 | open lewd conduct | up to 5 yrs. or up to $300 |
| 13, 2603 | fellation | 1 to 5 yrs. |
| 13, 2631 & 2632(8) | prostitution, lewdness, assignation - 1st offense | up to $100 or up to 1 yr. |
| 13, 3901 & 3902 | vagrancy | up to 6 mos. or up to $100 |
| common law | sodomy | fine, imprisonment, or both |
| **VIRGINIA** (Code of Virginia 1950 Annotated)  (Major revisions in Criminal Code effective 8-1-75) | | |
| 18.2-26 | attempt to commit a felony | 1 to 5 yrs.; or up to 1 yr., up to $1000, or both |
| 18.2-27 | attempt to commit a misdemeanor | same penalty as for the offense |
| 18.2-348 & 350 | aiding prostitution or illegal sex intercourse | up to 1 yr., up to $1000, or both; or commitment to state hospital |
| 18.2-361 & 18.2-10 | crime against nature (anal and oral) | 1 to 5 yrs.; or up to 1 yr., up to $1000, or both |
| 18.2-387 & 18.2-11 | indecent exposure | up to 1 yr., up to $1000, or both |
| 18.2-415 & 18.2-11 | disorderly conduct | up to 1 yr., up to $1000, or both |
| **WASHINGTON** (Revised Code of Washington Annotated)  (New Criminal Code allowing consensual sex acts at age 18 eff. 7-1-76) | | |
| 9A.88.010 & 9A.20.020(3) | public indecency, obscene exposure | up to 90 days, up to $500, or both |
| **WEST VIRGINIA** (West Virginia Code Annotated)(New Criminal Code allowing consensual sex acts at age 16 eff. 6-12-76) | | |
| 61.6.14(a) | loitering on school property - 1st offense | up to $100, up to 30 days, or both |
| 61.8.4 | open lewd conduct - 1st offense | up to $50 & (optional) up to 6 mos. |

| Citation | Offense | Penalty |
|---|---|---|
| 61.8.13 | crime against nature (anal and oral) | 1 to 10 yrs. |
| 61.8.28 | indecent exposure | $20 to $100, up to 30 days, or both |
| **WISCONSIN (West's Wisconsin Statutes Annotated)** | | |
| 343.06 & 343.30 | person convicted of sexual perversion | denial or revocation of driver's license |
| 939.32 | attempt to commit a felony | up to half the penalty for the offense |
| 944.17 | sexual perversion (anal and oral) | up to $500, up to 5 yrs., or both |
| 944.20 | lewd behavior, indecent exposure | up to $500, up to 1 yr., or both |
| **WYOMING (Wyoming Statutes 1957 Annotated)** | | |
| 6.90 & 93 | prostitution, lewdness, assignation | 4 to 12 mos. or 1 to 3 yrs. |
| 6.98 | sodomy (anal and oral) | up to 10 yrs. |
| 6.102 | public indecency, indecent exposure, obscene language | up to $100 & (optional) up to 3 mos. |
| 6.114 | breach of peace - obscene language | up to $50, up to 30 days, or both |
| 6.221 & 222 | vagrancy - immoral life | up to $100, up to 3 mos., or both |
| 7.348-352 | person convicted of sex offense | mental exam and possible commitment to state hospital |
| **UNITED STATES UNIFORM CODE OF MILITARY JUSTICE (Manual for Courts-Martial, 1968)** | | |
| 80) | attempt to commit (acts below) | same maximum as for the offense itself |
| 125) chap. 25 & | sodomy - unnatural carnal copulation (anal and oral) | dishonorable discharge, loss of all pay & allowances, & up to 5 yrs. |
| 134) appendix 12 | indecent exposure | up to 6 mos. & loss of 2/3 pay for up to 6 mos. |
| 134) | indecent and lewd acts | dishonorable discharge, loss of all pay & allowances, & up to 5 yrs. |
| **CANAL ZONE (Canal Zone Code)** | | |
| 6.371 | attempt to commit an offense | up to half the penalty for the offense |
| 6.1281 | indecent and immoral conduct | up to $100, up to 30 days, or both |
| 6.1282 | indecent exposure - 1st offense | up to $100, up to 30 days, or both |
| 6.2451 | sodomy (anal and oral) | up to 10 yrs. |
| 6.2541(16),(18)&(20) | vagrancy - loitering near school or toilet, obscene exposure | up to $100, up to 30 days, or both |
| **GUAM (Penal Code of the Territory of Guam)** | | |
| 9.286 | crime against nature | 1 to 10 yrs. |

| State and Statute | Offense | Penalty imprisonment & fine |
|---|---|---|
| **GUAM (Cont'd)** | | |
| 9.288a | sex perversion - oral copulation | 1 to 10 yrs. |
| 9.311.1 and 7 | indecent exposure | up to $2000, up to 1 yr., or both |
| 9.626.14 | attempt to commit crime against nature or sex perversion | up to 10 yrs. |
| 9.647.5 | vagrancy - lewd persons | up to $100, up to 6 mos., or both |
| **PUERTO RICO (Laws of Puerto Rico Annotated)** | | |
| 33.1118 | crime against nature | 1 to 10 yrs. |
| 33.1171(1) & 33.37 | public exposure | up to 2 yrs., up to $250, or both |
| 33.1439 | disturbing the peace - offensive conduct, indecent language | up to $200, up to 90 days, or both |
| **VIRGIN ISLANDS (Virgin Islands Code Annotated)** | | |
| 14.331 | attempt to commit an offense | up to half the penalty for the offense |
| 14.1022(1) & (6) | public exposure, obscene language | up to $100, up to 90 days, or both |
| 14.1191(1-3) | loitering near school or toilet | up to $100, up to 30 days, or both |
| 14.1621 & 1622 | prostitution, lewdness, assignation, solicitation | up to $100, up to 6 mos., or both |
| 14.2061 | sodomy (anal and oral) | up to 10 yrs. |
| 14.2221(10), (15) & (16) | vagrancy - indecent exposure, loitering near school or public toilet | up to $100, up to 30 days, or both |

# INDEX OF SUBJECTS

Lesbians (cont'd)
    Lesbian feminists, the Women's movement, and Gay lib-
        eration  16, 78, 96, 106, 210, 221, 239, 249, 261,
        283, 295, 308, 311-12, 338, 347, 349, 351, 372, 412,
        419, 491, 512, 547, 591, 602-05, 609, 612, 614, 639,
        650, 704, 879, 940, 948, 957, 959, 1004, 1113, 1186,
        1302, 1305, 1512, 2426, 2797
    Lesbians and employment  580, 1656, 2388
    Lesbians and religion  543, 844, 1469
    Lesbians and the law  104, 133, 391, 681, 913, 954-56,
        958, 1073, 1087-88, 1241-42, 1250, 1255, 1330, 1578,
        1629-30, 1649, 1652, 1659, 1699, 2462, 2616, 2710,
        2744
    Lesbians in arts and literature  32, 66, 230, 258, 446,
        563, 1133, 2265, 2333, 2398, 2475, 2910
    Personal experiences of lesbians (autobiography, bio-
        graphy, etc.)  21, 76-77, 85, 101a, 103, 107-09, 128,
        150, 153, 306, 350, 369, 385, 395, 447-48, 580, 627,
        633, 693, 812, 884, 892, 939, 1072, 1139, 1278, 2322,
        2396, 2743
    Scientific and specialized studies on lesbians  125, 249,
        266, 274, 276-77, 281, 289, 294, 381, 409, 450, 501-
        02, 559, 617, 660-61, 672, 1725, 1751, 1789-90, 1854,
        1858, 1880-81, 1890, 1896, 1914, 1919, 1922, 1934-35,
        1949, 1961, 1967, 1972-73, 2034, 2045, 2048, 2064,
        2070, 2087, 2105, 2107, 2128, 2130-31, 2134, 2161,
        2171-72, 2204, 2248, 2318, 2335, 2345, 2356, 2384,
        2409, 2424
Literature, homosexuality in  111, 134, 146, 166, 184, 193-
    94, 224, 230, 258, 269, 275, 307, 411, 446, 462,
    478, 483, 1199, 1214, 1256, 2220, 2229, 2231, 2239,
    2262, 2271, 2273, 2287, 2289, 2301, 2326, 2334, 2338,
    2341, 2348, 2354, 2359, 2367, 2377, 2415, 2440, 2449,
    2533, 2800, 2805
London  61, 535, 1137, 1182-83, 2516, 2611, 2802
Long-term or short-term relationships between male homo-
    sexuals  292, 1877
Los Angeles  576, 843, 889, 896, 965-71, 989, 1009-13,
    2491, 2496, 2501, 2545, 2573, 2614, 2679, 2707, 2716,
    2728, 2740-41, 2752-60, 2789, 2842, 2848
Loud, Lance  991, 1345, 2862.  See also Television programs


Mafia  740, 833
Male chauvinism, men's liberation, and heterosexual fears of
    homosexuality  323, 343, 364, 394, 496, 550, 624
Male groupies  2663

Population control, homosexuality as  536, 1810, 2339
Pornography and erotica  430, 678, 974, 1848, 1855, 1867,
    1930, 2005, 2223
Portugal  908
Prevention--see Therapy
Prisons and homosexuality  17, 158, 186, 252, 262, 274, 279,
    380, 409-10, 476, 507, 528, 534, 647, 680-81, 753,
    797, 909, 912-13, 922, 958, 988, 1033-34, 1061, 1408,
    1581, 1628, 1633, 1669, 1674, 1705, 1792, 2045, 2095,
    2219, 2228, 2318, 2329, 2337, 2409, 2430, 2531, 2577,
    2683, 2771.  See also Homosexual rape, Violence
    against homosexuals
Professionals' attitudes on homosexuality  220, 271, 460, 872,
    1800, 1829, 1854, 1858, 1871, 2035, 2062, 2123, 2346,
    2372, 2487, 2865-66, 2895, 2925
Psychological and personality characteristics of homosexuals
    1712, 1739, 1762, 1764, 1780, 1783, 1788, 1791, 1815,
    1819, 1868, 1875, 1877, 1880, 1890, 1962, 1989-90,
    2006, 2047, 2066-67, 2075, 2093, 2181, 2193, 2195,
    2204, 2467.  See also Comparisons of homosexuals and
    heterosexuals
Psychological functioning of homosexuals  50, 126, 179, 613,
    1732, 1780, 1832, 2128-29, 2171, 2313, 2675.  See
    also Comparisons of homosexuals and heterosexuals
Psychodrama  2187
Psychopathology and disease  41, 45, 63, 95, 208, 265, 297,
    310, 329, 331, 362, 382, 402, 480, 568, 621-22, 700-
    02, 1716, 1742-43, 1778-79, 1836, 1888, 1912, 1937,
    1951, 1968, 2051, 2106-07, 2143-44, 2146, 2233, 2437-
    38.  See also Health versus sickness argument, Therapy
Public attitudes  197, 229, 232, 248, 257, 278, 389, 399,
    460, 477, 521, 581, 675, 725, 740, 754, 769, 794,
    802-11, 824, 866, 894-95, 929, 961, 964, 967, 981,
    997, 1036, 1072, 1100, 1132, 1187, 1264, 1276, 1328,
    1359, 1383, 1391, 1405, 1409, 1586, 1758, 1811-12,
    1820, 1851, 1941, 1978, 2032, 2123, 2142, 2152, 2207,
    2255, 2267, 2274, 2357, 2365-66, 2369, 2383, 2385,
    2393, 2422, 2507, 2527, 2783, 2821-22, 2888, 2914,
    2920.  See also Federal policy, Gay demonstrations
    and protests, Gay public officials, Homophobia, The
    Law and homosexuality, Law reform, Police attitudes
    and practices
Public sex  69, 470, 673, 1590, 1685, 2325
Public welfare, homosexuals and  920, 2283, 2399


Quakers  2829

# INDEX OF AUTHORS

328

McAllister, H.   2074, 2212
McAllister, William   980
McArthur, Charles C.   331
McCabe, Charles   981
McCabe, H.   1515
McCaffrey, Joseph A.   101,
  555, 1516-17
McCandless, Boyd R.   2171-
  72
McCann, J. S.   1886
McCary, James L.   556-57
McCawley, Austin   2007
McCleary, Roland D.   2373
McConaghy, N.   558, 1733,
  2008-17
McConnell, Nancy F.   1518
McCormick, Richard A.
  1519
McCrady, Richard E.   2018
McCuen, Gary   320
McCullough, James P.   1933
McCullough, Patricia   2250
McCullough, Roy L.   2771
McDougall, Joyce   559,
  2019
McFarland, Arthur C.   2299
McGirr, Kevin J.   560
McGraw, James R.   1520
McGuinness, Richard   982
McGuire, B. P.   1521
McIntosh, Mary   561
McKenney, Mary   2374
McNally, Terrence   3094-95
McNamara, Francis J.
  2375
McNamee, Gil   2376
McNaught, Brian   1522,
  2772-73
McNeill, John J.   562, 1523-
  24
Meacock, Norma   3006
Mead, Margaret   1259
Meaker, Marijane   3007
Meeks, John E.   1525
Mellen, Joan   563
Melleno, Frank   217
Mellow, James R.   101a

Melville, Charles   2108
Mendenhall, George   2774-
  75
Menninger, W. Walter
  2206
Merrick, Gordon   3008-10
Meyer, Jon K.   2021
Meyer, Robert C.   1833,
  2022
Meyer, V.   2023
Meyers, Jeffrey   564, 1527,
  2377
Michael, Richard P.   565
Michaelson, Judith   991
Mileski, Maureen   2378
Miller, David   528
Miller, Derek   2024
Miller, Elizabeth   1747-48
Miller, Henry   1262
Miller, Isabel   3011
Miller, Jimmy   3012
Miller, Merle   102, 779,
  992-93, 1263-67, 3013
Miller, Michael M.   2025
Miller, Milton   2026
Miller, Peter   566
Miller, Stuart J.   2228
Millett, Kate   103, 567,
  1196, 1268, 1286
Milligan, Andy   3096
Milligan, Don   222
Millon, Renee   568
Millon, Theodore   568
Mills, Ivor H.   2379
Milo, Simcha   2039
Mintz, Elizabeth   569
Mitler, Merrill M.   2027
Mitzel, John   570, 2781-82
Moan, Charles E.   2028
Moeller, William S.   2177
Monahan, Jim   571
Money, John   572-73,
  2029-31, 2381
Monroe, Jack   2783
Monroe, John T.   2026
Montag, Tom   2382
Monteiro, G. E.   2089

Okum, Marjorie E.  278
Olivia  3020
Olivieri, Antonio  1622
Olson, A. K.  2121
Olson, Jack  113
O'Mary, Barbara  3131
One, Varda  230
O'Neal, Thomas P.  2049
Onge, Jack  114
O'Rourke, Thomas W.  2255
Orthner, H.  2036
Ortlieb, Chuck  2395
Orwin, Arnold  2050,
  2058, 2180-81
Osborn, David  3021
Osman, Shelomo  2396
Ostrander, Kenneth H.
  2397
Ovesey, Lionel  2051, 2065
Owen, Robert L.  2052

Pacion, Stanley J.  2053-
  56
Page, James D.  586
Pakalka, William R.  1623
Panati, Charles  1287
Panky, Ted  587
Papaevangeliou, George
  2057
Papatheophilou, R.  2058
Pariser, Harry  2059
Parisex  588
Parker, Robert B.  3022
Parker, William  115, 589-
  90, 1624-26, 2812-14
Parker, William C.  279
Parks, Adrienne  2398
Parks, Gary A.  2060
Parman, Leah  346, 591
Patrinos, Dan  1538
Pattison, E. Mansell
  1539, 2061
Pauly, Ira B.  2062
Peck, Ellen  530
Pedder, J. R.  2063
Penny, Robert L.  2411

Perew, T.  2818
Perkins, Muriel W.  2064
Perreault, Jeanne  592
Perry, Troy  116, 593
Person, Ethel  2051, 2065
Perutz, Kathrin  594
Petrilli, Anthony  2174,
  2176
Phanjoo, A. L.  1787
Phelps, Robert  595
Phillips, Gene D.  1540
Phillips, Howard  2399
Phillips, William  596
Philpott, Kent  117
Pielmaier, H.  2181
Pierce, David M.  2066-67
Pillard, Richard C.  2068
Pineda, Elia B.  280
Pinkett, Cil  48
Pinkus, Susan  1289
Pitchford, Kenneth  1541,
  3132
Pittenger, W. Norman
  118, 597-98, 598a,
  1542-44
Pittman, David J.  2400
Pittman, Frank S.  2069
Plowman, Edward E.  1545-
  46
Plummer, Kenneth  119
Poland, Jefferson F.  599
Poltergeist, Jaye V.  600
Pomeroy, Wardell B.  505-
  06, 1393
Poole, Kenneth  281, 2070
Poole, Lee  1547
Popenoe, P.  2401
Porcsa, Michael  3023
Powell, John R.  1548
Prescott, Kathryn F.  2146
Prescott, R. G. W.  2071
Presly, A. S.  1793
Pressman, Kurt  2824
Preston, John  1549
Prewett, Michael  1899
Pritt, Thomas E.  282
Proctor, N.  2017